Simplicity, Inference and Modelling

The idea that simplicity matters in science is as old as science itself, with the much cited example of Occam's razor, 'entia non sunt multiplicanda praeter necessitatem': entities are not to be multiplied beyond necessity. A problem with Occam's razor is that nearly everybody seems to accept it, but few are able to define its exact meaning and to make it operational in a non-arbitrary way. Using a multidisciplinary perspective, with contributions from philosophers, mathematicians, econometricians and economists, this monograph examines simplicity by asking six questions. What is meant by simplicity? How is simplicity measured? Is there an optimum trade-off between simplicity and goodness-of-fit? What is the relation between simplicity and empirical modelling? What is the relation between simplicity and prediction? What is the connection between simplicity and convenience? The book concludes with reflections on simplicity by Nobel laureates in economics.

ARNOLD ZELLNER is H. G. B. Alexander Distinguished Service Professor Emeritus of Economics and Statistics at the University of Chicago.

HUGO A. KEUZENKAMP is Professor of Economics at the University of Amsterdam and director of SEO Amsterdam Economics.

MICHAEL MCALEER is Professor of Economics at the University of Western Australia in Perth.

Simplicity, Inference and Modelling

Keeping it Sophisticatedly Simple

edited by

Arnold Zellner, Hugo A. Keuzenkamp and
Michael McAleer

CAMBRIDGE
UNIVERSITY PRESS

CAMBRIDGE UNIVERSITY PRESS
Cambridge, New York, Melbourne, Madrid, Cape Town, Singapore,
São Paulo, Delhi, Dubai, Tokyo

Cambridge University Press
The Edinburgh Building, Cambridge CB2 8RU, UK

Published in the United States of America by Cambridge University Press, New York

www.cambridge.org
Information on this title: www.cambridge.org/9780521121354

© Cambridge University Press 2001

First published 2001
This digitally printed version 2009

A catalogue record for this publication is available from the British Library

ISBN 978-0-521-80361-8 Hardback
ISBN 978-0-521-12135-4 Paperback

Contents

List of figures   *page* vii
List of tables   viii
List of contributors   ix

1   The enigma of simplicity   1
    HUGO A. KEUZENKAMP, MICHAEL MCALEER AND
    ARNOLD ZELLNER

PART I   The importance of simplicity   **11**
2   What is the problem of simplicity?   13
    ELLIOTT SOBER

3   Science seeks parsimony, not simplicity: searching   32
    for pattern in phenomena
    HERBERT A. SIMON

4   A macroeconomic approach to complexity   73
    MARCEL BOUMANS

5   The new science of simplicity   83
    MALCOLM R. FORSTER

6   What explains complexity?   120
    BERT HAMMINGA

7   Occam's bonus   128
    A. W. F. EDWARDS

PART II   Simplicity in theory and practice   **133**
8   Simplicity, information, Kolmogorov complexity   135
    and prediction
    PAUL VITÁNYI AND MING LI

9   Simplicity and statistical inference   156
     JORMA RISSANEN

10   Rissanen's theorem and econometric time series   165
     WERNER PLOBERGER AND PETER C. B. PHILLIPS

11   Parametric versus non-parametric inference: statistical   181
     models and simplicity
     ARIS SPANOS

12   The role of simplicity in an econometric model   207
     selection process
     ANTONIO AZNAR, M. ISABEL AYUDA AND
     CARMEN GARCÍA-OLAVERRI

13   Simplicity in a behavioural, non-parametric context   227
     DIRK TEMPELAAR

14   Keep it sophisticatedly simple   242
     ARNOLD ZELLNER

15   Communication, complexity and coordination in games   263
     MATTIAS GANSLANDT

16   The simplicity of an earnings frontier   277
     UWE JENSEN

17   Simplicity: views of some Nobel laureates in economic   292
     science
     MICHAEL MCALEER

Index   297

Figures

2.1	Pressure/temperature	*page* 14
3.1	A nearly completely decomposable matrix	65
5.1	Classical Neyman-Pearson hypothesis testing	92
5.2	The critical point at which the null hypothesis is rejected in cross-validation, BIC and AIC	93
5.3	The behaviour of various quantities in a nested hierarchy of models	104
5.4	Predictive accuracy	109
12.1	Difference of parsimony factors of Cp and AIC	214
12.2a	Parsimony factors of LM, LR and W $(k_1 = 1, k_2 = 2, \varepsilon = 5\%)$	215
12.2b	Parsimony factors of LM, LR and W $(k_1 = 1, k_2 = 2, \varepsilon = 1\%)$	215
12.2c	Parsimony factors of LM, LR and W $(k_1 = 1, k_2 = 4, \varepsilon = 5\%)$	216
12.2d	Parsimony factors of LM, LR and W $(k_1 = 1, k_2 = 4, \varepsilon = 1\%)$	216
12.3a	Difference of parsimony factors of BEC and SBIC $(k_2 \in (2,4), t \in (20,40))$	217
12.3b	Difference of parsimony factors of BEC and SBIC $(k_2 \in (5,10), t \in (20,100))$	217
12.4a	Parsimony factors of AIC, BEC and LR $(k_1 = 1, k_2 = 2, \varepsilon = 5\%)$	218
12.4b	Parsimony factors of AIC, BEC and LR $(k_1 = 1, k_2 = 2, \varepsilon = 1\%)$	218
12.4c	Parsimony factors of AIC, BEC and LR $(k_1 = 1, k_2 = 4, \varepsilon = 1\%)$	218

Tables

11.1	A generic parametric statistical model	*page* 182
11.2	A generic non-parametric statistical model	183
11.3	A non-parametric statistical model for smoothing	195
11.4	Sample correlation coefficients	200
11.5	The Probabilistic Reduction approach specification	204
11.6	Reduction versus model assumptions	204
12.1	Criteria	212
12.2	Mean square error of prediction	222
12.3	Results of the comparison for each DGP	223
15.1	Numerical simulation	274
16.1	Exogenous variables	280
16.2	Estimation results	281

Contributors

M. Isabel Ayuda *University of Zaragoza*
Antonio Aznar *University of Zaragoza*
Marcel Boumans *University of Amsterdam*
A. W. F. Edwards *University of Cambridge*
Malcolm R. Forster *University of Wisconsin, Madison*
Mattias Ganslandt *University of Lund and the Research Institute of Industrial Economics, Stockholm*
Carmen García-Olaverri *Public University of Navarra*
Bert Hamminga *Tilburg University*
Uwe Jensen *University of Kiel*
Hugo A. Keuzenkamp *University of Amsterdam*
Ming Li *University of Waterloo*
Michael McAleer *University of Western Australia*
Peter C. B. Phillips *Yale University*
Werner Ploberger *University of Rochester*
Jorma Rissanen *IBM Research Division, Almaden Research Centre, San Jose*
Herbert A. Simon† *Carnegie Mellon University*
Elliott Sober *University of Wisconsin, Madison*
Aris Spanos *Virginia Polytechnic Institute and State University*
Dirk Tempelaar *Maastricht University*
Paul Vitányi *University of Amsterdam*
Arnold Zellner *University of Chicago*

1 The enigma of simplicity

Hugo A. Keuzenkamp, Michael McAleer and Arnold Zellner

Introduction

Many scientists believe that simplicity is a crucial element in their quest for knowledge. The order, which is found in chaos, it is thought, facilitates understanding, prediction and intervention. This seems particularly proper in statistical science. Simplicity seems to be related to inductive power. Some even hold simplicity as a sign of beauty and assign it intrinsic value (see Derkse, 1992). Simplicity has many faces.

Still, exactly how simplicity is used in scientific reasoning remains enigmatic. Until recently, simplicity remained part of the realm of metaphysics. Recent arguments in the philosophy of science, statistics and econometrics generated wide agreement that the role of simplicity in scientific reasoning is in need of clarification. A multidisciplinary conference was organized and held at Tilburg University in January 1997 to help clarify the definition and role of simplicity in scientific reasoning.[1] The fruits of the conference are presented in this volume of papers.

The idea that simplicity matters in science is as old as science itself. Consider Occam's razor, 'entia non sunt multiplicanda praeter necessitatem': entities are not to be multiplied beyond necessity.[2] A problem with Occam's razor is that nearly everybody seems to accept it, but few are able to define its exact meaning and to make it operational in a non-arbitrary way. Hence, the theme for this volume might well be summarized by the general question of how to clarify the enigma of simplicity in scientific inference. This leads to several specific questions, namely:

---

[1] Conference on Simplicity and Scientific Inference, Tilburg, The Netherlands, 9–11 January 1997, sponsored by the Center for Economic Research. Eighteen participants from nine countries attended the conference, with the following disciplinary backgrounds (with numbers in parentheses): econometric theory (6), applied econometrics (3), philosophy of science (3), information theory (2), and one from each of statistical theory, probability theory, economic game theory and history of economic thought.
[2] See Keuzenkamp (2000, ch. 5) for further discussion.

1. What is meant by simplicity?
2. How is simplicity measured?
3. Is there an optimum trade-off between simplicity and goodness-of-fit?
4. What is the relation between simplicity and empirical modelling?
5. What is the relation between simplicity and prediction?
6. What is the connection between simplicity and convenience?

In this introduction, we will briefly discuss these questions and note how different contributions to this volume relate to them. The volume has two parts. Part I, 'The Importance of Simplicity', consists of six chapters where the epistemological issues are the main focus. Part II, 'Simplicity in Theory and Practice', consists of ten chapters in which statistical and econometric dimensions of simplicity are the main topic. Part II is concluded with contributions on communication, application and, finally, some reflections by Nobel laureates in economics.

1   What is meant by simplicity?

That simplicity matters in science is a fact which is revealed in scientific practice, but also more explicitly by the answers to a questionnaire which was sent to Nobel laureates in economics. McAleer reports on this in chapter 17. An interesting finding is that the preference for simplicity is almost (not completely – Lawrence Klein being an exception) universal. Equally interesting is that scientists admit to having little analytical understanding of simplicity. Kenneth Arrow made the point succinctly in writing 'I have not thought deeply about it, although it certainly plays a great role in my thinking and that of my colleagues. I know certainly that the term has a number of different meanings.'

Simplicity may mean 'paucity of parameters' (Simon and many others in this volume), 'plausibility' (e.g. Sober), 'strong falsifiability', 'communicability' and many other things. The contributions to this volume illustrate that different meanings do indeed prevail, but also that there is much common ground between scientists of totally different backgrounds.

2   How is simplicity measured?

Sober notes in his contribution that philosophers have little advice on the measurement of simplicity (or plausibility). Moreover, they fail to justify simplicity as a guide to hypothesis choice and have a hard time weighing the desideratum 'simplicity' against other desiderata of scientific models. For Sober, the conclusion is that simplicity may have no global justification, in which case its justification might be problem-specific. Hamminga sympathizes with that conclusion. In 'What explains complexity?', he argues that it is difficult to find anyone opposing simplicity as a desirable feature of a theory or model. However, facing some choice, the recommendation to maximize simplicity is in danger of being empty unless the problem is specified more precisely.

Despite the deep philosophical problems with an operational definition of simplicity, many attempts to make simplicity measurable have been made. A simple measure of complexity seems to be the number of parameters of a statistical model. Such a measure lies behind nearly all more sophisticated measures of simplicity. It is not without problems. Parametric simplicity implies a formal (mathematical) structure – which to some will be quite complex and may, therefore, violate another meaning of simplicity: communicability. Still, as the language of economics is by and large mathematical, this criticism does not seem to be fatal. Indeed, most authors in this volume suggest that simplicity is related in some way to paucity of parameters. But even then, the meaning may remain unclear.

The most prominent early contributor to the statistical literature on simplicity is Harold Jeffreys. His contribution is an integral part of his Bayesian theory of probability and philosophy of science. He summarized his view regarding simplicity pointedly as 'the simpler laws have the greater prior probability' (1961, p. 47).[3] Jeffreys has pioneered the theory of simplicity by providing an operational measure of simplicity (or its counterpart, complexity). The simplicity postulate of Jeffreys in its operational form attaches a prior probability of 2^{-c} to the disjunction of laws of complexity c, where c = order + degree + absolute values of the coefficients of scientific laws, expressed as differential equations.

Jeffreys, who regarded his proposal as a first step in the direction of measuring complexity, did not propose a formal justification for the simplicity postulate and its operational form. Therefore, some critics claim that the measure is arbitrary and sensitive to the choice of the operational 'language' and measurement system which are used in scientific models. Others regard it as a serious contribution to the understanding of the role of simplicity in scientific inference. Various chapters in this volume help to clarify and elaborate Jeffreys' intuitive definition and contribute to appraise its importance in scientific methodology.

The 'language problem' is well known in the philosophy of science, for example, as the so-called riddle of induction, due to Goodman (see the contribution of Sober). In this 'riddle', two propositions are compared:

---

[3] See also Wrinch and Jeffreys (1921).

(1) all emeralds are green; and (2) all emeralds are green until the year 2050, after that, they are blue. If one defines 'grue' as green until 2050 and blue afterwards, and 'bleen' as blue until 2050 and green afterwards, then the propositions can be rephrased as (1′) all emeralds are grue until the year 2050, after that, they are bleen; and (2′) all emeralds are grue. 'Why', asks Sober, 'should we adopt one language, rather than another, as the representational system within which simplicity is measured?' Philosophers have no answer to this question. Happily, it turns out that the intuitive measure of Jeffreys is an approximation of a formally justifiable measure of complexity, which has been derived in information theory (see below). It can be shown that, asymptotically, the measurement language is not relevant for this information-theoretic measure of simplicity.

In this volume, Zellner analyses and elaborates Jeffreys' approach in detail, and provides illustrative examples. Zellner has long advocated that economists should follow the advice of natural scientists and others to keep their models sophisticatedly simple, especially as simple models seem to work well in practice. Zellner reviews Jeffreys' measure of the complexity of differential equations. Subsequently, he extends it to the context of difference equations and other models that are frequently encountered in statistics and econometrics, among others, allowing for measurement equations as well as state equations, and introducing measures of complexity for various distributional assumptions for error terms.

As noted above, Jeffreys' measure can be related to the information-theoretical measure, due to Kolmogorov. Kolmogorov complexity theory is explained in the chapter by Vitányi and Li (chapter 8). The confrontation between philosophy and information theorists is a rare occasion for improving our understanding of simplicity. The benefit is even larger thanks to Rissanen's contribution on description length (see chapter 9). Those two chapters provide an exceptionally lucid introduction to a highly relevant theme. Ploberger and Phillips (chapter 10) expand this theme to the econometrics context.

Vitányi and Li define Kolmogorov complexity as 'the quantity of absolute information in an individual object'. Rissanen argues that the most appealing concrete complexity measure of a data set is the length of the shortest binary program for the data in a universal computer language. That language, however, is too large to provide a useful complexity yardstick for statistical applications because no algorithm exists to find it, so that finding such a model is a non-computable problem. It is possible to modify the idea by selecting a family of probability distributions as the language (as such, a non-trivial modelling problem), which provides codes as 'programs' for the data The shortest code length is then taken as the complexity of the data set relative to the chosen family, and the associated distribution is its 'best' description for inductive purposes. Stochastic complexity separates the model from the noise and enables the complexity of the model to be defined exactly. In his chapter, Rissanen provides an operational statistical device to implement those insights, which is the so-called 'minimum description length principle'. This principle also provides an answer to the question, is there an optimum trade-off between simplicity and goodness-of-fit? We turn to this question now.

3   Is there an optimum trade-off between simplicity and goodness-of-fit?

The idea that there is a trade-off between goodness-of-fit and simplicity is common knowledge in statistics. But just how the trade-off should be made remains unclear. Surprisingly, the theory of statistics does not provide a unique answer. Fisher's theory of reduction is based on 'sufficient statistics', where loss of information is measured against an arbitrary (or, should we say, conventional) significance level of mostly 5 per cent. In econometrics, parameter deletion tests are normally based on similar criteria, or on correlation indices, which are corrected for degrees of freedom (like Theil's corrected R^2). Alternatively, statistical information criteria are used to trade-off simplicity and goodness-of-fit. The latter approach is closest to most contributions in this volume.[4]

In chapter 5, Forster argues that simplicity has appeared in statistics with a form and precision that it never attained in the methodology of science. Forster lays a foundation for all forms of model selection, from hypothesis testing and cross-validation to Akaike's information criterion (AIC) and Schwarz's Bayesian information criterion (BIC). These methods are evaluated with respect to a common goal of maximizing predictive accuracy. The general theme is that, along with descriptive accuracy, simplicity is an important ingredient for predictive performance of statistical models.

'Occam's bonus' by Anthony Edwards (chapter 7) notes that the year of the Tilburg Simplicity Conference, 1997, coincided with the twenty-fifth anniversary of three classic contributions to the literature on the

---

[4] A perspective that is highly relevant to the issue at stake, but not elaborated on in this volume, is the method of posterior odds in Bayesian inference, due to Jeffreys. Posterior odds for alternative models (say a simple model versus a complicated model) reflect relative goodness-of-fit, the extent to which prior information is in agreement with sample information, prior odds and a penalty for relative complexity. See Zellner (1984, repr. 1987), chapters 3.6 (which relates the posterior odds ratio to the Akaike Information Criterion) and 3.7.

trade-off between simplicity and goodness-of-fit. They are Akaike's development of his AIC, Edwards' monograph on likelihood, and Nelder and Wedderburn's generalized linear models (which referred to the trade-off as the 'deviance'). Edwards examined the rate of exchange (trade-off) between support (log-likelihood) and simplicity. He discussed what increase in support is required to justify an increase in complexity of the model, such as the addition of a new parameter, with Occam's bonus referring to such a trade-off. There is a trade-off in allowing for the complexity of a probability model: too little complexity and the model will be so unrealistic as to make prediction unreliable; too much complexity and the model will be so specific to the particular data as to make prediction unreliable.

4   What is the relation between simplicity and empirical modelling?

There has been a long discussion in the econometric literature on the relation between empirical modelling and the complexity of models. One theme, discussed in Keuzenkamp and McAleer (1995), is whether 'general-to-specific' modelling strategies have specific merits (the answer was negative, which is consistent with earlier assessments of Jeffreys and Zellner). There are more issues that relate empirical modelling and simplicity.

Ploberger and Phillips, for example, explain why econometricians are interested in a particular aspect of Rissanen's theoretical results. In a typical empirical modelling context, the data-generating process (DGP) of a time series is assumed to be known up to a finite-dimensional parameter. In such cases, Rissanen's theorem provides a lower bound for the empirically achievable distance between all possible data-based models and the 'true' DGP.[5] This distance depends only on the dimension of the parameter space. Ploberger and Phillips examine the empirical relevance of this notion to econometric time series. Next, they discuss a new version of the theorem that allows for non-stationary DGPs. Non-stationarity is relevant in many economic applications and it is shown that the form of non-stationarity affects, and indeed increases, the empirically achievable distance to the true DGP.

In chapter 11 of this volume, on 'Parametric versus non-parametric inference: statistical models and simplicity', Aris Spanos compares and contrasts two approaches to statistical inference, parametric and non-parametric. The relation between simplicity and goodness-of-fit (or, in

---

[5] The notion of a 'true' DGP (with probability 1) is controversial, both in probability theory and in the philosophy of science.

his words, statistical adequacy) can best be analysed in a parametric setting. Spanos argues that simplicity is a pragmatic, as opposed to an epistemic, attribute, such as empirical adequacy, which constitutes a necessary condition for choosing among theories using simplicity as a criterion. Spanos relates the notion of simplicity to relevant themes in statistical modelling, such as misspecification testing, data mining and the pre-test bias problem.

Antonio Aznar, Isabel Ayuda and Carmen García-Olaverri examine 'The role of simplicity in an econometric model selection process' (chapter 12). The authors argue that the first condition to be met by any model to be used in empirical science is that it provides a good fit to the available data. However, in order to achieve a good model, this fit is a necessary, though not sufficient, condition. Agreement with the facts can take many forms, but not all of them are equally acceptable. Therefore, apart from goodness-of-fit, models should also satisfy a second condition, associated with the concept of simplicity. The authors justify and analyse a bipolar approach to the evaluation of econometric models, based on a trade-off between goodness-of-fit and simplicity, which move in opposite directions. Alternative forms in which different model selection criteria combine the two elements are also analysed.

Moving from a parametric to a non-parametric theme, Dirk Tempelaar examines 'Simplicity in a behavioural, non-parametric context' (chapter 13). As the concept of simplicity is inextricably related to models, the definition of simplicity depends critically on the modelling paradigm chosen – the theme which is discussed by Sober and Hamminga as well. Tempelaar argues that the parametric versions of the concept of simplicity constitute, in some sense, a paradox. Simplicity, or its mirror image, complexity, is particularly useful in modelling exercises in which theory plays a rather modest role, and the data are more important in deciding upon the model structure. Consequently, there is a need for principles such as Occam's razor. However, with weak theory and strong data, deep structural parameters are scarce, or even absent, thereby questioning the legitimacy of parametric implementations of Occam's razor. An alternative non-parametric definition of the concepts of simplicity and complexity, based on 'behavioural modelling', is sketched.

Uwe Jensen examines 'The simplicity of an earnings frontier' (chapter 16) and provides estimates of an extended human capital model with imperfect information on the employee's side as a stochastic earnings frontier. The costs of the information imperfection are measured by the inefficiency terms of the frontier model. This individual inefficiency in finding suitable jobs is shown to be considerable. The frontier function approach leads to a sensible interpretation of the deviations of empirical income from estimated maximum possible income. Jensen applies the concept of simplicity and descriptive accuracy to examine whether the standard least squares estimation approach or the frontier approach are to be preferred. Comparisons of the models are conducted verbally as there is no computable simplicity criterion in this context.

Herbert Simon contributed chapter 3, entitled 'Science seeks parsimony, not simplicity: searching for pattern in phenomena'. He argues that science aims at parsimony, the ratio of the number of symbols in raw data to the number that will describe their pattern, and thereby describe and explain the facts parsimoniously, enhancing the falsifiability of theories, and bringing simplicity in its wake. By synthesizing simple hypotheses before complex ones, the most parsimonious hypothesis that will account for the phenomena will be obtained. Theories built on structural relations allow predicting the behaviour of systems under partial change in structure. The approximately hierarchical structure of many phenomena admits relatively simple theories, each describing system behaviour at a different level of the hierarchy. Simon relates the roles that parsimony and simplicity have played in his own research, especially in economics and statistics.

Continuing in this vein, Marcel Boumans explores an approach in which complex systems are considered as hierarchic in 'A macroeconomic approach to complexity' (chapter 4). A system is hierarchic when it is composed of interrelated subsystems, each of them being, in turn, hierarchic until some lower level of subsystems that are treated as black boxes is reached. According to Jeffreys, the internal structure of a black box can be taken to be as simple as possible. If the complexity of the system arises from the complicated interaction of the parts, computer simulations are possible. However, if the complexity arises from the multitude of the parts, Simon suggests approximating the system by a nearly decomposable system to simplify the analysis. Boumans explores the development of Simon's approach and its methodology in macroeconomics.

5   What is the relation between simplicity and prediction?

One of the most important justifications for aiming at (some degree of) simplicity is that it supports the predictive performance of models. This justification has been given by Jeffreys and, explicitly or implicitly, many statisticians (see also Forster and Sober, 1994). Based on the principle of Occam's razor, it is widely believed that the better a theory compresses the data, the better the theory generalizes and predicts unknown data. This belief is vindicated in practice but, Vitányi and Li note, has apparently not been rigorously justified in a general setting. For that purpose, they propose the use of the Kolmogorov complexity. They examine the relation between data compression and learning, and show that compression is almost always the best strategy, both in hypothesis identification by using the minimum description length principle and in prediction methods.

6   What is the connection between simplicity and convenience?

In chapter 15, 'Communication, complexity and coordination in games', Mattias Ganslandt investigates how the transmission of information determines collective behaviour in coordination games. Pre-play communication should help players to avoid coordination failures. Furthermore, transmission of information should help players to optimize their collective behaviour. The complexity of an equilibrium is defined as the length of the description the players attach to the equilibrium strategy profile. Ganslandt shows that simplicity can be used to choose from multiple strict Nash equilibria, and that choosing an equilibrium is a trade-off between efficiency and ease of describability (the mirror image of complexity). It is also shown that simple patterns of behaviour occur if talk is costly.

Hamminga focuses on why an increase in complexity is such an almost universally observed empirical phenomenon in dynamic processes (chapter 6). From a philosophical point of view, econometrics is claimed to be a special case of this general process of the evolution of nature towards complexity. Simplicity discussions should be viewed from the perspective of individuals striving to maintain simplicity while their surroundings become more complex. Perhaps the comments by Jeffreys on Schrödinger's wave equation, discussed in Zellner's contribution (chapter 14), clarify some of the issues raised here. Jeffreys suggests that this apparently highly complex differential equation may be the gradual result of successively better approximations: it was likely to be the simplest among competing partial differential equations, not the simplest in an absolute sense.

7   Conclusion

The chapters in this volume clarify the enigma of simplicity, without providing the final answers to all questions raised above. The growing interest in the analysis of simplicity and scientific inference merits further research, where it is likely that interactive contributions from different disciplines will yield much synergy. We hope that this volume stimulates such research and, paraphrasing Occam, would like to thank our contributors for their enormous effort in making their chapters not complex beyond necessity.

REFERENCES

Derkse, W. (1992). *On Simplicity and Elegance*. Delft: Eburon.

Forster, M. R. and E. Sober (1994). How to tell when simpler, more unified, or less *ad hoc* theories will provide more accurate predictions. *British Journal for the Philosophy of Science* 45: 1–35.

Jeffreys, H. (1961). *Theory of Probability*. Oxford: Clarendon Press.

Keuzenkamp, H. A. (2000). *Probability, Econometrics and Truth*. Cambridge: Cambridge University Press.

Keuzenkamp, H. A. and M. McAleer (1995). Simplicity, scientific inference and econometric modelling. *Economic Journal* 105: 1–21.

Wrinch, D. and H. Jeffreys (1921). On certain fundamental principles of scientific inquiry. *The London, Edinburgh and Dublin Philosophical Magazine and Journal of Science* 42: 369–90.

Zellner, A. (1984, repr. 1987). *Basic Issues in Econometrics*. Chicago: University of Chicago Press.

Part I

The importance of simplicity

2   What is the problem of simplicity?

Elliott Sober

Scientists sometimes choose between rival hypotheses on the basis of their simplicity. Non-scientists do the same thing; this is no surprise, given that the methods used in science often reflect patterns of reasoning that are at work in everyday life. When people choose the simpler of two theories, this 'choosing' can mean different things. The simpler theory may be chosen because it is aesthetically more pleasing, because it is easier to understand or remember, or because it is easier to test. However, when philosophers talk about the 'problem of simplicity', they are usually thinking about another sort of choosing. The idea is that choosing the simpler theory means regarding it as *more plausible* than its more complex rival.

Philosophers often describe the role of simplicity in hypothesis choice by talking about the problem of curve-fitting. Consider the following experiment. You put a sealed pot on a stove. The pot has a thermometer attached to it as well as a device that measures how much pressure the gas inside exerts on the walls of the pot. You then heat the pot to various temperatures and observe how much pressure there is in the pot. Each temperature reading with its associated pressure reading can be represented as a point in the coordinate system depicted below (figure 2.1). The problem is to decide what the *general* relationship is between temperature and pressure for this system, given the data. Each hypothesis about this general relationship takes the form of a line. Which line is most plausible, given the observations you have made?

One consideration that scientists take into account when they face curve-fitting problems is goodness-of-fit. A curve that comes close to the observed data fits the data better than a curve that is more distant. If goodness-of-fit were the only consideration relevant to the curve-fitting problem, scientists would always choose curves that pass exactly through the data points. They do not do this (and even if they did, the question would remain of how they choose among the infinity of curves that fit the

I am grateful to Malcolm Forster for useful discussion.

13

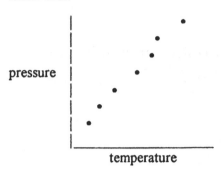

Figure 2.1 Pressure/temperature

data perfectly). Another consideration apparently influences their decisions, and this is simplicity. Extremely bumpy curves are often thought to be complex, whereas smoother curves are often thought to be simpler. Scientists sometimes reject an extremely bumpy curve that fits the data perfectly and accept a smoother curve that fits the data a little less well. Apparently, scientists care about both goodness-of-fit *and* simplicity; both considerations influence how they choose curves in the light of data.

The fact that scientists use simplicity considerations to help them choose among competing hypotheses gives rise to a philosophical problem. In fact, the problem of simplicity decomposes into three parts. The task is to show how simplicity should be *measured*, how it can be *justified*, and how it should be traded off.

1　Measuring simplicity

To strive for simplicity in one's theories means that one aims to minimize something. The minimization might involve a semantic feature of what a set of sentences says or a syntactic feature of the sentences themselves. An example of the first, semantic, understanding of simplicity would be the idea that simpler theories postulate fewer causes, or fewer changes in the characteristics of the objects in a domain of inquiry. An example of the second, syntactic, understanding of simplicity would be the idea that simpler theories take fewer symbols to express, or are expressible in terms of a smaller vocabulary.

If simplicity involves minimization, why should there be a problem in determining how simple a theory is? The problem is to figure out what to count. Theory X may seem simpler than theory Y when the counting is done one way, but the opposite conclusion may be reached if the counting is done differently. Consider, for example, the longstanding dispute in psychology and the social sciences about psychological egoism. Egoism claims that all of our ultimate motives are focused on some benefit to self. The rival of egoism is motivational pluralism, which allows that some of our ultimate motives are egoistic, but maintains that other ultimate motives are focused on the welfare of others. Motivational pluralism says that people have both egoistic and altruistic ultimate desires. It may seem, at first glance, that egoism is simpler than pluralism, since egoism postulates just one type of ultimate desire, whereas pluralism postulates two (Batson, 1991). This may be why social scientists often favour the egoism hypothesis in spite of the fact that both egoism and pluralism are consistent with observed behaviour.

Complications arise when one considers other implications that egoism and pluralism have. Egoism says that people want to help others only because they think that helping will benefit themselves. Egoism therefore attributes to people a certain *causal belief.* Motivational pluralism postulates no such belief about the selfish benefits that helping will produce. If the simplicity of the two theories were calculated by counting such causal beliefs, the conclusion would be drawn that motivational pluralism is simpler. Egoism postulates fewer types of ultimate desire, but it postulates a larger number of causal beliefs (Sober and Wilson, 1998). What is gained on the one hand is lost on the other.

Theories have many implications. Which of those implications should be considered when one calculates how simple a theory is? This problem is not solved merely by stipulating a metric. One must show why simplicity should be measured in one way rather than another. This task inevitably affects the second and third parts of the problem of simplicity – the problem of justifying simplicity and of trading it off.

Another example of the measurement problem is suggested by Nelson Goodman's (1965) 'new riddle of induction'. Consider the following two hypotheses:

(H1) All emeralds are green.
(H2) All emeralds are green until the year 2050; after that, they are blue.

(H1) seems to be the simpler hypothesis. It says that emeralds do not change colour, whereas (H2) says that they do. Here simplicity involves minimizing the number of postulated changes. If the emeralds we have observed to date are all green, then (H1) and (H2) fit the observations equally well. If simplicity is a reason to prefer one hypothesis over another, then perhaps we are entitled to choose (H1) on grounds of its greater simplicity.

Problems arise when we consider the predicate 'grue'. Let us say that an object is grue at a time if and only if the object is green and the time is before the year 2050, or the object is blue and the time is after the year 2050. Symmetrically, we will say that an object is 'bleen' at a time if and only if it is blue and the time is before the year 2050 or it is green and the time is after the year 2050. Just as blue and green are colours, we can say that grue and bleen are 'grulers'. We now can reformulate (H1) and (H2) in terms of the vocabulary just introduced:

(H1′) All emeralds are grue until the year 2050; after that, they are bleen.

(H2′) All emeralds are grue.

(H1′) and (H1) are logically equivalent; so are (H2′) and (H2). Which of (H1′) and (H2′) is simpler? (H2′) says that emeralds do not change gruler; (H1′) says they do. So if simplicity is calculated by seeing which theory minimizes change in gruler, (H2′) is simpler. This means that it is not an adequate solution to the measurement problem to say that simplicity should be measured by seeing how many changes a theory postulates. The proposal is incomplete. Is it change in colour or change in gruler that matters?

A similar question may be raised about the proposal that the simplicity of a proposition should be measured by considering the length of the shortest sentence that expresses it (Rissanen, 1978, 1989). In a language that contains colour predicates, but not gruler predicates, the proposition that all emeralds are green can be encoded more briefly than the proposition that all emeralds are grue. In a language that contains gruler predicates, but not colour predicates, the reverse is true. And in a language that contains both types of predicate, the two propositions have the same minimum description length. Stipulating which language should be used resolves this ambiguity, but a further question needs to be answered. Why should we adopt one language, rather than another, as the representational system within which simplicity is measured?

Syntactic measures of simplicity inevitably encounter this sort of problem. Since a proposition can be encoded in many different ways, depending on the language one adopts, measuring simplicity in terms of code features will fail to be linguistically invariant. This will not be true of measures of simplicity that are purely semantic, since semantic measures focus on features of what a proposition says, not on how the proposition is expressed in any particular language. Any measure of simplicity in terms of probability will be semantic in this sense. The conditional probability $Pr(Q|P)$ describes a relationship between the two propositions Q and P; once values for such quantities are specified, they remain the same regardless of what language one uses to encode the propositions. Another way to put this point is that if two sentences are logically equivalent, then they must have the same probability. (H1) and (H1') must be equiprobable, as must (H2) and (H2').

These comments about the difference between syntactic and semantic measures of simplicity may sound odd, given the fact that the minimum description length proposal and the Bayesian approach of Schwarz (1978) are asymptotically equivalent (Rissanen, 1978, 1989). In fact, this type of result does not contradict the point just made about the difference between syntactic and semantic proposals. Suppose a probability model is adopted for a set of propositions, and that the simplicity of a proposition is then identified with some probabilistic property that it possesses. This semantic measure of simplicity does not rule out the possibility that some suitable language might be constructed in which the simplicity of a proposition in the set is identified with the length of the shortest sentence in that language that expresses the proposition. It is possible that the semantic and syntactic definitions might induce precisely the same ordering of propositions. This would be no more surprising than the fact that the relation of logical entailment can be defined both syntactically and semantically in propositional logic, and the two definitions are equivalent.

One reason the problem of measuring simplicity is difficult is that intuitive descriptions of what simplicity means lead to opposite measurement proposals. It is often said that simpler theories make fewer assumptions. It also is often said that simpler theories have fewer adjustable parameters. These intuitive statements come into conflict when we examine families of models that are nested. Consider, for example, the following two hypotheses; the first says that x and y are linearly related, the second says that their relation is parabolic:

(LIN) $y = a + bx$

(PAR) $y = a + bx + cx^2$

(LIN) has two adjustable parameters (a and b); (PAR) has three (a, b, and c). Once values for these parameters are specified, a unique straight line and a unique parabola are obtained. Notice that (LIN) is simpler than (PAR) if simplicity is calculated by counting adjustable parameters. However, if simplicity involves paucity of assumptions, the opposite conclusion follows. (LIN) is equivalent to the conjunction of (PAR) and the further assumption that $c = 0$. Since (LIN) is a special case of (PAR), (LIN) says more, not less.

2   Justifying simplicity

To justify simplicity is to show why it should be taken into account in judging how plausible a theory is. Ideally, this task would be accomplished by giving a general theory about what makes one hypothesis more plausible than another, and then explaining how simplicity contributes to plausibility.

I am using 'plausibility' as an informal and neutral term. There are a number of philosophical theories about what this concept means. Bayesians suggest that one theory is more plausible than another when the first is more probable. Popperians say that one theory is more plausible than another if it is better 'corroborated'; this will be true if both are consistent with the observations and the first is more falsifiable (Popper, 1959). Likelihoodists understand plausibility in terms of evidential support, which they define in terms of the probability that a hypothesis confers on the observations (Edwards, 1984). The Akaike framework maintains that one theory is more plausible than another when it has a higher expected degree of predictive accuracy; here predictive accuracy is a technical term, defined in the context of a specific type of inference problem in which one selects a specific hypothesis from a family of hypotheses, based on the data at hand, and uses that hypothesis to predict new data (Akaike, 1973; Sakamoto et al., 1986; Forster and Sober, 1994).

Although most of these approaches attempt to provide a 'global' theory of inference that applies to all hypotheses, no matter what their logical form and no matter what their subject matter, it is important to realize that these approaches can be understood as 'local' proposals as well. Perhaps Bayesianism works well in some contexts, but not in others; the same may be true for the other frameworks. It may turn out that inference obeys different rules in different settings, and that simplicity has to be justified in different ways in different contexts. Even though theories of inference have traditionally been global, it is possible that only local analyses can be constructed (Sober, 1988, 1994). Maybe there is no such thing as *the* justification of simplicity.

It may seem pessimistic to suggest that there might be no single unified justification of simplicity in scientific inference. An even more pessimistic suggestion is that the project of justification – whether global or local – is itself impossible. Perhaps simplicity can't be justified in terms of something else. If this is right, then there are two options. Either simplicity should be rejected as an irrelevant consideration in hypothesis evaluation, or it needs to be regarded as an ultimate consideration – something that is valuable for its own sake, not because it contributes to some broader aim.

Just as the question 'why be rational?' may have no non-circular answer, the same may be true of the question 'why should simplicity be considered in evaluating the plausibility of hypotheses?'

Even if local justifications of simplicity are developed for certain types of hypotheses in certain sorts of evidential contexts, the possibility remains that simplicity may not be justifiable in other settings. For example, I have argued, following Reichenbach (1938), that the justification for using simplicity to choose between theories that make different predictions does not furnish a reason for choosing between theories that are predictively equivalent (Sober, 1996). Does this mean that simplicity has some quite different rationale in the latter type of problem, or that it has no justification at all?

Another feature of the problem of justification is worth noting. If simplicity is used to justify choosing theory X over theory Y, then it must be shown that the greater simplicity of theory X makes it more plausible. What are the assumptions on which this demonstration will rest? One possibility is that purely *a priori* considerations will suffice; perhaps logic and mathematics are enough to show why simplicity contributes to plausibility in the context at hand. Although this style of justification might be desirable, it is reasonable to expect that the justification of simplicity cannot, in general, be so minimal in its empirical assumptions. Typically, substantive empirical assumptions are needed to explain why, in a particular inference problem, the simplicity of a hypothesis contributes to its plausibility (Sober, 1988). I'll illustrate this point by discussing a simple example later in this chapter.

If justifying simplicity means showing why simpler theories are more plausible, then Rissanen's idea that simplicity should be measured by minimum description length cannot stand on its own. Minimum description length is an intuitive representation of what simplicity means and an impressive body of mathematical results has been developed around this thought. However, the problem remains of saying what minimum description length has to do with plausibility. It is here that the asymptotic equivalence with Schwarz's (1978) Bayesian proposal may be important.

3   Trading off simplicity

The task of justifying simplicity involves showing that simplicity 'breaks ties'. That is, if two theories are equally good in all other respects, then the simpler of the two should be regarded as more plausible. However, theories are almost never equally good in all other respects. For example, in the curve-fitting problem discussed at the beginning of this chapter, simplicity influences our judgments about plausibility, but so does good-ness-of-fit. It almost never happens that two curves that we wish to test fit the data equally well. This means that a justification of simplicity, if it is to be relevant to scientific practice, can't merely show that the simpler of two theories is more plausible, all else being equal. Additionally, one needs to establish how sacrifices in simplicity are to be 'traded off' against gains in the other factors that affect a theory's plausibility. If curve X is simpler than curve Y, but curve Y fits the data better than curve X, how are these two pieces of information to be combined into an overall judgment about the plausibility of the two curves?

The trade-off problem shows why the problem of measuring simplicity involves more than saying which of two theories is simpler. Additionally, one must be able to say *how much* simpler one theory is than another, and the constraints on this answer go beyond merely preserving judgments of comparative simplicity. Consider, for example, the dispute between the Akaike information criterion (AIC) and the Bayesian information criterion (BIC) (Schwarz, 1978). Both approaches can be thought of as equating the complexity of a family of curves with k – the number of adjustable parameters it contains. However, AIC and BIC disagree on the weight that simplicity deserves, when compared with the other factor that is said to affect a family of curve's plausibility. For a data set of fixed size, the two proposals may be formulated as follows:

The AIC estimate of family F's plausibility =

log-likelihood{L[F]} − k

The BIC estimate of family F's plausibility =

log-likelihood{L[F]} − klog(n)/2.

L(F) is the likeliest curve in the family – i.e., the one that confers the highest probability on the data at hand. For large data sets, BIC places more emphasis on simplicity than AIC does.

Regardless of how the dispute between AIC and BIC is resolved, it is important to recognize that both approaches not only provide a way of measuring simplicity, but do so in a way that is commensurable with the measurement of other properties of hypotheses that affect their plausibility. This is an essential feature of any adequate solution to the problem of simplicity. It is not enough to be told that the complexity of a family of curves is measured by the number of adjustable parameters it contains. This information is useless until one is also told how simplicity and goodness-of-fit together affect a hypothesis' plausibility.

Several philosophers have asserted, without providing much of a supporting argument, that the trade-off problem has no objective solution.

For example, Kuhn (1977) claimed that scientists differ in how much importance they assign to one virtue of a theory as opposed to another, and that this difference is just a matter of taste. One scientist may think that the most important demand on a theory is that it should make accurate predictions; another may hold that the first duty of a theory is that it be elegant and general. Kuhn does not offer much of an argument for this claim; it merely constitutes his *impression* of what would be left open by any compelling and reasonably complete set of epistemological standards. Of course, it is not in dispute that scientists have different temperaments. But from the point of view of normative theory, it is far from obvious that no uniquely best trade-off exists between simplicity and the other factors that affect a theory's plausibility. Once again, this cannot be settled in advance of examining particular proposals – the AIC, the BIC and others.

4   A simple example

These various points about the problem of simplicity can be illustrated by considering a simple example. Suppose Al and Beth are students in a philosophy seminar, which is held in a seminar room in Madison whose wall of windows looks out on a lake. Students in philosophy seminars sometimes find that their attention wanders; it is possible to concentrate on the Eternal Forms for only so long. This, apparently, is what happens during one of the seminar sessions. At a certain point in the afternoon, Al and Beth both find themselves thinking 'there is a sailboat with a red sail on the lake'.

There are two hypotheses I want to consider, each of which might explain this matching of Al's and Beth's mental states. The common cause explanation (COM) says that Al and Beth were both looking at the same thing on the lake. The separate cause explanation (SEP) says that they were looking at different things. The two hypotheses might be represented as follows:

$$A \quad B \qquad A \quad B$$
$$\nwarrow \quad \nearrow \qquad \uparrow \quad \uparrow$$
$$C \qquad\qquad C_1 \quad C_2$$

$$(\text{COM}) \qquad (\text{SEP})$$

The (COM) hypothesis seems to be simpler than the (SEP) hypothesis. After all, one is a smaller number than two. The question I now want to explore is why this difference in simplicity should make a difference when we decide how to evaluate (COM) and (SEP). Why is simplicity relevant?

I propose to identify a set of assumptions that suffices to guarantee that (COM) is more likely than (SEP). As noted before, I am using likelihood in the technical sense introduced by R. A. Fisher (1925). To say that (COM) is likelier than (SEP) means that (COM) confers a higher probability on the observations than (SEP) does. First, let's introduce some abbreviations for various propositions:

> A = Al believes that there is a sailboat on the lake with a red sail.
> B = Beth believes that there is a sailboat on the lake with a red sail.
> C = The object that Al and Beth both looked at was a sailboat on the lake with a red sail.
> −C = The object that Al and Beth both looked at was not a sailboat on the lake with a red sail.

Notice that C and −C are both part of the (COM) explanation – both say that Al and Beth were looking at the same object; C and its negation differ over what the characteristics of that common cause were. Next, let's introduce abbreviations for some relevant probabilities:

> $Pr(A \mid C) = a$ $Pr(A \mid -C) = m$
> $Pr(B \mid C) = b$ $Pr(B \mid -C) = n$
> $Pr(C) = c$

These allow us to represent the likelihood of the (COM) explanation as follows:

> $Pr(A\&B|COM) = cab + (1 - c)mn.$

This way of expressing the probability of the two observations, given the existence of a common cause, assumes that the belief states of Al and Beth were conditionally independent, given the state of the object they were both looking at. This is not an implausible assumption about vision – Al's probability of having a certain belief, given the state of the object that he and Beth are examining, is not affected by what Beth comes to believe. Or, at least, this is plausible, if we assume that Al and Beth don't have a conversation as they look out at the lake.

We now need to develop a similar representation of the likelihood of the (SEP) hypothesis. First, we need some new propositions:

> C_1 = The object that Al was looking at, but Beth was not, was a sailboat on the lake with a red sail.

$-C_1$ = The object that Al was looking at, but Beth was not, was not a sailboat on the lake with a red sail.

C_2 = The object that Beth was looking at, but Al was not, was a sailboat on the lake with a red sail.

$-C_2$ = The object that Beth was looking at, but Al was not, was not a sailboat on the lake with a red sail.

Notice that C_1 and its negation are propositions that are specific to the (SEP) hypothesis ; they agree that Al and Beth were looking at different things, but disagree about the characteristics of one of those objects. The same holds, of course, for C_2 and its negation.

We now need to introduce some symbols for the probabilities that will figure in our representation of the likelihood of the (SEP) hypothesis. We do this by borrowing letters from our representation of the (COM) hypothesis:

$$\Pr(A \mid C_1) = a \qquad \Pr(A \mid -C_1) = m$$
$$\Pr(B \mid C_2) = b \qquad \Pr(B \mid -C_2) = n$$
$$\Pr(C_1) = \Pr(C_2) = c$$

We now can represent the likelihood of the (SEP) hypothesis as follows:

$$\Pr(A\&B|SEP) = [ca + (1 - c)m][cb + (1 - c)n].$$

Our use of a, b, m, n and c involves a set of empirical assumptions. The fact that the letter 'a' appears in the likelihood expression for (COM) and the likelihood expression for (SEP) means that the probability of Al's believing what he does, given the state of what he is looking at, isn't affected by whether Beth is looking at that object, or at something else. The fact that 'c' occurs in both expressions means that the probability that an object on the lake is a sailboat with a red sail isn't affected by whether two people look at it, or only one does. These assumptions seem reasonable for the case at hand.

Now that we have characterized the likelihoods of the (COM) and the (SEP) hypotheses, we can derive a result that describes which hypothesis will be more likely:

(1) If $0 < c < 1$, then $\Pr(A\&B \mid COM) > \Pr(A\&B \mid SEP)$
     if and only if $(a - m)(b - n) > 0$.

Assuming that c is neither 0 nor 1, the common cause hypothesis is more likely precisely when a and m differ, b and n differ, and a and m differ in the same direction that b and n do. This will be true if Al and Beth are, in a certain broad sense, similar causal systems. Suppose that Al's probability of believing that there is a sailboat on the lake with a red sail is increased if he in fact is looking at such an object. If the same is true of Beth, then the (COM) hypothesis has the higher likelihood. The common cause hypothesis also would be more likely if Al and Beth were both 'counter-suggestible' in the same way. If Al's probability of believing that a red-sailed sailboat is present were lowered by a red-sailed sailboat's being present, and if the same were true of Beth, then the (COM) hypothesis would be more likely in this circumstance as well. Assuming that (COM) is simpler than (SEP), the assumptions just described entail that the simpler hypothesis is more likely.

Proposition (1) provides a criterion for determining which hypothesis has the higher likelihood. For a Bayesian, this result provides only half of the needed analysis. The ultimate goal is to compare the posterior probabilities of the two hypotheses. So far, we have analysed only one of the factors that influence this result. A fuller specification of what needs to be examined is provided by the following criterion, which follows from Bayes' Theorem:

(2) $Pr(COM \mid A\&B) > Pr(SEP \mid A\&B)$ if and only if
      $Pr(A\&B \mid COM)Pr(COM) > Pr(A\&B \mid SEP)Pr(SEP)$.

Likelihood influences which posterior probability is greater, but so do the prior probabilities. If simplicity is relevant to this problem because of its connection with likelihood, the question remains of how simplicity should be traded off against the other factor that affects a hypothesis' overall plausibility.

How should we understand the prior probability of the hypotheses in question? How probable was it that Al and Beth looked at the same object on the lake? There is no way to answer this question *a priori*. However, if we adopt the following model of the process of looking, an answer can be obtained. Let us suppose that Al and Beth independently select an object at random from the ones on the lake to look at. This would not be true if some objects were far more interesting to look at than others, but let's assume that Al and Beth are as described. Then, if there are r objects on the lake, the probability that Al and Beth are looking at the same object is $r(1/r)(1/r) = 1/r$. This means that the prior probabilities of the two hypotheses are $Pr(COM) = 1/r$ and $Pr(SEP) = (r - 1)/r$. For large r, the common cause hypothesis is vastly less probable *a priori*. If the common cause hypothesis is to have the higher posterior probability, then it must overcome this deficiency by having a very superior likelihood. Rewriting (2) and substituting the two prior probabilities just obtained, the result is:

(3) $Pr(COM \mid A\&B) > Pr(SEP \mid A\&B)$ if and only if
$Pr(A\&B \mid COM)/Pr(A\&B \mid SEP) > (r - 1)$.

Proposition (1) says that the (COM) hypothesis will have a higher likelihood than the (SEP) hypothesis in a wide range of circumstances. Now proposition (3) tells us how much greater this likelihood needs to be, if the (COM) hypothesis is to be more probable, given the evidence at hand. Of course, just as empirical assumptions entered into our derivation of proposition (1), the same is true for the reasoning behind proposition (3).

This example, I think, illustrates the main ingredients that are needed for the problem of simplicity to be solved in a given type of inference problem. The common cause explanation is simpler than the separate cause explanation of why Al and Beth have the same thought. This should affect our judgment about which explanation is more plausible only to the extent that simplicity can be connected to some independently acceptable conception of what plausibility means. This task is accomplished by showing that the common cause hypothesis has the higher likelihood, on the assumption that likelihood is relevant when we assess the plausibility of competing hypotheses. Empirical assumptions that are fairly reasonable entail that the simpler hypothesis is more likely in this problem. However, there apparently is more to a hypothesis' plausibility than its likelihood. Prior probability also enters, and the common cause hypothesis, though it is more likely, has a lower prior probability. We therefore need a principle that tells us how simplicity (in the guise of likelihood) should be traded off against prior probability. Further empirical assumptions allow this rate of exchange to be calculated. Simpler theories aren't always more probable, given the evidence at hand. Proposition (3) allows us to determine when this is true for the problem under analysis.

In this example, it is interesting that the relevance of simplicity to inference does not depend on the assumption that 'nature is simple' or that it usually is so. It is more likely, in Fisher's sense, that Al and Beth were looking at the same thing, rather than at different things, given that their beliefs matched. This is wholly independent of the question of whether people usually look at the same or at different things. The simpler hypothesis is more *likely*; this does not entail that the simpler hypothesis is more *probable*. In fact, it is not unreasonable to suspect that the very reverse may be true, in terms of the prior probabilities involved. If I tell you that Al and Beth are both looking at the lake, but don't tell you what they are thinking, is it more probable that they are looking at the same object on the lake, or at different objects? Unless there is a single enormously attention-grabbing object there (for example, a giant fire-breathing sea serpent rising from the lake's centre), it is reasonable to think that the latter hypothesis has the higher prior probability.

I am not suggesting that the analysis of this example provides a satisfactory model for how the entire problem of simplicity should be addressed. However, besides illuminating the general character of 'the problem of simplicity', it also applies to an interesting type of scientific inference. When evolutionists seek to reconstruct the phylogenetic relationships that connect different species to each other, they generally prefer hypotheses that allow them to view similarities as homologies. For example, consider the fact that numerous mammalian species have hair. One could explain this by saying that the shared characteristic is a homology inherited from a common ancestor, or by saying that it is a homoplasy – that it evolved independently in separate lineages. Common sense and scientific practice both embody a preference for the common cause explanation. This preference has a likelihood justification, if the processes occurring in lineages obey a principle that I have called the backwards inequality (Sober, 1988):

> Pr(Descendant has hair | Ancestor has hair) >
>
> Pr(Descendant has hair | Ancestor lacks hair).

This inequality formally resembles the constraint that $a > m$ and $b > n$ discussed in connection with Al and Beth. The backwards inequality is independent of the question of whether stasis is more probable than change – that is, of whether the following forwards inequality obtains:

> Pr(Descendant has hair | Ancestor has hair) >
>
> Pr(Descendant lacks hair | Ancestor has hair).

The forwards inequality is a contingent matter that may be true for some traits in some lineages and false for others. The backwards inequality, however, is much more robust; it follows from the idea that evolution can be modelled as a Markov process in which there is a small constant probability of change per small interval of time (Sober, 1988).

5   Model selection

The example about Al and Beth makes Bayesianism look like a very promising approach to the problem of simplicity. Bayesianism says that the relative plausibility of hypotheses in the light of evidence is to be assessed by calculating likelihoods and prior probabilities. In the problem just analysed, fairly plausible empirical assumptions can be used to make sense of both these quantities, and one of them seems to explain why simplicity should influence our judgment of a hypothesis' plausibility. If simplicity could always be understood in this format, the problem of simplicity would be solved and its solution would count as a major triumph for Bayesianism.

Unfortunately, matters are not so simple. The role of simplicity in the curve-fitting problem is hard to understand within a Bayesian framework. In this type of inference problem, two quite different kinds of proposition are discussed. There are specific curves, and there are the families of curves to which those specific curves belong. The straight line hypothesis 'y = 3x + 4' is an example of the former; the family (LIN) – the set of all straight lines – is an example of the latter. Specific curves have no adjustable parameters; families contain at least one adjustable parameter. Let us consider how prior probabilities and likelihoods might be assigned to hypotheses of both these types.

Whether one is talking about specific curves or families of curves, it is usually quite difficult to know how to make sense of their prior probabilities. Harold Jeffreys' (1957) Bayesian proposal is instructive in this regard. Although he provided slightly different proposals in different publications, his idea basically was that the complexity of a differential equation should be measured by summing the absolute values of the integers (degrees and derivative orders) in it, along with the number of adjustable parameters it contains. Jeffreys further suggested that simpler equations should be assigned higher prior probabilities (Hesse, 1967).

A consequence of this proposal is that (LIN) is said to be more probable than (PAR). As Popper (1959) pointed out, this contradicts the axioms of probability; if one hypothesis entails another, the former cannot have the higher probability, no matter what the evidence is on which one conditionalizes. To rescue Jeffreys' idea from contradiction, it is sometimes suggested that the families under comparison be disjoint. Rather than compare (LIN) and (PAR), one should compare (LIN) and (PAR'), where (PAR') says that $y = a + bx + cx^2$ *and* that $c \neq 0$. There is no logical barrier to stipulating that (LIN) has a higher prior probability than (PAR').

However, an important question still needs to be addressed. *Why* should (LIN) be assigned a higher prior probability than (PAR')? I suggest that Bayesians should feel uncomfortable with this proposal, since it says that it is more probable that $c = 0$ than that $c \neq 0$. If I told you I was about to drop a very sharp dart onto a line that is one mile long, would you think it more probable that the dart will fall exactly at the beginning of the line than that it will fall elsewhere? Although this assumption is logically consistent, it cannot be said to be very plausible. The proposal that (LIN) be assigned a higher prior probability than (PAR$'$) seems to be an act of desperation, one that conflicts with the intuitions that usually motivate Bayesian reasoning.

Setting aside the difficulty of what should be said about nested models, the general problem here is that the prior probability assignments that Bayesians propose often seem to lack justification. The prior probabilities assigned to the (COM) and (SEP) hypotheses that I discussed in connection with Al and Beth were based on empirical facts about how often two people look at the same thing when they look at a lake. These assignments of priors can be rationally assessed because we are able to view each hypothesis as a possible outcome of a chance process; in this case, frequency data are relevant and in principle available. It is a familiar criticism of Bayesianism that many of the hypotheses that are of interest in science cannot be understood in this way. As a result, assigning them prior probabilities has only a subjective significance, representing someone's degrees of belief.

If prior probabilities don't offer much promise as a vehicle by which Bayesians can explain the relevance of simplicity in the problem of model selection, what about likelihoods? The idea that specific curves have likelihoods – that they confer probabilities on the data – makes perfectly good sense, once an error distribution is specified. The usual model of error entails that a curve that is near the data will have a higher likelihood than a curve that is more distant; goodness-of-fit is relevant to curve fitting because goodness-of-fit reflects likelihood. However, the fact that the likelihoods of specific curves are well defined does not help explain why simplicity is relevant to model evaluation. The reason is that a complex curve can always be found that fits the data better than a simpler curve that fits the data imperfectly. If our only goal is to maximize likelihood, there is no reason to value simplicity.

Since the likelihoods of specific curves cannot explain why simplicity is desirable, perhaps we should consider the likelihoods of families of curves. This approach requires that we ask, for example, what the probability is of obtaining the data, if (LIN) is correct? This quantity is an average over all the specific straight lines (L_1, L_2, ...) that belong to the family:

$$Pr(\text{Data} \mid \text{LIN}) = \sum Pr(\text{Data} \mid L_i)Pr(L_i \mid \text{LIN}).$$

Some of the L_i's are very near the data, so the value of $Pr(\text{Data} \mid L_i)$ for those straight lines will be large; however, many straight lines will be quite far away, and so the value of $Pr(\text{Data} \mid L_i)$ for them will be small. The *average* straight line is further from the data than any finite number, so $Pr(\text{Data} \mid \text{LIN}) = 0$, if we assume that $Pr(L_i \mid \text{LIN}) = Pr(L_j \mid \text{LIN})$, for all straight lines L_i and L_j.

One way around this problem is to use some of the data to induce a weighting among these straight lines. Straight lines close to the data are assigned higher weight; $Pr(L_i \mid \text{LIN})$ is said to be greater than $Pr(L_j \mid \text{LIN})$, if L_i is close to the data and L_j is far away. This is essentially the approach of Schwarz (1978). When the average likelihood $Pr(\text{Data} \mid \text{LIN})$ is computed using this system of weights, it can turn out, depending on the data, that (LIN) has a higher average likelihood than (PAR'). Schwarz assumes that the competing models have the same prior probability (in this respect he differs from Jeffreys), with the net result that (LIN) can turn out to have the higher posterior probability.

As mentioned earlier, Schwarz's BIC gives more emphasis to simplicity than the AIC does. However, it is important to notice that Schwarz's analysis of the problem focuses on estimating the average likelihood of families of curves. Akaike's theorem, on the other hand, says that the AIC is an unbiased estimator of predictive accuracy, not of average likelihood. In a sense, the AIC and the BIC provide estimates of different things; yet, they almost always are thought to be in competition. If the question of which estimator is better is to make sense, we must decide whether the average likelihood of a family or its predictive accuracy is what we want to estimate. The predictive accuracy of a family tells you how well the best-fitting member of that family can be expected to predict new data; a family's average likelihood tells you how well, on average, the different members of the family fit the data at hand. Both quantities might be of interest, but they are different.

If we fix on predictive accuracy as our goal, what is the upshot? This decision doesn't automatically mean that AIC is better than BIC. After all, BIC might be a good device for estimating predictive accuracy, even though it was derived to estimate average likelihood. In any event, a very important fact here is that Akaike proved that the AIC is an unbiased estimator of predictive accuracy; it follows that the BIC must be a biased estimator of that quantity. On the other side, it is often said that the AIC is statistically inconsistent, but that BIC is statistically consistent; Malcolm Forster's chapter in the present volume addresses this claim and shows that it rests on using an inappropriate definition of predictive accuracy. Other optimality properties need to be considered as well, if a full assessment of AIC and BIC is to be obtained.

Even though it is important to resolve this question, we should not lose sight of what the AIC and the BIC approaches have in common. The idea that the goal of curve-fitting (and model selection, generally) is to achieve predictive accuracy helps explain why simplicity is relevant in this inferential context. The more adjustable parameters a family contains, the greater its risk of *over-fitting* the data, of mistaking noise for signal (Forster and Sober, 1994). Simplicity is relevant because complex families often do a bad job of predicting *new* data, though they can be made to fit the *old* data quite well. This is part of the practical experience that model builders have in different sciences. The mathematical framework constructed by Akaike and his co-workers allows one to understand *why* complexity contributes to over-fitting, and even to predict, from the data at hand, the degree to which this is apt to happen.

6   Conclusion

Simplicity considerations are relevant in many inference problems. In some, simplicity matters because simpler hypotheses have higher likelihoods; in others, simplicity matters because simpler hypotheses have higher prior probabilities; and in still others, simplicity matters because it reduces the risk of over-fitting. This 'local' approach has thrown considerable light on the longstanding philosophical problem of simplicity; we now have available a set of ideas that indicates how simplicity should be measured, justified and traded off against other desirable properties that hypotheses may possess. The progress that has been made on this problem is encouraging. If the near future resembles the recent past (a simple assumption!), this progress can be expected to continue.

REFERENCES

Akaike, H. (1973). Information theory and an extension of the maximum likelihood principle. In B. Petrov and F. Csaki (eds.), *Second International Symposium on Information Theory*. Budapest: Akademiai Kiado.

Batson, D. (1991). *The Altruism Question*. Hillsdale, NJ: Erlbaum.

Edwards, A. (1984). *Likelihood*. 2nd edition. Baltimore: Johns Hopkins University Press.

Fisher, R. A. (1925). *Statistical Methods for Research Workers*. Edinburgh: Oliver & Boyd.

Forster, M. and E. Sober (1994). How to tell when simpler, more unified, or less *ad hoc* theories will provide more accurate predictions. *British Journal for the Philosophy of Science* 45: 1–35.

Goodman, N. (1965). *Fact, Fiction, and Forecast*. Indianapolis: Bobbs-Merrill.

Hesse, M. (1967). Simplicity. *The Encyclopedia of Philosophy*. Vol. 7, pp. 445–8.

Jeffreys, H. (1957). *Scientific Inference*. 2nd edition. Cambridge: Cambridge University Press.

Kuhn, T. (1977). Objectivity, value judgment, and theory choice. In *The Essential Tension*, pp. 320–39. Chicago: University of Chicago Press.

Popper, K. (1959). *The Logic of Scientific Discovery*. London: Hutchinson.

Reichenbach, H. (1938). *Experience and Prediction*. Chicago: University of Chicago Press.

Rissanen, J. (1978). Modeling by the shortest data description. *Automatica* 14: 465–71.

(1989). *Stochastic Complexity in Statistical Inquiry*. Singapore: World Books.

Sakamoto, Y., M. Ishiguro and G. Kitagawa (1986). *Akaike Information Criterion Statistics*. Dordrecht: Kluwer.

Schwarz, G. (1978). Estimating the dimension of a model. *Annals of Statistics* 6: 461–5.

Sober, E. (1988). *Reconstructing the Past: Parsimony, Evolution, and Inference*. Cambridge, MA: MIT Press.

(1994). Let's razor Ockham's razor. In *From a Biological Point of View*. New York: Cambridge University Press.

(1996). Parsimony and Predictive Equivalence. *Erkenntnis* 44: 167–97.

Sober, E. and D. Wilson (1998). *Unto Others – the Evolution and Psychology of Unselfish Behavior*. Cambridge, MA: Harvard University Press.

3 Science seeks parsimony, not simplicity: searching for pattern in phenomena

Herbert A. Simon

Karl Popper (1961) is perhaps best known for reminding us that facts can falsify theories but cannot validate them. The theme of this chapter derives from another, less well known, dictum of Popper's: science does not aim at simplicity; it aims at parsimony. First, I will make some preliminary remarks about the goals of science. Then I will comment on the contributions of parsimony and simplicity to these goals. Finally, I will say something about the role that parsimony and simplicity have played in my own research and, in particular, my research in economics and statistics.

1   The goals of science

I will assume, for the purposes of this discussion, that the scientist may be concerned with one or more of the following goals:

1. (Basic science) The central goals of basic science are (1) to describe the world (reality, if you please): both (a) specific facts about it ('The Earth revolves about the Sun each 365 1/4 days') and (b) generalizations (laws) that describe collections of phenomena ('The periods of the planets around the Sun vary as the 3/2 power of their distances from it', Kepler's Third Law) and/or (2) to provide explanations of these phenomena ('Each planet is accelerated toward the Sun by a force that varies with the ratio of its mass to the square of its distance from the Sun'). Basic science is aimed at knowing and understanding.

2. (Applied science) Laws connecting sets of variables allow inferences or predictions to be made from known values of some of the variables to unknown values of other variables. Inferences and predictions can be used, in turn, to invent and design artifacts (e.g., arches) that perform desired functions (support the weight and other stresses placed on them), or to anticipate and adapt to future events on the basis of knowledge about the present and past. At the times the predictions are to be realized, the new data can be used, of course, to test whether the laws continue to hold.

3. (Science as art) Although conforming to empirical truth is the central imperative of science, the working scientist, like every other professional, also responds to an aesthetic imperative in which simplicity plays an important role. In general, beauty is thought (and felt) to lie in explaining much with little, and in finding pattern, especially simple pattern, in the midst of apparent complexity and disorder. Of course, these two aspects of beauty are closely connected: to be able to sum up a complex body of data in a relatively simple generalization (a pattern) is to explain much with little.

Daniel Berlyne (1960), in his research on curiosity, found that the length of time during which people will attend to a stimulus is a nonlinear function of its simplicity. A stimulus that is very simple (relative to the knowledge and experience of the viewer) will soon become boring: such obvious pattern as it possesses will soon exhaust its interest and attention will flag. If the stimulus is very complex (again, relative to the knowledge and experience of the viewer), no pattern will be recognized in it and attention will also soon flag.

Only if the viewer can continue, over some time, to detect new pattern in the stimulus, or to elaborate the pattern that has been detected, will his or her attention continue to focus on it. What is moderately complex relative to the viewer is interesting and beautiful because it can be perceived in terms of parsimonious patterns that can be extracted with reasonable effort. The overly simple or overly complex is boring and ugly, because of the poverty of its perceived patterns. In this chapter, I will show that, in consistency with Berlyne's evidence about interestingness and beauty, the scientist does not seek simplicity, per se, but parsimony: that is, pattern in the phenomena.

It is not easy to decide when scientists are interested in parsimony for its own sake (i.e. for its beauty), or when they seek it because the same patterns they find beautiful are also the patterns that describe and explain, and allow them to design and predict. One can speculate that the human emotional response to the beauty of parsimony has evolved through natural selection because it is useful for survival to be able to detect pattern in nature. Certainly the search for pattern in the environment is a very basic and persistent human drive.

2   Patterns in data

At the outset, it will be useful to define a few of the terms I have been using, especially simplicity, parsimony and pattern. I am not going to proceed in a highly formal fashion, but will refer to some formalisms, mostly derived from information theory, that have been discussed extensively in the literature. In particular, my discussion is based on the early work of R. J. Solomonoff (1964), (see also Barron and Cover, 1991). For the rest, I will count on the reader to generalize my definitions of the key concepts to the more complex cases. For a formal account of these matters, generally consistent with what I shall say here, and an excellent review of the literature, see Keuzenkamp and McAleer (1995).

Definitions of simplicity, parsimony and pattern

Simplicity Consider a data set represented as a one-dimensional ordered string of 0s and 1s. By the *complexity* of this string, I will mean simply its length, and by its *simplicity*, the reciprocal of its complexity.[1] Now suppose that there is a formula, also encoded as a string of 0s and 1s (possibly with the addition of a small finite number of special symbols), that can be used to describe with precision the data set. The formula might take the form of a program for generating the successive members of the string. For example, if * is the symbol for indefinite repetition, then the formula (01)* would represent the particular data set that is an alternation of 0s and 1s, and (1)* the data set that is a string of 1s. I can measure the complexity and simplicity of the formula in the same way as the complexity and simplicity of the data set – by the formula's length and the reciprocal of the length, respectively.

Notice that we are concerned with measuring only the complexity of finite strings, representing observed data sets or formulae we have generated. There is no occasion to deal with the behaviour of the measures as the sets and formulae grow without limit, although notice from the examples above that a finite formula can represent a data set of arbitrary length. The scientist is interested in how well a formula fits a set of data. Whether the formula will continue to fit as new data are obtained is a separate question, of interest for theory verification (or falsification), but irrelevant to discovery. Hence, by restricting our attention to finite sets, we avoid some of the difficulties that plague most theories of induction. We will return to this issue from time to time.

Parsimony and pattern Parsimony is a relation between two strings: one representing a data set, the other representing a formula for that set. In general, we will be interested in data sets represented as sequences of raw observations, before they have been recoded to take

---

[1] On occasion, I will use the term 'simplicity' in other ways, but I will always indicate when I am departing from the definition just given

advantage of any redundancy they may possess. The function of formulas is to exploit such redundancy when it can be discovered.

We could view the formula based on observed pattern as simply a recoding of the data – a different representation of the same data. We could then talk of finding the pattern *in the data*. Alternatively, we can view the pattern as separate from the data, but denoting it. We will employ the second viewpoint here, for it is convenient and customary to distinguish between data and a theory of the data, and viewing the pattern as simply a recoding of the data confounds the two. Moreover, by keeping pattern and data separate, it is easier to talk about what parts of the data are captured by any given pattern, and also to use multiple patterns to capture different components of the data (e.g., to distinguish between the gravitational term and the term for air resistance in a law of falling bodies).

Specifically, *parsimony* is the ratio of the complexity of the data set to the complexity of the formula. To the extent to which a data set can be represented parsimoniously, we say that it is patterned, and we call the representing formula a *pattern*. We will not always insist that the formula represent a data set exactly; in fact, in the real world of science, such representations are almost inevitably approximate (does one need the 'almost'?). We can speak of the parsimony of the formula's representation of the data set *up to such and such an approximation*. Except for occasions when we are concerned specifically with goodness of approximation, we will leave implicit the closeness with which the formula describes the data. Whether explicit or implicit, a criterion of goodness of fit is always present in the background of the processes of discovering or testing laws.

Consider two data sets, the second of which includes the first, and is thereby the more complex. Suppose that the same formula describes both sets. Then the parsimony of the relation of the formula with the larger data set is greater than the parsimony of its relation with the smaller set. Similarly, if two formulae describe the same data set, the parsimony of the relation with the simpler formula is greater than the parsimony of the relation with the more complex. As we are most often concerned with comparing the fit of two laws to the same data or the same law to an expanded data set (new observations), our comparisons will generally only depend on ordinal properties of the complexity measures, as long as goodness-of-fit issues do not arise.

Whatever the scientist's motives, an invariable characteristic of laws is that they simplify the data they describe or explain. We cannot find laws in data unless there are patterns in the data. If there are patterns, the data are to that extent redundant and the patterns may be used to provide a parsimonious description that is more concise than the data themselves. In this sense, the search for laws *is* a search for simplicity, where simplicity here mean terseness of description relative to the original representation of the data.

The primordial acts of science are to observe phenomena, to seek patterns (redundancy) in them, and to redescribe them in terms of the discovered patterns, thereby removing redundancy. The simplicity that is sought and found beautiful is the simplicity of parsimony, which rests, in turn, on the exploitation of redundancy. We do not seek the absolutely simplest law but the law that is simplest in relation to the range of phenomena it explains, that is most parsimonious.

The Platonist in search of pattern

I can recount five anecdotes from my personal experience that illustrate my Platonic urge to search for pattern. The first three date back to high school mathematics, where I was delighted to discover from examples that $(x - y)(x + y) = x^2 - y^2$. I wasn't able, at first, to prove the relation in general, but I could show empirically that it worked for any example I tried. It summed up an infinity of facts in a simple formula, which I found beautiful.

A little later in algebra, I found an ugly fact: quadratic equations could have two solutions, one solution or none. I was only reconciled to that apparent lack of pattern when I later learned about imaginary and complex numbers, and that all quadratic equations had exactly two solutions in this extended number system.

Similarly, it was ugly, I thought, that a set of n linear equations in n variables, where at least k of these variables appeared in every subset of k equations, might or might not have a solution, depending on the ranks of certain determinants. Some years later I was delighted to discover that, if an appropriate measure is defined over the sets of coefficients of the equations, all such equations that do not have a solution lie in a subspace of measure zero (Hall, 1934). (Needless to say, this subspace can be defined by the ranks of the same determinants, but the 'rarity' of the exceptions somehow consoled me to their existence.) All of these examples show that discovery of pattern plays a critical role in understanding not only empirical data but also data in which the patterns are created tautologically by the laws of mathematics and logic.

My next two examples relate to empirical matters. At the University of Chicago, while studying econometrics with Professor Henry Schultz, a homework problem required me to fit a function to data where the independent variable was the length of young infants ranging from three to twelve months in age, and the dependent variable was their weight. My Platonist urges led me to fit the function $y = Ax^3$, on the hypothesis that an infant's density and shape would remain approximately constant over this period. Schultz graded the paper B, noting that I should have fitted $y = Ax^B$, and then tested the significance of the difference, $B - 3$. I am still uncertain whether the criticism was justified; after fitting the cubic function I could simply have computed what percentage of the variance in the data was explained by the fitted curve.

On another occasion, Professor Schultz called my attention to A. J. Lotka's wonderful book, *Elements of Physical Biology* (1924, 1956), full of fascinating and often mysterious facts. A fact that especially struck my fancy was that if we rank the cities of the United States (or many other countries) by size, we find that a city's population varies (to a very close approximation) with $1/R$, where R is its rank. So the eightieth largest city in the US is almost exactly one tenth as large as the eighth largest city. (In recent decades the rule fits best for metropolitan areas.)

I worked off and on for a number of years before I found an appropriate formula to fit these data (the so-called Yule distribution, which is approximated by the Pareto distribution), and an explanation of why it worked that satisfied me (Simon, 1955). Patterns essentially the same as the rank-size pattern for cities also appear in many other social and biological phenomena: word frequencies in texts, frequency of authorship, sizes of business firms (I'll return to this example later), sizes of biological genera in terms of numbers of species in each, etc. It turned out that the (statistical) explanation of the Yule distribution, with a little reinterpretation of the underlying probability mechanisms, also worked for these other phenomena, thus greatly extending the range of application of the pattern without loss of simplicity.

Some notable examples of pattern in science

A little reading in the history of science assured me that I was not alone in my passion for pattern in data and the parsimony that could be obtained from it. Let me cite a few examples of notable cases where the pattern was found with essentially no help from any pre-existing theory – cases of pure empiricism. One case already mentioned is Kepler's Third Law, which was probably (the evidence is scant) discovered by Kepler in a wholly inductive way, and which, as we will see, has been rediscovered by a computer program using a path that is demonstrably inductive (or abductive, if we prefer Peirce's term for it), receiving no help from theory (Langley et al., 1987).

A second case is Prout's Law (announced about 1815) asserting that all atomic weights are integral multiples of the atomic weight of hydrogen (see Prout's Hypothesis, in Bynum et al., 1981). The observed facts were that many atomic weights (for example, all but two of the first twenty) were close to fitting the law although there were egregious exceptions (e.g., the atomic weight of chlorine is 35.5). Chemists took sides on the reality of Prout's pattern and Stoney tested statistically whether the large number of near-integers could have arisen by chance (the odds were very long against it). The issue was settled (in Prout's favour) about a century later with the discovery by Aston of isotopes, and the hypothesis that all atomic nuclei are made up of protons and neutrons with nearly equal masses. The correct law, taking isotopes into account, was a little less simple than Prout's first approximation, but everyone would now prefer the more exact one.[2]

A third case is Bode's Law (actually first suggested by Titus in 1766), that the successive planets, Mercury $= 0$, Venus $= 1, \ldots, i, \ldots$ are at (approximate) distances $D_i = 4 + 3 * 2^{(i-1)}$ from the Sun (see Bode's Law in Bynum et al., 1981). As the 'law' is only very approximate, does not hold for the two outer planets, Neptune and Pluto, and has found no clear theoretical explanation, it remains an open question whether there is a law here or a coincidence. A very similar regularity does hold, however, for the satellites of Jupiter, and astrophysicists still seek an explanation, perhaps based on the dynamics of the planetary origins and separation from the Sun.

Notice that in the case of Prout's Law, what tipped the balance to acceptance was a new pattern (involving isotopes) that provided not only a much better fit to the data, but also an explanation – something that is still missing in the case of Bode's Law. The explanation also made more acceptable the remaining deviations, which were very small compared with those that had been removed, hence might be expected to require a different explanation (a different pattern or mechanism) to remove them. Today, we attribute them to the nuclear packing fraction.

A fourth case, the last I shall mention, is Balmer's Law (1885) for the wave lengths of successive lines in the hydrogen spectrum: $i^2/(i^2 - 4)$, $i = 3, 4, \ldots, \ldots$ (soon generalized to $i^2/(i^2 - j^2)$) (Banet, 1966). It fits the data with extraordinary precision, was discovered by a non-physicist by pure induction – perhaps 'numerology' would better describe the process – and

---

[2] Even the revised law is not exact, for it does not take care of the packing fractions, whose explanation depends on the mass-energy equivalence introduced by special relativity. Hence physicists today might prefer for some purposes a second approximation by a still more complex law.

had no explanation until 1913 when Bohr provided one with his new quantum model of the hydrogen atom. Here the fit was so good and the parsimony so great that the law obtained immediate acceptance in 1885 even without an explanation.

So finding pattern is the name of the game – or at least of one very important game in science. I mention again that we are speaking both of exact patterns discovered inductively in mathematical 'data' (my high school examples) and *approximate* patterns in real data. In a few cases, e.g., Balmer's Law, the pattern may fit the data extremely well; often, the fit is quite approximate. Later, I will return to the question of approximation, and how we should judge whether an approximation is satisfactory or unsatisfactory.

3   The uses of parsimony

We see that parsimony is at the root of what we mean by a scientific law. With simplicity, it also plays several roles in the discovery of laws and their verification. Parsimony is not only the end product of scientific activity, but it also helps to guide the discovery and verification processes. Let us see how this comes about.

Discovery versus verification of laws

Philosophers of science commonly distinguish between the discovery of laws and their verification (Reichenbach, 1938). Early writers, including Sir Francis Bacon, in *The New Organon* (1960), John Stuart Mill, in *A System of Logic* (1963), and William Whewell, in *The Philosophy of Inductive Sciences* (1847, 1966), paid considerable attention to law discovery, and laid down normative principles to guide efficient experimentation. Consider, for example, John Mill's Canon of Difference:

If an instance in which a phenomenon occurs and one in which it does not differ in only one other circumstance, it is the cause or the effect, or an indispensable part of the cause, of the phenomenon.

If we observe a phenomenon to occur from time to time but not always, we can seek to determine its causes and effects by searching for the circumstances that distinguish its appearance from its non-appearance. If we find such a circumstance, we can never be sure that it is unique, but that need not discourage us, for we are not looking for an infallible method of scientific discovery – something that no one has promised us. Discovery is a process of heuristic search whose success cannot be guaranteed.

Because the search for laws is a heuristic process carrying no guarantees of success or validity, many philosophers of science in this century, perhaps the most notable being Karl Popper,[3] denied the possibility of formulating normative rules of discovery. Only during the past thirty-five years, beginning with Norwood Hanson's *Patterns of Discovery* (1958), has this view been seriously challenged. However, with the construction in recent years of a number of computer programs that incorporate successful mechanisms of discovery, we possess a rather conclusive constructive demonstration that normative (heuristic) theories of discovery are possible (Langley et al., 1987).

We will consider separately the roles of simplicity and parsimony in discovering (generating) theories and their roles in verifying or falsifying (testing) them. Then we will say something also about simplicity in the application of theory and simplicity in experimentation. We will see that simplicity is not always used in the sense we defined earlier, but has somewhat different meanings and different roles in each of these activities.

Parsimony and simplicity in law discovery

We may take as common, though not universal, the case of some observed phenomena in need of description and explanation: that is, which call for a law that fits them – if possible, a law representing a mechanism that explains them. There may or may not already exist some theory that could play the role of this law. As a first subcase, let us assume that no such theory exists. We are then confronted with the task of data-driven law discovery.

Data-driven discovery The BACON program (Langley et al., 1987) has shown itself to be capable of discovering laws by fitting functions to data. At the most general level, BACON consists of a hypothesis generator and a test. The hypothesis generator produces functions, the test fits them to the data and decides that the fit is or is not satisfactory. (The programmer sets the standard of approximation that must be met.) Now the easiest way in which to build such a hypothesis generator is to begin with a small set of simple functions, and generate successively more complex ones from combinations of these primitives. The next function

---

[3] He calls on the authority of, among others, Albert Einstein, who is quoted (*The Logic of Scientific Discovery*, p. 32) as saying: 'there is no logical path leading to these ... [highly universal] ... laws. They can only be reached by intuition, based upon something like an intellectual love of the objects of experience.'

to be generated is selected on the basis of information about the fit or misfit of the functions already generated.

As the functions are not simple binary strings, hence have no obvious unique order, our earlier definition of simplicity does not apply without extension. One meaning of simplicity in this case is just the order of generation. We call a function simple if it is generated early in the sequence. This order may be different for different sets of data for, as remarked above, observed relations with the data of the functions already generated affect what function will be generated next. As a function is complex (in an informal sense) to the extent that it is formed as some kind of combination of previously generated functions, the new definition of simplicity is not wholly unrelated to the basic one for binary strings.

Consider again the specific example of Kepler's Third Law. The given data (we can use Kepler's actual data) are the distances from the Sun (x) and periods of revolution (y) of the then-known planets. BACON observes that as x grows larger y also grows larger, and forms the hypothesis that $y/x = k$, a constant. When this function fails to fit the data, BACON observes that as x grows larger y/x also grows larger and hypothesizes that $x/(y/x) = x^2/y = k$, a constant. The fit is now closer, but the test fails again.[4] Persevering, BACON next observes that as y/x grows larger x^2y grows larger, and hypothesizes that $(y/x)/(x^2/y) = (y^2/x^3) = k$, a constant. In this case, the test succeeds, yielding Kepler's Third Law: a planet's period of revolution varies as the 3/2 power of its distance.

Now it seems quite natural to build the BACON system from a small set of primitives that themselves are simple in another sense: simple in having only a few parameters. Just as Peano's Axioms generate all the integers from zero with the help of the single operation of succession, so BACON generates a large set of functions from the linear function with the help of the two operations of multiplication and division, applied in response to cues provided by the data. By moving from the simple to the complex (in this new sense) we increase the likelihood that we will find first the function that provides greatest parsimony.

It is of some interest with respect to the trade-off between simplicity and parsimony that Kepler, ten years before he found the 3/2-power law, had published the hypothesis that the planets' period varied as the square of the distance. Only some years later did he become dissatisfied with the fit of hypothesis to data and search for a law that gave better agreement. It happens that BACON's generator also discovers the square law before

---

[4] As in all such procedures in science, the closeness of fit that is regarded as acceptable is an arbitrary parameter. Accepting or rejecting Prout's Law (or any other) is a matter of taste – or should we call it free will?

the 3/2-power law. Whether it accepts the former, or rejects it and goes on to the latter, depends on the goodness-of-fit criterion it applies (determined by the programmer). BACON, like Kepler and Prout (and everyone else), needs a separate parameter (a 'propensity for simplicity') to determine what degree of approximation is acceptable.

For a wider range of applications in science, we might want to supply BACON with a few more primitives (e.g., the log function, the exponential, the sine function), but it is remarkable that with the linear function as its sole primitive, it discovers not only Kepler's Third Law, but also Joseph Black's law of the equilibrium temperatures of mixtures of liquids, Ohm's law of current and resistance, Snell's law of refraction, the law of conservation of momentum and a host of others. What is more remarkable, it achieves each of these successes after only a small number of trials. What it definitely doesn't do is to 'try out all possible functions'. Instead, its search is highly selective and guided by cues.

In the course of discovering laws that fit data, BACON also discovers a number of theoretical concepts, including inertial mass, specific heat, voltage, molecular weight, atomic weight (distinguishing the latter two) and others. The motivation for these discoveries of theoretical concepts is that, by introducing them, laws previously found can be simplified, hence can explain the same data more parsimoniously (Simon, 1985).

For example, BACON finds that when bodies A and B are accelerated by a stretched spring connecting them, the ratio of their accelerations is always the same constant k_{AB}. Bodies A and C provide another constant, k_{AC}, and bodies B and C a third, k_{BC}. BACON, finding a new pattern, that k_{AB} times k_{BC} equals k_{AC}, postulates a constant associated with each body, m_A, m_B, and m_C, respectively, and hypothesizes that the ratio of the accelerations of I and J, $k_{IJ} = m_J/m_I$, for all I and J. If we have N objects, we can now state the law relating the accelerations of all pairs of them in terms of N constants, the m_I, instead of N^2 constants, the k_{IJ}. The m's are, of course, familiar to us as inertial masses. By introducing theoretical terms we have gained a new source of parsimony.

From this brief (and somewhat oversimplified) description of BACON, we see at least three roles for simplicity in law discovery or generation. First, as hypotheses must be tried in some order, the easiest way to build a hypothesis-generator of some generality is to start with a *simple primitive function, or a small set of simple primitive functions*, and generate successively more complex functions by the application of *simple combinatorial operations* (in our example, multiplication and division).

The second role of simplicity is to make as small as possible the number of functions that have to be generated before one is found that fits the data. In discovery systems like BACON, the order of function generation is not fixed, but responds to the form of the misfit in unsuccessful applications. This feedback serves as a powerful heuristic that often permits satisfactory functions to be found with very little search.

The third role of simplicity is to make more parsimonious the laws that are found, by introducing new theoretical terms (new properties that are not directly observable but are inferred from observables). Thus, important theoretical terms in physics (e.g., mass, specific heat, voltage and the like) can be discovered in response to the goal of simplifying the forms of laws (Langley et al., 1987).

In all of these roles, simplicity goes hand in hand with parsimony. That is to say, we seek to explain the data with simple functions, containing few constant parameters, before we test complex functions. Similarly, in introducing theoretical terms, we greatly reduce the number of independent parameters whose values must be fixed to explain the data. This is the aspect of parsimony, that Popper, with his emphasis on verification, defended. In fact, he argued (1961, p. 140) that '[t]he epistemological questions which arise in connection with the concept of simplicity can all be answered if we equate this concept with *degree of falsifiability*' (his italics). Popper did not, however, see that the concern for parsimony can lead to normative rules for discovery systems: that such systems should be designed, as far as possible, to generate simple rules before generating complex ones.

The progression in hypothesis generation from simple to complex is not peculiar to the BACON program but is seen in most of the other extant examples of law-finding programs. For example, Valdes-Perez's MECHEM (1992) accepts data on the substances that are input to a chemical reaction and some of the substances that are produced by it, and then attempts to find a sequence of reaction steps that will account quantitatively for these inputs and outputs.

MECHEM does this by first trying all possible one-step reactions (1) with no unobserved intermediate products, (2) that are consistent with applicable constraints derived from chemical theory. Then, if it fails to match the data, it gradually increases the number of steps and the number of postulated unobserved reactants until a reaction chain is found that fits the data. In this respect MECHEM is like theorem-proving programs that first search for one-step proofs, then for two-step proofs, building each new structure on those previously generated. The architecture that proceeds from simplicity to complexity in the generation of hypotheses discovers the maximum redundancy in the data and is easily implemented.

Theory-guided discovery The examples discussed thus far, except MECHEM, deal with discovery when no theory, or essentially no theory, exists to guide the search for pattern. This is, in fact, a common case in the history of science, but certainly not universal. Often existing theory, while not adequate to account for the phenomena of interest, can provide powerful help in the search. Consider the question of finding a law that gives the equilibrium temperature of the mixture of a liquid contained in two vessels, each with its own initial mass and temperature (Black's Law). If it is hypothesized that the law must be symmetrical with respect to the two liquids (a hypothesis that itself contributes to simplicity of the law) then, after the form of the function for the first liquid is determined, the same form can be postulated for the second. Likewise, if it is hypothesized that the mass and the heat (the product of temperature by mass) will be conserved, this additional constraint will further limit the set of functions to be generated.

In fact, when BACON is given these three constraints, of symmetry and mass and heat conservation, it finds the law without any superfluous search whatsoever. In this case, in fact, it *deduces* the law from previously accepted theory, just as Newton deduced Kepler's Third Law from his own laws of mechanics. Later on, we will have occasion to look at other cases of law discovery where the relation between prior theories and new patterns is more complex than in these two examples.

Parsimony and simplicity in verification

I have already mentioned the important role of simplicity in enhancing parsimony, thereby making a theory easier to falsify. Of course we know today, as a result of the work of Lakatos and others, that the matter is not quite as simple as Popper made it. What we usually falsify by our observations or experiments is not a single law but the consistency with the evidence of a whole complex of laws, together with assumed initial and boundary conditions. We can usually save any particular part of this complex by sacrificing some other part. I will not go into the whole Lakatosian story of progressive and degenerating research programs, but simply, for the present, ignore this added complication and speak of falsification in a simple Popperian sense.

Direct comparison of theory with data Each degree of freedom – each parameter in our theory that must be estimated from the set of data that is being used to test the theory – both adds to the complexity of the theory and weakens our ability to falsify it if it is wrong. Consider Ohm's Law, $I = kV/R$, where I is the current, V the voltage, R the resistance, and k a constant. In Ohm's original experiment, he could measure the resistance (the length of a wire) and the current (the angle of the needle on an ammeter), but not the voltage. Thus, he 'used up' one set of observations to estimate the product, kV, and this single trial could not falsify the hypothesis. Only after estimating kV could he then test his theory by modifying R (changing the length of the resistance wire) and inserting in the equations the values observed in a second experimental trial (with kV held constant by using the same battery).

In Ohm's experiment, the problem of fitting parameters is very simple, whereas the usual situation in econometrics (or in most observational, as distinguished from experimental, sciences) is far more difficult, not in principle but quantitatively, because we often want to consider the simultaneous interaction of many variables. Suppose we wish to fit N data points in V variables by a system of simultaneous linear equations. As we must estimate $V^2 + V$ parameters from the data, we will always obtain a perfect fit unless $N > V^2 + V$, hence only in the latter case can we test the hypothesis that the data fit the model.

If we wish to experiment with functional forms that have more parameters, the situation gets progressively worse. If we have a sufficient number of data points so that the model can be falsified, we can then introduce an error term into each equation, apply the method of least squares and use the percent of variance in the data that is explained to determine whether we wish to accept the equations as describing the pattern of the phenomena. In the first case, of falsifiability, we say that the equations are *over-identified*; with the introduction of the error terms and the minimization of the variance, we say that they are *just identified*. The underlying rationale is essentially the same as BACON's. As in all statistical testing, the criterion of acceptance is arbitrary.

Identification of structural relations It would take me too far afield in this chapter to discuss the whole concept of identification and the reasons why, both in order to understand mechanisms and in order to apply theories to practical affairs, sciences always strongly prefer over-identified structural equations to equations that are incompletely identified (Koopmans, 1949). The relation of identifiability to parsimony may be briefly characterized as follows. Suppose we have a theory that postulates k mechanisms governing the behaviour of k variables. We now come to a situation where we have reason to believe that $k - 1$ of the mechanisms remain effective, but the remaining one has been altered. For reasons of parsimony, we would prefer to carry over the unaltered parts of the theory, making modifications only in the equation corresponding to the mechanism that has been changed. If we have information about the nature of the change, we may even be able to use this information to infer the modified mechanism. We do not have to recreate the theory, whenever it has suffered a structural change, from whole cloth.

Structural equation systems are parsimonious descriptions of reality, factoring complex systems into simpler subsystems. The approximate effect of successive factorization, when it is possible, is to reduce the complexity of a system from a linear to a logarithmic function of the number of its elements.

To the extent that we can match the components of the equation systems to corresponding components of the systems they describe, we can build theories of complex systems in combinatorial fashion from the theories of their components. The existing body of theory in molecular biology is a striking example of the pay-off that can be obtained from this divide-and-conquer strategy. Factorability is a powerful source of simplicity, and parsimony. (See the discussion of near-decomposability in the last pages of this chapter.)

Matching inferences from theory to data We turn now to another verification issue. In the situations examined so far, we have been concerned with matching laws directly to data. However, in many situations, we must draw out the implications of theories before we can test them against available data. For example, Einstein had to reason from his theory of time and synchronization of clocks to the Lorentz transformations and from these to the invariance of Maxwell's equations under Lorentz transformations in order to test special relativity (assuming that Maxwell's equations had already been found to agree with the data on electromagnetism). To take a simpler example, Newton had to deduce Kepler's laws from the laws of motion and the inverse square law of gravitational attraction in order to show that the latter laws were consistent with the planetary motions.

Simplicity in computation In these inference processes, another kind of simplicity may be important: simplicity that facilitates computation. Drawing out the implications of a theory requires deduction or simulation or some other form of computation, which may be simple or complex. If a set of differential equations can be solved in closed form, the paths that the equations define can be compared directly with data to test their fit. In the literature of theoretical mechanics, we find many papers that solve a system of simultaneous equations for the stresses in a board with, say, an infinite slit or other unrealistic boundary conditions. In these cases, the boundary conditions are not selected because there are many real boards in the world with infinite slits, but because if these boundary conditions, rather than more realistic ones, are used, the equations can be solved in closed form.

Even in our present world of supercomputers, it is still a trivial matter to find problems of deep scientific interest where heroic simplification is required to make feasible the computations needed to understand the behaviour of the system of interest – either by solving in closed form or by simulation. The recent focus of attention on chaotic systems has greatly increased our sensitivity to computational feasibility. The computer has reduced but not eliminated the need for simplification and approximation as practical necessities for testing and applying theory.

The field of computer science has been much occupied with questions of computational complexity, the obverse of computational simplicity. But in the literature of the field, 'complexity' usually means something quite different from my meaning of it in the present context. Largely for reasons of mathematical attainability, and at the expense of relevance, theorems of computational complexity have mainly addressed worst-case behaviour of computational algorithms as the size of the data set grows larger. In the limit, they have even focused on computability in the sense of Gödel, and Turing and the halting problem.[5] I must confess that these concerns produce in me a great feeling of ennui.

When I speak here of computational complexity (or simplicity), I refer to the amount of computation we have to do to solve a problem of some kind in the average case, and what percentage of the problems of that kind we are likely, on the basis of previous experience, to solve with an acceptable amount of computation ('acceptable' being a flexible word like 'significant'). Just as in the long run we are all dead, so, as problems grow in size without limit, we don't solve them. Scientists do not ask for guarantees (and certainly not guarantees in the form of theorems) that they will solve any given problem, or even that the problem has a solution (a parsimonious formula for the data). They follow various procedures in search of patterns (like the BACON procedures described earlier) and sometimes they are successful – often enough to maintain their addiction to science. (Experimental psychology has shown that random partial

---

[5] I have been startled, in the past several years, to find that the phrase 'bounded rationality', for which I can claim some authorship, has now been borrowed by rational expectationists (e.g. Sargent, 1993) and game theorists (e.g. Aumann, 1986) to refer to worst-case complexity theory and the limits on computation imposed by Gödel and Turing. Bless me, the actual bounds on the powers of computation that we mortals possess are so severe that we almost never have occasion, in our scientific practice, to regret that we are only Turing machines and cursed with Gödel incompleteness! Our difficulties with computation start at much lower levels, not even including the worst case. But then, I belong to a generation that remembers how matrices were inverted with hand-operated desk calculators.

reinforcement is more conducive to addiction than consistent reinforcement.)

Finally, the advantages of simplicity (in my sense of the term) for computation must be balanced against the loss of fit of theory to data through approximation. I will take up this issue at some length after considering other implications of simplicity for the application of theories.

Simplicity in the application of science

From our discussion of computational simplicity, we can see that simplicity plays a role in applying accepted theories that is similar to the role it plays in testing new theories. Parsimony enhances our ability to make strong predictions about the behaviour of the systems of interest, whether they be systems we are designing or natural systems, by decreasing the number of degrees of freedom we lose through parameter estimation. At the same time, computational simplicity increases our ability to deduce or to simulate system behaviour under the anticipated conditions of application.

Notice that parsimony and computational simplicity are not always compatible. When we limit ourselves to functional forms that facilitate computation, we may have to introduce additional parameters in order to obtain sufficiently close approximations to the real phenomena. For example, Fourier's series and Taylor's series provide powerful formalisms for approximating wide classes of functions, but at the expense of introducing a potentially infinite number of parameters. These formalisms afford computational simplicity but not necessarily parsimony. The problem thereby created is serious if our goal is to test a theory but not if we are simply applying an accepted theory whose validity we are not questioning. Even in the latter case, lack of parsimony makes it impossible for us to make strong predictions from the theory when we have to estimate most or all of the parameters from the data.

Simplicity in experimentation

I will distinguish two classes of experiments (or observational procedures), one of which may be called well-structured, the other exploratory. They call for quite different heuristics in their design.

Well-structured experiments The design of experiments, as usually described, provides an obvious application of yet another kind of simplicity. According to the standard doctrine, we vary one variable at a time, controlling other variables that are known to be or suspected of being influential, and we randomize where we cannot control. We seek situations where the variables we are measuring will sound loud and clear against the background of unwanted noise. Strong structure and controls of this kind are of special value when we already have a specific hypothesis, originating from a theory or elsewhere, that we want to test. Then a good experimental design clears away irrelevancies and focuses attention on the variables of interest.

Exploratory procedures Well-structured experiments fit well the Popperian picture of science in which the main concern is the verification or falsification of hypotheses that already exist. The generation of hypotheses is a different matter. Let us distinguish two cases. In one case, we already have a general theory. We deduce some new consequences from the theory and then design an experiment to test whether these consequences are supported empirically. This is the pattern of what Kuhn called 'normal science'. In the other case, there are some phenomena of interest – bacteria, say – but at the moment we have no hypothesis about them that we wish to test. Then we can design experiments, or merely opportunities for observation, that may reveal new and unexpected patterns to us. Having found such patterns, we can search for explanations of them.

Most of my earlier examples of law discovery fit this latter description of scientific activity. In my algebra classes I noticed certain patterns in equations: when the sum and difference of two quantities were multiplied, the product always had the same form: the difference of their squares. A quadratic function usually had two solutions (but there were exceptions), and n linear equations in n variables generally had a unique solution (but again there were exceptions). Prout found lots of elements whose atomic weights were integral multiples of the atomic weight of hydrogen, an improbable result if only chance were at work. Balmer found a regularity in the spectral lines of hydrogen. Kepler found a relation between the distances and periods of revolution of the planets.

Let us consider two examples of a somewhat more complex sort. Fleming observed, in a Petri dish that he had left unwashed in his laboratory when he had gone on vacation, some bacteria being lysed, and near them, a growth of fungus that he recognized as belonging to the genus *Penicillium*. You and I (unless you are a bacteriologist) would have noticed nothing, for we would see nothing unusual in bacteria cells that were dissolving in the proximity of a fungus (or even *that* it was a fungus). As Pasteur observed, accidents happen to the prepared mind.

Fleming's observation led him to a very vague hypothesis: that there might be a cause and effect relation between the presence of the fungus and the fate of the bacteria. He (like many other scientists) had a standard way (a heuristic) for approaching unexpected patterns when only vague hypotheses (or none) were available: (1) to design experiments to test the scope of the phenomena, and (2) to look for a mechanism capable of producing them. Fleming's (incomplete) follow-up pursuing this heuristic, and its later completion by Florey and Chain, brought the discovery of antibiotics.

The second example concerns the young Hans Krebs, who took as his first major independent research project designing a sequence of experiments to elucidate the chemical reaction path that produces urea in living mammals (Holmes, 1991). He did not have a strong hypothesis but a question (and some research tools he thought might help find the answer). He did know (a weak hypothesis) that the likely sources of the nitrogen in urea were ammonia and the amino acids. However, the task he set himself was not to test that hypothesis but to accept it and design experiments that might disclose the mechanism (the reaction path).

Consequently, he added various mixtures of ammonia and particular amino acids to slices of living liver tissue and measured the products. In many such experiments, he observed only a minimal production of urea, but on an occasion when he tested ammonia together with the amino acid ornithine, he obtained a large yield. For his prepared mind, and on the basis of his recent experiments, this was a contrasting pattern and a surprising one. He responded by doing exactly what Fleming did: (1) he tested the scope of the phenomenon ((a) did it require ornithine, or would similar substances do the trick?; (b) what happened to the product when the quantities of ammonia and ornithine were varied?), (2) he searched for a plausible chemical reaction path. Within a few months he had found the path for urea synthesis. Interestingly enough, on this path, ornithine did *not* serve as a source of the nitrogen in urea, but as a catalyst for the reaction that extracted the nitrogen from ammonia; so the answer Krebs obtained to his original question about the origins of the nitrogen *disconfirmed* the hypothesis that led him to experiment with ornithine. He had carried out the right experiment for the wrong reason!

The cases of Fleming and Krebs are not unusual in the history of science. One could easily produce another dozen that led to Nobel prizes. A person who is expert in some domain exposes himself or herself to phenomena, watches for the unexpected (a pattern), then designs new observations or experiments to account for it. One attractive feature of this procedure is that it is tolerant of complexity in the phenomena being observed. All that is required is that these phenomena have a variety of properties (a pattern) which someone skilled in the art will come to know. Then a 'surprising' pattern is just one that is different from the familiar and expected patterns.

A simpler example of pattern finding helps to show what is going on here. Standard intelligence tests often make use of the Thurstone Letter Series Completion task (Simon and Kotovsky, 1963). A series of numbers or letters is presented, say, ABMCDMEF. . . , and the test-taker is asked to supply the continuation (in this case, MGHM would be the 'right' answer). A strong case can be made for this task as a good measure of aptitude for high-level cognitive skills. Studies of how answers are found reveal a very simple picture. Subjects notice two kinds of relations, repetitions of the *same* symbol and relations of *next* between pairs of symbols, where 'next' refers to succession on some familiar 'alphabet'. For example, speakers of English in our culture would find relations of next between X and Y, Tuesday and Wednesday, October and November, the integers 16 and 17, and so on.

Having noticed such relations in the test series, the test-taker finds a simple pattern, usually involving periodic repetition and hierarchies of the relations, that accounts for the presented sequence and allows it to be extrapolated. A very small number of primitive relations, those we usually associate with the concept of symmetry, account for the major patterns that have been found in sciences ranging from molecular genetics to particle physics. The pattern that is discovered is formed combinatorially from the small set of primitive relations.

Which form of experiment? In observing the natural world we do not have these luxuries of varying things one at a time and removing noise; and therein lies the superior power of laboratory experiments for disclosing the underlying structural relations in which we are interested, *once we know what variables we should segregate and examine.* Therein also lies the weakness of formal experimentation when it is designed tightly to test particular hypotheses: it does not usually provide us with the surprises that often lead to our most exciting and important scientific discoveries. For these – for the initial hypotheses that guide our experiments – we must depend largely on observation of complex phenomena against the background of a large body of stored expert knowledge, with the aim of encountering surprises.

Exploration, as distinct from systematic experimentation, is not regarded very favorably in typical normative theories of experimental design. 'Random' search in complex situations is thought to be a highly inefficient procedure. On the contrary, for a scientist who has built up a wide body of knowledge about some domain, any situation that conflicts with that knowledge, hence violates expectations, is a starting point for a program of experimentation, using the 'surprise' heuristic described earlier in the cases of Fleming and Krebs as a basis for guiding search.

Rapid scanning of the environment until an unexpected pattern, a surprise, occurs has proved historically to have been a highly productive scientific strategy (not to the exclusion, of course, of other strategies). A plausible account in terms of the surprise mechanism can be given for many instances of the 'aha' phenomena that are so greatly treasured by historians of science, and thought so mysterious by the layperson.

4   Simplicity versus closeness of fit

In building theories, there is almost always a trade-off between simplicity and close approximation to the facts. My anecdote about the 'theory' relating lengths and weights of infants, $W = aL^3$, illustrates the point well. By assuming that density and shape do not change with growth, we save one degree of freedom in our equation. Should we make this assumption or should we weaken the theory by substituting a parameter, b, for the number 3? Or should we further decompose b into a product of two parameters, one for change in density, the other for change in shape? The obvious answer is that 'it depends'. Depends on what? It depends on how close our assumptions approximate the reality and on how accurate a theory we need or want.

The principle of 'unrealism'

In economics, Milton Friedman's advocacy of the 'principle of unrealism' (Friedman, 1953) has provided a frequent battleground for the contention between simplicity and closeness of approximation. One of his examples, Galileo's law of uniform acceleration, celebrates Galileo's genius in sticking with simplicity (parsimony in relation to the data). For understanding the movement of bodies in space where air resistance is negligible, or even close to Earth at low velocities, extracting the relation between a constant force and a velocity that grows steadily with time ($v = gt$) was a stellar scientific achievement. It also provides an excellent illustration of the experimental strategy of varying one variable at a time in order to determine the underlying mechanisms that are present in, and interact in, more complex situations. In fact, its value for law discovery and perhaps for verification is far more obvious than its value for application of the law in either design or prediction.

For example, Galileo's discovery fails to advance the science far enough to support the design and manufacture of parachutes. The maker of parachutes might prefer, to $v = gt$ or its equivalent $dv/dt = g$, a formula that looked more like $dv/dt = (g - fv)$, (leading to the even more complex $v = (g/f)(1 - e^{-ft})$) where f is a parameter representing the air resistance on the body. True, there is another parameter here to be estimated, and it will take on different values for bodies of different sizes and shapes, and air of different densities. But the new formula has the virtue that, these estimates having been made, it might predict the behaviour of parachutes (e.g., their terminal velocity, (g/f)), which the simpler formula can not. Hence, as the two formulae have different ranges of application, it is meaningless to ask which is the more parsimonious. The first thing we must ask of a formula, before considering its parsimony, is whether it describes the data of interest to an acceptable level of approximation.

Simplicity and complexity in modern biology

Before turning to examples drawn from economic theory, let me discuss one more example from the natural sciences: simplicity and approximation in genetics (Watson, 1976). We start with Mendel, who in his experiments with sweet peas, arrives at the important concept of the gene and a simple probabilistic law of inheritance for combinations of genes that (by good luck in his choice of experimental material) are inherited independently and exhibit a full dominant/recessive contrast. Mendel was able to explain his data by means of an extremely simple theory (which is still retained as a special case in the modern genetic model) as a result of the lucky fact that the particular situations he investigated had these particular special properties.

Before the end of the nineteenth century, chromosomes were observed under the microscope and were identified as the agents of inheritance because of their behaviour (splitting) during meiosis. These observations produced new data that, interpreted within the existing model, produced a great gain in parsimony.

The next major steps occurred at the turn of the twentieth century when, along with the rediscovery of Mendel's work and its association with chromosomes, crossovers of chromosomes were observed (accounting for statistical dependence between genes). The observation of chromosomes had strengthened the theory (by providing a hypothetical mechanism for the observed phenomena), but certainly complicated it. The discovery of crossover complicated it further by introducing the parameters that described the dependence between pairs of genes, but also provided a potential explanation in terms of actual location of the genes on the same or different chromosomes. Here we have a classic case of the trade-offs among simplicity of hypotheses, range of phenomena explained and falsifiability.

The idea that genes could be assigned particular locations on particular chromosomes suggested new experimental manipulations – for example, increasing mutation frequency by irradiation – and led to curiosity about the chemical structure of genes and chromosomes. Nearly a half century passed before answers began to be found for these questions: first, identifying DNA rather than proteins as the basis for differentiation among chromosomes (which contain both); and second, identifying protein synthesis as the key process governed by genes, through the mapping of nucleotide triads upon amino acids. The introduction of these mechanisms produced a far more complex theory (which became still more complex as myriads of details were discovered), but a theory that could begin to explain the entire process in terms of accepted principles of physical chemistry, hence was actually enormously parsimonious.

During the entire century to which I am referring, there appeared to be no reluctance whatsoever to moving from simpler theories to more complex ones that gave far more complete explanations (and predictions) of the phenomena. Parsimony was valued highly, as was a detailed understanding of complex phenomena, but bare simplicity of theory, which could only be obtained by sacrificing explanatory power, was valued hardly at all.

Laws of qualitative structure

Along with the formal genetic models that have been developed, with their exquisitely detailed picture of the chemical processes, there have also emerged some broad qualitative generalizations of great importance – what Allen Newell and I, in another context (Newell and Simon, 1976), called 'Laws of Qualitative Structure'. In genetics, an example of such a law is: 'A protein is a sequence of amino acids that is (often) synthesized in vivo on a template consisting of a linear sequence of nucleotides (RNA), the latter mapped 1-1 from a corresponding sequence (DNA) in the chromosome.' This is the meaning of the slogan: 'One gene, one protein.'

Notice the 'usually', and 'often' in the statement of the law, as well as its general vagueness. Many of the most important laws of biology (and of physics, for that matter) have this qualitative and slogan-like character: two examples are the germ theory of disease and the cell theory. The germ theory of disease simply amounts to the advice that: 'If you encounter a disease, look for a micro-organism as cause; there may often be one. Of course there are many diseases that don't involve micro-organisms.' The cell theory suggests that: 'Organisms are divided into cells each of which has many organelles, including (at least in eukaryotes) a nucleus which contains (most of) the genetic material, and various organelles capable of carrying out metabolic processes.'

While these laws of qualitative structure are no substitute for detailed and relatively rigorous theories, they play an important role in organizing the thinking of experts in scientific domains about the phenomena with which they deal, and in guiding their search for solutions of the problems they attack. For example, the germ theory of disease suggests the heuristic of applying to an ailing organism the known methods for detecting and identifying micro-organisms in tissue. One might say that they provide simple, but very rough, statements of very complex but powerful theories. Scientists carry both the 'slogans' and the detailed theories around, and alternate between using one or the other as circumstances dictate. I will have more to say later about what these circumstances might be.

5   Parsimony and simplicity in economics

The same principles of theory building and choices between simplicity and complexity that I have been illustrating with examples drawn from physics and biology apply, with little need for modification, to economics. Again, concrete examples (which I have drawn from my own work) will help us see why (Simon, 1997).

Utility maximization v. bounded rationality

The maximization of expected utility, the central axiom of neoclassical economics, is usually regarded as an exceedingly simple theory, because all that it postulates is a consistency of choice behaviour over the whole set of choices that an actor makes. Given the subject's utility function, income and probability distributions over future events, and the full set of market prices, his or her demands for all goods are determined. Income and the market prices can be observed, hence create no problem; but as the utility function is completely undetermined apart from the requirement of consistency, virtually any pattern of demands is consistent with the theory; and in spite of 'revealed preference', there is generally no practical way to describe empirically the content of the utility function, hence the actual pattern of demand, at any given moment of time.

Matters are a little better if we compare two situations that are close in time, the second being identical to the first except that the price of one commodity has increased. Now, with a few additional 'harmless' assumptions about the utility function (essentially that it is unchanged and that there are no inferior commodities) we can predict that less of the commodity whose price has risen will be demanded than before. However, without yet another assumption – or information – (about elasticities), we cannot predict whether the total amount spent on that commodity will increase or decrease, much less what the magnitude of the change will be. Thus, each bit of additional prediction seems to call for empirical evidence about one or more additional parameters. The theory may be thought simple, but it is not especially parsimonious.

Measuring demand elasticities Henry Schultz, in his monumental *The Theory and Measurement of Demand* (1938), did what scientists in other fields usually do in such circumstances: he attempted to determine the parameters, in particular the elasticities of demand, empirically. In the process he revealed the difficult issues of identification of structural equations that face such an undertaking. What was further discouraging was that the parameters, if estimated, could hardly be expected to retain their values over any great length of time. Measuring demand elasticities was more like measuring the magnetic field of the Earth, or even the changing patterns of barometric pressures, than it was like measuring the velocity of light, the gravitational constant, or Planck's constant.

Moreover, it was not clear what should be taken as the independent variables. The theory of choice under uncertainty was in a primitive state at that time, and although Schultz was well aware that he had to make assumptions about the predictive process, the assumptions he chose looked much more like the cobweb than like rational expectations. (There was, of course, no empirical evidence available in the 1930s – and there is precious little today – that would have led very readily to the choice of either of these models or some other.)

Marginal utilities and budgets Let me turn to my own first research encounter with marginal utilities. In 1935, I studied at first hand the administration of public recreation programmes in my native city of Milwaukee. Among other things, I was interested in the budget process that required choices between planting more trees on playgrounds, say, and hiring additional recreation leaders. Obviously (or so my economics courses had taught me) the money should be put where the marginal return was greatest. There were only a few difficulties in applying this principle: (1) you had to be able to estimate the results produced by the alternative expenditures, and (2) you had to be able to determine the increments in utility produced by these results.

As a practical matter, my observations and interviews showed that none of the participants in the process were thinking of the matter in this way, as they had not the slightest idea of how to carry out the requisite measurements. The observations showed further that, in the two departments involved in operating the programme, administrators affiliated with the city's public works department almost always preferred the first alternative (trees), whereas administrators affiliated with the school board almost always preferred the second (recreation leaders).

Nevertheless, budget decisions were made. In the process, the principal references to data were references to last year's expenditures for these same purposes. If it was possible to spend more in the coming year, the increment was usually allocated more or less proportionately to previous spending levels. Of course the process was more complex than this (at least more wordy), but these remarks convey its flavour. Out of my observations (and the accompanying surprise at the irrelevance of what I had learned in Henry Simons' excellent course in price theory) emerged some laws of qualitative structure dealing with budget processes and human decision-making processes in general.

Bounded rationality and organizational loyalties The first of these new laws of qualitative structure was the principle of bounded rationality: human beings have reasons for what they do, but they seldom maximize utility. They do not maximize because, given the complexities and uncertainties of the choice situations they face, they have neither the knowledge (theories and facts) nor the computational abilities to carry out the necessary inference processes. The principle of bounded rationality is, like the germ theory of disease (and like utility theory, for that matter), a scientist's hunting license rather than a definite answer to the question of what behaviour will be observed. Its simplicity is deceptive, for applying it requires one to ascertain a myriad of facts.

Fortunately (and in contrast to utility theory), forty years of research in cognitive psychology within the information processing framework has disclosed many of these facts, especially the mechanisms that are used in decision making when maximization of subjective expected utility (SEU) is impossible. The resulting theory is not simple (see, for example, Newell and Simon, 1972, ch. 14), but it is parsimonious, allowing prediction of behaviour in some detail and with some accuracy in a large number of situations that have been studied, including some within the domain of economics. It looks much more like theory in molecular biology than like Newton's laws of motion.

The second law of qualitative structure that came out of my recreation study was that members of organizations identify, cognitively and motivationally, with the goals of the organizations or organization units to which they belong. This principle also has central importance to economics: specifically (1) to the question of the nature of altruism and the role that altruism plays in human choice, and (2) to the motivations that underlie behaviour in organizations and the consequences of these motivations for the respective roles of organizations and markets in an economy (Simon, 1990, 1991).

Both laws of qualitative structure that emerged from my first adventure in research had some of the same seductive simplicity that is possessed by SEU maximization. As in the latter case, the attempt to apply them revealed what a vast amount of empirical information must be provided before broad principles of this kind (or even more rigorous ones that are expressible in equations) can make predictions about specific situations.

Explanation of supply and demand changes Before leaving this issue, let us look at one more example, which I think not atypical, of an application of SEU maximization theory: Gary Becker's 'explanation' of the movement of women after World War II into the labour market (Becker, 1981). Clearly, the SEU theory requires that something change either in womens' utility functions (and hence in the supply function) or in the demand for their labour. Becker opts for the latter without providing any empirical evidence for his choice or even discussing the possibility of changes in the utility function.

Surely it is not implausible to suppose that, as a result of the gradual change of women's role in society during the first half of this century, smaller families and the experience of women in the workplace during World War II, there have been large continuing changes in their preferences for outside employment versus managing a household. Clearly the question of whether the increase in employment resulted from a shift in demand or supply (hence utility) is an empirical one and the theory, without such evidence, does not support one explanation over the other.

The 'work' of arriving at Becker's explanation is not done by the theory but by unsupported empirical assumptions which could only be validated by data – data that were not provided. Even more damaging to Becker's claims, the same phenomenon of increasing employment of women could have resulted from mechanisms consistent with bounded rationality, without appeal to the SEU maximization hypothesis. Just to suggest two from among numerous possibilities, the wartime experience may have called women's attention to the possibilities of outside employment, of which they had been only dimly aware, or may have redefined what constituted a satisfactory pattern of life activities.

Are we better or worse off with respect to simplicity or parsimony if we substitute bounded rationality for utility maximization to explain this and other concrete phenomena? We have seen that the principle of bounded rationality is clearly a law of qualitative structure, subject to many kinds of imprecision. It advises us that, in order to predict behaviour, we must know something not only about the preferences of the actor and the environment in which he or she is acting (which utility theory also requires) but also about the actor's knowledge (of alternatives and of consequences) and ability to compute and draw inferences.

What does bounded rationality propose as a replacement for utility maximization? It says that we must examine human behaviour empirically to find out what procedures are actually used to make decisions. These procedures may vary considerably, depending on what knowledge and information is available and upon the complexity of the situation. They may change in the course of history with the acquisition of new knowledge and computational techniques, and with shifts in public attention. The procedures that are used in decision are not constructed arbitrarily and anew, however, for each decision situation, but themselves derive from more general principles.

The psychological research I mentioned earlier has brought together and tested some much more specific models of the decision process, which incorporate such mechanisms as heuristic search (including search to enlarge the commodity space), satisfying and aspiration levels (finding alternatives that meet 'satisfactory' levels, where what is satisfactory is constantly modified by experience), means-ends analysis, focus of attention, recognition, the content and organization of expert memories and so on.

We might say that this body of theory resembles, qualitatively if not quantitatively, theory in molecular biology. It postulates a large number of specific mechanisms, and a great deal of empirical knowledge is required before it can be applied in any particular circumstances. Neither SEU maximization nor bounded rationality are exceptionally parsimonious theories. Nor are they simple, except when they are posed in the forms of laws of qualitative structure – rough qualitative guides to the phenomena. How are we to choose between them?

I would propose that we should choose in much the same way that we choose in other sciences. First, we should seek empirical evidence of whether the mechanisms advanced by each theory do in fact operate as postulated. To the extent that they do, the theory at least has explanatory value, if not predictive value. Of course, we might conclude that there is no way of finding out about these mechanisms. To that extent, we would have to regard the theory as vacuous: 'metaphysical' or 'non-operational' in positivist language.

If our interests are more applied than basic, we might choose between theories, as Friedman proposes, on the basis of predictive power rather than explanatory value. But if we do that, we must include not just the bare bones of the theory but the parameters that have to be estimated in order to make the predictions. Here again, a theory is essentially helpless unless there are practical means for estimating these parameters, and the success of the prediction is apt to rest at least as heavily on the parameter measurements as on the exact form of the axioms.

Firm size distributions I turn to another example from my own economic research to illustrate the points I have just made. In the chapters on the theory of the firm in neoclassical economics textbooks, some attention is usually given to the determinants of firm size. The standard theory transmitted by all the textbooks with which I am familiar stems from Jacob Viner and his celebrated debate with Wang, his draftsman. Each firm, according to Viner as amended by Wang, has a U-shaped short-term cost curve, determined by the level of operation for which it was designed, and a U-shaped long-term cost curve which is the envelope of the short-run curves for all possible levels of operation. In the long run, firms will operate on a scale that corresponds to the point of minimum cost on the long-term cost curve.

What does this theory (deduced from profit maximization) allow one to say about the distribution of firms by size in an industry or in an entire economy? Essentially nothing unless all the firms in the industry face the same long-term cost curve. In that case, all firms will be predicted to be about the same size, a prediction that is in egregious conflict with all of the known facts. If, on the other hand, each firm has an idiosyncratic cost curve, then each will have its size determined by that curve. In this case, nothing at all can be said about the size distribution of firms in the industry without previous knowledge of the optimum for each firm – not a very parsimonious prediction.

As I mentioned earlier in this chapter, I came to the firm size question from the opposite direction: from empirical data of actual size distributions, which almost always fit quite well the Yule (or Pareto) distribution, a distribution related to, but even more asymmetrical than, the lognormal distribution (Ijiri and Simon, 1977). For the phenomena of firm sizes, this distribution can be derived from assumptions that make very much weaker demands on human calculation than does SEU maximization, and that are compatible with human bounded rationality. The basic assumption (usually called the Gibrat assumption) is that the average rates of growth of firms of all sizes are independent of present size. If, on average, small firms grow by 5 per cent per year, then medium-sized firms also grow 5 per cent on average, and large firms, 5 per cent.

This Gibrat assumption has several things to commend it. First it is simple – much simpler than SEU maximization, hence far more parsimonious. Second, it is easy to find data to test it. Third, and perhaps most important, it fits the facts very well in almost all cases where it has been tested. Fourth, the Gibrat assumption itself follows from some rather plausible assumptions about the underlying mechanisms: roughly, that the amount of money a firm can borrow at reasonable cost for expansion, the speed with which it can expand its production and marketing facilities and markets at reasonable cost, and all of the similar magnitudes that govern overall expansion will be roughly proportionate to the present size of the firm. (If we want to put the matter in terms of U-shaped cost curves, we should begin with curves for the cost of *changing* the rate of production, rather than curves for the cost of production at different output levels.) I don't know that these hypotheses about ease of expansion have ever been tested systematically, but such casual data as I am familiar with fits them, and they 'resonate' when proposed to people experienced in business.

In the case of business firm sizes, it seems clear that the principles usually applied in science to choose among theories – whether simplicity, parsimony, or predictive power and accuracy – will pick the explanation of firm size distributions based on the Gibrat assumption over the nearly vacuous explanation based on profit maximization. That the Viner–Wang theory persists in the textbooks, which seldom mention the Gibrat theory, can only be explained by the mystique of SEU that continues to dominate the profession of economics. It is as if physicists continued to believe that space was occupied by an ether for forty years after the results of the Michelson–Morley experiments had been published.

6   Parsimony and simplicity in the world

Up to this point, we have been concerned with the meaning of simplicity and parsimony in scientific theories. In this final section, still focusing on my own research, I would like to propose some generalizations about simplicity in the phenomena that we study. I will examine two examples – one relating to the human sciences, the other more abstract and general. The lessons I will draw are, first, that simplicity (as distinguished from parsimony) is attainable in science to the extent that the phenomena we are studying are simple; and second, that, fortunately for us, we find in many domains a particular kind of simplicity that enables us to pursue a divide-and-conquer strategy in our research.

Is human behaviour simple?

In the discussion thus far of simplicity and parsimony in science, I have made no distinction between the human sciences and the so-called 'natural' sciences. Some special considerations arise when we are building theories about the behaviour of adaptive organisms, among which human beings are of particular interest to us. Our investigations will lead to some generalizations about the relation between the complexity of the environments in which adaptive systems live and the simplicity or complexity of the systems themselves (and hence of theories about them).

In another context (Simon, 1996) I claim that, if we set aside for a moment the contents of human memory, then '[a] man, viewed as a behaving system, is quite simple. The apparent complexity of his behaviour over time is largely a reflection of the complexity of the environment in which he finds himself.' The reason for exempting memory from this characterization is that the contents of memory largely reflect the complexity (or simplicity) of the environment. They are not part of the built-in human architecture, but are acquired and shaped through experience of the world (including, of course, social experience).

Here we have another law of qualitative structure. What does it assert about the simplicity or complexity of theory? It asserts that if we divide our theory of human behaviour into two parts – (1) architecture, and (2) learned knowledge and skill – the former will be relatively simple (at least at the level of detail of information processes, although not necessarily at the neuronal level) in comparison with the latter. The learning processes themselves, being part of the architecture, will be simple, but the body of knowledge and skill acquired through them will not be. Contemporary theories of cognition, including theories of problem solving and of perception, learning and memory, partition matters in this way, acquiring thereby enormous parsimony. Let me comment on one such theory which has been employed to explain, among other things, the bases for specialized human expertise.

EPAM is a model of human perception, learning, memory (short-term and long-term) and recognition. The theory was first proposed by Feigenbaum (1961) to account for the phenomenon of human rote verbal learning, and in the succeeding third of a century has been gradually extended to explain a wide range of phenomena that have been studied by experimental psychologists. In recent years, EPAM has been of particular value for explaining the vast differences between the performances of novices and experts in any particular domain (Richman et al., 1996). To accomplish this, it interacts with another theory, the General Problem Solver (GPS), whose history dates back to 1958, and which provides an explanation of human problem-solving processes (Newell and Simon, 1972). EPAM and GPS, taken together, may be regarded as specifications at the symbolic level of the main mechanisms that implement bounded rationality in human beings.

I will not attempt to describe either EPAM or GPS, but will simply show how they provide a simple theory of expertise – one that is simple at least at the level of qualitative structure, and not too complex even when we look at the nitty-gritty details of implementation. However we assess its simplicity, the theory is surely parsimonious – probably the more important assessment – for EPAM and GPS use only a few basic mechanisms to account for exceedingly complex behaviour (e.g. playing grandmaster chess, making medical diagnoses, discovering scientific laws, steering an automobile, writing music, making drawings).

The central mechanisms of GPS are heuristic search and, in particular, means–ends analysis, which I have already discussed. The central mechanisms of EPAM are a learning process and a recognition process. Through the learning process EPAM acquires the ability to distinguish among stimuli that are presented to it. It does this by using very simple processes to build a discrimination net of unlimited size (nets of more than 200,000 terminal nodes have been grown) that performs successive tests on stimulus features and sorts them accordingly. The discrimination process enables EPAM to recognize stimuli already familiarized through learning, and thereby to access information about them that has been stored previously.

In brief, the theory of expertise asserts that experts are able to perform as they do because (1) by virtue of GPS-like structures and processes, they have powerful heuristics that makes their problem solving in the domain of expertise orders of magnitude more powerful and efficient than the problem solving of novices; (2) by virtue of EPAM-like structures and processes, they recognize a great many situations from the cues they perceive in them, and thereby gain access to knowledge and skills relevant to these situations that enable them to solve many problems by immediate recognition and that greatly enhance their search efficiency in solving the others. One might say that the expert operates like a well-indexed encyclopedia, EPAM serving as index, with capabilities (GPS) for selective search.

The evidence supporting this account of expertise has been gathered in many domains and is by now overwhelming. One can say with assurance, for example, that a great deal of medical diagnosis is achieved by recognition (of symptoms), and when this does not suffice, the rest of the job is done by heuristic search that guides the collection of additional evidence and its interpretation. The theory has not lacked application to economic phenomena, elucidating, among others, the processes used by a financial analyst to determine a firm's problem areas, the processes used to select an investment portfolio, systems for scheduling complex phenomena when optimization is not computationally feasible, job choice processes, the processes used to analyse a business case of the kind commonly used in business policy courses, and the investment decision processes of business firms (see references to this research in Simon, 1997). Recently, it has scored some major successes in showing how bounded rationality (it might in this case be called minimal rationality) can bring about relatively efficient equilibration of markets in the absence of mechanisms for utility maximization.

By constructing a domain-independent theory of heuristic search (GPS) and recognition (EPAM) mechanisms, and by supplying domain knowledge that has been determined independently to be available to experts in specific domains, theories in the form of running computer models have been able to account for expert performance in these domains. Because the computer models can themselves perform professional tasks in the domain, they make direct predictions of expert behaviour that can be compared with observations of human experts in the laboratory or in real-life settings. As the examples of the previous paragraph show, these methods can be used to study and explain, in a way that can be empirically verified or refuted, the decision making of economic actors.

Are large systems simple?

The final topic that I shall discuss had its beginnings in economics, but has important implications for such distant domains as evolutionary biology and computer science, and indeed, for the organization of the sciences in general. It concerns the relation between particular kinds of pattern in the phenomena under study, on the one hand, and the parsimony of the theories that describe the phenomena, on the other. It goes under the labels of 'near decomposability' and 'nearly complete decomposability' of dynamic systems, and the core of it is found in the Simon–Ando Theorem, first published in *Econometrica* (Simon and Ando, 1961).

Block triangular and diagonal dynamic systems Shortly after its publication, my attention was attracted to a paper by Richard M.

Goodwin (1947). Goodwin was concerned with the justification of partial equilibrium analysis, especially the legitimacy of treating sets of variables as unconnected if their connection is very weak or if they are coupled unilaterally (systems with unilateral coupling of subsets of variables are called block triangular).

Exploring this idea further, I was led to a formal characterization of causal ordering and its relation to identifiability (Simon, 1953). In 1957, Albert Ando and I, returning again to Goodwin's ideas, saw how to simplify dramatically, without serious loss of information, the description of systems that were nearly completely decomposable, and in this way to make their descriptions much more parsimonious. Nearly completely decomposable systems are systems made up of blocks of variables, where each block is only weakly connected with the others (Simon and Ando, 1961). For example, in the input–output matrices of economic systems, it is typical for variables within particular clusters of industries to be tightly bound with one another, but only weakly bound with the variables of other clusters. The variables and equations of nearly completely decomposable systems can be arranged so that their matrices are nearly block diagonal (figure 3.1).

It occurred to us that this hierarchical structure of relations among variables and sets of variables was not peculiar to economic systems or human organizations; it was also commonly observed in both inorganic nature (layers from quarks through atoms to molecules) and organic

X	X	X			ε			
X	X	X				ε		
X	X	X		ε		ε		
			X	X	X	X		
	ε		X	X	X	X		ε
			X	X	X	X	ε	
ε			X	X	X	X		
		ε					X	X
ε				ε			X	X

Figure 3.1 A nearly completely decomposable matrix: X represents a possibly strong link; ε, a weak (epsilon) link

nature (layers from organic molecules through complex reactions to cells, organs and organisms).

This led us to the hypothesis (a law of qualitative structure) that systems in nature that appear to be complex will usually be found to be patterned in hierarchies; and that they will be describable simply and parsimoniously if advantage is taken of this special and powerful property.

We were able to prove (the Simon–Ando Theorem) that in a stable dynamic system whose matrix of coefficients is nearly block diagonal (figure 3.1), each of the diagonal blocks rapidly approaches its steady state almost independently of the others. Over a longer period of time, the entire matrix gradually approaches a long-term steady state; and during this second period the diagonal blocks move monolithically, nearly preserving their individual steady states. Thus, to describe the entire system approximately, it is necessary only to solve the equations for each of the diagonal blocks, replace each block by a single element that is a weighted average of the elements of its principal eigenvector, and then solve this aggregated system (with one degree of freedom for each block) for the long-term behaviour of the system.

Multilevel systems This possibility of simplifying nearly completely decomposable systems through aggregation is not limited to systems of two levels, like the one depicted in figure 3.1. Each of the diagonal blocks in that figure could itself represent a nearly completely decomposable system, and so on, to any number of levels. In terms of time scales, events at the lowest level of the hierarchy would occur very rapidly, then on slower and slower time scales as we ascend toward higher levels. Aggregation amounts to selecting out the processes that operate on each particular time scale and studying their behaviour independently of the faster and slower processes.[6] For the time scale selected, dynamic phenomena are observed at a particular level of aggregation; variables at the higher levels of aggregation remain approximately constant; and subsystems at lower levels are seen only as aggregates in steady-state motion.

Near-decomposability and the specialization of science In a world built on this plan, as large aspects of our world are, phenomena on different time scales can be studied nearly independently of each other; and a good deal of the specialization among the sciences is based pre-

---

[6] Physicists, struggling with certain problems in quantum electrodynamics, appear to have rediscovered a closely similar idea, which they employ under the label of 'renormalization'.

cisely on this possibility for decomposition and aggregation. Each of the sciences selects phenomena on a particular time scale, treats variables on slower time scales as constant parameters, and treats subsystems operating on faster time scales as aggregates whose internal details are irrelevant at the scale of special interest. This partitioning is perhaps seen in its sharpest form in physics and chemistry, in the progression from quarks, through the so-called elementary particles, atomic components, to small molecules, macromolecules, etc.

Near-decomposability is of great importance for the social sciences also. For example, the cognitive theories that I have described in this chapter postulate processes that have durations ranging from tens of milliseconds to a few seconds. (It may take about 10 milliseconds to test a single feature in a stimulus; about 500 milliseconds to recognize a stimulus; about 8 seconds to store a simple new stimulus in long-term memory.) At the next level below are neural processes that are one or more orders of magnitude faster. (It takes about one millisecond for a signal to cross the synapse between two neurons.) It is this difference between the speeds of processes at the two levels that permits us to build a theory of cognition at the symbol-processing level which is reducible, in principle, to a neuro-psychological theory, but which can be developed independently of the details of the latter theory. To understand problem solving, we don't need to know much detail about the operation of neurons.

A second way of representing the near-decomposability of complex systems is by means of computer programs that employ closed subroutines. In such programs, each routine is executed by executing in sequence its component routines, until we come down to the level of primitive instructions, which are executed directly (translated directly into machine language). A routine will execute correctly as long as it provides the correct inputs to its subroutines, and the subroutines, in return, produce correct outputs. Beyond this requirement, the operation of a routine is wholly independent of the structure and operation of its subroutines (and of their sub-subroutines, down to the level of the primitives). Just as markets reduce the information that economic actors must have about the other parts of the economic system, so the architecture of closed subroutines, and the closely related architecture of nearly complete decomposability, reduce the dependence of each component on the detailed structure and operation of the others.

'Natural' simplicity in theories The suspension of theories from hierarchical sky-hooks is characteristic of all of science. One might describe it as Nature's concession to the bounded rationality of scientists:

phenomena do not have to be understood all at once, but can be divided into components that can be studied separately. But the subdividing process, if it is to be successful, must respect the structure of the natural systems. The hierarchical structure of many complex systems, and the divide-and-conquer strategy it enables, is a major source of simplicity in scientific theories just because it is a major source of pattern. The independent treatment of system components does not represent simplicity for simplicity's sake, but the exploitation of the parsimony that is present in nature. In particular, near-decomposability gains this parsimony with little loss in accuracy of approximation. The simplicity that is achieved is a by-product of the way things are, not a celebration of a 'principle of unrealism'.

Evolutionary basis of near-decomposability It is natural to ask how we are so fortunate as to find nature structured in this way. A plausible answer can be given in terms of natural selection. As I have given that answer at considerable length in *The Sciences of the Artificial* (Simon, 1996), I will only outline it briefly here. Although it has not been shown conclusively, there are reasons to believe that the rate at which complex systems are likely to evolve is very much accelerated if they are composed of stable subsystems, each of which can be altered without major alterations to the others. At any level of complexity (measured, say by system size) hierarchically ordered systems will evolve more rapidly than systems that are not so ordered. As a result, most of the very complex systems that have evolved, and that we are able to observe in the world, have hierarchical structure.

In inorganic nature, and organic nature up to the level of single-celled organisms, the advantage of near-decomposition is gained whenever simpler stable systems combine into more complex stable systems (e.g. atoms into molecules). At the level of multi-celled organisms, similar advantages are obtained because the interrelations of the stable chemical processes of specialized tissues and organs resemble the interrelations of closed subroutines: each depends only on the outputs of the others and provides inputs to the others. The success of each is nearly indifferent to the details of how its inputs are produced by the providers.

The liver converts ammonia previously derived from amino acids into urea, which it delivers to the kidneys for excretion. Provided that the urea is synthesized and delivered, the operation of the kidneys is unaffected by the exact sequence of urea-synthesizing reactions in the liver. Increased efficiency of the liver will not affect the kidneys in the short run; over a longer run the ratio of sizes of the two organs may change if one gains efficiency more rapidly than the other. The important fact is that the rate of evolution is accelerated by the mutual independence of subsystems from sensitivity to each other's details of structure and process.

The implications of near-decomposability for efficiency and evolution of complex systems is still only imperfectly understood. We can expect that progress in molecular developmental biology will soon throw a great deal of light on these matters.

7   Conclusion

What have we learned from this exploration of simplicity and parsimony in science? In particular, what are the principal laws of qualitative structure that we can carry away from our investigation? I will not attempt a detailed summary of the many issues that I have discussed, but simply point to some of the most important of the generalizations that emerged from the discussion.

The basic desideratum in science, whether pursued for understanding, for its practical products or for its beauty, is parsimony, which may be measured by the ratio of the number of symbols required to describe the data individually to the number required to describe the patterns they form. We aim to discover pattern in observed facts that can be used to describe and explain these facts parsimoniously.

Parsimony brings simplicity in its wake; but simplicity in theory without parsimony in the relation between the theory and data is bought only at the price of weakening the goodness of approximation of our descriptions, narrowing the range of phenomena over which they extend, and impoverishing our understanding of the phenomena.

Law discovery requires us to synthesize hypotheses, and it is usually advantageous to synthesize simple hypotheses before complex ones, both (1) because it is easiest to generate hypotheses by combinatoric operations on a few primitive hypotheses, and (2) because we are seeking the simplest hypothesis that will account for the phenomena (that is, the most parsimonious).

Parsimony, measured by the ratio of number of data points to number of parameters that need to be estimated from the data, enhances the falsifiability of theories.

Simplicity, when it can be attained without unacceptable sacrifice of descriptive, explanatory and predictive power, can facilitate computation with theories and reasoning about them. Computational simplicity, simplicity of statement of theories, and simplicity of the mechanisms that implement theories are not always synonymous. Computational simplicity is a principal ground for choosing between alternative representations of the same theory.

We must distinguish between the simplicity of a theory and the simplicity of the mechanisms at the next level down, implied by the theory. However one regards the simplicity of SEU theory, its implementation implies unattainably complex computational mechanisms for the theory's human actors. On the other hand, bounded rationality can be implemented by computational mechanisms that are within human capabilities.

Describing data in terms of theories that are built on structural relations provides means for predicting the behaviour of systems under partial change in structure. The validity of the structural relations in a theory can only be tested if the theory is over-identified.

Important features of theories are often encapsulated in laws of qualitative structure, which are heuristic and not rigorous, and which provide high-level generalizations, and representations useful in organizing problem-solving search.

The source of simplicity in a theory is the existence of discoverable pattern in the phenomena the theory describes and explains. The hierarchical structure of many of the phenomena of our world provides a basis for constructing independent, and relatively simple, theories for different problem domains, each dealing with system behaviour at a different level of the hierarchy. The levels are distinguishable in terms of the speeds and durations of their processes, and nearly-independent theories can be provided for the phenomena at each hierarchical level. Among large systems, evolution will select favourably for those that are hierarchical.

REFERENCES

Aumann, R. J. (1986). *Rationality and Bounded Rationality*, Nancy L. Schwartz Lecture, delivered May 1986 at the J. L. Kellogg School of Management, Northwestern University.

Bacon, Sir Francis (1960). *The New Organon*. New York: Liberal Arts Press.

Banet, L. (1966). Evolution of the Balmer Series. *American Journal of Physics* 34: 496–503.

Barron, A. R. and T. M. Cover (1991). Minimum complexity density estimation. *IEEE Transactions on Information Theory* 37: 1034–54.

Becker, G. S. (1981). *A Treatise on The Family*. Cambridge, MA: Harvard University Press.

Berlyne, D. E. (1960). *Conflict, Arousal, and Curiosity*. New York: McGraw-Hill.

Bynum, W. F., E. J. Browne and R. Porter (1981). *Dictionary of the History of Science*. Princeton, NJ: Princeton University Press.

Feigenbaum, E. A. (1961). The simulation of verbal learning behavior. *Proceedings of the 1961 Western Joint Computer Conference* 19: 121–32.

Friedman, M. (1953). *Essays in Positive Economics*. Chicago: University of Chicago Press.

Goodwin, R. M. (1947). Dynamical coupling with especial reference to markets having production lags. *Econometrica* 15: 181–204.

Hall, P. (1934). On representations of subsets. *Journal of the London Mathematical Society* 10: 26.

Hanson, N. (1958). *Patterns of Discovery*. Cambridge: Cambridge University Press.

Holmes, F. L. (1991). *Hans Krebs: the Formation of a Scientific Life*. New York: Oxford University Press.

Ijiri, Y. and H. A. Simon (1977). *Skew Distributions and the Sizes of Business Firms*. New York: North-Holland Publishing Co.

Keuzenkamp, H. A. and M. McAleer (1995). Simplicity, scientific inference and econometric modelling. *The Economic Journal* 105: 1–21.

Koopmans, T. C. (1949). Identification problems in economic model construction. *Econometrica* 17: 125–44.

Langley, P., H. A. Simon, G. L. Bradshaw and J. M. Zytkow (1987). *Scientific Discovery*. Cambridge, MA: MIT Press.

Lotka, A. J. (1924, 1956). *Elements of Mathematical Biology*. New York: Dover Publications. (Originally published as *Elements of Physical Biology*.)

Mill, J. S. (1963). *A System of Logic*. London: Routledge & Keegan Paul.

Newell, A. and H. A. Simon (1972). *Human Problem Solving*. Englewood Cliffs, NJ: Prentice-Hall.

(1976). Computer science as empirical inquiry: symbols and search. *Communications of the ACM* 19: 113–26.

Popper, K. (1961). *The Logic of Scientific Discovery*. New York: Science Editions.

Reichenbach, H. (1938). *Experience and Prediction*. Chicago: University of Chicago Press.

Richman, H. B., F. Gobet, J. J. Staszewski and H. A. Simon (1996). Perceptual and memory processes in the acquisition of expert performance: the EPAM model. In K. A. Ericsson (ed.), *The Road to Excellence: the Acquisition of Expert Performance in the Arts and Sciences, Sports and Games*, pp. 167–88. Mahwah, NJ: Lawrence Erlbaum Associates.

Sargent, T. J. (1993). *Bounded Rationality in Macroeconomics*. Oxford: Oxford University Press.

Schultz, H. (1938). *The Theory and Measurement of Demand*. Chicago: University of Chicago Press.

Simon, H. A. (1953). Causal ordering and identifiability. In W. Hood and T. C. Koopmans (eds.), *Studies in Econometric Methods*. New York: John Wiley.

(1955). On a class of skew distribution functions. *Biometrika* 52: 425–40.

(1985). Quantification of theoretical terms and the falsifiability of theories. *British Journal for Philosophy of Science* 36 : 291–8.

(1990). A mechanism for social selection and successful altruism. *Science* 250: 1665–8.

(1991). Organizations and markets. *Journal of Economic Perspectives* 5: 25–44.

(1996). *The Sciences of the Artificial*. 3rd edition. Cambridge, MA: MIT Press.

(1997). *Models of Bounded Rationality*, vol. 3. Cambridge, MA: MIT Press.

Simon, H. A. and A. Ando (1961). Aggregation of variables in dynamic systems. *Econometrica* 29: 111–38.

Simon, H. A. and K. Kotovsky (1963). Human acquisition of concepts for sequential patterns. *Psychological Review* 70: 534–46.

Solomonoff, R. (1964). A formal theory of inductive inference. *Information and Control* 7: 1–22, 224–54.

Valdes-Perez, R. E. (1992). Theory-driven discovery of reaction pathways in the MECHEM system. *Proceedings of National Conference on Artificial Intelligence.*

Watson, J. D. (1976). *Molecular Biology of the Gene.* 3rd edition. Menlo Park, CA: W. A. Benjamin.

Whewell, W. (1847, 1966). *Philosophy of the Inductive Sciences.* 2nd edition. New York: Johnson Reprint Corp.

4 A macroeconomic approach to complexity

Marcel Boumans

1 Introduction: the problem of complexity

complexity, correctly viewed, is only a mask for simplicity (Simon, 1969, p. 1)

An economy is a complex system, in the sense that it is a system made up of a large number of parts that interact in a non-simple way (see Simon, 1962, p. 468). The Walrasian programme was an answer to this problem of complexity by setting up a manageable interdependent system of a whole economy. A modern version of this programme is the Cowles approach: a combination of the Walrasian method to construct a mathematical system without empirical content and econometrics to put empirical flesh and blood on this system. The Cowles method to treat complexity was to build more and more comprehensive models.

This development was not justified by its results, more comprehensiveness did not lead to better predictions than very simple univariate naive models (e.g. random walks, low-order autoregressive (AR) models, or simple autoregressive moving average (ARMA) models; see Zellner, 1994 for a brief survey). In interpreting these results, Milton Friedman (1951), who was influential in having such forecasting tests performed, suggested that the Cowles programme of building large-scale macroeconomic models was probably faulty and needed reformulation. He saw the disappointing test results as evidence of the prematurity of macromodelling of a whole economy, which sent him in another research direction, namely that of partitioning. This opinion became increasingly shared in the applied circle. Many applied modellers shifted their interest in macromodelling away from a whole economy to parts of economic activities where economic theories were relatively well developed (Qin, 1993, pp. 138–9).

I am grateful to Mary Morgan, Margie Morrison, Hans Amman, and the research group colleagues at the University of Amsterdam and at the Centre for Philosophy of Natural and Social Science, London School of Economics, for their comments on earlier drafts of this paper. I also thank Arnold Zellner and the other participants of the Simplicity conference for their suggestions.

An alternative response to the 'failure' of the Cowles approach is Zellner's advice to 'Keep it sophisticatedly simple' (KISS; see elsewhere in this volume), in other words, start with models as simple as possible and improve the model each time in the direction indicated by all kinds of diagnostic checks on the properties of the model. This approach, the so-called SEMTSA approach, is a synthesis of the Cowles approach and time-series analysis (Zellner, 1979, 1994).

A third reaction came from a consultant of the Cowles Commission, who did not try to get round the problem of complexity but dealt explicitly with it. Herbert Simon's approach, which considers complex systems as hierarchic, is the point of departure of much research dealing with complexity. For his work he can rightly be called one of the founders of artificial intelligence and computer science.

The aim of this chapter is to explore the development of this last approach and its methodology in macroeconomics. This development is influenced by a simultaneous development in computer science into both model building and tests. In particular, I will discuss the work of Herbert Simon in which one can find a methodology for building models to analyse complexity.

2   Simon's AI approach to complexity

To avoid discussions about the correct naming of the techniques and methodology discussed here – the candidates are computer science, computational economics, artificial intelligence, artificial life, sciences of the artificial etc. – the original name is chosen: artificial intelligence (AI). Artificial intelligence can briefly be characterized as the discipline that tries to gain an understanding of systems of such complexity (like the mind) that they are beyond the scope of mathematics alone. To put it in other words, the relevant point is the following: 'Given a certain model with a certain parameterization, can one reason, i.e. without running a simulation, *which* functions of the parameterization the outcomes are?' (Vriend, 1995, p. 212n). If not, computer simulations are appropriate.

Typical of the AI method is the top–down approach of dealing with complexity. John von Neumann's 1951 paper, 'The General and Logical Theory of Automata', is paradigmatic to this approach. In that paper he introduces what he calls the 'axiomatic procedure':

The natural systems are of enormous complexity, and it is clearly necessary to subdivide the problem that they represent into several parts. One method of subdivision, which is particularly significant in the present context, is this: The organisms can be viewed as made up of parts which to a certain extent are independent, elementary units. We may, therefore, to this extent, view as the first part of the problem the structure and functioning of such elementary units individually. The second part of the problem consists of understanding how these elements are organized into a whole, and how the functioning of the whole is expressed in terms of these elements. (von Neumann, 1951, repr. 1963, p. 289)

The first part of the problem belonging to the discipline in question, in this case physiology, could be removed by the 'process of axiomatization':

We assume that the elements have certain well-defined, outside, functional characteristics; that is, they are to be treated as 'black boxes'. They are viewed as automatisms, the inner structure of which need not to be disclosed, but which are assumed to react to certain unambiguously defined stimuli, by certain unambiguously defined responses. (von Neumann, 1951, repr. 1963, p. 289)

John von Neumann presented his 'General Theory of Automata' at the Harvard Meeting of the Econometric Society in 1950. In his talk von Neumann warned against taking the brain–computer analogy too literally. But Simon, who was discussant in this session on the theory of automata, observed that 'the significant analogy was not between the hardware of computer and brain, respectively, but between the hierarchic organizations of computing and thinking systems' (Simon, 1977, p. 180).

Simon's (1962) 'The Architecture of Complexity' is an elaboration of the axiomatic procedure. The central thesis of this article is that complex systems frequently take the form of hierarchic systems. An hierarchic system is a system that is composed of interrelated subsystems, each of the latter being, in turn, hierarchic in structure until we reach some lowest level of elementary subsystems. Each subsystem can be treated as a black box whose inputs and outputs, but not its internal structure, are of interest. So, there is some arbitrariness, depending on the researcher's interest, as to where the partitioning is left off and what subsystems are taken as elementary.

A system is decomposable when the subsystems are independent of each other. Decomposable systems are much easier to investigate, but complex systems are by definition not decomposable. It was Simon's solution for the description and comprehension of complex systems to approximate hierarchic systems by nearly decomposable systems. These are systems in which the interactions among the subsystems are weak but not negligible.

The contributions of Simon are extremely vast and diverse, ranging from philosophy and methodology of science, applied mathematics, through various aspects of economics, computer science, management science, political science, cognitive psychology to the study of human problem-solving behaviour. In his review of Simon's contributions to economics, Ando (1979) formulates a theme that runs consistently throughout Simon's writings: 'to construct a comprehensive framework for modelling and analysing the behaviour of man and his organizations faced with a complex environment, recognizing the limitation of his ability to comprehend, describe, analyse and to act, while allowing for his ability to learn and to adapt' (Ando, 1979, p. 83). One of the research areas was therefore to find a description of that complex environment so that it is both comprehensible and manageable for decision makers. Very early in his career Simon already found that the description of very complex systems can be simplified by considering them as hierarchic. This strategy can be found in several of Simon's articles dealing with complexity. Ando refers to two economic contributions, which will be discussed below.

3   Causal ordering

The first application of the top–down approach can be found in Simon's (1953) 'Causal Ordering and Identifiability' paper written for the Cowles Foundation. The context of this paper was a debate between the Cowles Commission, as proponent of simultaneous equations models, and Herman Wold as proponent of recursive chain models.[1] One of the issues in the debate was causality, and its representation and interpretation in economic models. Although the Cowles Commission group mainly ignored the issue, it was taken seriously and discussed in greater depth by Simon (1953). While Simon and Wold disagreed on certain notions about causal systems – asymmetries and relationships versus time sequences and variables – they came closer to each other with respect to the necessity of causal chain system models for policy evaluation (see Morgan, 1991, p. 249).

The aim of the paper was to provide 'a clear and rigorous basis for determining when a causal ordering can be said to hold between two variables or groups of variables in a model' (Simon, 1953, p. 51). The discussion was limited to systems of linear equations without random disturbances. To introduce the notion of causal ordering, it appeared to be essential that the structure is complete ('self-contained' in Simon's terminology). A linear structure is complete when the number of variables in the structure equals the number of structural equations.

The first step was to show that a complete linear structure can be decomposed into a sum of disjunct 'minimal' complete subsets and a

---

[1] For a comprehensive discussion of this debate, see Morgan (1991).

remainder. Minimal subsets were defined as complete subsets of a linear structure that do not themselves contain complete (proper) subsets. When there are one or more minimal complete proper subsets of the structure and the remainder is not null, the structure is said to be 'causally ordered'. The next step was to repeat the partitioning as follows. The equations of the minimal subsets are solved and substituted in the equations of the remainder. The result is again a complete structure, called the 'derived structure of first order'. When this structure is also causally ordered, the process can be repeated. The derived structure is of second order. And so on. Finally the point will be reached at which the remainder of the nth decomposition is null. The result of this process is a complete ordering of disjunct subsets of the equations of the original structure. A consequence of this ordering is that each variable appears as an endogenous variable in one and only one complete subset, and that it appears in a structure of higher order as an exogenous variable. Thus, there exists a one-to-one correspondence between the minimal subsets of equations and the subsets of variables occurring as endogenous variables in these equations. From this, Simon defined a causal ordering of the sets of variables endogenous to the corresponding complete subsets of equations:

Let β designate the set of variables endogenous to a complete subset B, and let γ designate the set endogenous to a complete subset C. Then the variables of γ are *directly causally dependent* on the variables of $\beta(\beta \to \gamma)$ if at least one member of β appears as an exogenous variable in C. (Simon, 1953, p. 57)

The second part of Simon's paper was to show how the concept of causal ordering was connected with the concept of identifiability, which lies beyond the scope of this chapter. More relevant to the discussion of the top–down approach in Simon's work is that the above definition of causal ordering is based on a particular partitioning of a system into subsystems and that causal ordering is a special chain of asymmetrical connections between these subsystems.

4   Aggregation of variables

The second example of Simon's approach to complexity is also a partitioning of a linear equation system, now represented by matrices, to discuss the links among the parts. The aim of his 1961 paper, co-written with Albert Ando, 'Aggregation of Variables in Dynamic Systems', was 'to determine conditions that if satisfied by a (linear) dynamic system, will permit approximate aggregation of variables' (Simon and Ando, 1961, p. 114). This discussion of aggregation was actuated by the disappointing facilities of computer capacities to 'handle matrices of about any desired size, and hence would obviate the need for aggregation' (Simon and Ando, 1961, p. 112).

It appeared that in 'nearly decomposable' systems aggregation can be performed. The notion of near decomposability was clarified by the definition of a decomposable matrix. When a matrix can be arranged in the following form:

$$P^* = \begin{Vmatrix} P_1^* & & \\ & P_i^* & \\ & & P_n^* \end{Vmatrix}$$

where the P_i^*'s are square submatrices and the remaining elements, not displayed, are all zero, then the matrix is said to be completely decomposable. A nearly decomposable matrix is the slightly altered matrix P:

$$P = P^* + \varepsilon C$$

where ε is a very small real number, and C is an arbitrary matrix of the same dimension as P^*.

With the aid of both definitions the dynamic behaviour of the following systems was investigated:

$$x(t+1) = x(t)P \text{ and } x^*(t+1) = x^*(t)P^*$$

To present Simon's result, the following notations for the vector x(t) on which P operates, and the vector $x^*(t)$ on which P^* operates, should be adopted:

$$x(t) = \{x_1(t), \dots, x_i(t), \dots, x_n(t)\}$$

and

$$x^*(t) = \{x_1^*(t), \dots, x_i^*(t), \dots, x_n^*(t)\}$$

where $x_i(t)$ and $x_i^*(t)$ are row vectors of a subset of components of x(t) and $x^*(t)$ respectively.

The results were (Simon and Ando, 1961, pp. 116–17):

(1) In the short run, the behaviour of $x_i(t)$ will be dominated by roots belonging to P_i, so that the time path of $x_i(t)$ will be very close to the time path of $x_i^*(t)$, and almost independent of $x_j(t)$, and P_j. 'If we are interested in the behavior of the system at this stage, we can treat the system as though it were completely decomposable' (Simon and Ando, 1961, p. 116).

(2) Unlike P^*, P is not completely decomposable, so that weak links among the subsystems will eventually make their influence felt. But the time required for these influences to appear is long enough so that

when they do become visible, within each subsystem the largest root will have dominated all other roots. Thus, at this stage, the variables within each subset, $x_i(t)$, will move proportionally, and the behaviour of the whole system will be dominated by the largest roots of each subsystem.

(3) At the end, however, the behaviour of $x(t)$ will be dominated by the largest root of P, as in any linear dynamic system.

Since the variables in each subsystem, after a while, move roughly proportionately according to (2), they may be aggregated into a single variable.

The main theoretical findings of the analysis of the structure of dynamic systems represented by nearly decomposable matrices were summed up in two propositions, which were also mentioned in slightly more general terms in 'The Architecture of Complexity':

(a) in a nearly decomposable system, the short-run behavior of each of the component subsystems is approximately independent of the short-run behavior of the other components; (b) in the long run, the behavior of any one of the components depends in only an aggregate way on the behavior of the other components. (Simon, 1962, p. 474)

By considering a complex system as nearly decomposable, the description of the system can be simplified: only aggregative properties of its parts enter into the description of the interactions of those parts (Simon, 1962, p. 478).

5   Causality in dynamic systems

The insights of both his papers on causal ordering and near decomposability were synthesized in a more recent paper on causality: 'Causal Ordering, Comparative Statics, and Near Decomposability' (1988). The purpose was to extend the account of causality to dynamic and nearly decomposable systems. The question was 'to what extent the causal analysis of a system is invariant as we pass from a description of the system's dynamics to a description of its equilibrium or steady state, and as we pass from a coarse-grained to a fine-grained description of the system, or vice versa, by disaggregation or aggregation' (Simon, 1988, p. 149). The conclusion is that for hierarchical, nearly decomposable systems the causal ordering is not sensitive to the 'grain size' of the analysis. At any level in the hierarchy, the causal ordering that relates to the relative movement of the variables within any single component is (nearly) independent of the causal ordering among components (Simon, 1988, p. 168).

Because of the indescribable complexity of the world we live in, we necessarily restrict our analyses of events to small or middle-size worlds, abstracted from their large environments and characterized by very small numbers of equations. We see that the notion of causal ordering provides us with a rigorous justification of this essential practice. If the small worlds we choose for study correspond to complete subsets of the mechanisms of the larger world of which they are parts, then simplifying our analysis in this way does not at all invalidate our conclusions. (Simon, 1988, p. 160)

6   Artifical worlds

Simon's AI-approach to complexity is a top–down decomposition of the complex system till a certain level is reached on which the subsystems are treated as black boxes, of which the input–output relation is well-defined. The purpose of simulation is to discover what kind of organization will emerge and how it will depend on the input–output specifications. The procedure of considering systems as hierarchic, thus facilitating the investigation of complex systems, is the point of departure of much research dealing with complexity. For example, David Lane's 'artificial worlds' (1993) are in particular designed to study hierarchic systems.

Artificial worlds (AWs) are computer-implementable stochastic models, which consist of a set of 'microlevel entities' that interact with each other and an 'environment' in prescribed ways. AWs are designed to give insight into processes of emergent organization. In his survey-article Lane (1993) gives, among others, an example of an artificial economy. An artificial economy is an artificial world whose microentities represent economic agents and products. Interactions between these microentities model fundamental economic activities – production, exchange and consumption. The purpose of an artificial economy experiment is to discover what kinds of structured economic regimes can occur and to see how they depend on system parameters and the characteristics of the constituent agents. For example, one of the problems of a general equilibrium model is the problem of coordination: where does this order come from? While general equilibrium modellers start by assuming a Walrasian equilibrium, the designer of an artificial economy is first of all concerned to model how economic agents interact. Whether a Walrasian equilibrium will emerge depends on the system parameters and agent's characteristics.

7   Comments

Complexity arises from the interaction of simple systems or from the interaction of a simple system with its complex environment. The latter was one of the main theses of Simon's *Sciences of the Artificial*

An ant/a man viewed as a behaving system, is quite simple. The apparent complexity of its/his behavior over time is largely a reflection of the complexity of the environment in which it/he finds himself. (Simon, 1969, pp. 24, 25, 52)

So, complex behaviour can be explained by the complexity of the environment. In Simon's work the complexity of a system can mean two different things: (1) the system is complex because a large number of interacting parts are involved, or (2) the parts interact in a non-simple way, that is, one is not able to describe mathematically the resulting behaviour. In the latter case it is appropriate to turn to computer simulations. In the case of the first interpretation of complexity, Simon has shown that if the system can be approximated by a nearly decomposable system, the analysis can be simplified considerably.

However, for both interpretations the point is to find an adequate partitioning and the choice of the elementary systems which can be treated as black boxes. When models are only meant to be a forecasting device, it is possible to consider the whole economy as a black box and to use simple models containing only a set of rules of thumb. When partitioning is carried out further, one comes closer to Simon's method of hierarchic decomposition till we reach a lower level of simple worlds.

To regard the black boxes as simple models can be justified by Jeffreys' (1967) advice to consider all variation random unless shown otherwise, based on the Jeffreys–Wrinch simplicity postulate that simpler models have a higher plausibility. Simon (1968) refers explicitly to this postulate when he discusses the plausibility of theories, generalizations or hypotheses. This postulate served also as the basis of Zellner's SEMTSA approach, but this latter approach avoids the explicit treatment of complexity (in both senses).

When complexity refers to systems which cannot be analysed mathematically there are two alternatives: the usage of computer simulations or the approximation of the system to an analysable system. Simon's treatment of near decomposability is closely related to the so-called 'perturbation theory' in physics. Perturbation theory is based on the idea of studying a system deviating slightly from an ideal system for which the complete solution of the problem under consideration is known. The ideal system is in the above cases a decomposable system and one investigates systems that are slightly different from that system: nearly decomposable systems.

Perturbation theory for linear operators was created by Rayleigh and Schrödinger. Mathematically speaking, the method is equivalent to an approximate solution of the eigenvalue problem for a linear operator, slightly different from a simple operator for which the problem is completely solved. Simon introduced this method to economics.

REFERENCES

Ando, A. (1979). On the contributions of Herbert A. Simon to economics. *Scandinavian Journal of Economics* 81: 83–114.

Friedman, M. (1951). Comment on 'A Test of an Econometric Model for the United States, 1921–1947', by Carl F. Christ. In *Conference on Business Cycles*, pp. 107–14. New York: National Bureau of Economic Research.

Jeffreys, H. (1967). *Theory of Probability*. Oxford: Clarendon Press.

Lane, D. A. (1993). Artificial worlds and economics. *Journal of Evolutionary Economics* 3: 89–107, 177–97.

Morgan, M. S. (1991). The stamping out of process analysis in econometrics. In N. De Marchi and M. Blaug (eds.), *Appraising Economic Theories: Studies in the Methodology of Research Programs*, pp. 237–65. Aldershot: Edward Elgar.

Neumann, J. von [1951] (1963). The general and logical theory of automata. In A. H. Taub (ed.), *John von Neumann, Collected Works*, vol. 5, pp. 288–318. Oxford: Pergamon Press. Reprint from L. A. Jeffress (ed.) (1951), *Cerebral Mechanisms in Behavior: the Hixon Symposium*, pp. 1–31. New York: Wiley.

Qin, D. (1993). *The Formation of Econometrics: a Historical Perspective*. Oxford: Clarendon Press.

Simon, H. A. (1951). Theory of automata: discussion. *Econometrica* 19: 72.

    (1953). Causal ordering and identifiability. In W. C. Hood and T. C. Koopmans (eds.), *Studies in Econometric Method*, Cowles Foundation Monograph 14, pp. 49–74. New Haven and London: Yale University Press.

    (1962). The architecture of complexity. *Proceedings of the American Philosophical Society* 106: 467–82.

    (1968). On judging the plausibility of theories. In B. Van Roostelaar and J. F. Staal (eds.), *Logic, Methodology and Philosophy of Sciences III*, pp. 439–59. Amsterdam: North-Holland.

    (1969). *The Sciences of the Artificial*. Cambridge, MA: MIT Press.

    (1977). *Models of Discovery*. Dordrecht: Reidel.

    (1988). Causal ordering, comparative statics, and near decomposability. *Journal of Econometrics* 39: 149–73.

Simon, H. and A. Ando (1961). Aggregation of variables in dynamic systems. *Econometrica* 29: 111–38.

Vriend, N. J. (1995). Self-organization of markets: an example of a computational approach. *Computational Economics* 8: 205–31.

Zellner, A. (1979). Statistical analysis of econometric models. *Journal of the American Statistical Association* 74: 628–43.

    (1994). Time-series analysis, forecasting and econometric modelling: the structural econometric modelling, time-series analysis (SEMTSA) approach. *Journal of Forecasting* 13: 215–33.

5 The new science of simplicity

Malcolm R. Forster

1 The problem

No matter how often billiard balls have moved when struck in the past, the next billiard ball *may not* move when struck. For philosophers, this 'theoretical' possibility of being wrong raises a problem about how to *justify* our theories and models of the world and their predictions. This is the *problem of induction*. In *practice*, nobody denies that the next billiard ball *will* move when struck, so many scientists see no practical problem. But in recent times, scientists have been presented with competing methods for comparing hypotheses or models (classical hypothesis testing, BIC, AIC, cross-validation, and so on) which do not yield the same predictions. Here there is a problem.

Model selection involves a trade-off between simplicity and fit for reasons that are now fairly well understood (see Forster and Sober, 1994, for an elementary exposition). However, there are many ways of making this trade-off, and this chapter will analyse the conditions under which one method will perform better than another. The main conclusions of the analysis are that (1) there is no method that is better than all the others under all conditions, even when some reasonable background assumptions are made, and (2) for *any* methods A and B, there are circumstances in which A is better than B, and there are other circumstances in which B will do better than A. Every method is fraught with some risk even in well-behaved situations in which nature is 'uniform'. Scientists will do well to understand the risks.

It is easy to be persuaded by the wrong reasons. If there is always a situation in which method A performs worse than method B, then there is a computer simulation that will display this weakness. But if the analysis of this chapter is correct, then there is always a situation in which any

My thanks go to the participants of the conference for a stimulating exchange of ideas, and to Martin Barrett, Branden Fitelson, Mike Kruse, Elliott Sober and Grace Wahba for helpful discussions on material that appeared in previous versions of this paper. I am also grateful to the Vilas Foundation, the Graduate School, and sabbatical support from the University of Wisconsin–Madison.

method A will do worse. To be swayed by a single simulation is to put all your money on the assumption that the examples of interest to you are the same in all relevant respects. One needs to understand what is relevant and what is not.

Another spurious argument is the (frequently cited) claim that AIC (Akaike's information criterion) is inconsistent – that AIC does not converge in the limit of large samples to what it is trying to estimate. That depends on what AIC is trying to estimate. Akaike (1973) designed AIC to estimate the expected log-likelihood, or equivalently, Kullback–Leibler discrepancy, or predictive accuracy (Forster and Sober, 1994). In section 7, I show that AIC is consistent in estimating this quantity. Whether it is the most efficient method is a separate question. I suspect that no method has a universally valid claim to that title. The bottom line is that the comparison of methods has no easy solution, and one should not be swayed by hasty conclusions.

The way to avoid hasty conclusions is to analyse the problem in three steps:

(1) The specification of a *goal*. What goal can be reached or achieved?
(2) The specification of a *means* to the goal. What is the *criterion*, or method?
(3) *An explanation* of how a criterion works in achieving the goal.

This chapter is an exercise in applying this three-step methodology to the problem of model selection.

The chapter is organized as follows. Section 2 introduces scientific inference and its goals, while section 3 argues that standard model selection procedures lack a clear foundation in even the *easiest* of examples. This motivates the need for a deeper analysis, and section 4 describes a framework in which the goal of predictive accuracy is precisely defined. The definition of predictive accuracy is completely general and assumption free, in contrast to section 5 which develops the framework using a 'normality assumption' about the distribution of parameter estimates.[1] Even though the assumption is not universal, it is surprisingly general and far reaching. No statistician will deny that this is a very important case, and it serves as concrete illustration of how a science of simplicity should be developed. Section 6 compares the performance of various methods for optimizing the goal of predictive accuracy when the normal-

---

[1] 'Normality' refers to the bell-shaped normal distribution, which plays a central role in statistics. Physicists, and others, refer to the same distribution as Gaussian, after Carl Friedrich Gauss (1777–1855), who used it to derive the method of least squares from the principle of maximum likelihood.

ity assumption holds approximately, and explains the limitations in each method. The clear and precise definition of the goal is enough to defend AIC against the very common, but spurious, charge that it is inconsistent. I discuss this in section 7. Section 8 summarizes the main conclusions.

2   Preliminaries

A model is a set of equations, or functions, with one or more adjustable parameters. For example, suppose LIN is the family of linear functions of a dependent variable y on a single independent variable x, $\{y = a_0 + a_1 x + u | a_0 \in \mathbb{R}, a_1 \in \mathbb{R}\}$, where $\mathbb{R}$ is the set of real numbers and u is an error term that has a specified probability distribution. The error distribution may be characterized by adjustable parameters of its own, such as a variance, although it is always assumed to have zero mean. Note that there can be more than one dependent variable, and they can each depend on several independent variables, which may depend on each other (as in causal modelling). The family LIN is characterized by two adjustable parameters, while PAR is a family of parabolic functions $\{y = a_0 + a_1 x + a_2 x^2 + u | a_0 \in \mathbb{R}, a_1 \in \mathbb{R}, a_2 \in \mathbb{R}\}$, characterized by at least three adjustable parameters.

The distinction between variables and adjustable parameters is sometimes confusing since the adjustable parameters are variables in a sense. The difference is that x and y vary within the context of each member of the family, while the parameters only vary from one member to the next. The empirical data specify pairs of (x, y) values, which do not include parameter values. Parameters are introduced *theoretically* for the purpose of distinguishing competing hypotheses within each model.

A typical inferential problem is that of deciding, given a set of seen data (a set of number *pairs*, where the first number is a measured x-value, and the second number is a measured y-value), whether to use LIN or whether PAR is better for the purpose of predicting new data (a set of unseen (x,y) pairs). Since LIN and PAR are competing models, the problem is a problem of *model selection*. After the model is selected, then standard statistical methods are used to estimate the parameter values to yield a *single* functional relation between x and y, which can be used to predict y-values for novel x-values. The second step is fairly well understood. Model selection is the more intriguing part of the process although model selection is usually based on the properties of the estimated parameter values.

The philosophical problem is to understand exactly how scientists should compare models. Neither the problem, nor its proposed solutions, are limited to curve-fitting problems. That is why econometricians or physicists, or anyone interested in prediction, should be interested in how to trade off fit with simplicity, or its close cousin, unification. For example, we may compare the solutions of Newton's equations with the solutions of Einstein's mechanics applied to the same physical system or set of systems. Here we would be comparing one huge nexus of *interconnected* models with another huge nexus where the interconnections amongst the parts follow a different pattern. Einstein's solution of the problem of explaining the slow precession of the planet Mercury's orbit around the sun depends on the speed of light, which connects that precession phenomenon to quite disparate electromagnetic phenomena. There is wide consensus that Einsteinian physics would come out on top because it fits the data at least as well as the Newtonian equations, and sometimes better, without fudging the result by introducing *new parameters* (the speed of light was already in use, though not in explaining planetary motions). It seems that the overall number of parameters is relevant here. These vague intuitions have swayed physicists for millennia. But physicists have not formalized them, nor explained them, nor understood them, even in very simple cases.

Recent research in statistics has lead to a number numerically precise criteria for model selection. There is classical Neyman–Pearson hypothesis testing, the Bayesian information criterion (BIC) (Schwarz, 1978), the minimization of description length (MDL) criterion (Rissanen, 1978, 1987, Wallace and Freeman, 1987); Akaike's information criterion (AIC) (Akaike, 1973, 1974, 1977, 1985; see also Sakamoto et al., 1986; Forster and Sober, 1994); and various methods of cross validation (e.g., Turney, 1994, Xiang and Wahba, 1996). In a few short years we have gone from informal intuition to an embarrassment of riches. The problem is to find some way of critically evaluating competing methods of scientific inference. I call this the 'new science of simplicity' because I believe that this problem should be treated as a scientific problem: to understand when and why model selection criteria succeed or fail, we should model the process of model selection itself. There is no simple and no universal model of model selection, for the success of a selection method depends greatly on the circumstances, and to understand the complexities, we have to model the situation in which the model selection takes place. For philosophers of science, this is like making assumptions about the uniformity of nature in order understand how induction works. The problem is the same: How can we make assumptions that don't simply assume what we want to prove? For example, it would not be enlightening to try to understand why inductive methods favour Einstein's physics over Newton's if we have to assume that Einstein's theory is true in order to model the inferential process. Fortunately, the new work on simplicity makes use of weaker assumptions. An example of such an assumption is the 'normality assumption'. It simply places constraints on how the estimated values of parameters are distributed around their true values without placing any constraints on the true values themselves.

This is why it is so important not to confuse what I am calling the normality assumption, which is about the distribution of repeated parameter estimates, with an assumption about the normality of error distributions. For example, in the case of a binary event like coin tossing, in which a random variable[2] takes on the values 0 and 1, there is no sense in which the deviation of this random variable from the mean is normal. The error distribution is discrete, whereas the normal distribution is continuous. However, the distribution of the sample mean, which estimates the propensity of the coin to land heads, is approximately normal. A normality assumption about errors is stronger and more restrictive than an assumption of normality for the repeated parameter estimates. It is the less restrictive assumption that is used in what follows.[3]

It is true that models of model selection are a little different from standard scientific models. Scientific models are descriptive, while models of model selection are what I will call weakly normative.[4] For example, models of planetary motion describe or purport to describe planets. But models of model selection relate a model selection criterion to a goal. The goal might be predictive accuracy, empirical adequacy, truth, probable truth, or approximate truth. But whatever the goal, the project is to understand the *relationship* between the methods of scientific inference and the goal. Of this list, predictive accuracy is the one epistemic goal (minimizing description length is a non-epistemic goal) whose relationship with simplicity is reasonably well understood thanks to recent work in mathematical statistics. So, predictive accuracy is the goal considered in this chapter.

Bayesianism is the dominant approach to scientific inference in North America today, but what does it take as the goal of inference? Fundamentally, Bayesianism is a theory of decision making, and can consider *any* goal. It then defines the *method* of deciding between two competing models as the maximization of the expected pay-off with

---

[2] A random variable is a variable whose possible values are assigned a probability.
[3] Kiessepä (1997) shows that a normality assumption for the error distribution is not always sufficient to ensure normality of the parameter estimators. However, Cramér (1946), especially chapters 32 and 33, explains how the conditions are met asymptotically for large sample sizes in a very general class of cases.
[4] A strongly normative statement is one which says we *should* or we *ought* to do such and such. A weakly normative statement is one that says we should do such and such *in order to optimize a given goal*, without implying that it is a goal we should optimize.

respect to that goal. The simplest idea is that the pay-off of scientific theories lies in their truth. With that in mind, it is simplest to assign a pay-off of 1 to a true model and 0 to a false model. Let me refer to this kind of Bayesian philosophy of science as *classical* Bayesianism, or *standard* Bayesianism.[5] Consider a choice between model A and model B. Is the expected pay-off in selecting A greater than the expected pay-off in selecting B? The answer is given in terms of their probabilities. If Pr(A) is the probability that A is true, and Pr(B) is the probability that B is true, then the expected pay-off for A is, by definition, Pr(A) times the pay-off if it's true plus the Pr(not-A) times the pay-off if it's false. The second term disappears, so the expected pay-off for believing A is Pr(A). Likewise, the expected pay-off for believing B is Pr(B). The expected pay-off for believing A is greater than the expected pay-off for believing B if and only if Pr(A) is greater than Pr(B). This leads to the principle that we should choose the theory that has the greatest probability, which is exactly the idea behind the model selection criterion derived by Schwarz (1978), called BIC.

Whatever the goal, a scientific approach to model selection is usefully divided into three parts:

1. The specification of a *goal*. What goal can be reached or achieved in model selection? Approximate truth is too vague. Probable truth is also too vague unless you tell me what the probability is of. Truth is too vague for the same reason. Are we aiming for the truth of a theory, a model, or a more precise hypothesis?
2. The specification of a *criterion*, or a *means* to the goal. This is where simplicity will enter the picture. What kind of simplicity is involved and exactly how it is to be used in combination with other kinds of information, like fit?
3. *An explanation* of how the criterion works in achieving the goal. For example, Bayesians explain the criterion by deducing it from specific assumptions about prior probability distributions. The Akaike explanation makes no such assumptions about prior probabilities, but instead, makes assumptions about the probabilistic behaviour of parameter estimates. The style of the explanation is different in each case, and is a further ingredient in what I am calling the framework.

---

[5] The classical Bayesian approach is currently dominant in the philosophy of science. See Earman (1992) for a survey of this tradition, and Forster (1995) for a critical overview. For alternative 'Akaike' solutions to standard problems in the philosophy of science, see Forster and Sober (1994). For an 'Akaike' treatment of the ravens paradox, see Forster (1994). For an 'Akaike' solution to the problem of variety of evidence, see Kruse (1997).

It should be clear from this brief summary that the difference between the Bayesian and Akaike modelling of model selection marks a profound difference between statistical *frameworks*. What I have to say about the modelling of model selection goes to the very heart of statistical practice and its foundations. Anyone interested in induction agrees that, in some sense, truth is the *ultimate* goal of inference, but they disagree about how to measure *partial success* in achieving that goal. Classical Bayesians do not tackle the problem of defining partial success. They talk of the *probability* that a hypothesis is true, but most Bayesians deny that such probabilities are objective, in which case they do not define partial success in an objective way. There is no sense in which one Bayesian scientist is closer to the truth than another if neither actually reaches the true model.

The same criticism applies to decision-theoretic Bayesians as well. These are Bayesians who treat model selection as a decision problem, whose aim is to maximize a goal, or utility (Young, 1987), or minimize a loss or discrepancy (Linhart and Zucchini, 1986). They are free to specify any goal whatsoever, and so they are free to consider predictive accuracy as a goal. But, again, the expectation is a *subjective* expectation defined in terms of a subjective probability distribution. Typically, these Bayesians do not evaluate the *success* of their method with respect to the degree of predictive accuracy *actually achieved*. They could, but then they would be evaluating their method within the Akaike framework.

Nor do Bayesians consider the *objective* relationship between the method (the maximization of *subjectively* expected utilities) and the goal (the utilities). That is, they do not consider step 3, above. At present, it appears to be an article of faith that there is nothing better than the Bayesian method, and they provide no explanation of this fact (if it is a fact). And even if they did, I fear that it would depend on a *subjective* measure of partial success. That is why the Akaike approach is fundamental to the problem of comparing methods of model selection.

The Akaike framework defines the success of inference by how close the selected hypothesis is to the true hypothesis, where the closeness is measured by the Kullback–Leibler distance (Kullback and Leibler, 1951). This distance can also be conceptualized as a measure of the accuracy of predictions in a certain domain. It is an objective measure of partial success, and like truth, we do not know its value. That is why predictive accuracy plays the role of a goal of inference, and not a means or method of inference. The issue of how well any method achieves the goal is itself a matter of *scientific* investigation. We need to develop models of model selection.

The vagueness of the notion of simplicity has always been a major worry for philosophers. Interestingly, all three methods already mentioned, the MDL criterion, BIC and AIC, define simplicity in exactly the same way – as the paucity of adjustable parameters, or more exactly, the dimension of a family of functions (when the two differ, then it is the dimension that is meant, for it does not depend on how the family is described; see Forster, 1999). So, the definition of simplicity is not a source of major disagreement.

In fact, I am surprised that there is *any* disagreement amongst these schools of thought at all! After all, each criterion was designed to pursue an entirely different goal, so each criterion might be the best one for achieving its goal. The MDL criterion may be the best for minimizing description length, the BIC criterion the best for maximizing probability, and the AIC criterion the best at maximizing predictive accuracy. The point is that the claims are *logically independent*. The truth of one does not entail the falsity of the others. There is no reason why scientists should not value all three goals and pursue each one of them separately, for none of the goals are wrong-headed.

Nevertheless, researchers do tend to think that the approaches are competing solutions to the same problem. Perhaps it is because they think that it is impossible to achieve one goal without achieving the others? Hence, there is only one problem of induction and they talk of *the* problem of scientific inference. If there is only one problem, then the Akaike formulation is a precise formulation of the problem, for it provides a definition of partial success with respect to the ultimate goal of truth. For that reason, I will compare all model selection criteria within the Akaike framework.

3   A milieu of methods and an easy example

Here is a very simple example of a statistics problem. Suppose that a die has a probability θ^* of an odd number of dots landing up, which does not change over time, and each toss is independent of every other toss. This fact is not known. The two competing models are M_1 and M_2. Both models get everything right except that they disagree on the probability of an odd number of dots landing up, denoted by θ.

M_1 asserts that $\theta = \frac{1}{2}$. This model specifies an exact probability for all events. If M_1 is a family of hypotheses, then there is only one hypothesis in the family. M_1 has no *adjustable* parameters. This is a common source of confusion, since it does mention a parameter; namely θ. But θ is given a value, and is therefore adjus*ted*, and not adjustable. M_2, on the other hand, is uncommitted about the value of θ. θ is now an adjustable parameter, so M_2 is more complex than M_1 in one sense of 'complex'. Also note that M_1 is *nested* in M_2, since all the hypotheses in M_1 also appear in

M_2. The problem is to use the observed data to estimate the probability of future events. There is no precise prediction involved, but we think of it as a prediction problem of a more general kind. The problem of induction applies to this kind of problem.

In classical statistics, there are two steps in the 'solution' of this problem. The first step is to test M_1 against M_2. This is the process that I am calling model selection. The second step is to estimate the value of any adjustable parameters in the winning model by choosing the best-fitting hypothesis in the family that best fits the seen data. This picks out a single hypothesis which can be used for the prediction or explanation of unseen data. While different statistical paradigms have different definitions of 'best fit', those differences usually make little difference, and I will ignore them here. I will assume that everyone measures fit by the likelihood (or log-likelihood). The naïve empirical method that ignores simplicity and goes by fit alone is called the method of maximum likelihood (ML). In the case of M_1 the maximum likelihood hypothesis has to be $\theta = \frac{1}{2}$, since there are no others that can do better. In the case of M_2 there is a well-known result that tells us that the maximum likelihood hypothesis is $\theta = \hat{\theta}$, where $\hat{\theta}$ is the relative frequency of heads-up in the observed data. Note that the second step is essential, since M_2 by itself does not specify the value of its adjustable parameter, and cannot be used to make probabilistic assertions about future data.

Here is how classical Neyman–Pearson hypothesis testing works. The simpler of two models is the null hypothesis, in this case M_1 (see figure 5.1). The decision to accept the null hypothesis or reject the null hypothesis (and therefore accept M_2) depends on how probable the data would be if the null hypothesis were true. If the data are improbable given the null hypothesis, then reject the null hypothesis, otherwise accept it. The degree of improbability is determined by the size or the level of significance of the test. A size of 5% is fairly standard ($p < .05$), which means that the null hypothesis is rejected if the observed data is a member of a class of possible data sets that collectively has a probability of 5% given the null hypothesis. The observed relative frequencies that would lead to such a rejection are those that fall under the shaded area in figure 5.1. The value of the relative frequency shown in figure 5.1 lies in that region, so that the null hypothesis is accepted in that case.

Notice that the hypothesis $\theta = \hat{\theta}$ in M_2 fits the observed facts better than the null hypothesis, yet the null hypothesis is still accepted. *Therefore classical model selection trades off fit for simplicity*, provided that the simpler hypothesis is chosen as the null hypothesis.

There are a number of peculiar features of the classical method of model selection. First, there is nothing to prevent the more complex

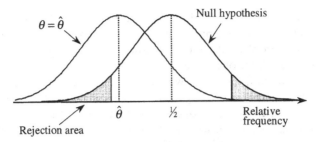

Figure 5.1 Classical Neyman–Pearson hypothesis testing

model being chosen as the null hypothesis, and there is no reason against this practice except to say that it is not common practice. Nor is there any reason for choosing a 5% level of significance other than common practice. Finally, it is odd that the same trade-off would be made even if M_2 had many more adjustable parameters than M_1. There is no obvious method for adjusting the size of the test to take account of these features of the context. Neyman–Pearson methods do not appear to have the kind of rationale demanded by the three steps described in the introduction.

I have heard only one reply to this charge. The reply is that classical statistics aims to minimize the probability of rejecting the null hypothesis when it is true (i.e. minimize type I error), and minimize the probability of accepting the null hypothesis when it is false (i.e. minimize type II error), and it does this successfully. I doubt that this is the only aim of the procedure because I think that working scientists are also interested in predictive accuracy, and it is not obvious that classical testing brings us closer to that goal. And, in any case, the two parts to the goal stated above are incompatible. To minimize type I error, we should choose the size of the test to be 0%. But that will maximize the type II error. At the other extreme, one could minimize type II errors by choosing a 100% significance level, but that would maximize the type I error. The actual practice is a trade-off between these two extremes. Classical statisticians need to specify a third goal if the trade-off is to be principled.

Another objection to the Neyman–Pearson rationale for hypothesis testing is that it fails to address the problem when both models are false. For then I would have thought that any choice is in error, so trading off type I and type II errors, which are conditional on one or other of the models being true, is an irrelevant consideration. In other words, there is no criterion of partial success. Note that these are criticisms of the *rationale* behind the methods, and not the methods themselves.

In order to explain the AIC and BIC model selection *methods* in this example, it is sufficient to think of them as classical Neyman–Pearson tests, with some special peculiarities. In particular, AIC chooses a greater rejection area (about 15.7%), while BIC recommends a smaller rejection area, which further diminishes as the number of data increases. This is the situation when the competing models differ by one adjustable parameter, as is the case in our example. Figure 5.2 plots the critical point (the point defining the boundary of the rejection area) as a function of the number of coin tosses. Notice that as the number of tosses increases, a smaller deviation of the proportion of heads up from the null result of 50% will succeed in rejecting the null hypothesis, although BIC requires greater deviation in all cases. Therefore BIC gives greater weight to simplicity in the sense that it requires that there be stronger evidence against the hypothesis before the simpler null hypothesis is rejected.

When the models differ by a dimension greater than one (such as would be the case if we were to compare LIN with a family of 10-degree polynomials), the size of the rejection areas decrease. This is significantly different from classical Neyman–Pearson testing, which makes no adjustment.

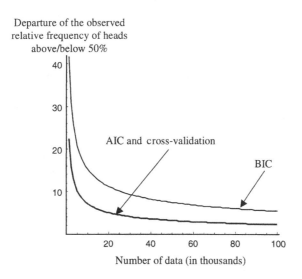

Figure 5.2 The critical point at which the null hypothesis is rejected in cross-validation, BIC and AIC. Classical hypothesis testing would be between BIC and AIC

Bayesians have responded to the conceptual difficulties facing classical statisticians by bringing in the prior probabilities of the competing hypotheses and their likelihoods. The posterior probability of a model is proportional to the product of the prior probability and the likelihood of the model. Therefore, the Bayesian method of comparing posterior probabilities appears to address the problem. Certainly, this approach does make a decision that depends on both of the competing models, but is it the best policy for comparing the predictive accuracy of competing models?

Perhaps Bayesians could argue like this: truth is connected to predictive accuracy in the sense that there is no hypothesis that can be more predictively accurate than a true hypothesis, so to maximize the expected predictive accuracy of a model, we should maximize its probability. However, this argument is flawed. First, the premise is false. It is true that for a *maximally specific* hypothesis – one that gives precise values to all parameters – no hypothesis can be more accurate than the true hypothesis. However, this statement does not extend to models, which assert only that one of its hypotheses is true – models are very large disjunctions. Therefore, the predictive accuracy of a *model* is either undefined, or it depends either on the probabilistic weights given to its members, or it is identified with the predictive accuracy of the maximum likelihood hypothesis (if 'point' estimation is used). In either case, if the predictive accuracy is well defined, then the predictive accuracy of a true model will be less than the predictive accuracy of the true hypothesis. It also follows that the predictive accuracy of a false model can be higher than the predictive accuracy of a true model.

Second, even if the premise were true, the conclusion does not follow. Maximizing the probability of truth does not always maximize the expected predictive accuracy. To show this, suppose I predict the reading (plus or minus a second) on an atomic clock using my watch, which is 3 seconds fast. My predictive accuracy (suitably defined) is pretty good, but the probability that my prediction is true is zero. Contrast that to someone who makes the same prediction on the basis of a stopped clock. The probability of their prediction being true is higher than mine, yet their predictive accuracy is lousy.

Another incongruity of this Bayesian approach arises in the case of nested models, like the ones we are considering. As an independent example, consider a curve-fitting example in which the model of all linear functions, LIN, is nested in the model of all parabolic functions, PAR, since all the members of LIN are contained in PAR. This can be seen by examining the equations: if the coefficient of the squared term in the equation for PAR is zero, then the equation reduces to the equation for a straight line. Logically speaking, this nested relationship means that LIN logically entails PAR, in the sense that it is impossible for LIN to be true and PAR false. It is now a consequence of the axioms of probability that the LIN can never be more probable than PAR, and this is true for all probabilities, prior or posterior (Popper, 1959, ch. 7). So, the Bayesian idea that we should select the model with the highest posterior probability leads to the conclusion that we should never choose LIN over PAR. In fact, we should never choose PAR over CUBE, where CUBE is the family of third-degree polynomials, and so on. But if we are interested in predictive accuracy, there will be occasions on which we should choose LIN over PAR. Therefore, the Bayesian principle cannot serve the goal of predictive accuracy in this case.

Of course, Bayesians can simply refuse to consider this case. They might consider LIN versus PAR⁻, where PAR⁻ is PAR minus LIN. Then the models are not nested, and the Bayesian criterion could lead to the choice of LIN over PAR⁻. But it is puzzling why this difference should make a difference if we are interested in predictive accuracy, since the presence or absence of LIN nested in PAR makes no difference to any prediction, and *ipso facto*, no difference to the *accuracy* of any predictions. The failure of Bayesian principles to yield the same answer in both cases is a clear demonstration that their methods are not designed to maximize predictive accuracy. If they succeed in achieving this goal, then it is a lucky accident.

The goals of probable truth and predictive accuracy are clearly different, and it seems that predictive accuracy is the one that scientists care about most. Whenever parameter values are replaced by point estimates, there is zero chance of that specific value being the true one, yet scientists are not perturbed by this. Economists don't care whether their predictions of tomorrow's stock prices are *exactly* right; being close would still produce huge profits. Physicists don't care whether their current estimate of the speed of light is *exactly* true, so long as it has a high degree of accuracy. Biologists are not concerned if they fail to predict the exact corn yield of a new strain, so long as they are approximately right. If the probability of truth were something they cared about, then point estimation would be a puzzling practice. But if predictive accuracy is what scientists value, then their methodology makes sense.

This does not work as a criticism of *all* Bayesians. Decision-theoretic Bayesians could take predictive accuracy as their utility, and derive a criterion to maximize the expected predictive accuracy. This decision-theoretic approach is discussed in Young (1987), for example. However, the classical Bayesian approach is the most influential amongst scientists, perhaps because it has led to the useable BIC criterion which appears to implement Occam's razor.[6]

A decision-theoretic Bayesianism that takes predictive accuracy as its utility still requires the use of prior probability distributions over propositions about the predictive accuracies of hypotheses. If we had such prior knowledge, then the Bayesian approach would make sense. But we don't. Another way of stating the criticism is that there are infinitely many Bayesian theories, and there is no way of deciding amongst them, besides using computer simulations, testing their success on real predictions, and mathematically analysing the various criteria under a variety of assumptions. But this is just to revert to the Akaike approach, and one might wonder whether Bayesianism is anything more than the background machinery for generating criteria.

A counter-consideration is that Bayesian decision theory allows us to incorporate background information in decision-making. Certainly, when such information is available, it should be used. But Bayesians do not have a monopoly on background knowledge. It is not even true that the AIC criterion takes no account of background information, since it can be applied more globally when there are data relevant to the hypothesis that fall outside of the prediction problem at hand. For example, a model of stock market movement may take global economic parameters into account, and this may be done by considering a broader base of economic data. AIC requires that the relevance be built explicitly into the model, whereas Bayesians allow it to be represented in the prior probabilities. I believe that the background information is better built into the model, where it is publicly displayed and subjected to debate.

Cross-validation is a method widely used in learning algorithms in neural networks and in machine learning (e.g. Turney, 1994). It is an interesting method because it appears to make no assumptions at all. The idea is that a curve is fitted to a subset of the observed data – often the whole data minus one data point. Such a subset of data is called a *calibrating data set*. The predictive accuracy of the fitted model is tested against the data point or points left out, which may be averaged over all possible calibrating data sets. Note that this method cannot be applied to a single specific curve, since the average fit for each data point in the set is

---

[6] The earliest reference to this idea I know is Rosenkrantz (1977), except he does not derive the BIC approximation, which was derived by Schwarz (1978). MacKay (1995) discusses the same version of Occam's razor in apparent ignorance of previous work. Cheeseman (1990) also discusses the classical Bayesian approach with even less sophistication and even fewer references.

just the fit with respect to the total data set, which reduces to the naïve empiricism of ML.

However, if the method is used to compare *models* rather than particular hypotheses, then it has different properties. Each calibrating data set produces a slightly different best-fitting curve in the family and there will be a penalty for large, complex families of curves because large families will tend to produce greater variation in the curve that best fits a calibrating data set (Turney, 1990). This leads to an average fit that is poorer than the fit of the curve that best fits the total data set. There is no need to explicitly define simplicity or to quantify its effects on the stability of estimation; it is taken into account implicitly rather than explicitly. It is a remarkable fact that this simple method leads to approximately the same criterion of model selection as AIC in our simple coin-tossing example (see figure 5.2). It is remarkable exactly because AIC factors in simplicity explicitly while cross-validation does not. But perhaps it is not so surprising once we note that they are both designed with the same goal in mind – predictive accuracy.[7] Methods of cross-validation are worthy of serious attention from scientists, either as a way of complementing other criteria or as an alternative criterion. I don't know which, but I believe that the Akaike framework provides the right tools for such an investigation.

This section has surveyed the variety of inference methods that can be applied to the easiest example imaginable. Very often the methods give similar results, but the *foundations* of those methods vary greatly. Nevertheless, they should all be considered seriously. The solution is to evaluate all of them within the Akaike framework (or some natural extension of it). As you can see, this has been an argument for the Akaike *framework*, and not the Akaike criterion (AIC).

4 Predictive accuracy as a goal of model selection

How should we define predictive accuracy? First, we need to distinguish between seen and unseen data. As a *goal*, we are interested in the prediction of unseen data, rather than the data used to construct the hypothesis. The seen data is the *means* by which we can forecast how well the hypothesis will predict unseen data.

However, any particular set of data may exhibit idiosyncrasies due to random fluctuations of observational error. If we took the goal to be the

---

[7] I have since learned that Stone (1977) proved that AIC is equivalent to leave-one-out cross-validation asymptotically for large samples, so the result I got is to be expected because I assumed the same conditions.

prediction of a *single* set of unseen data, then the goal is too hard in the sense that particular errors are impossible to predict, and in other cases the goal may be achieved by dumb luck. It is therefore customary to define predictive accuracy differently. The idea is that a predictively accurate curve is one that is as close as possible to the *trend*, or *regularity*, *behind* the data. The technical trick used to unpack that idea is to imagine many data sets generated repeatedly by that regularity (the true curve) and define the predictive accuracy of an arbitrary hypothesis as the average fit of the curve with respect to all such data sets. In that way no particular set of error fluctuations is given undue emphasis. In the language of probability, predictive accuracy is the expected fit of data sets generated by the true probability distribution. The expected value is therefore objectively defined. It is not the subjective expectation that would appear in a Bayesian analysis of the problem. This point is worth examining in greater detail.

Consider a curve-fitting example in which y is a function of x. Define the *domain of prediction* in terms of a probability distribution defined over the independent variable, $p(x)$. This distribution will define the range of x-values over which unseen data sets are sampled. There is no claim that $p(x)$ is objective in the sense of representing an objective chance, or a propensity of some kind. But it is objectively given once the domain of prediction is fixed. There are now three cases to consider:

1. There is a true conditional probability density $p^*(y/x)$, which is an objective propensity. Since $p(x)$ is objective (given the domain of prediction), the joint distribution $p(x, y)$ is objective, because it is the product of the two.
2. The probability density $p(y/x)$ is an average over the propensities $p^*(y/x, z)$, where z refers to one or more variables that affect the value of y. In this case, one needs to specify the domain of prediction more finely. One needs to specify the probability distribution $p(x, z)$. Once $p(x, z)$ is fixed, $p(x, y)$ is determined by $p^*(y/x, z)$, and is again objective.
3. The independent variable x determines a unique, error-free, value of y. This is the case of noise-free data. The true curve is defined by the value of y determined by each value of x. What this means is that all points generated by the $p(x, y)$ will lie exactly on the true curve. The distribution $p(y/x)$ is a Dirac delta function (zero for all values of y except for one value, such that it integrates to 1). The probability $p(x, y)$, is still objectively determined from $p(x)$, which defines the *domain of prediction*. Moreover, $p(x, y)$ allows for a statistical treatment of parameter estimation, so it fits into the Akaike framework.

Case 3 is important for it shows how a probabilistic treatment of parameter estimation may be grounded in a probabilistic definition of the domain of prediction. There is no need to assume that nature is probabilistic. The only exception to this is when a family of curves actually contains the true curve, for in that case, there can be no curve that fits the data better than the true curve, and the estimated parameter values are always the true ones, and there will be no variation from one data set to the next. In this case, the framework will not apply. I believe that this is not a severe limitation of the framework since it is plausible to suppose that it arises very rarely. Therefore, in general, *once the domain is fixed*, the probability of sets of data generated by the true distribution in this domain is objectively determined by the true distribution.

The relativization of predictive accuracy to a domain has meaningful consequences. In many cases, a scientist is interested in predictions in a domain different from the one in which the data are sampled. For example, in time series, the observed data are sampled from the past, but the predictions pertain to the future. In the Akaike framework, the default assumption is that the domain of prediction is the same as the domain in which the data are sampled. It is imagined, in other words, that new data are re-sampled from the past. If the time series is stationary, then the past is effectively the same as the future. But in general this is not true, in which case it is an open question whether the standard model selection criteria apply (for discussion, see Forster, 2000). It is an advantage of the Akaike framework that such issues are raised explicitly.

Predictive accuracy is the expected fit of unseen data in a domain, but this definition is not precise until the notion of fit is precise. A common choice is the sum of squared deviations made famous by the method of least squares. However, squared deviations do not make sense in every example. For instance, when probabilistic hypotheses are devised to explain the relative frequency of heads in a hundred tosses by the fairness of the coin, the hypothesis does not fit the data in the sense of squared deviations. In these cases, an appropriate measure of fit is the likelihood of the hypothesis relative to the data (the probability of the data given the hypothesis).

However, does the likelihood measure apply to all cases? In order for the hypothesis to have a likelihood, we need the hypothesis to be probabilistic. In curve fitting, we do that by associating each hypothesis with an error distribution. In that way, the fit of a hypothesis with any data set is determined by the hypothesis itself, and is therefore an entirely objective feature of the hypothesis. When the error distribution is normal (Gaussian), then the log-likelihood is proportional to the sum of squared deviations. When the error distribution is not normal, then I take the log-likelihood to be the more fundamental measure of fit.

Before we can state the goal of curve fitting, or model selection in general, we need a clear definition of the predictive accuracy of an arbitrary hypothesis. We are interested in the performance of a hypothesis in predicting data randomly generated by the true hypothesis. We have already explained that this can be measured by the expected log-likelihood of newly generated data. But we do not want this goal to depend on the number of data n because we do not really care whether the unseen data set is of size n or not. It is convenient to think of the unseen data sets as the same size as the seen data set, but it is surely not necessary. Unfortunately, the log-likelihood relative to n data increases as n increases. So, in order that the goal not depend on n we need to define the predictive accuracy of a hypothesis h as the expected *per datum* log-likelihood of h relative to data sets of size n. Under this definition, the predictive accuracy of a fixed hypothesis will be the same no matter what the value of n, at least in the special case in which the data are probabilistically independent and identically distributed.[8]

Formally, we define the predictive accuracy of an arbitrary hypothesis h as follows. Let E^* be the expected value with respect to the objective probability distribution $p^*(x, y)$, and let $Data(n)$ be an arbitrary data set of n data randomly generated by $p^*(x, y)$. Then the predictive accuracy of h, denoted by $A(h)$, is defined as

$$A(h) = \tfrac{1}{n} E^*[\text{log-likelihood}(Data(n))],$$

where E^* denotes the expected value relative to the distribution $p^*(x, y)$. The goal of curve fitting, and model selection in general, is now well defined once we say what the h's are.

Models are families of hypotheses. Note that, while each member of the family has an objective likelihood, the model itself does not. Technically speaking, the likelihood of a model is an average likelihood of its members, but the average can only be defined relative to a *subjective* distribution over its members. So, the predictive accuracy of a model is undefined (except when there is only one member in the model).[9]

Model selection proceeds in two steps. The first step is to select a model, and the second step is to select a particular hypothesis from the

---

[8] For in that case, the expected log-likelihood is n times the expected log-likelihood of each datum.

[9] There are ways of defining model accuracy (Forster and Sober, 1994), but I will not do so here.

model. The second step is well known in statistics as the *estimation* of parameters. It can only use the seen data, and I will assume that it is the method of maximum likelihood estimation. Maximizing likelihood is the same as maximizing the log-likelihood, which selects the hypothesis that best fits the seen data. If an arbitrary member of the model is identified by a vector of parameter values, denoted by θ, then $\hat{\theta}$ denotes the member of the model that provides the best fit with the data. Each model produces a different best-fitting hypothesis, so *the goal of model selection is to maximize the predictive accuracy of the best-fitting cases drawn from rival models*. This is the first complete statement of the goal of model selection.

In science, competing models are often constrained by a single background theory. For example, Newton first investigated a model of the earth as a uniformly spherical ball, but found that none of the trajectories of the earth's motion derived from this assumption fit the known facts about the precession of the earth's equinoxes. He then complicated the model by allowing for the fact that the earth's globe bulges at the equator and found that the more complicated model was able to fit the equinox data. The two models are Newtonian models of the motion. However, there is no reason why Newtonian and Einsteinian models cannot compete with each other in the same way (Forster, 2001). In fact, we may suppose that there are no background theories. All that is required is that the models share the common goal of predicting the same data.

In the model selection literature, the kind of selection problem commonly considered is where the competing models form a nested hierarchy, like the hierarchy of k-degree polynomials. Each model in the hierarchy has a unique dimension k, and the sequence of best-fitting members is denoted by $\hat{\theta}_k$. The *predictive accuracy* of $\hat{\theta}_k$ is denoted by $A(\hat{\theta}_k)$. This value does not depend on the number of data, n. In fact, the predictive accuracy is not a property of the *seen* data at all – except in the sense that $\hat{\theta}_k$ is a function of the seen data. The aim of model selection in this context is to choose the value of k for which $A(\hat{\theta}_k)$ has the highest value in the hierarchy.

Note that $\hat{\theta}_k$ will not be the predictively most accurate hypothesis in the model k. $\hat{\theta}_k$ fits the *seen* data the best, but it will not, in general, provide the best average fit of unseen data. The random fluctuations in any data set will lead us away from the predictively most accurate hypothesis in the family, which is denoted by θ_k^*. However, from an epistemological point of view, we don't know the hypothesis θ_k^*, so we have no choice but to select $\hat{\theta}_k$ in the second step of curve fitting. So, our goal is to maximize $A(\hat{\theta}_k)$, and not $A(\theta_k^*)$. In fact, the maximization of $A(\theta_k^*)$ would lead to the absurd result that we should select the most complex model in the hierarchy, since $A(\theta_k^*)$ can never decrease as k increases.

While I am on the subject of 'what the goal is not', let me note that getting the value of k 'right' is not the goal either. It is true that in selecting a model in the hierarchy we also select the value of k. And in the special case in which $A(\theta_k^*)$ stops increasing at some point in the hierarchy, then that point in the hierarchy can be characterized in terms of a value of k, which we may denote as k^*. In other words, k^* is the smallest dimensional family in the hierarchy that contains the most predictively accurate hypothesis to occur anywhere in the hierarchy (if the true hypothesis is in the hierarchy, then k^* denotes the smallest true model). But model selection aims at selecting the best hypothesis $\hat{\theta}_k$, and this may not necessarily occur when $k = k^*$. After all, $\hat{\theta}_k$ could be closer to the optimal hypothesis when k is greater than k^* since the optimal hypothesis is also contained in those higher dimensional models. I will return to this point in section 7, where I defend AIC against the common charge that it is not statistically consistent.

5   A 'normality' assumption and the geometry of parameter space

There is a very elegant geometrical interpretation of predictive accuracy in the special case in which parameter estimates conform to a probabilistic description that I shall refer to as the *normality condition*. It is good to separate the condition from the question about what justifies the assumption. I will concentrate on its consequences and refer the interested reader to Cramér (1946, chs. 32–4) for the theory behind the condition.

Consider the problem of predicting y from x in a specified domain of prediction. As discussed in the previous section, there is a 'true' distribution $p(x, y)$, which determines how the estimated parameter values in our models vary from one possible data set to the next. We can imagine that a large dimensional model K contains the true distribution, even though the model K is too high in the hierarchy to be considered in practice. In fact, we could define the hierarchy in such a way that it contains the true distribution, even though every model considered in practice will be false. So, let the point θ^* in the model K represent the true distribution. The maximum likelihood hypothesis in K is $\hat{\theta}_K$, which we may denote more simply by $\hat{\theta}$. There are now two separate functions over parameter space to consider. The first is the probability density for $\hat{\theta}$ over the parameter space, which we could denote by $f(\theta)$. The second is the likelihood function, $L(Data|\theta)$, which records the probability of the data given any particular point in parameter space. Both are defined over points in parameter space, but each has a very different meaning. The normality assumption describes the nature of each function, and then connects them together.

1. The distribution $f(\theta)$ is a multivariate normal distribution centred at the point θ^* with a bell-shaped distribution around that point whose spread is determined by the covariance matrix Σ^*. The covariance matrix Σ^* is proportional to $1/n$, where n is the sample size (that is, the distribution becomes more peaked as n increases).
2. The likelihood function $L(Data|\theta)$ is *proportional* to a multivariate normal distribution centred at the point $\hat{\theta}$ with a covariance matrix Σ.[10] As n increases, $\log L(Data|\theta)$ increases proportionally to n, so that Σ is proportional to $1/n$.
3. Σ is equal to Σ^*.

The exact truth of condition 3 is an unnecessarily strong condition, but its implications are simple and clear. Combined with 1 and 2, it implies that log-likelihoods and the predictive accuracies defined in terms of them vary in parameter space according to the same metric; namely proportional to the squared distances in parameter space. More precisely, there is a transformation of parameter space in which Σ is equal to I/n, where I is the identity matrix and n is the sample size. The log-likelihood of an arbitrary point θ is equal to the log-likelihood of $\hat{\theta}$ minus $\frac{1}{2}n|\theta - \theta^*|^2$, where $|\theta - \hat{\theta}|^2$ is the square of the Euclidean distance between θ and $\hat{\theta}$ in the transformed parameter space. Moreover, the predictive accuracy of the same point θ is equal to the predictive accuracy of θ^* minus $\frac{1}{2}|\theta - \theta^*|^2$ (remember that predictive accuracy is defined in terms of the *per-datum* log-likelihoods, so that n drops out of the equation). Since $\hat{\theta}$ is a multivariate normal random variable distributed around θ^* with covariance matrix I/n, $\sqrt{n}(\hat{\theta} - \theta^*)$ is a multivariate normal random variable with mean zero and covariance matrix I. It follows that $n|\hat{\theta} - \theta^*|^2$ is a chi-squared random variable with K degrees of freedom, and that $|\theta - \theta^*|^2$ is a random variable with mean K/n.

Similar conclusions apply to lower models in the hierarchy of models, assuming that they are represented as subspaces of the K-dimensional parameter space. Without loss of generality, we may suppose that the parameterization is chosen so that an arbitrary member of the model of dimension k is $(\theta_1, \theta_2, \ldots, \theta_k, 0, \ldots, 0)$, where the last $K - k$ parameter values are 0. The predictively most accurate member of model k, denoted θ_k^*, is the projection of θ^* onto the subspace and $\hat{\theta}_k$ is the projection of $\hat{\theta}$ onto the same subspace.

---

[10] The likelihood function is not a probability function because it does not integrate to 1.

We may now use the normality assumption to understand the relationship between $A(\hat{\theta}_k)$ and $A(\theta_k^*)$. First note that θ_k^* is fixed, so $A(\theta_k^*)$ is a constant. On the other hand, $\hat{\theta}_k$ varies randomly around θ_k^* according to a k-variate normal distribution centered at θ_k^*. We know that $A(\theta_k^*)$ is greater than $A(\hat{\theta}_k)$, since $A(\theta_k^*)$ is the maximum by definition. Moreover, $A(\hat{\theta}_k)$ is less than $A(\theta_k^*)$ by an amount proportional to the squared distance between $\hat{\theta}_k$ and θ_k^* in the k-dimensional subspace. Therefore,

$$A(\hat{\theta}_k) = A(\theta_k^*) - \frac{\chi_k^2}{2n},$$

where χ_k^2 is a chi-squared random variable of k degrees of freedom. It is a property of the chi-squared distribution that χ_k^2 has a mean, or expected value, equal to k. This leads to the relationship between the bottom two plots in figure 5.3. It is not merely that $A(\theta_k^*)$ can never decrease (because the best in $k + 1$ is at least as good as the best in k), but $A(\theta_k^*)$ is also bounded above (since it can never exceed the predictive accuracy of the true hypothesis). This implies that the lower plot of $A(\hat{\theta}_k)$ will eventually reach a maximum value and then decrease as k increases. *Hence model selection aims at a model of finite dimension*, even though the predictive accuracy $A(\theta_k^*)$ of the best hypothesis in the model will keep increasing as we move up the hierarchy (or, at least, it can never decrease). The distinction between $\hat{\theta}_k$ around θ_k^* is therefore crucial to our understanding of model selection methodology.

As an example, suppose that a Fourier series is used to approximate a function. Adding new terms in the series can improve the *potential* accu-

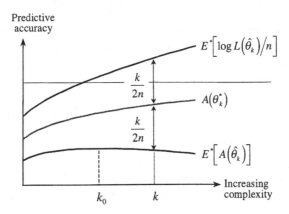

Figure 5.3 The behaviour of various quantities in a nested hierarchy of models

racy of fit indefinitely; however, the problem of overfitting is overwhelming when there are too many parameters to estimate. An historical illustration of this phenomenon is the case of ancient Ptolemaic astronomy, where adding epicycles can improve the approximation to the planetary trajectories indefinitely, yet adding epicycles beyond a certain point does not improve the prediction in practice. The present framework explains this fact.

Denote the k for which $A(\hat{\theta}_k)$ is maximum as k_0. The value of k_0 depends on $\hat{\theta}_k$, which depends on the actual data at hand. There will be a tendency for k_0 to increase as the number of seen data increases. This is observed in figure 5.3. The middle curve (the curve for $A(\theta_k^*)$) is entirely independent of the data, and the mean curve for $A(\hat{\theta}_k)$ hangs below it by a distance k/n. As n increases, it will hang closer to the middle curve, and so its maximum point will move to the right. Therefore a richer data set justifies an increase in the complexity – something that is intuitively plausible given the idea that more data allow for a more accurate estimation of complex regularities. For example, a parabolic trend in a small set of data is more readily explained away as an accidental deviation from a linear regularity, while the same parabolic trend in a large number of data is not so easily dismissed.

The relationship between $A(\hat{\theta}_k)$ and $A(\theta_k^*)$ exhibits what is commonly called the bias/variance trade-off (Geman et al., 1992). Let me first explain the terms 'bias' and 'variance'. *Model bias* is the amount that the best case in the model is less predictively accurate than the true hypothesis. By 'best case', I mean the hypothesis in the model with the highest predictive accuracy, not the best-fitting case. In other words, model bias is the difference between $A(\theta_k^*)$ and the predictive accuracy of the true hypothesis. As $A(\theta_k^*)$ increases (see figure 5.3), it gets closer to the best possible value, so the model bias decreases. Of course, we do not know which hypothesis is the most predictively accurate. So, model bias is not something that models wear on their sleeves. Nevertheless, we can make some reasonable guesses about model bias. For example, the model that says that planets orbit the sun on square paths is a very biased model because the best possible square orbit is not going to fit the true orbit very well. At the other extreme, any model that contains the true hypothesis has zero bias. In nested models, the bias is less for more complex hypotheses.

The variance, on the other hand, refers to the squared distance of the best-fitting hypothesis $\hat{\theta}_k$ from the most predictively accurate hypothesis θ_k^*. It is governed by the chi-squared random variable in the previous section. The variance of estimated hypotheses from the best case favours simplicity.

In conclusion, complexity is good for reduction of bias, whereas simplicity reduces the tendency to overfit. The optimum model is the one that makes the best trade-off between these two factors. The bias/variance dilemma refers to the fact that as we go up in a hierarchy of nested models, the bias decreases, but the expected variance increases. A model selection criterion *aims* at the best trade-off between bias and variance, but neither bias nor variance is known, so this theoretical insight does not lead directly to any criteria. It tells us what we *aim* to do, not how to do it.

An interesting special case is where a family k_1 at some point in the hierarchy already contains the true hypothesis. In that case, there is no decrease in bias past that point. But going higher in the hierarchy leads to some loss, because the additional parameters will produce a tendency to overfit. This means that going from model k_1 to $k_1 + 1$ has no *expected* advantages in terms of predictive accuracy. So, it would be best to stop in this case. However, this fact does not lead to a criterion either, unless we know that the k_1 model is true. If we already knew that, we would need no criterion.

6   Comparing selection criteria

In this section I will compare the performance of AIC and BIC in the selection of two nested models differing by one adjustable parameter in contexts in which the normality assumption holds. While the normality condition will not hold for many examples, it is a central case in statistics because the Central Limit theorems show that it holds in a wide variety of circumstances (see Cramér, 1946, chs. 32 and 33). More importantly, the arguments levelled against AIC in favour of BIC are framed in this context. So, my analysis will enable us to analyse those arguments in the next section.

The normality assumption also determines the stochastic behaviour of the log-likelihood of the seen data, and we can exploit this knowledge to obtain a criterion of model selection. Let $\log L(\hat{\theta}_k)$ be the log-likelihood of $\hat{\theta}_k$ relative to the seen data. If $\hat{\theta}_k$ is a random variable, then $\log L(\hat{\theta}_k)/n$ is also a random variable. Its relationship to $A(\hat{\theta}_k)$ is also displayed in figure 5.3: $\log L(\hat{\theta}_k)/n$ is, on average, higher than $A(\hat{\theta}_k)$ by a value of k/n (modulo a constant, which doesn't matter because it cancels out when we compare models). So, an unbiased[11] estimate of the predictive accuracy

---

[11] An estimator of a quantity (in this case an estimator of predictive accuracy) is *unbiased* if the expected value of the estimate is equal to the quantity being estimated. This sense of 'bias' has nothing to do with model bias.

of the best-fitting curve in any model is given by $\log L(\hat{\theta}_k)/n - k/n$. If we judge the predictive accuracies of competing models by this estimate, then we should choose the model with the highest value of $\log L(\hat{\theta}_k)/n - k/n$. *This is the Akaike information criterion* (AIC).

The BIC criterion (Schwarz, 1978) maximizes the quantity $\log L(\hat{\theta}_k)/n - k\log[n]/2n$, giving a greater weight to simplicity by a factor of $\log[n]/2$. This factor is quite large for large n, and has the effect of selecting a simpler model than AIC. As we shall see, this is an advantage in some cases and a disadvantage in other cases. There is an easy way of understanding why this is so. Consider two very extreme selection rules: the first I shall call the Always-Simple rule because it always selects the simpler model no matter what the data say. Philosophers will think of this rule as an extreme form of rationalism. The second rule goes to the opposite extreme and always selects the more complex model no matter what the data, which I call the Always-Complex rule. In the case of nested models, the Always-Complex rule always selects the model with the best-fitting specification and is therefore equivalent to a maximum likelihood (ML) rule. It is also a rule that philosophers might describe as a naïve form of empiricism, since it gives no weight to simplicity. BIC and AIC are between these two rules: BIC erring towards the Always-Simple side of the spectrum, while AIC is closer to the ML rule.

Consider any two nested models that differ by one adjustable parameter, and assume that normality conditions apply approximately. Note we need *not* assume that the true hypothesis is in either model (although the normality conditions are easier to satisfy when it is). The simple example in section 3 is of this type, but the results here are far more general. The only circumstance that affects the expected performance of the rules in this context is the difference in the model biases between the two models. The model bias, remember, is defined as the amount that the most predictively accurate member of the family is less predictively accurate than the true hypothesis. Under conditions of normality, the difference in model bias is proportional to the squared distance between the most accurate members of each model. In our easy example, this is proportional to $(\theta^* - \frac{1}{2})^2$. Note that the Always-Simple rule selects the hypothesis $\theta = \frac{1}{2}$ and the ML rule selects the hypothesis $\theta = \hat{\theta}$, where $\hat{\theta}$ is the maximum likelihood value of the statistic (the relative frequency of 'heads up' in our example). Under the normality assumption the predictive accuracies of these hypotheses are proportional to the squared distance to θ^* in parameter space. That is,

$$A\left(\theta = \tfrac{1}{2}\right) = -const.\left(\theta^* - \tfrac{1}{2}\right)^2 \text{ and } A\left(\theta = \hat{\theta}\right) = -const.\left(\theta^* - \hat{\theta}\right)^2.$$

Therefore, the null hypothesis $\hat{\theta} = \frac{1}{2}$ is a better choice than the alternative $\theta = \hat{\theta}$ if and only if $\frac{1}{2}$ is closer to θ^* than $\hat{\theta}$ is to θ^*. Notice that the first distance is proportional to the complex model's advantage in bias, while the expected value of the second squared distance is just the variance of the estimator $\hat{\theta}$. Therefore, the ML rule is more successful than the Always-Simple rule, on average, if and only if, the advantage in model bias outweighs the increased variance, or expected overfitting, that comes with complexity. This is the bias/variance dilemma.

A simple corollary to this result is that the two extreme rules, Always-Simple and Always-Complex, enjoy the same success (on average) if the model bias advantage exactly balances the expected loss due to variance. It is remarkable that two diametrically opposed methods can be equally successful in some circumstances. In fact, we may expect that any rules, like BIC and AIC, will perform equivalently when the bias difference is equal to the variance difference.

The situation in which the bias and variance differences are equal is a *neutral point* between two kinds of extremes – at one end of the spectrum the variance is the dominant factor, and at the other extreme, the bias difference is the overriding consideration. In the first case simplicity is the important factor, while in the second case goodness of fit is the important criterion. So, when the model bias difference is less than the expected difference in variance, we may expect BIC to perform better since it gives greater weight to simplicity. And when the model bias is greater than the variance, we may expect AIC to perform better than BIC, though neither will do better than ML.

These facts are confirmed by the results of computer computations shown in figure 5.4. In that graph, the expected gain in predictive accuracy, or what amounts to the same thing, the gain in expected predictive accuracy, is plotted against the model bias difference between the two models in question. Higher is better. The expected performance of the naïve empiricist method of ML is taken as a baseline, so the gain (or loss if the gain is negative) is relative to ML. The performance is therefore computed as follows. Imagine that a data set of size n is randomly generated by the true distribution in a domain of prediction. The method in question then selects its hypothesis. If it is the same as the ML hypothesis, then the gain is zero. If it chooses the simpler model, then the gain will be positive if the resulting hypothesis is predictively more accurate, and negative if it is less accurate, on average. The overall performance of the method is calculated as its expected gain. The expectation is calculated by weighting each possible case by the relative frequency of its occurrence as determined by the true distribution.

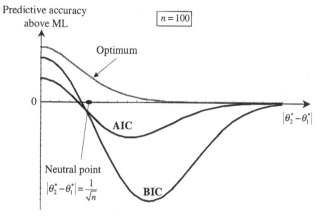

Figure 5.4 At the neutral point, the advantage of bias had by the complex model balances its disadvantage in variance, and all selection rules result in roughly the same expected predictive accuracy. In situations where the difference in model bias is smaller, methods that favour simplicity do better, like BIC, while in all other contexts, it is better to give less weight to simplicity, in which case AIC does better than BIC. The plot looks the same for a very wide variety of values of n

The performance of any method will depend on the difference in bias between the two models. The horizontal axis is scaled according to raw (un-squared) distances in parameter space, so it actually represents the square root of the model bias differences.[12] On the far left is the special case in which both models have the same bias. That is, the point at which there is no advantage in complexity. To the right are points for which the model bias is decreased in the more complex model. For nested models, the bias factor will always favour the more complex model, although this is not always true for non-nested models.

The rest of the context is held fixed: the models differ by one adjustable parameter, the number of seen data is fixed, and normality conditions hold. Remember that the seen data set itself is not held fixed. We are interested in the expected performance averaged over all possible seen data sets of size n, where the expectation is determined by the true distribution.

The curve labelled the 'optimum rule' in figure 5.4 records the performance of the following 'perfect' method of selection: of the two hypoth-

---

[12] If it were scaled by the squared distances, then the results would look even less favourable to BIC.

eses, choose the one that is the most predictively accurate. Sometimes the simpler model will 'win', sometimes the more complex model will 'win'. In the cases in which the simpler model is chosen, the policy is doing the opposite from the ML method. This 'policy' does better than ML when the model bias gain is relatively small, which reflects the fact that the decreased overfitting outweighs the loss in model bias. But when the model bias advantage of complex models is large enough, the complex model is almost always doing better in spite of its greater tendency to overfit. Note that the optimum rule cannot be implemented in practice, for it supposes that we know the predictive accuracies of the hypotheses in question. Of course, we do not know this. 'Real' methods can only make use of things we know, like the number of adjustable parameters, the number of seen data, and the fit with seen data. The optimum curve is shown on the graph because it marks the absolute upper bound in performance for any real criterion.

BIC manages to meet that optimum for the special case (on the far left in figure 5.4) in which both models are equally biased. In our easy example, this corresponds to the case in which the null hypothesis is actually true ($\theta^* = \frac{1}{2}$). If we knew this were the case, then we would want to choose the null hypothesis no matter what the data are, which is to say that the Always-Simple rule is also optimum in this situation. It is hardly surprising that both these rules do better than AIC in this situation.

Nevertheless, this situation may be relevant to scientific research. Raftery (1994) argues that this situation is likely to arise in regression problems in which scientists consider many possible independent variables when few, if any, are truly relevant to the dependent variable. In an extreme case we can imagine that a set of 51 variables are all probabilistically independent. Pick one as the depend variable and consider all models that take this variable to be a linear function of some proper subset of the remaining variables. Since the coefficients of each term in the equation can be zero, all of the models contain the true hypothesis (in which all the coefficients are zero). Therefore all the models are unbiased (in fact, they are all true). That means that complex models lose by their increased tendency to overfit, and have no compensating gains in bias. For instance, in comparing two nested models in which one adds a single independent variable, AIC will incorrectly add the variable 15.7% of the time no matter how many data we collect. BIC will make this mistake less often, and the frequency of the mistake diminishes to zero as we collect more data.

While AIC is making a mistake in this situation, the mistake is not as bad as it sounds. The goal is to maximize predictive accuracy, and the severity of the mistake is measured by the loss in predictive accuracy. If the estimated value of the coefficient of the added variable is close to zero, then the loss in predictive accuracy may be very small. Even in the extreme case of adopting the maximum likelihood rule (ML), which adds all 50 variables, the loss in predictive accuracy due to overfitting is equal to $50/n$, on average, which diminishes as n increases.[13] AIC will tend to add about 8 variables, instead of 50, although the loss will be more than $8/n$ because it will add the variables with the larger estimated coefficients. The plot in figure 5.4 suggests that the loss is around $28/n$. For smaller n, this may be quite a large loss, but notice that the loss tends to zero as n increases, despite that fact that the proportion of wrongly added variables does not tend to zero. That is why it is important to be clear about the goal (I will return to this point in the next section).

In the plot in figure 5.4, $n = 100$. But, surprisingly, the plots look the same for a wide variety of values I tested, from $n = 100$, and up. Again, the reason that the *relative* performance of BIC and AIC does not change much is because of the fact that the relative *cost* of each BIC mistake goes up even though the frequency of BIC mistakes diminishes for BIC. Note that the *absolute* cost, in terms of predictive accuracy, decreases to zero for both methods as n tends to infinity.

Before leaving the special case, it is important to emphasize that scientists do not *know* that they are in such a situation. If they did know, there would be no need for any method of model selection – just pick the simplest model. It is precisely because the context is unknown that scientists want to use a selection rule. So, it would be wrong to prefer BIC solely on the basis of what happens in this special case.

The raison d'être of model selection is the possibility of facing the situations represented further to the right on the x-axis in figure 5.4. There we quickly approach the neutral point at which all 'real' methods perform approximately the same. This point occurs when the model bias difference equals the variance of the true distribution (of the parameter estimator). With the units we have chosen, this occurs at the point marked $1/\sqrt{n}$. At points of greater difference in model bias, the fortunes of BIC and AIC change dramatically, and at model bias differences corresponding to about three standard deviations, BIC is paying a huge price for weighing simplicity so heavily.

In the case illustrated, the competing models differ by just one adjustable parameter ($\Delta k = 1$). In other computer computations, I have found that BIC has an even greater disadvantage on the right-hand side of the

---

[13] This is because the maximum likelihood hypothesis is, on average, a (squared) distance of $1/n$ from the optimum hypothesis, θ^* (see figure 5.4). (This depends on an appropriate scaling of distances in parameter space.) The loss is then multiplied for each variable.

neutral point, while its advantage over AIC on the left is less. The near optimality of BIC in one case exposes us to considerable risk in other contexts.

It is interesting to consider what happens when the number of seen data, n, increases. I have defined model bias in a way that does not depend on n, so the point on the x-axis in figure 5.4 that represents the context we are in does not change as n changes. As n increases, the relative shapes of the curves do not change, but they shrink in size. That is, the heights above and below the x-axis get smaller inversely proportionally to n, *and the neutral point moves to the left.* If we imagine that the graph is magnified as it shrinks, so it appears the same size to us, then the only change is that the point on the x-axis that represents the current context moves to the right. So, what happens if we steadily increase the number of seen data over time? We start out at an initial value of n, call it n_0. Then we collect more data, and n increases. At the beginning, we are either to the left of the neutral point or we are not. If we start at the left, then BIC will be better than AIC initially. But as the data number increases, we *must* move through the region in which BIC is performing poorly. If we do not start out to the left of the neutral point, then AIC is never worse than BIC. So, no matter what happens, we are exposed to a case in which BIC is worse than AIC as the sample size increases. In the limit as n tends to infinity, all methods approximate the optimal curve. So, the risks associated with BIC appear at intermediate values of n. Analyses that look only at the behaviour of the methods for asymptotically large values of n will overlook this weakness of BIC at intermediate sample sizes.

The analysis of this section has looked at the comparison of two fixed nested models. These results do not extend straightforwardly to the case of selecting models in a *hierarchy* of nested models (some remarks will address this in the next section). However, the special case considered here does substantiate my thesis that BIC pays a price for its near optimality in one special case.

7   The charge that AIC is inconsistent

It is frequently alleged that AIC is inconsistent,[14] while BIC is not, thereby suggesting that BIC performs better in the limit of large n. This allegation is repeated in many publications, and in so many con-

---

[14] Philosophers unfamiliar with statistical terminology should note that this does *not* refer to *logical* inconsistency. Rather, an estimator is statistically *consistent* if it converges in probability to the true value of what it is trying to estimate (the target value).

versations, that I am unable to document all of them. I will pick on just one example. Keuzenkamp and McAleer (1995, p. 9) state that AIC 'fails to give a consistent estimate of k', which they attribute to Rissanen (1987, p. 92) and Schwarz (1978). Bozdogan (1987) takes the criticism to heart, and derives an extension of AIC that is consistent in this sense. My conclusion will be that there is no sensible charge to answer, and so there is no need to modify AIC (at least, not for this reason). An immediate corollary is that all the competing criteria are consistent in the relevant sense. In any case, even if it did turn out unfavourably for AIC, it would be wrong to place too much emphasis on what happens in the long term, when scientists are only interested in finite data.[15]

There are actually many different questions that can be asked about the consistency of AIC. The first is whether AIC is a consistent method of *maximizing* predictive accuracy in the sense of converging on the hypothesis with the greatest predictive accuracy in the large sample limit. The second is whether AIC is a consistent estimator of predictive accuracy, which is a subtly different question from the first. And the third is whether AIC converges to the smallest true *model* in a nested hierarchy of models. The answer to the first two questions will be 'yes, AIC is consistent in this sense' while the answer to the third is 'no, AIC is not consistent in this sense, but this fact does not limit its ability to achieve its goal'. Here are the details.

Whatever it means to 'estimate k', it is certainly not what AIC was *designed* to estimate. The goal defined by Akaike (1973) was to estimate predictive accuracy. Because Akaike is the author of this approach, the charge that AIC is inconsistent might be read by many observers as saying that AIC is an inconsistent estimate *of predictive accuracy*. I will begin by showing that this charge of inconsistency is false, and then return to the quoted charge.

Akaike's own criterion minimizes the quantity $-2(\log L(\hat{\theta}_k) - k)$, which estimates $-2nA(\hat{\theta}_k)$. But note that this is a strange thing to estimate, since it depends on the number of seen data, n. It is like estimating the *sum* of heights of n people drawn from a population. The target value would be $n\mu$, where μ is the mean height in the population. Rather, the target *should* be a feature of the population alone, namely μ. To proceed otherwise is to mix up the *means* to the goal, which *is* a function of n, and the goal itself (which is not a function of n). So, the correct procedure is to use the sample mean, $\bar{x}$, to estimate μ, and this is a consistent estimate.

---

[15] See Sober (1988) for a response to the inconsistency of likelihood estimation in some situations, and Forster (1995, especially section 3) for a critique of the Bayesian idea that priors are harmless.

Now suppose we were to use $n\bar{x}$ to estimate $n\mu$. Then of course the estimator would be inconsistent because the error of estimation grows with increasing n. This is hardly surprising when the target value keeps growing. The correct response to this problem would be to say, as everyone does, that $\bar{x}$ is a consistent estimate of μ. Surprisingly, this is exactly the situation with respect to AIC. AIC, in Akaike's formulation, *is* an inconsistent estimate because its target value grows with n. Akaike (1973, 1974, 1977, 1985) sets up the problem in a conceptually muddled way.

The correct response to the 'problem' is to divide the estimator and target by n, so that the target does not depend on the sample size. This is exactly what I have done here, and what Forster and Sober (1994) were careful to do when they introduced the term 'predictive accuracy' to represent what the AIC criterion aimed to estimate (Akaike does not use this term). AIC does provide a consistent estimate of predictive accuracy when it is properly defined.

Now, let us return to the earlier charge of inconsistency. When there is talk of 'estimating k' the discussion is typically being restricted to the context of a nested hierarchy of models. Here there are two cases to consider. The first is the case in which the true hypothesis appears somewhere in the hierarchy, while in the second it does not. Let me consider them in turn.

In the former case, the true hypothesis will first appear in a model of dimension k^*, *and in every model higher in the hierarchy.* When one talks of estimating k, one is treating the value of k determined by the selected model as an estimate of k^*. But why should it be desirable that k be as close as possible to k^*? In general it is not desirable. For example, consider the hierarchy of nested polynomials and suppose that the true curve is a parabola (i.e. it is in PAR). If the data is sampled from a relatively narrow region in which the curve is approximately linear (which is to say that there is not much to gain by going from LIN to PAR), then for even quite large values of n, it may be best to select LIN over PAR, and better than any other family of polynomials higher in the hierarchy. Philosophically speaking, this is the interesting case in which a false model is better than a true model. However, for sufficiently high values of n, this will change, and PAR will be the better choice (because the problem of overfitting is then far less). Again, this is an example in which asymptotic results are potentially misleading because they do not extend to intermediate data sizes.

Let us consider the case in which n is large enough to make PAR the best choice (again in that case in which the true curve is in PAR). Now AIC will eventually overshoot PAR. Asymptotically, AIC will not converge on PAR (Bozdogan, 1987; Speed and Yu, 1991). This is the basis for the quoted charge that AIC is inconsistent. But how serious are the consequences of this fact? After all, AIC does successfully converge on the true hypothesis!

One might object: 'But how can it converge on the true parabola if it doesn't converge on PAR?' But the objector is forgetting that the true curve in all the models is also higher in the hierarchy because the models are nested. So, there is no need for the curve favoured by AIC to be in PAR in order for it to converge to a member of PAR. The fact that I am right about this is seen independently from the fact that the maximum likelihood estimates of the parameter values converge to their true values. This implies that even ML converges on the true hypothesis, and certainly ML overshoots k^* far more than AIC!

In the second case the true hypothesis does not appear anywhere in the hierarchy of models. In this case the model bias will keep decreasing as we move up the hierarchy, and there will never be a point at which it stops decreasing. The situation is depicted in figure 5.3. For each n, there will be an optimum model k_0, and this value will keep increasing as n increases. The situation here is complicated to analyse, but one thing is clear. There is no *universally valid* theorem that shows that BIC does better than AIC. Their relative performances will depend on the model biases in the hierarchy in a complicated way.

In both cases, the optimum model moves up the hierarchy as n increases. In the first case, it reaches a maximum value k^*, and then stops. The crucial point is that in all cases, the error of AIC (as an estimate of predictive accuracy) converges to zero as n tends to infinity. So, there is no *relevant* charge of inconsistency to be levelled against AIC in any situation. In fact, there is no such charge to be levelled against any of the methods I have discussed, which is to say that asymptotic results do not succeed in differentiating any method from any other. The crucial question concerns what happens for intermediate values of n. Theoreticians should focus on the harder questions, for there are no easy knock-down arguments against one criterion or another.

8   Summary of results

The analysis has raised a number of issues: is there any universal proof of optimality, or more realistically, is one criterion more optimal than known competitors? Or does it depend on the circumstances? What is the sense of optimality involved? I believe that the framework described in this chapter shows how to approach these questions, and has yielded some answers in special cases. The main conclusion is that the performance of model selection criteria varies dramatically from one context to another. Here is a more detailed summary of these results:

- All model selection criteria may be measured against the common goal of maximizing predictive accuracy.
- Predictive accuracy is always relative to a specified domain of prediction, and different domains define different, and perhaps conflicting, goals.
- It is commonly claimed that AIC is inconsistent. However, *all* criteria are consistent in the sense that they converge on the optimum hypothesis for asymptotically large data sizes.
- Because all methods are consistent in the relevant sense, this asymptotic property is irrelevant to the comparison of selection methods.
- The relevant differences in the selection criteria show up for *intermediate* sized data sets, although what counts as 'intermediate' may vary from one context to the next.
- When the more complex model merely adds adjustable parameters without reducing model bias, then BIC makes a better choice than AIC, but no method does better than always choosing the simpler model in this context.
- When a more complex model does reduce bias, but just enough to balance the expected loss due to overfitting, then this is a 'neutral point' at which all methods enjoy roughly the same degree of success.
- When a more complex model reduces model bias by an amount that exceeds the expected loss due to overfitting, then AIC does quite a lot better than BIC, though ML performs better than both.

The demonstration of these results is limited to the comparison of two nested models under conditions of normality, and it supposes that the domain of prediction is the same as the sampling domain (it deals with interpolation rather than extrapolation – see Forster, 2000 for some results on extrapolation). This leaves a number of open questions. How do these results extend to hierarchies of nested models, and to non-nested models? What happens when normality conditions do not apply? What if the domain of prediction is different from the domain from which the data are sampled? While I have few answers to these questions, I have attempted to describe how such an investigation may proceed.

What are the *practical* consequences of these results? In the case investigated here, I have plotted the relative performances of model selection criteria against the biases of the models under consideration. The problem is that the model biases are generally unknown.

A sophisticated Bayesian might assign a prior probability distribution over the model biases. For example, if the model biases along the x-axis in figure 5.4 have approximately the same weight, then the expected performance of AIC will be better than BIC. If such a prior were available, it would not only adjudicate between AIC and BIC, but it would also allow one to *design* a third criterion that is better than both. However, it is difficult to see how any such prior could be justified.

If such priors are unavailable, then it seems sensible to favour AIC over BIC, if that were the only choice.[16] After all, AIC is a better estimator of predictive accuracy than BIC, since BIC is a biased[17] estimator of predictive accuracy. When you correct for the bias in BIC you get AIC. BIC merely sacrifices bias with no known gain in efficiency or any other desirable property of estimators.

Irrespective of any practical advice available at the present time, the main conclusion of this chapter is that the Akaike *framework* is the right framework to use in the investigation of practical questions.

REFERENCES

Akaike, H. (1973). Information theory and an extension of the maximum likelihood principle. In B. N. Petrov and F. Csaki (eds.), *2nd International Symposium on Information Theory*, pp. 267–81. Budapest: Akademiai Kiado.

(1974). A new look at the statistical model identification. *IEEE Transactions on Automatic Control,* AC-19: 716–23.

(1977). On the entropy maximization principle. In P. R. Krishniah (ed.), *Applications of Statistics*, pp. 27–41. Amsterdam: North-Holland.

(1985). Prediction and entropy. In A. C. Atkinson and S. E. Fienberg (eds.), *A Celebration of Statistics*, pp. 1–24. New York: Springer.

Bearse, P. M., H. Bozdogan and A. Schlottman (1997). Empirical econometric modeling of food consumption using a new informational complexity approach. *Journal of Applied Econometrics.* October 1997.

Bozdogan, H. (1987). Model selection and Akaike's information criterion (AIC): the general theory and its analytical extensions. *Psychometrika* 52: 345–70.

(1990). On the information-based measure of covariance complexity and its application to the evaluation of multivariate linear models. *Communications in Statistics–Theory and Method* 19: 221–78.

Bozdogan, H. and D. Haughton (forthcoming). Information complexity criteria for regression models. *Computational Statistics and Data Analysis.*

Burnham, K. P. and D. R. Anderson (1998). *Model Selection and Inference: a Practical Information-Theoretic Approach.* New York: Springer.

---

[16] Of course, they are not the only choices. For example, Bearse et al. (1997) and Bozdogan and Haughton (forthcoming) derive alternative criteria to AIC and BIC. Burnham and Anderson (1998) provide a recent survey of variations on AIC.

[17] An estimator of a quantity, in this case an estimator of predictive accuracy, is *biased* if the expected value of the estimate is not equal to the quantity being estimated. This sense of 'bias' has nothing to do with model bias.

Cheeseman, P. (1990). On finding the most probable model. In Jeff Shrager and Pat Langley (eds.), *Computational Models of Scientific Discovery and Theory Formation*, pp. 73–93. San Mateo, CA: Morgan Kaufmann Inc.

Cramér, H. (1946). *Mathematical Methods of Statistics*. Princeton, NJ: Princeton University Press.

Earman, J. (1992). *Bayes or Bust? A Critical Examination of Bayesian Confirmation Theory*. Cambridge, MA: MIT Press.

Forster, M. R. (1994). Non-Bayesian foundations for statistical estimation, prediction, and the Ravens example. *Erkenntnis* 40: 357–76.

(1995). Bayes and bust: the problem of simplicity for a probabilist's approach to confirmation. *British Journal for the Philosophy of Science* 46: 399–424.

(1999). Model selection in science: the problem of language variance. *British Journal for the Philosophy of Science* 50: 83–102.

(2000). Key concepts in model selection: performance and generalizability, *Journal of Mathematical Psychology* 44: 205–31.

(2001). Hard problems in the philosophy of science: idealisation and commensurability. In R. Nola and H. Sankey (eds.), *After Popper, Kuhn, and Feyerabend: Issues in Theories of Scientific Method*. Dordrecht: Kluwer.

Forster, M. R. and E. Sober (1994). How to tell when simpler, more unified, or less ad hoc theories will provide more accurate predictions. *British Journal for the Philosophy of Science* 45: 1–35.

Geman, S., E. Bienenstock and R. Doursat (1992). Neural networks and the bias/variance dilemma. *Neural Computation* 4: 1–58.

Keuzenkamp, H. and M. McAleer (1995). Simplicity, scientific inference and economic modelling. *The Economic Journal* 105: 1–21.

Kiessepä, I. A. (1997). Akaike information criterion, curve-fitting, and the philosophical problem of simplicity. *British Journal for the Philosophy of Science* 48: 21–48.

Kruse, Michael (1997). Variation and the accuracy of predictions. *British Journal for the Philosophy of Science* 48: 181–93.

Kullback, S. and R. A. Leibler (1951). On information and sufficiency. *Annals of Mathematical Statistics* 22: 79–86.

Linhart, H. and W. Zucchini (1986). *Model Selection*. New York: Wiley.

MacKay, D. J. C. (1995). Probable networks and plausible predictions – a review of practical Bayesian methods for supervised neural networks. *Network: Computation in Neural Systems* 6: 496–505.

Popper, K. (1959). *The Logic of Scientific Discovery*. London: Hutchinson.

Raftery, A. E. (1994). Bayesian model selection and social research. Working Paper no. 94–12. Center for Studies in Demography and Ecology, University of Washington.

Rissanen, J. (1978). Modeling by the shortest data description. *Automatica* 14: 465–71.

(1987). Stochastic complexity and the MDL principle. *Economic Reviews* 6: 85–102.

(1989). *Stochastic Complexity in Statistical Inquiry*. Singapore: World Books.

Rosenkrantz, R. D. (1977). *Inference, Method, and Decision*. Dordrecht: Reidel.

Sakamoto, Y., M. Ishiguro and G. Kitagawa (1986). *Akaike Information Criterion Statistics*. Dordrecht: Kluwer.

Schwarz, G. (1978). Estimating the dimension of a model. *Annals of Statistics* 6: 461–5.

Sober, Elliott (1988). Likelihood and convergence. *Philosophy of Science* 55: 228–37.

Speed, T. P. and Bin Yu (1991). Model selection and prediction: normal regression. Technical Report No. 207, Statistics Dept, University of California at Berkeley.

Stone, M. (1977). An asymptotic equivalence of choice of model by cross-validation and Akaike's criterion. *Journal of the Royal Statistical Society* B 39: 44–7.

Turney, P. D. (1990). The curve fitting problem – a solution. *British Journal for the Philosophy of Science* 41: 509–30.

(1994). A theory of cross-validation error. *The Journal of Theoretical and Experimental Artificial Intelligence* 6: 361–92.

Young, A. S. (1987). On a Bayesian criterion for choosing predictive sub-models in linear regression. *Metrika* 34: 325–39.

Wallace, C. S. and P. R. Freeman (1987). Estimation and inference by compact coding. *Journal of the Royal Statistical Society* B 49: 240–65.

Xiang, D. and G. Wahba (1996). A generalized approximate cross validation for smoothing splines with non-Gaussian data. *Statistica Sinica* 6: 675–92.

6   What explains complexity?

Bert Hamminga

This chapter is perhaps an outlier in this volume because, though concerned with simplicity and econometrics, it is written from the somewhat
distant viewpoint of general philosophy.

As many contributions to this volume show, it is hard to find anyone
opposing simplicity, *ceteris paribus*. However, facing some choice, the
recommendation 'maximize simplicity' strongly resembles the well-
known advice 'maximize utility': unless specified, the recommendation
is in danger of being empty.

1   Everything in nature tends to become more complex

There is also the obvious *paradox of simplicity*: while simplicity is generally favoured, in reality everything becomes more complex all the time!

The first example is the physical evolution of the universe: since the Big
Bang, more and more different types of matter and force unfolded themselves, according to the physical theories modern man believes.

In the evolution of the living, more recently developed species usually
strike us as more complex than earlier ones. The same holds for the
growth to maturity of an individual of a certain species: individuals,
developing in a short time from a single cell to a complicatedly organized
billion-cell structure, seem to favour a kind of complexity that is even
beyond our present scientific grasp. Species that do not favour this, one-
cell beings, strike us as primitive, even though we know very well they can
kill, and can thus in a sense be 'stronger' than even such complex crea-
tures as mammals.

In human history, society, except for some spectacular episodes of
cultural decline in some regions, systematically unfolds itself to higher
levels of complexity. The crucial aspect of complexity increase in societies
is the technique and division of labour. In early societies, different types
of socially important activities, such as agriculture, trade, warfare and
leadership in secular and spiritual matters, tend to assume a largely her-

editary attribution to specialized classes within the society, unable to survive on their own.

It must be conceded that many cultures have experienced quite long episodes with relatively little growth of complexity: periods of relative stagnation if compared to periods of more rapid development like the transition from the stone to bronze age, from bronze to iron and, for instance, the transitions in Europe in the eleventh and twelfth centuries and later. The relatively stagnant nature of such periods tends, naturally, to be challenged by specialists who study the societies of these periods closely. As in so many fields, including econometrics, the general rule is that once you zoom in on something, you'll see more movement.

Secondly, it must be conceded that complex societies are not always more viable than their primitive neighbours. In cases where primitive neighbours succeed in overrunning a more complex, 'civilized', society, usually the structure of the more complex society is preserved by the quick learning of the invaders as they become the new ruling class. The notable exception is the overrunning of the Roman Empire in the fourth and fifth centuries. In this case, Christianity was taken over by the invaders, but clearly insufficient economic and social structure remained intact to keep up late Roman Christian sophistication. The savages coming into the Roman Empire from the East were too numerous to allow for quick individual learning by personal intercultural contact. Though this is a clear example of the rare exception of the socially simple winning over the socially complex (like the less rare, above-mentioned case of one-cell beings killing mammals), the resulting dramatic drop in welfare might make us doubt whether simplicity is desirable, had we anything to choose. As an analogy to econometrics, this may remind us of random walk techniques, which sometimes predict better than complex models containing all the know-how that has been carefully collected by able economists over many years.

Proceeding to the social products of the human mind, first turning our attention to legislation and jurisdiction, their growth of complexity goes without saying. As economists, we like to concentrate on substructures like taxation systems, and none of us, to say the least, lives in a country where these systems become more simple.

Finally, we arrive at the subject of this volume, as an aspect of the general trend observed thus far: simplicity in theory. In the fifteenth century, it was still possible for some to master the science of the time as a whole. Who nowadays could sensibly pretend to master completely even the field of economics alone? No matter how we measure simplicity, isn't it clear to us all that, say, dissertations become more complex all the time?

Our interest in simplicity as such in this volume is raised by the process of (over?)sophistication of the tools and procedures of econometrics. Our starting point should be to note that it is the rise of complexity that is the rule rather than the exception in nature.

No matter who likes it, everywhere it happens naturally.[1]

2   How can we explain the increase of complexity?

If we restrict our question 'Why is there complexity?' to theory and society, much of the complexity is really the result of all kinds of *competitions*: natural, social and economic.

Acquiring what a species needs from nature requires wit. Man belongs to the animals that survive by co-operating in groups. One rarely gets enough for one's family, because enough will make your family grow, and spur you to get more. Both larger food supply and larger families create larger complexity. Families, then tribes, then societies of ever increasing size, and finally the whole world system of societies divide labour to secure supply.

Another way to increase your supply is not to acquire from nature, but from others, by agreement, trade, or robbery. Robbery especially is a major cause of the increase of complexity: in order to rob you need a technique to outwit the robbed. In order not to get robbed, you need a technique to outwit the potential robber. This is a highly dynamic arms race which has occupied many noble and outstanding minds in history. It explains how acquiring and keeping rapidly became more complicated in the course of human history.

In the relationship between rulers and their people, supply to the ruler, whether in the form of gifts of honour or taxation, has a dynamics of its own, known until the present day in the form of tax regulations and the development of the techniques to evade them. The mechanism towards complexity roughly resembles the dynamics of robbery and the protection against it: great minds on both sides of the line swiftly increase the body of techniques to levy and evade tax and other contributions to the sovereign.

---

[1] Many a philosopher's hero on this subject is Gottfried Friedrich Wilhelm Hegel, writing in the early nineteenth century. His main idea is that, in history, any force provokes a counterforce. Together they form a new system with its own dynamics, which is in itself a force on a higher level, and provokes again its own counterforce, etc. Due to lack of knowledge of physics, even of his own time, he explains the physical nature in quite an erroneous way, and while dealing with logic and pure thinking he locks himself up in his own dialectical concepts, but many of his views on the genesis and structure of society (for some basic ideas of which he was inspired by the economists James Stuart and Adam Smith; Hegel (1807, 1821)) are still stimulating reading for amateurs of complexity.

The early economist's arguments for free trade rested largely upon the capacity of markets to spur suppliers to meet the needs of consumers. Thus economic competition led to the marketing of commodities of ever increasing complexity, made in increasingly complicated production processes. More generally, markets helped to make *progress* a pervasive value all over market societies, even in fields of science and scholarship where progress has no direct market value. *Progress* is not at all an obvious value in many traditional non-market societies, though from a secular viewpoint most of them at least grow more complex.

3   Seeming simplicity

In spite of this pervasive universal tendency towards increased complexity, simplicity has a natural attraction. Why?

In the historic course of the increase the division of labour, society becomes more complex but individual life may be experienced as becoming simpler: in a complex society, a worker may earn his living in a comparatively simple job, for which he needs to know relatively little about his environment. He spends his wage on products that are highly complex, like cars, TVs, PCs and food ready-made for his microwave, but these require for their use only very simple knowledge about a few buttons. In Uganda, a country I frequently visit, people normally do not employ sophisticated consumer goods, and consequently need to possess complicated capabilities, the acquisition of which by members of Western societies would need a lot of effort, to feed and house themselves starting from scratch in their natural environment. As a society develops towards more complexity, 'primitive' know-how is abolished and the education efforts of individuals shifts to the acquisition of more specialized techniques, making the 'civilized' individual utterly helpless if left on his own in nature.[2] This is a good model for what happened in econometrics: the first techniques of econometrics in the 1940s and 1950s created a further division of labour in economics. To an individual economist, life may have seemed to become simpler: techniques became available replacing his own cumbersome and unsystematic procedures leading him to decide whether or not somewhere there was a relationship. For those individuals specializing in econometrics life became simpler too: their techniques *in*

---

[2] But since the age at which a Ugandan individual has normally acquired all technical (not the social!) capabilities, largely unknown to a normal Western citizen, necessary to produce and consume is about fourteen, and standard education in Western society is longer, one might be inclined to think that *per saldo* the life to which the *individual* Western adolescent is introduced is more complex.

themselves simply required variables, equations and data sets, and the application of the techniques in themselves did not require much consideration of what the variables *mean* economically. But those who tried to retain an embracing consciousness, like for instance Solow and Salter, saw the dramatic rise of complexity.[3] The results of efforts to mould econometric models with the help of basic economic wisdom corrected by the resistance of data sets were hard to interpret and the subject of fierce debate from the very beginning. John Maynard Keynes was one of the earliest advocates of the simplicity of *keeping econometricians out*: economic parameters are inherently unstable, he claimed, only somewhat less unstable than the variables in their relations. Economics shall never be the physics of markets, it should remain the logic of markets: reasoning from sound and plausible behavioural axioms should keep doing the job (Keynes, 1939, 1940).

The danger of applied econometricians becoming like, say, TV-consumers, easily pressing buttons to see what they like, unconsciously enjoying the complicated efforts of designers of TV sets and programmes to create their world, became greater in the computer era.

4   The complexity of 'professionals' barring 'laymen'

From ancient times, another important explanation for complexity is the need to create a gap between insiders and outsiders of a profession that claims certain knowledge and abilities. The primary examples are the priests in antiquity, able to stun ordinary people with their 'magic', like temple doors opening 'by themselves' or 'by the hand of the god', when in fact this was due, for instance, to the thermodynamic effects of water boiling on fires. The maturity of a science plays no role here: medicine, until a century ago, cured even less than it does now, but has always been highly complicated (you definitely had to catch the bat at full moon, and it should definitely come flying from the left, etc.). The explanation for the complexity of medicine in former times has nothing to do with its success as a science; it stems primarily from the need to bar outsiders from the trade, and, secondly, from the incurable inclination of mankind to believe something *because* it is incomprehensible, that is, *incomprehensibility as a marketing technique*. As we all know, alas, economists some-

---

[3] In Salter (1960) and Solow (1955, 1960), for instance, explicit reference is made to the complex interrelations of the tasks of econometrics and economics respectively, in the context of modelling the causal chain investment–technical change–growth, a discussion I treated in Hamminga (1992).

times have to suffer similar qualifications of their trade nowadays, and likewise have to face the severity of social demand for their skills.

Everything that persists in nature must have an explanation. Complexity resulting from arms races has its roots directly in self-preservation, a point which many find satisfactory to take as axiomatic. The use *to the insiders* of the barring of outsiders and the uncritical belief by outsiders of the complexities of insiders are quite understandable. But the use of such phenomena for the ecological survival of *a society as a whole* is not so clear. Barring outsiders with seemingly unnecessary complexity is pervasive in human society: most trades and professions have codes and secrets, some complexity meant to prevent easy access. This holds for advanced viable, strong societies as well. Sometimes one hears people amusing themselves with the supposed vanity these codes and secrets seem to have, but there must be explanations for the survival of societies that have this feature and the apparent unviability – inferred from their non-existence – of those that do not have it. It is the task of science to find explanations, not uncritically to criticize them.

As for econometrics, its complexity as an 'access-reducing' or selection device is no different from any other academic profession: the best should prevail. This requires the definition of clear rules and criteria, and fierce competition according to them. Standards should continuously be sharpened and elevated to reduce the crowd succeeding in meeting them. There is not a place for everyone in the econometrics section, neither is there on the pages of the econometrics journal. This produces complexity: *scarcity, that is the ratio of the available space (demand) to the number of aspirants (supply), determines not only the wages of econometricians, but also the growth of complexity.* To aspire to simplicity, which feels like a natural thing to do, could, in part, be to voice a romantic dissatisfaction with the causal chains in the hard, real world in which econometricians find themselves; it could be an aspiration to be pondered seriously only by those elderly *éminences grises* who no longer feel the heat of academic competition on their necks.

5 Dynamics of scientific progress

Philosophers of science following Kuhn explain the growing complexity of science as the natural result of 'normal science', the activity of applying an established paradigm (a 'world view', a basic theory and a set of standard research routines) to an ever wider set of intended applications of the theory. However, every now and then this process results in persistent and disturbing problems that, according to a steadily growing number of pioneer experts in the field of science involved, requires drastic, or 'revolutionary' revision of overall ideas and methods in that field. Usually pioneers consider their new approach to be 'simpler' than the old one, but unfortunately only so in some key applications, where other areas of phenomena, successfully explained by the old paradigm, still have to be 'conquered' by the new. In this process of completion of the whole list of desired intended applications, the new network of theories quickly becomes more complex, and a measure to compare the complexity of the new approach to the old one will be hard to come by. In practice, adherents of different paradigms often agree on simplicity as a value *per se*, but they maintain *criteria of simplicity* suggested by the paradigm they adhere to. Disagreement persists: 'old-fashioned' experts maintain that all newly explained phenomena might be explained more simply by the old theory, provided one could keep spending the energy on attempts to do so. What one expert considers simple seems complex to others.[4]

This results in an image of the development of the theories in some field from simple T1 to complex T2, T3, etc., until persisting problems appear. There are attempts to cope with these with a new 'simple', incomplete but promising T'1, and forward again to more complex encompassing versions T'2,T'3, etc, where the T-series is hard to compare to the T'-series, first of all while your criteria of simplicity depend upon which of the series (T1, T2, etc. or T'1,T'2, etc.) you favour, secondly while, even if you can agree on a criterion, the requirements such a criterion needs to meet to yield a conclusive result are unlikely to be met. To make things worse, other criteria like predictive and explanatory power, or even economic earning capacity, if yielding clearly different scores for the theories under scrutiny, may lightly overrule simplicity as a criterion.

Special logical studies on theoretical steps towards complexity have been done, also in economics, on the basis of the ideas of Leszek Nowak, who claims that in a field of science, experts have a 'significance structure' (a list of exogenous variables partially ordered according to significance: e.g. when bodies fall, gravity principally 'comes before' air resistance, since gravity is needed to explain air density and not (or, strictly, far less) vice versa; when goods are exported, foreign demand is more significant than tariffs for the same reason, etc.). Basic laws explain the operation of 'deep', 'first' factors only, hence they are simple.

---

[4] Popper (1936) hoped that his criterion of falsifiability would constitute a 'neutral' criterion of simplicity too. Alas, the defining notion of 'empirical content' makes his criterion only applicable in very special theory comparisons unlikely to occur in real science discussions. Cf. Hamminga (1991).

'Concretizations' are modifications of the law, made to cope with the complications of including secondary, tertiary, etc. considerations. Nowak's position on this subject would be, I guess, that simplicity is desirable for deep explanations, because simple starting points are best equipped to survive theoretical steps towards complexity.

These seem to be useful basic tools that philosophy of science has provided for the kind of research that aims to explain (the degree of) complexity. Obviously, the best harvest obtainable for the time being, as many papers in this volume clearly show, is precise answers to questions restricted to small, well-defined subspaces of the vast area to which our questions are directed.

REFERENCES

Hamminga B. (1992). Learning economic method from the invention of vintage-models. In N. B. de Marchi (ed.), *Post-Popperian Methodology of Economics: Recovering Practice*, pp. 327–54. Dordrecht: Kluwer.

(1991). Comment on Hands: meaning and measurement of excess content. In N. B. de Marchi and M. Blaug, *Appraising Economic Theories*, pp. 76–84. Brookfield, Hants: Edward Elgar.

Hegel, G. W. F. (1807). *Phänomenologie des Geistes*. Frankfurt am Main: Suhrkamp, 1973.

(1812). *Wissenschaft der Logik, Erster Teil, Die objective Logik*. Hamburg: Meiner, 1986.

(1812). *Wissenschaft der Logik*. Hamburg: Meiner, 1986.

(1821). *Grundlinien der Philosophie des Rechts*. Frankfurt am Main: Suhrkamp, 1970.

(1830). *Enzyklopädie der philosophischen Wissenschaften im Grundrisse*. Hamburg: Meiner, 1992.

Keynes, J. M. (1939). Official Papers. The League of Nations. Professor Tinbergen's method. *Economic Journal*, Sept. 1939, pp. 558–68.

(1940). Comment (on 'On a method of statistical business-cycle research'. A reply by J. Tinbergen). *Economic Journal* 50.

Kuhn, T. S. (1962). *The Structure of Scientific Revolutions*. 2nd edn. Chicago: University of Chicago Press, 1970.

Nowak, L. (1980). *The Structure of Idealisation*. Synthese Library vol. 139. Dordrecht: Reidel.

Popper, K. R. (1936). *The Logic of Scientific Discovery*. London, 1972.

Salter, W. E. G. (1960). *Productivity and Technical Change*. Cambridge: Cambridge University Press, 1969.

Solow, R. M. (1955). The production function and the theory of capital. *Review of Economic Studies* 23: 101–8.

(1960). Investment and technical progress. In K. Arrow, S. Karlin and P. Suppes (eds.), *Mathematical Methods in the Social Sciences*. Stanford University Press.

7   Occam's bonus

A. W. F. Edwards

The year of the Tilburg Conference on Simplicity, 1997, coincided with
the twenty-fifth anniversary of the publications of three classic contribu-
tions to the literature on the concerns of the conference (Akaike, 1973;
Edwards, 1972; Nelder and Wedderburn, 1972). Taking my book
Likelihood first (Edwards, 1972), it contains a section headed
'Simplicity' which may still serve to introduce the problem:

We seek scientific laws that adequately account for what we have observed in the
belief that, next time a similar situation arises, they will account for what we then
observe. We formulate our laws in probability terms because there is always a
residuum of uncertainty in our predictions; and we weigh our laws in likelihood
terms because there is always a residuum of uncertainty about them. Ramsey
(1931) wrote 'In choosing a system we have to compromise between two principles: subject always to the proviso that the system must not contradict any facts
we know, we choose (other things being equal) the simplest system, and (other
things being equal) we choose the system which gives the highest chance to the
facts we have observed. This last is Fisher's "Principle of Maximum Likelihood",
and gives the only method of verifying a system of chances.' It is the inequality of
'other things' to which we must now pay attention.

I went on to write of 'the rate of exchange between support and simplicity' and asked 'What increase in support [log-likelihood] do we
require to justify an increase in complexity of the model, say the addition
of a new parameter?' Jeffreys, as I reminded my readers, had tried to give
simpler laws higher prior probabilities in his Bayesian scheme, but I was
more circumspect and offered 'no specific guidance on the "rate-of-
exchange" problem, but only a general warning to eschew dogmatism'.
Within a page, though, I had mentioned a rate of exchange of 2. I went
on to recall the graphic phrase my brother, J. H. Edwards, had coined for
it in 1969 by analogy with Occam's razor: *Occam's bonus* (Edwards,
1969). As Keuzenkamp and McAleer (1995) point out, Jeffreys' ideas
go back to Wrinch and Jeffreys (1921), and are expounded in his book
Scientific Inference (Jeffreys, 1973).

We are here trying to allow for the *complexity* of a probability model. Too little complexity and the model will be so unrealistic as to make prediction unreliable; too much complexity and the model will be so specific to the particular data as to make prediction – yes – unreliable. As long ago as the seventeenth century we find Galileo (1623) replying to the criticism that when hypothesizing about cometary orbits he did not consider irregular curves, in the following words:

Lines are called regular when, having a fixed and definite description, they are susceptible of definition and of having their properties demonstrated. Thus the spiral is regular, and its definition originates in two uniform motions, one straight and the other circular. So is the ellipse, which originates from the cutting of a cone or a cylinder. Irregular lines are those which have no determinacy whatever, but are indefinite and casual and hence indefinable; no property of such lines can be demonstrated, and in a word nothing can be known about them. Hence to say 'Such events take place thanks to an irregular path' is the same as to say 'I do not know why they occur'. The introduction of such lines is in no way superior to the 'sympathy', 'antipathy', 'occult properties', 'influences', and other terms employed by some philosophers as a cloak for the correct reply, which would be 'I do not know'.

It would be admirable if R. A. Fisher had given an opinion as to what Occam's bonus should be, but I am not aware that he ever compared likelihoods for models with different numbers of parameters, or even models with the same number of parameters but which were discretely separate. In 1922 he applied the method of maximum likelihood to the genetic linkage estimation problem (its first application, as a matter of fact), and might have compared the maximum likelihoods for the different possible orders of the eight loci he considered; but, alas, he assumed the order known (Fisher, 1922a).

Since there has been much discussion of the appropriate rate of exchange in recent years, the so-called Akaike Information Criterion proposal being especially popular, it is pertinent to review the history. Professor Akaike wrote to me in July 1972 upon the publication of *Likelihood*, finding it 'very interesting' and expressing surprise at the 'deep connection between the content of your book and my recent work'. 'You might find it interesting to note that in these papers [which he sent me] a figure exactly equal to 2 is adopted for the evaluation of the improvement in log-likelihood of a model fit with introduction of a new parameter.' I nervously replied that 'although I agree that a 2-unit support level is about right for one parameter, I am not in agreement that $2n$ is right for n parameters. I regret the implication of my page 202 [where the suggestion of 2 was made].' By October 1972 I was advocating $\frac{1}{2}$ on the basis of the fact that twice the log-likelihood ratio is approximately distributed as χ^2 whose expected value is equal to its degrees of freedom (Edwards, 1973). Notwithstanding Akaike's letter, his Information Criterion value is in fact 1, not 2: the 2 refers not to the increase in log-likelihood but to the increase in twice the log-likelihood, or the *deviance* in Nelder and Wedderburn's (1972) terminology. Nelder and Wedderburn's choice for Occam's bonus was $\frac{1}{2}$, like mine.

Akaike's (1973) starting point was a rule to maximize the expected log-likelihood function, or what I had called the expected support function, which he then justified in terms of the Kullback–Leibler mean information measure for discrimination between two distributions (which goes back to Jeffreys, 1948). I have been unable to follow his reasoning, since the expected support function obviously does not involve the data, but it is a concept which I thought must be important whilst I was writing *Likelihood*, though I could find very little about it in the literature. I considered the whole population of support functions, and argued that both the distribution of their maxima and their expectation (still expressed as a function of the parameters) must be important. All I could find was a paper by Huzurbazar (1949), who had studied for his PhD with Jeffreys, but no one I consulted in Cambridge had read it. I could see that a consequence of Huzurbazar's result was the following general theorem (Theorem 7.2.4 of *Likelihood*):

For a distribution which admits k jointly sufficient statistics t for its k parameters θ, the expectation of the support function taken at θ^* is identical to the support function for which θ^* is the evaluate [my word for the maximum likelihood estimate].

O. Barndorff-Nielsen tells me that this will be related to the fact that for the exponential family the expectation of t taken at the evaluate is equal to the evaluate. It follows from the theorem that the true value, say θ^*, has maximum expected support.

My difficulty with Akaike's proposal is that one cannot write down the expected support function without knowing this true value of the parameter, and to use the maximum-likelihood value seems like begging the question. In practice statisticians are now inclining to my view that 1 is too big a value for Occam's bonus. Various smaller values are circulating, but I will limit myself to enlarging on reasons why $\frac{1}{2}$ deserves consideration as a starting point.

I begin with the close relationship between likelihood and χ^2 which arises through the fact that the first term of the Taylor expansion of twice the log-likelihood is simply Pearson's χ^2, as Fisher noted in 1922 (Fisher, 1922b). Now the expected value of χ^2 is equal to its degrees of freedom, so that adjusting parameter values by minimising χ^2 rather than equating it to its degrees of freedom is obviously going to lead to lower-than-expected values for χ^2. If we now think of this in terms of the log-likelihood, or support, instead, we can ask ourselves the question 'By how much is the expected support at the true parameter value θ^* less than the maximum support?' In the theorem I quoted above I said that the expected support function was identical to the support function with the same maximum, but of course I was disregarding the additive constant, as one usually does with support functions. Now we need to know what that constant is.

Consider the evaluation of the mean θ of a $N(\theta, 1)$ distribution. From one observation x the support function is

$$S = \frac{1}{2}(x - \theta)^2,$$

with a maximum of $S = 0$ of course. Taking expectations with respect to the true value θ^* we have

$$\mathrm{E}(S) = -\tfrac{1}{2}\mathrm{E}\{(x - \theta)^2\} = -\tfrac{1}{2}\mathrm{E}\{(x - \theta^* + \theta^* - \theta)^2\}$$
$$= -\tfrac{1}{2}[\mathrm{E}\{(x - \theta^*)^2\} + 2(\theta^* - \theta)\mathrm{E}(x - \theta^*) + (\theta^* - \theta)^2]$$
$$= -\tfrac{1}{2}[1 + (\theta^* - \theta)^2].$$

At the maximum $\theta = \theta^*$, therefore, $\mathrm{E}(S) = -\tfrac{1}{2}$. By estimating one parameter we expect to gain half a unit. Occam's bonus is one half, and this argument, though really equivalent to the χ^2 argument, is perhaps a more persuasive one. Presumably it works for the exponential family generally. But I must reiterate my warning in *Likelihood* to 'eschew dogmatism' over this rate of exchange. Forster and Sober (1994), in their development of Akaike's result, attribute the additional value of $\tfrac{1}{2}$ to the predictive part of the argument.

As the contributions to this volume make clear, it is unlikely that any one value for Occam's bonus is going to be acceptable under all circumstances. Rather like with Laplace's Rule of Succession, the best we can do is to analyse the very simplest cases as a guide to the real world of model choice.

REFERENCES

Akaike, H. (1973). Information theory and an extension of the maximum likelihood principle. In B. N. Petrov and F. Csàki (eds.), *Second International Symposium on Information Theory*, pp. 267–81. Budapest: Akadémiai Kaidó.

Edwards, A. W. F. (1972). *Likelihood*. Cambridge: Cambridge University Press; (1992) Baltimore: Johns Hopkins University Press.

(1973). The likelihood treatment of linear regression. *Biometrika* 60: 73–7.

Edwards, J. H. (1969). In N. E. Morton (ed.), *Computer Applications in Genetics*. Honolulu: University of Hawaii Press.

Fisher, R. A. (1922a). The systematic location of genes by means of crossover observations. *American Naturalist* 56, 406–11.

(1922b). On the mathematical foundations of theoretical statistics. *Philosophical Transactions of the Royal Society* A 222: 309–68.

Forster, M. and E. Sober (1994). How to tell when simpler, more unified, or less *ad hoc* theories will provide more accurate predictions. *British Journal of the Philosophy of Science* 45: 1–35.

Galilei, G. (1623). *The Assayer*. Transl. in *Discoveries and Opinions of Galileo*, by S. Drake. New York: Doubleday Anchor, 1957.

Huzurbazar, V. S. (1949). On a property of distributions admitting sufficient statistics. *Biometrika* 36: 71–4.

Jeffreys, H. (1948). *Theory of Probability*. 2nd edition. Oxford: Clarendon Press.

(1973). *Scientific Inference*. 3rd edition. Cambridge: Cambridge University Press.

Keuzenkamp, H. A. and M. McAleer (1995). Simplicity, scientific inference and econometric modelling. *Journal of the Royal Economic Society* 105: 1–21.

Nelder, J. A. and R. W. M. Wedderburn (1972). Generalized linear models. *Journal of the Royal Statistical Society* A 135: 370–84.

Ramsey, F. P. (1931). *The Foundations of Mathematics and other Logical Essays*. London: Routledge & Kegan Paul.

Wrinch, D. M. and H. Jeffreys (1921). On certain fundamental principles of scientific enquiry. *London, Edinburgh and Dublin Philsophical Magazine* 42: 369–90.

Part II

Simplicity in theory and practice

8 Simplicity, information, Kolmogorov complexity and prediction

Paul Vitányi and Ming Li

1 Introduction

'We are to admit no more causes of natural things (as we are told by Newton) than such as are both true and sufficient to explain the appearances. To this purpose the philosophers say that Nature does nothing in vain, and more is in vain when less will serve; for Nature is pleased with simplicity, and affects not the pomp of superfluous causes.'

The conglomerate of different research threads drawing on an objective and absolute form of this approach appears to be part of a single emerging discipline, which will become a major applied science like information theory or probability theory. Intuitively, the amount of information in a finite string is the size (number of binary digits or *bits*) of the shortest program that, without additional data, computes the string and terminates. A similar definition can be given for infinite strings, but in this case the program produces element after element forever. Thus, a long sequence of 1's such as

$$\underbrace{11111\ldots1}_{10,000 \text{ times}}$$

contains little information because a program of size about log 10,000 bits outputs it:

```
for i := 1 to 10,000
    print 1
```

Likewise, the transcendental number $\pi = 3.1415\ldots$, an infinite sequence of seemingly 'random' decimal digits, contains but a few bits of information. (There is a short program that produces the consecutive digits of π forever.) Such a definition would appear to make the amount of information in a string (or other object) depend on the particular programming language used.

Fortunately, it can be shown that all reasonable choices of programming languages lead to quantification of the amount of 'absolute' information in individual objects that is invariant up to an additive constant. We call this quantity the 'Kolmogorov complexity' of the object. If an object contains regularities, then it has a shorter description than itself. We call such an object 'compressible'.

The application of Kolmogorov complexity takes a variety of forms, for example, using the fact that some strings are extremely compressible; using the compressibility of strings as a selection criterion; using the fact that many strings are not compressible at all; and using the fact that some strings may be compressed, but that it takes a lot of effort to do so.

Here we are concerned with the induction problem: given a body of data concerning some phenomenon under investigation, we want to select the most plausible hypothesis from among all appropriate hypotheses, or predict future data. 'Occam's razor' tells us that, all other things being equal, the simplest explanation is the most likely one. Interpreting 'simplest' as 'having shortest description', the most likely hypothesis is the most compressed one. The length of the shortest effective description of some object is its Kolmogorov complexity. The argument says that among all hypotheses consistent with the data the one with least Kolmogorov complexity is the most likely one. This idea of hypothesis identification is closely related to Solomonoff's original 'universal prior' which is used for prediction (Solomonoff, 1964).

The classical method for induction is Bayes' rule. The problem with applying Bayes' rule is that one requires the prior probabilities of the hypotheses first. Unfortunately, it is often impossible to obtain these. In the unlikely case that we possess the true prior distribution, it is still the case that in practice the data tend to be noisy due to the measuring process or other causes. The latter confuses Bayes' rule into overfitting the hypothesis by adding random features while trying to fit the data.

One way out of the conundrum of *a priori* probabilities is to require prediction or inference of hypotheses to be completely or primarily data driven. For prediction this was achieved using the Kolmogorov-complexity-based universal distribution (Solomonoff, 1964, 1978), and for hypothesis identification by the minimum description length (MDL or MML) approach (Rissanen, 1978, 1989; Wallace and Boulton, 1968; Wallace and Freeman, 1987).

Ideally, the description lengths involved should be the shortest effective description lengths. (We use 'effective' in the sense of 'Turing computable' (Turing, 1936).) Shortest effective description length is asymptotically unique and objective and known as the *Kolmogorov complexity* of the object being described. Such shortest effective descriptions are 'effective' in the sense that we can compute the described objects from them. Unfortunately, it can be shown, see Li and Vitányi (1997), that one cannot compute the length of a shortest description from the object being described. This obviously impedes actual use. Instead, one needs to consider computable approximations to shortest descriptions, for example by restricting the allowable approximation time. This course is followed in one sense or another in the practical incarnations such as MML and MDL. There one often simply uses the Shannon–Fano code, which assigns prefix code length $-\log P(x)$ to x irrespective of the regularities in x. If $P(x) = 2^{-l(x)}$ for every $x \in \{0, 1\}^n$, with the length of x denoted by $l(x)$, then the code word length of an all-zero x equals the code word length of a truly irregular x. While the Shannon–Fano code gives an expected code word length close to the entropy, it does not distinguish the regular elements of a probability ensemble from the random ones.

The code of the shortest effective descriptions, with the Kolmogorov complexities as the code word length set, also gives an expected code word length close to the entropy and additionally compresses the regular objects until all regularity is squeezed out. All shortest effective descriptions are completely random themselves, without any regularity whatsoever. Kolmogorov complexity can be used to develop a theory of (idealized) minimum description length reasoning. In particular, shortest effective descriptions enable us to rigorously analyse the relation between shortest description length reasoning and Bayesianism. This provides a theoretical basis for, and gives confidence in, practical uses of the various forms of minimum description length reasoning mentioned.

In Li and Vitányi (1995) and Vitányi and Li (2000) we rigorously derive and justify this Kolmogorov-complexity-based form of minimum description length, 'Ideal MDL', via the Bayesian approach using a particular prior distribution over the hypotheses (the so-called 'universal distribution'). This leads to a mathematical explanation of correspondences and differences between Ideal MDL and Bayesian reasoning, and in particular it gives some evidence of the conditions under which the latter is prone to overfitting while the former isn't. Namely, for *hypothesis identification* Ideal MDL using Kolmogorov complexity can be reduced to the Bayesian approach using the universal prior distribution, provided the minimum description length is reached for those hypotheses with respect to which the data sample is *individually random* in the sense of Martin-Löf (1966). Under those conditions Ideal MDL, Bayesianism, MDL and MML select pretty much the same hypothesis.

In this chapter we focus on *prediction* rather than hypothesis identification. We explain Solomonoff's prediction method using the universal distribution. We show that this method is not equivalent to the use of shortest descriptions. Nonetheless, we demonstrate that in almost all cases compression of descriptions gives optimal prediction. A final version combining the material of the current chapter together with Li and Vitányi (1995) and Vitányi and Li (1996) and full details on the mathematical background of Kolmogorov complexity, incompressibility, and individual randomness, appeared as Vitányi and Li (2000). A popularized account of the miraculous universal distribution and its applications is given in Kirchherr, Li and Vitányi (1997). First we look at some pertinent lacunas of classical probability theory and information theory.

1.1   A lacuna of classical probability theory

An adversary claims to have a true random coin and invites us to bet on the outcome. The coin produces a hundred heads in a row. We say that the coin cannot be fair. The adversary, however, appeals to probability theory which says that each sequence of outcomes of a hundred coin flips is equally likely, $1/2^{100}$, and one sequence had to come up.

Probability theory gives us no basis to challenge an outcome *after* it has happened. We could only exclude unfairness in advance by putting a penalty side-bet on an outcome of 100 heads. But what about 1010...10? What about an initial segment of the binary expansion of π?

Regular sequence $\Pr(00000000000000000000000000) = \frac{1}{2^{26}}$,
Regular sequence $\Pr(01000110110000010100111001) = \frac{1}{2^{26}}$,
Random sequence $\Pr(10010011011000111011010000) = \frac{1}{2^{26}}$.

The first sequence is regular, but what is the distinction of the second sequence and the third? The third sequence was generated by flipping a quarter. The second sequence is very regular: 0, 1, 00, 01, ... The third sequence will pass (pseudo-)randomness tests with overwhelming probability.

In fact, classical probability theory cannot express the notion of *randomness of an individual sequence*. It can only express expectations of properties of outcomes of random processes, that is, the expectations of properties of the total set of sequences under some distribution.

Only relatively recently, this problem of defining a proper notion of *individual* unpredictability has found a satisfactory resolution by combining notions of computability and statistics to express the complexity of a finite object. This complexity is the length of the shortest binary program from which the object can be effectively reconstructed. It may be called the *algorithmic information content* of the object. This quantity turns out to be an attribute of the object alone, and absolute (in the technical sense of being recursively invariant). It is the *Kolmogorov complexity* of the object.

1.2   A lacuna of information theory

Shannon's classical information theory assigns a quantity of information to an ensemble of possible messages. All messages in the ensemble being equally probable, this quantity is the number of bits needed to count all possibilities. This expresses the fact that each message in the ensemble can be communicated using this number of bits. However, it does not say anything about the number of bits needed to convey any individual message in the ensemble. To illustrate this, consider the ensemble consisting of all binary strings of length 9999999999999999.

By Shannon's measure, we require 9999999999999999 bits on average to encode a string in such an ensemble. However, the string consisting of 9999999999999999 1's can be encoded in about 55 bits by expressing 9999999999999999 in binary and adding the repeated pattern '1'. A requirement for this to work is that we have agreed on an algorithm that decodes the encoded string. We can compress the string still further when we note that 9999999999999999 equals $3^2 \times 1111111111111111$, and that 1111111111111111 consists of 2^4 1's.

Thus, we have discovered an interesting phenomenon: the description of some strings can be compressed considerably, provided they exhibit enough regularity. This observation, of course, is the basis of all systems of expressing very large numbers and was exploited early on by Archimedes in his treatise *The Sand Reckoner*, in which he proposes a system to name very large numbers:

There are some, King Golon, who think that the number of sand is infinite in multitude [... or] that no number has been named which is great enough to exceed its multitude. ... But I will try to show you, by geometrical proofs, which you will be able to follow, that, of the numbers named by me ... some exceed not only the mass of sand equal in magnitude to the earth filled up in the way described, but also that of a mass equal in magnitude to the universe.

However, if regularity is lacking, it becomes more cumbersome to express large numbers. For instance, it seems easier to compress the number 'one billion', than the number 'one billion seven hundred thirty-five million two hundred sixty-eight thousand and three hundred ninety-four', even though they are of the same order of magnitude.

1.3   Lacuna in randomness

In the context of the above discussion, random sequences are sequences that cannot be compressed. Now let us compare this with the common notions of mathematical randomness. To measure randomness, criteria have been developed that certify this quality. Yet, in recognition that they do not measure 'true' randomness, we call these criteria 'pseudo' randomness tests. For instance, statistical surveys of initial sequences of decimal digits of π have failed to disclose any significant deviations from randomness. But clearly, this sequence is so regular that it can be described by a simple program to compute it, and this program can be expressed in a few bits.

The notion of randomness of individual objects has a long history which goes back to the initial attempts by von Mises (1919) to formulate the principles of application of the calculus of probabilities to real-world phenomena. Classical probability theory cannot even express the notion of 'randomness of individual objects'. Following almost half a century of unsuccessful attempts, the theory of Kolmogorov complexity (Kolmogorov, 1965) and Martin-Löf tests for randomness (Martin-Löf, 1966) finally succeeded in formally expressing the novel notion of individual randomness in a correct manner, see Li and Vitányi (1997). Objects which are random in this sense will satisfy *all* effective tests for randomness properties – those which are known and those which are yet unknown alike.

2   Kolmogorov complexity

The Kolmogorov complexity (Kolmogorov, 1965; Zvonkin and Levin, 1970; Li and Vitányi, 1997) of x is simply *the length of the shortest effective binary description of* x. Formally, this is defined as follows. Let $x, y, z \in \mathcal{N}$, where $\mathcal{N}$ denotes the natural numbers and we identify $\mathcal{N}$ and $\{0, 1\}^*$ according to the correspondence

$$(0, \in), (1, 0), (2, 1), (3, 00), (4, 01), \ldots$$

Here $\in$ denotes the *empty word* '' with no letters. The *length* $l(x)$ *of* x is the number of bits in the binary string x. For example, $l(010) = 3$ and $l(\in) = 0$.

The emphasis is on binary sequences only for convenience; observations in any alphabet can be so encoded in a way that is 'theory neutral'.

A binary string y is a *proper prefix* of a binary string x if we can write $x = yz$ for $z \neq \in$. A set $\{x, y, \ldots\} \subseteq \{0, 1\}^*$ is *prefix-free* if for any pair of distinct elements in the set neither is a proper prefix of the other. A prefix-free set is also called a *prefix code*. Each binary string $x = x_1 x_2 \ldots x_n$ has a special type of prefix code, called a *self-delimiting code*,

$$\bar{x} = 1 x_1 x_1 x_2 x_2 \ldots x_n\, x_n,$$

where $\neg x_n = 0$ if $x_n = 1$ and $\neg x_n = 1$ otherwise. Additionally, we define $\bar{\varepsilon} = 0$. This code is self-delimiting because we can determine where the code word $\bar{x}$ ends by reading it from left to right without backing up. Using this code we define the standard self-delimiting code for x to be $x' = \overline{l(x)}x$. It is easy to check that $l(\bar{x}) = 2n + 1$ and $l(x') = n + 2\log n + 1$.

Let $T_1, T_2, \ldots$ be a standard enumeration of all Turing machines (or, what is equivalent and perhaps more familiar, all programs in a general universal programming language like G'^{++} or Java) and let $\phi_1, \phi_2, \ldots$ be the enumeration of corresponding functions which are computed by the respective Turing machines. That is, T_i computes ϕ_i. These functions are the *partial recursive* functions or *computable* functions. The Kolmogorov complexity $C(x)$ of x is the length of the shortest binary program from which x is computed. Formally, we can define this as follows (in a simplified, but formally correct manner):

Definition 1 The *Kolmogorov complexity* of x given y (for free on a special auxiliary input tape) is

$$C(x|y) = \min_{p,i}\{l(i'p) : \phi_i(p, y) = x, p \in \{0, 1\}^*, i \in \mathcal{N}\}.$$

Define $C(x) = C(|x| \in)$.

The Kolmogorov complexity is absolute in the sense of being recursively invariant by Church's Thesis and the ability of universal machines to simulate one another (Li and Vitányi, 1997). For technical reasons we also need a variant of complexity, so-called prefix complexity, which is associated with Turing machines for which the set of programs resulting in a halting computation is prefix free. We can realize this by equipping the Turing machine with a one-way input tape, an auxiliary input tape, a separate work tape, and a one-way output tape. Such Turing machines are called prefix machines since the halting programs for any one of them form a prefix-free set. As before, let $P_1, P_2, \ldots$ be a standard enumeration of prefix machines, and let $\psi_1, \psi_2, \ldots$ be an enumeration of the corresponding function being compared. It can be shown that these coincide (again) precisely with the partial recursive functions. Taking the prefix machine P we can define the prefix complexity analogously with the plain Kolmogorov complexity. If x^* is a program for x then the set $\{x^* : P(x^*) = x, x \in \{0, 1\}^*\}$ is a *prefix code*. That is, each x^* is a code word for some x, and if x^* and y^* are code words for x and y with $x \neq y$ then x^* is not a prefix of y^*.

Let $\langle \cdot \rangle$ be a standard invertible effective one-one encoding from $\mathcal{N} \times \mathcal{N}$ to prefix-free recursive subset of $\mathcal{N}$. For example, we can set $\langle x, y \rangle = x'y'$. We insist on prefix-freeness and recursiveness because we want a prefix

Turing machine to be able to read an image under $\langle \cdot \rangle$ from left to right and determine where each constituent string ends.

Definition 2 The *prefix Kolmogorov complexity* of x given y (for free) is

$$K(x|y) = \min_{p,i}\{l(\langle i, p \rangle) : \psi_i(\langle p, y \rangle) = x, p \in \{0, 1\}^*, i \in \mathcal{N}\}.$$

Define $K(x) = K(x| \in)$.

The nice thing about $K(x)$ is that we can interpret $2^{-K(x)}$ as a probability distribution. Namely, $K(x)$ is the length of a shortest prefix-free program for x. By the fundamental Kraft's inequality, see for example Li and Vitányi (1997), we know that if $l_1, l_2, \ldots$ are the code-word lengths of a prefix code, then $\sum_x 2^{-l_x} \leq 1$. This leads to the notion of universal distribution – a rigorous form of Occam's razor-below.

3   Universal distribution

A Turing machine T computes a function on the natural numbers. However, we can also consider the computation of real valued functions. For this purpose we consider both the argument of ϕ and the value of ϕ as a pair of natural numbers according to the standard pairing function $\langle \cdot \rangle$. We define a function from $\mathcal{N}$ to the reals $\mathcal{R}$ by a Turing machine T computing a function ϕ as follows. Interpret the computation $\phi(\langle x, t \rangle) = \langle p, q \rangle$ to mean that the quotient p/q is the rational valued tth approximation of $f(x)$.

Definition 3 A function $f : \mathcal{N} \to \mathcal{R}$ is *enumerable* if there is a Turing machine T computing a total function ϕ such that $\phi(x, t+1) \geq \phi(x, t)$ and $\lim_{t \to \infty} \phi(x, t) = f(x)$. This means that f can be computably approximated from below. If f can also be computably approximated from above then we call f *recursive*.

A function $P : \mathcal{N} \to [l, \infty]$ is a *probability distribution* if $\sum_{x \in \mathcal{N}} P(x) \leq 1$. (The inequality is a technical convenience. We can consider the surplus probability to be concentrated on the undefined element of $u \notin \mathcal{N}$.)

Consider the family $\mathcal{EP}$ of *enumerable* probability distributions on the sample space $\mathcal{N}$ (equivalently, $\{0, 1\}^*$). It is known (Li and Vitányi, 1997), that $\mathcal{EP}$ contains an element $\mathbf{m}$ that multiplicatively dominates all elements of $\mathcal{EP}$. That is, for each $P \in \mathcal{EP}$ there is a constant c such that $c\mathbf{m}(x) > P(x)$ for all $x \in \mathcal{N}$. We call $\mathbf{m}$ a *universal distribution*.

The family $\mathcal{EP}$ contains all distributions with computable parameters which have a name, or in which we could conceivably be interested, or which have ever been considered. The dominating property means that **m** assigns at least as much probability to each object as any other distribution in the family $\mathcal{EP}$ does. In this sense it is a universal *a priori* by accounting for maximal ignorance. It turns out that if the true *a priori* distribution in Bayes' Rule is recursive, then using the single distribution **m**, or its continuous analogue the measure **M** on the sample space $\{0, 1\}^\infty$ (defined later), is provably as good as using the true *a priori* distribution. We also know, Li and Vitányi (1997) that

Lemma 1

$$-\log \mathbf{m}(x) = K(x) \pm O(1). \tag{1}$$

That means that **m** assigns high probability to simple objects and low probability to complex or random objects. For example, for $x = 00 \ldots 0$ (n 0's) we have $K(x) = K(n) + O(1) \le \log n + 2\log\log n + O(1)$ since the program

```
print n_ times a '0'
```

prints x. (The additional $2 \log \log n$ term is the penalty term for a self-delimiting encoding.) Then, $1/(n \log^2 n) = O(\mathbf{m}(x))$. But if we flip a coin to obtain a string y of n bits, then with overwhelming probability $K(y) \ge n - O(1)$ (because y does not contain effective regularities which allow compression), and hence $\mathbf{m}(y) = O(1/2^n)$.

4   Betting against a crooked player

Let us apply this to the betting problem on a not-known-to-be-false coin we identified in section 1.1 as a lacuna in probability theory. We borrow a little story from Kirchherr et al. (1997):

Alice, walking down the street, comes across Bob, who is tossing a coin. He is offering odds to all passers-by on whether the next toss will be heads or tails. The pitch is this: he'll pay you two dollars if the next toss is heads; you pay him one dollar if the next toss is tails. Should she take the bet? If Bob is tossing a fair coin, it's a great bet. Probably she'll win money in the long run. After all, she would expect that half Bob's tosses would come up heads and half tails. Giving up only one dollar on each heads toss and getting two for each tails – why, in a while she'd be rich!

Of course, to assume that a street hustler is tossing a fair coin is a bit of a stretch, and Alice is no dummy. So she watches for a while, recording how the coin comes up for other betters, writing a '1' for 'heads' and a '0' for 'tails'. After a while she has written 01010101010101. This doesn't look good. So Alice makes the following offer.

Alice pays Bob \$1 first and proposes that Bob pays her $2^{1000-K(x)}$ dollars, where x is the binary sequence of the 1,000 coin flip results to come. This is fair since Bob is only expected to pay her

$$\sum_{|x|=1000} 2^{-1000} 2^{1000-K(x)} \leq \$1,$$

by Kraft's inequality. So Bob should be happy to accept the proposal. But if Bob cheats, then, for example, Alice gets $2^{1000-\log 1000}$ dollars for a sequence like 0101010101... 1

In the 1 versus 2 dollars scheme, Alice can propose to add this as an extra bonus play. This way, she is guaranteed to win big: either polynomially increasing her money (when Bob does not cheat) or exponentially increasing her money (when Bob cheats).

5   Randomness tests

One can consider as non-random those objects in which one can find sufficiently many regularities. In other words, we would like to identify 'incompressibility' with 'randomness'. This is proper if the sequences that are incompressible can be shown to possess the various properties of randomness (stochasticity) known from the theory of probability. That this is possible is the substance of the celebrated theory developed by the Swedish mathematician Per Martin-Löf.

There are many known properties which probability theory attributes to random objects. To give an example, consider sequences of n tosses with a fair coin. Each sequence of n zeros and ones is equiprobable as an outcome: its probability is 2^{-n}. If such a sequence is to be random in the sense of a proposed new definition, then the number of ones in x should be near to $n/2$, the number of occurrences of blocks '00' should be close to $n/4$, and so on.

It is not difficult to show that each such single property separately holds for all incompressible binary strings. But we want to demonstrate that incompressibility implies all conceivable effectively testable properties of randomness (both the known ones and the as yet unknown ones). This way, the various theorems in probability theory about random sequences carry over automatically to incompressible sequences. We do not develop the theory here but refer to the exhaustive treatment in Li and Vitányi (1997) instead. We shall use the properties required in the sequel of this paper.

6   Bayesian reasoning

Consider a situation in which one has a set of observations of some phenomenon, and also a finite or countably infinite set of hypotheses which are candidates to explain the phenomenon. For example, we are given a coin and we flip it 1000 times. We want to identify the probability that the coin has outcome 'head' in a single coin flip. That is, we want to find the bias of the coin. The set of possible hypotheses is uncountably infinite if we allow each real bias in $[0, 1]$, and countably infinite if we only allow each rational bias in $[0, 1]$.

For each hypothesis H we would like to assess the probability that H is the 'true' hypothesis, given the observation of D. This quantity, $\Pr(H|D)$, can be described and manipulated formally in the following way.

Consider a sample space Ω. Let D denote a sample of outcomes, say experimental data concerning a phenomenon under investigation. Let $H_1, H_2, \ldots$ be an enumeration of countably many hypotheses concerning this phenomenon, say each H_i is a probability distribution over Ω. The list $\mathcal{H} = \{H_1, H_2 \ldots\}$ is called the *hypothesis space*. The hypotheses H_i are exhaustive and mutually exclusive.

For example, say the hypotheses enumerate the possible rational (or computable) biases of the coin. As another possibility there may be only two possible hypotheses: hypothesis H_1 which says the coin has bias 0.2, and hypothesis H_2 which puts the bias at 0.8.

Suppose we have *a priori* a distribution of the probabilities $P(H)$ of the various possible hypotheses in $\mathcal{H}$ which means that $\sum_{H \in \mathcal{H}} P(H) = 1$. Assume furthermore that for all $H \in \mathcal{H}$ we can compute the probability $\Pr(D|H)$ that sample D arises if H is the case. Then we can also compute (or approximate in case the number of hypotheses with non-zero probability is infinite) the probability $\Pr(D)$ that sample D arises at all

$$Pr(D) = \sum_{H \in \mathcal{H}} \Pr(D|H)P(H).$$

From the definition of conditional probability it is easy to derive **Bayes' formula**[1]

$$\Pr(H|D) = \frac{\Pr(D|H)P(H)}{\Pr(D)}. \tag{2}$$

The prior probability $P(H)$ is often considered as the learner's *initial degree of belief* in hypothesis H. In essence Bayes' rule is a mapping

---

[1] Some Bayesians prefer replacing $\Pr(D|H)P(H)$ by a joint probability of data and hypotheses together, the prior $P(D, H) = \Pr(D|H)P(H)$.

from *a priori* probability $P(H)$ to *a posteriori* probability $\Pr(H|D)$ determined by data D.

Continuing to obtain more and more data, this way the total inferred probability will concentrate more and more on the 'true' hypothesis. We can draw the same conclusion of course, using more examples, by the law of large numbers. In general, the problem is not so much that in the limit the inferred probability would not concentrate on the true hypothesis, but that the inferred probability gives as much information as possible about the possible hypotheses from only a limited number of data. Given the prior probability of the hypotheses, it is easy to obtain the inferred probability, and therefore to make informed decisions. However, in general we don't know the prior probabilities. The following MDL approach in some sense replaces an unknown prior probability by a fixed 'universal' probability.

7   Prediction by minimum description length

Theoretically the idea of predicting time sequences using shortest effective descriptions was first formulated by R. Solomonoff (1964). He uses Bayes' formula equipped with a fixed 'universal' prior distribution. In accordance with Occam's dictum, it tells us to go for the explanation that compresses the data the most – but not quite as we shall show.

The aim is to *predict* outcomes concerning a phenomenon μ under investigation. In this case we have some prior evidence (prior distribution over the hypotheses, experimental data) and we want to predict future events. This situation can be modelled by considering a sample space S of one-way infinite sequences of basic elements $\mathcal{B}$ defined by $S = \mathcal{B}^\infty$. We assume a prior distribution μ over S with $\mu(x)$ denoting the probability of a sequence starting with x. Here $\mu(\cdot)$ is a *semimeasure*[2] satisfying

$$\mu(\epsilon) \leq 1$$
$$\mu(x) \geq \sum_{a \in \mathcal{B}} \mu(xa).$$

Given a previously observed data string x, the inference problem is to predict the next symbol in the output sequence, that is, to extrapolate the sequence x. In terms of the variables in formula 2, H_{xy} is the hypothesis that the sequence starts with initial segment xy. Data D_x consists of the fact that the sequence starts with initial segment x. Then, $\Pr(D_x|H_{xy}) = 1$,

---

[2] Traditional notation is '$\mu(\Gamma_x)$' instead of '$\mu(x)$', denoting the probability concentrated on the cylinder $x = \{\omega \in S : \omega \text{ starts with } x\}$. We use notation '$\mu(x)$' for convenience. Recall, μ is a *measure* if equalities hold.

that is, the data is forced by the hypothesis, or $\Pr(D_z|H_{xy}) = 0$ for z is not a prefix of xy, that is, the hypothesis contradicts the data. For $P(H_{xy})$ and $\Pr(D_x)$ in formula 2 we substitute $\mu(xy)$ and $\mu(x)$, respectively. For $P(H_{xy}|D_x)$ we substitute $\mu(y|x)$. This way the formula is rewritten as

$$\mu(y|x) = \frac{\mu(xy)}{\mu(x)}. \tag{3}$$

The final probability $\mu(y|x)$ is the probability of the next symbol string being y, given the initial string x. Obviously we now only need the prior probability μ to evaluate $\mu(y|x)$. The goal of inductive inference in general is to be able to either (i) predict, or extrapolate, the next element after x or (ii) to infer an underlying effective process that generated x, and hence to be able to predict the next symbol. In the most general deterministic case such an effective process is a Turing machine, but it can also be a probabilistic Turing machine or, say, a Markov process (which makes its brief and single appearance here). The central task of inductive inference is to find a universally valid approximation to μ which is good at estimating the conditional probability that a given segment x will be followed by a segment y.

In general that is impossible. But suppose we restrict the class of priors μ to the *recursive* semimeasures and restrict the set of basic elements B to $\{0, 1\}$. Under this relatively mild restriction on the admissible semimeasures μ, it turns out that we can use the single universal semimeasure **M** as a 'universal prior' (replacing the real prior μ) for prediction. The notion of universal semimeasure **M** is a continuous version of **m** we saw before, and which is explained in Li and Vitányi (1997), defined with respect to a special type of Turing machine called the *monotone* Turing machine. The universal semimeasure **M** multiplicatively dominates all enumerable (computable from below) semimeasures. A central notion in the theory of computability is the following: A 'universal' Turing machine for a given class of Turing machines is a machine from the class that, given a description of any other machine in the class, precisely imitates its computation with respect to any supplied input. If we flip a fair coin to generate the successive bits on the input tape of the universal reference monotone Turing machine, then the probability that it outputs $x\alpha$ (x followed by something) is **M**(x).

It can be shown that the universal distribution *itself* is directly suited for prediction. The universal distribution combines a weighted version of the predictions of all enumerable semimeasures, including the prediction of the semimeasure with the shortest program. It is not *a priori* clear that the shortest program dominates in all cases – and, as we shall see, it does not. However, we show that in the overwhelming majority of cases – the typical cases – the shortest program dominates sufficiently to validate the approach that only uses shortest programs for prediction. The properties of $\mathbf{M}(x)$ allow us to demonstrate that a minimum description length procedure is almost always optimal for prediction.

Given a semimeasure on $\{0, 1\}^\infty$ and an initial binary string x, our goal is to find the most probable $\mathbf{m}$-bit extrapolation of x. That is, taking the negative logarithm on both sides of equation 3, we want to determine y with $l(y) = \mathbf{m}$ that minimizes

$$-\log \mu(y|x) = -\log \mu(xy) + \log \mu(x).$$

We assume that μ is a *recursive* semimeasure.

This theory of the *universal semimeasure* $\mathbf{M}$, the analogue in the sample space $\{0, 1\}^\infty$ of $\mathbf{m}$ in the sample space $\{0, 1\}^*$ equivalent to $\mathcal{N}$, is developed in Li and Vitányi (1997, chs. 4 and 5). A celebrated result of Solomonoff (1978) says that $\mathbf{M}$ is very suitable for prediction. Let S_n be the μ-expected value of the square of the difference in μ-probability and $\mathbf{M}$-probability of 0 occurring at the nth prediction

$$S_n = \sum_{l(x)=n-1} \mu(x)(\mathbf{M}(0|x) - \mu(0|x))^2.$$

We may call S_n the *expected squared error at the nth prediction*.

Theorem 1 *Let μ be a recursive semimeasure. Using the notation above, $\sum_n S_n \leq k/2$ with $k = K(\mu) \ln 2$. (Hence, S_n converges to 0 faster than $1/n$.)*

A proof using Kulback–Leibler divergence is given in Li and Vitányi (1997). There it is additionally demonstrated that for almost all unbounded x the conditional probability of $\mathbf{M}$ converges to the conditional probability of μ. Note that while the following theorem *does* imply the convergence of the conditional probabilities similarly to theorem 1, it *does not* imply the speed of convergence estimate. Conversely, theorem 1 does not imply the following.

Theorem 2 *Let μ be a positive recursive measure. If the length of y is fixed and the length of x grows to infinity, then*

$$\frac{\mathbf{M}(y|x)}{\mu(y|x)} \to 1$$

with μ-probability one. The infinite sequences ω with prefixes x satisfying the displayed asymptotics are precisely the μ-random sequences.

Proof. We use an approach based on the Submartingale Convergence Theorem (Doob, 1953, pp. 324–5), which states that the following property holds for each sequence of random variables $\omega_1, \omega_2, \ldots$ If $f(\omega_{1:n})$ is a μ-submartingale, and the μ-expectation $E|f(\omega_{1:n})| < \infty$, then it follows that $\lim_{n \to \infty} f(\omega_{1:n})$ exists with μ-probability one.

In our case,

$$t(\omega_{1:n}|\mu) = \frac{M(\omega_{1:n})}{\mu(\omega_{1:n})}$$

is a μ-submartingale, and the μ-expectation $Et(\omega_{1:n}|\mu) \leq 1$. Therefore, there is a set $A \subseteq B^\infty$ with $\mu(A) = 1$, such that for each $\omega \in A$ the limit $\lim_{n \to \infty} t(\omega_{1:n}|\mu) < \infty$. These are the μ-random ω's by corollary 4.8 in Li and Vitányi (1997). Consequently, for fixed m, for each ω in A, we have

$$\lim_{n \to \infty} \frac{M(\omega_{1:n+m})/\mu(\omega_{1:n+m})}{M(\omega_{1:n})/\mu(\omega_{1:n})} = 1,$$

provided the limit of the denominator is not zero. The latter fact is guaranteed by the universality of M: for each $x \in B^*$ we have $M(x)/\mu(x) \geq 2^{-K(\mu)}$ by theorem 4.4 and equation 4.10 in Li and Vitányi (1997).

Example 1 Suppose we are given an infinite decimal sequence ω. The even positions contain the subsequent digits of $\pi = 3.1415\ldots$, and the odd positions contain uniformly distributed, independently drawn random decimal digits. Then, $M(a|\omega_{1:2i}) \to 1/10$ for $a = 0, 1, \ldots, 9$, while $M(a|\omega_{1:2i+1}) \to 1$ if a is the $(i+1)$th digit of π, and to 0 otherwise. $\diamond$

There are two possibilities to associate complexities with machines. The first possibility is to take the length of the shortest program, while the second possibility is to take the negative logarithm of the universal probability. In the discrete case, using prefix machines, these turned out to be the same by the coding theorem 1. In the continuous case, using monotone machines, it turns out they are different.

Definition 4 The complexity KM is defined as

$$KM(x) = -\log M(x).$$

In contrast with C and K complexities, in the above definition the greatest prefix-free subset of *all* programs which produce output starting with x contribute to the complexity in weighed form. Again, let $M_1, M_2, \ldots$ be a standard enumeration of monotone machines, and let $\mu_1, \mu_2, \ldots$ be an enumeration of the corresponding functions being computed. It can be shown that these coincide precisely with the set of partial recursive functions over $\{0,1\}^\infty$.

Definition 5 Let U be the reference monotone machine. The complexity Km, called *monotone complexity*, is defined as

$$Km(x/y) = \min_{p,i}\{l(\langle i, p\rangle) : \mu_i(\langle p, y\rangle) = x, p \in \{0, 1\}^*, i \in \mathcal{N}\}$$

By definition, $KM(x) \leq Km(x)$. But the difference can only be logarithmic. In fact, all proper complexities coincide up to a logarithmic additive term. It has been shown that equality does not hold: the difference between $KM(x)(= -\log \mathbf{M}(x))$ and $Km(x)$ is very small, but still rises unboundedly. This contrasts with the equality between $-\log \mathbf{m}(x)$ and $K(x)$ in theorem 1. Intuitively, this phenomenon is justified by exposing the relation between $\mathbf{M}$ and $\mathbf{m}$.

The coding theorem 1 states that $K(x) = -\log \mathbf{m}(x) + O(1)$. L. A. Levin (1973), conjectures that the analogue would hold for the unrestricted continuous version. But it has been shown (Gács, 1983)

$$\sup_{x \in \mathcal{B}^*} |KM(x) - Km(x)| = \infty,$$

There it is shown that the exact relation is (for each particular choice of basis $\mathcal{B}$ such as $\mathcal{B} = \mathcal{N}$, the natural numbers, or $\mathcal{B} = \{0, 1\}$):

Lemma 2

$$KM(x) \leq Km(x) \leq KM(x) + Km(l(x)) + O(1). \tag{4}$$

This shows that the differences between $Km(x)$ and $KM(x)$ must in some sense be very small. The next question to ask is whether the quantities involved are usually different, or whether being different is a rare occurrence. In other words, whether for *a priori* almost all infinite sequences x, the difference between Km and KM is bounded by a constant. The following facts have been proven (Gács, 1983).

Lemma 3 (i) *For the individually random strings $x \in \mathcal{B}^*$ we have $Km(x)\text{-}KM(x) = O(1)$.*

(ii) There exists a function $f(n)$ which goes to infinity with $n \rightarrow \infty$ such that $Km(x) - KM(x) \geq f(l(x))$, for infinitely many x. If x is a finite binary string ($\mathcal{B} = \{0, 1\}$), then we can choose $f(n)$ as the inverse of some version of Ackermann's function.

An infinite binary sequence ω is μ-random iff

$$\sup_n \mathbf{M}(\omega_1 \ldots \omega_n)/\mu(\omega_1 \ldots \omega_n) < \infty,$$

and the set of μ-random sequences has μ-measure one, see Li and Vitányi (1997, ch. 4). Let ω be a μ-random infinite binary sequence and xy be a finite prefix of ω. For $l(x)$ grows unboundedly with $l(y)$ fixed, we have by theorem 2

$$\lim_{l(x)\to\infty} \log\mu(y|x) - \log \mathbf{M}(y|x) = 0. \tag{5}$$

Therefore, if x and y satisfy above conditions, then maximizing $\mu(y|x)$ over y means minimizing $-\log \mathbf{M}(y|x)$. It shows in lemma 3 that $-\log \mathbf{M}(x)$ is slightly smaller than $Km(x)$, the length of the shortest program for x. For binary programs this difference is very small, lemma 2, but can be unbounded in the length of x.

Together this shows the following. Given xy that is prefix of a (possibly not μ-random) ω, optimal prediction of fixed length extrapolation y from an unboundedly growing prefix x of ω need not necessarily be reached by the shortest programs for xy and x minimizing $Km(xy) - Km(x)$, but is reached by considering the weighted version of all programs for xy and x which is represented by

$$-\log \mathbf{M}(xy) + \log \mathbf{M}(x) = (Km(xy) - g(xy)) - (Km(x) - g(x)).$$

Here $g(x)$ is a function which can have unbounded growth in between the inverse of the Ackermann function and $Km(l(x)) \leq \log\log x$ – but only in case x is not μ-random.

Therefore, for certain x and y which are *not* μ-random, optimization using the minimum length programs may result in very incorrect predictions. However, for μ-random x we have that $-\log \mathbf{M}(x)$ and $Km(x)$ coincide up to an additional constant independent of x, that is, $g(xy) = g(x) = O(1)$, lemma 3. Hence, together with equation 5, we find the following.

Theorem 3 *Let μ be a recursive semimeasure, and let ω be a μ-random infinite binary sequence and xy be a finite prefix of ω. For $l(x)$ grows unboundedly and $l(y)$ fixed,*

$$\lim_{l(x)\to\infty} -\log\mu(y|x) = Km(xy) - Km(x) \pm O(1) < \infty,$$

where $Km(xy)$ and $Km(x)$ grow unboundedly.

By its definition Km is monotone in the sense that always $Km(xy) - Km(x) \geq 0$. The closer this difference is to zero, the better the shortest effective monotone program for x is also a shortest effective monotone program for xy and hence predicts y given x. Therefore, for all large enough μ-random x, predicting by determining a y that minimizes the difference of the minimum program lengths of xy and x gives a good prediction. Here y should preferably be large enough to eliminate the influence of the $O(1)$ term.

Corollary 1 (prediction by data compression) Assume the conditions of theorem 3. With μ-probability going to one as $l(x)$ grows unboundedly, a fixed-length y extrapolation from x maximizes $\mu(y|x)$ iff y can be maximally compressed with respect to x in the sense that it minimizes $Km(xy) - Km(x)$. That is, y is the string that minimizes the length difference between the shortest program that outputs $xy\ldots$ and the shortest program that outputs $x\ldots$

8   Hypothesis identification by minimum description length

The minimum description length principle is an algorithmic paradigm that is widely applied. That is, it is widely applied at least in spirit; to apply it literally may lead to computation difficulties since it involves finding an optimum in an exponentially large set of candidates, as noted for example in Li and Vitányi (1997). Yet in some cases one can approximate this optimum (Vovk, 1995, 1997; Yamanishi, 1996). For the theoretical case where the minimum description lengths involved are the Kolmogorov complexities, we mathematically derived the minimum description length paradigm from first principles, that is, Bayes' rule (Li and Vitányi, 1995, 1997; Vitányi and Li, 1996, 2000). To do so we needed auxiliary notions of *universal distribution* and *randomness of individual objects*.

Before proceeding it is useful to point out that the idea of a two-part code for a body of data D is natural from the perspective of Kolmogorov complexity. If D does not contain any regularities at all, then it consists of purely random data and there is no hypothesis to identify. Assume that the body of data D contains regularities. With the help of a description of those regularities (a model) we can describe the data compactly. Assuming that the regularities can be represented in an effective manner (that is, by a Turing machine), we encode the remaining, accidental, data as a program for that machine. Squeezing all effective regularity out of the data, we end up with a Turing machine representing the meaningful regular information in the data together with a program for that Turing machine representing the remaining meaningless randomness of the data. This is the intuition, which finds its basis in the definitions 1 and 2. However, it is difficult to find a valid mathematical way to force a sensible division of the information at hand in a meaningful part and a meaningless part.

A practice-oriented form of this theory like MDL, although often lacking in justification, apparently works and is used by practitioners. The MDL principle is very easy to use in some loose sense, but it is hard to justify. A user of the MDL principle needs to choose a concept that can be described shortly and without causing too many errors (and he needs to balance these two things).

In various forms aimed at practical applications this idea of doing induction or data modelling in statistical hypothesis identification or prediction was proposed by C. Wallace and co-authors (Wallace and Boulton, 1968; Wallace and Freeman, 1987), who formulated the *minimum message length (MML)* principle and J. Rissanen (1978, 1979) who formulated the *minimum description length (MDL)* principle. Here we abstract away from epistemological and technical differences between MML and MDL, and other variants, and their concessions to reality in the name of feasibility and practicability. We focus only on the following central ideal version involved. Indeed, we do not even care about whether we deal with statistical or deterministic hypotheses. All effectively describable hypotheses are involved.

Definition 6 *Given a sample of data, and an effective enumeration of models,* ideal MDL *selects the model which minimizes the sum of*

- *the length, in bits, of an effective description of the model; and*
- *the length, in bits, of an effective description of the data when encoded with the help of the model.*

Intuitively, with a more complex description of the hypothesis H, it may fit the data better and therefore decrease the misclassified data. If H describes all the data, then it does not allow for measuring errors. A simpler description of H may be penalized by increasing the number of misclassified data. If H is a trivial hypothesis that contains nothing, then all data are described literally and there is no generalization. The rationale of the method is that a balance in between seems required. Similarly to the analysis of prediction above, in Li and Vitányi (1995) and especially Vitányi and Li (2000) we have shown that in almost all cases maximal compression finds the best hypothesis.

9   Conclusion

The analysis of both hypothesis identification by Ideal MDL and prediction shows that maximally compressed descriptions give good results on the data samples which are random with respect to probabilistic hypotheses. These data samples form the overwhelming majority and occur with probability going to one when the length of the data sample grows unboundedly. This validates by mathematical proof a rigorous formal version of Occam's razor – the ancient simplicity-based method to infer the true cause of the data.

REFERENCES

Breiman, L., J. Friedman, R. Olshen and C. Stone (1984). *Classification and Regression Trees*. Wadsworth International Group, Belmont, CA.
Doob, J. L. (1953). *Stochastic Processes*. New York: Wiley.
Gács, P. (1974). On the symmetry of algorithmic information. *Soviet Mathematical Doklady* 15: 1477–80. Correction: ibid., 15: 1480.
—— (1983). On the relation between descriptional complexity and algorithmic probability. *Theoretical Computer Science* 22: 71–93.
Kirchherr, W. W., M. Li and P. M. B. Vitányi (1997). The miraculous universal distribution. *Mathematical Intelligencer* 19 (4): 7–15.
Kolmogorov, A. N. (1965). Three approaches to the quantitative definition of information. *Problems in Information Transmission* 1 (1): 1–7.
Levin, L. A. (1973). On the notion of a random sequence. *Soviet Mathematical Doklady* 14: 1413–16.
Li, M. and P. M. B. Vitányi (1995). Computational machine learning in theory and praxis. In J. van Leeuwen (ed.), *Computer Science Today*, Lecture Notes in Computer Science, vol. 1000, pp. 518–35. Heidelberg: Springer.
—— (1997). *An Introduction to Kolmogorov Complexity and its Applications*. 2nd edition. New York: Springer.
Martin-Löf, P. (1966). The definition of random sequences. *Information and Control* 9: 602–19.
Mises, R. von (1919). Grundlagen der Wahrscheinlichkeitsrechnung. *Mathematische Zeitschrift* 5: 52–99.
Rissanen, J. J. (1978). Modeling by the shortest data description. *Automatica – Journal of the International Federation of Automatic Control* 14: 465–71.
—— (1989). *Stochastic Complexity and Statistical Inquiry*. Singapore: World Scientific.
—— (1996). Fisher information and stochastic complexity. *IEEE Transactions on Information Theory* IT-42 (1): 40–7.
Segen, J. (1980). *Pattern-Directed Signal Analysis*. PhD Thesis, Carnegie-Mellon University, Pittsburgh.
Solomonoff, R. J. (1964). A formal theory of inductive inference, Part 1 and Part 2. *Information and Control* 7: 1–22, 224–54.
—— (1978). Complexity-based induction systems: comparisons and convergence theorems. *IEEE Transactions on Information Theory* IT-24: 422–32.

Turing, A. M. (1936). On computable numbers with an application to the Entscheidungsproblem. *Proceedings of the London Mathematical Society*, ser. 2, 42: 230–65; correction, ibid., 43 (1937), 544–6.

Vitányi, P. M. B. and M. Li (1996). Ideal MDL and its relation to Bayesianism. *Proceedings of ISIS: Information, Statistics and Induction in Science*, pp. 282–91. Singapore: World Scientific.

(2000). Minimum description length induction, Bayesianism, and Kolmogorov complexity. *IEEE Transactions on Information Theory* IT-46 (2): 446–64.

Vovk, V. (1995). Minimum description length estimators under the universal coding scheme. In P. Vitányi (ed.), *Computational Learning Theory*, Proceedings of the 2nd European Conference (EuroCOLT '95), Lecture Notes in Artificial Intelligence, vol. 904, pp. 237–51. Heidelberg: Springer.

(1997). Learning about the parameter of the Bernoulli model. *Journal of Computer and System Sciences* 55 (1): 96–104.

Wallace, C. S. and D. M. Boulton (1968). An information measure for classification. *Computing Journal* 11: 185–95.

Wallace, C. S. and P. R. Freeman (1987). Estimation and inference by compact coding. *Journal of the Royal Statistical Society*, Series B 49: 240–51. Discussion: ibid., 252–65.

Yamanishi, K. (1996). A randomized approximation of the MDL for stochastic models with hidden variables. *Proceedings of the 9th ACM Computational Learning Conference*. ACM Press.

Zvonkin, A. K. and L. A. Levin (1970). The complexity of finite objects and the development of the concepts of information and randomness by means of the theory of algorithms. *Russian Mathematical Surveys* 25 (6): 83–124.

9 Simplicity and statistical inference

Jorma Rissanen

1 Introduction

The intuitive idea of a model is like a smooth, low-order polynomial curve fitted to a cloud of points on a plane. It, then, represents the proverbial 'law' which the data are supposed to follow except for the inevitable 'noise'. We see already in this simple example the basic difficulty in modelling problems: it is not at all clear how to formalize the idea of a 'smooth' curve, or what is considered to be a 'low'-order polynomial. Needless to add that by assuming some probability distribution for the noise and then calculating the conditional mean contributes nothing towards the solution of the problem. And the same goes for any Bayesian approach, where not only the data but even the parameters must be assumed to be samples from a distribution.

One can argue that a conceptually ideal model of an observed data string is the shortest program that generates the string in a universal programming language; for a thorough account of the algorithmic theory of information or complexity, see Li and Vitányi (1993). Indeed, if the data string has any regular features, i.e. if there is a 'law' that holds even approximately, the shortest program must take advantage of it. In this spirit, then, the length of the shortest program, the Kolmogorov complexity, which really is due to Solomonoff, serves as a measure of the string's complexity. However, to find such a model is a non-computable problem, which is why such a model must remain just a conceptual one. But there is something else unsettling about this idea of a model and the length of the shortest program as the measure of its complexity. And, perhaps justifiably, these notions corresponding to our intuition of what we feel a model and its complexity should be have been questioned. For instance, clearly, a sequence of a given fixed and large length n, such as 1010 . . ., has a low complexity, because it has a simple generating 'law' as the model. But for all intents and purposes, some argue, so has the purely random binary string of the same length, obtained by flipping a coin, even though it has the maximum Kolmogorov complexity. Indeed, the 'law' is just the Bernoulli distribution, given by $Prob(head) = 1/2$. In other words, what the algorithmic theory of complexity does not deal with is the separation of the idea of a 'model' as the mechanism for the data, the 'go of it' in the words of Maxwell, from the 'noise', and hence it does not provide us with the means to talk about the complexity of the model.

There is another, non-algorithmic theory of complexity, which, to be sure, builds on the ideas of the algorithmic theory, where there is a separation of the model as the 'law' from the 'noise', and where the complexity of the model can be exactly defined. This is the theory of the so-called stochastic complexity (Rissanen, 1984, 1985, 1996) and the associated MDL (minimum description length) principle for statistical inference, which we shall outline in this chapter.

2   Models and their complexity

The idea to avoid the non-computability problem is to replace the set of programs by a smaller set of probability measures as models. Indeed, each such measure, often defined by a density function $f(x^n)$ for the data strings $x^n = x_1, x_2, \ldots, x_n$, can be used to define a code with the (ideal) length for the string given by $-\log f(x^n)$. Hence, we may identify the measure with the code it defines, which in turn gives the codeword for the data as a 'program', from which the data string can be recovered. The base of the logarithm doesn't matter; we usually take it as the natural logarithm. In addition, we frequently want the density function to be defined on the set of all finite data strings such that the marginality condition of a random process

$$\int f(x^n, x_{n+1}) dx_{n+1} = f(x^n)$$

holds for all n.

The most frequently used models are parametric $f(x^n|\theta)$, where the parameter vector $\theta = \theta_1, \ldots, \theta_k$ ranges over a suitable subset of the k–dimensional Euclidean space. We can then take the model class either as $\mathcal{M}_k = \{f(x^n|\theta)\}$ or the union $\mathcal{M} = \cup_k \mathcal{M}_k$. In the latter form such models include virtually all models that can be fitted to data. The more general models of the type $f(x^n|y^n)$, where y^n is another observed data sequence, add nothing new to the theory.

We now face the problem of how to define the shortest code length for the data sequence, called *stochastic complexity*, given a model class. We can no longer do it the same way as in the algorithmic theory of complexity, because clearly, somehow or other, we must restrict the coding operations so as to take advantage of the restrictions for the data predicated by the model class and only them. An appropriate way to do this is either to give a formula for it or an algorithm for the computation of a code length, and then justify the result. A great help in this is provided by a theorem, which for many classes of models states that there is no code that would give a shorter code length for the data than a certain amount, except for rare sequences, or sequences generated by rare models in the class. Then to complete the justification we exhibit a code with which the lower bound is reached together with a formula for the shortest code length, the stochastic complexity, which breaks up into two parts, the first representing the code length of the 'noise', without our having to define what noise is, and the second representing the code length for the optimal model itself. Clearly, the latter ought to depend on the 'size' of the model class, its complexity as it were, which is precisely what happens.

Before continuing with further detail let us give some examples of model classes.

Example 1 The Bernoulli class $\mathcal{B} = \{\theta\}, \theta = Prob(X_i = 0)$. Then $P(x^n) = \theta^{n_0}(1 - \theta)^{n_1}$, where n_j denotes the number of times symbol j occurs in the string $x^n, j \in \{0, 1\}$.

Example 2 The class of AR-processes, each defined by

$$x_{t+1} = a_0 x_t + \ldots + a_p x_{t-p} + e_{t+1}$$

for some p and the parameter values, where e_t is a normally distributed independent sequence of zero mean and variance σ^2. There are then $p + 2$ parameters $\theta = a_0, \ldots, a_p, \sigma$, which define a dependent normal process $f(x^n|\theta)$.

Example 3 The class of equal-bin width histogram densities on the unit interval, where each model has m non-negative parameters $\theta = \theta_1, \ldots, \theta_m$, some m, satisfying $\sum_i \theta_i = 1$. The model assigns, to a point x in the unit interval, the density $f(x|\theta) = \theta_{i(x)}m$, where $i(x)$ denotes the bin in which x falls.

Remarks. Similarly to example 2, we could define the set of all ARMA processes, where actually for each number of parameters k we would have several types of processes depending on the number of poles p and zeros q in their transfer function such that $p + q = k - 1$. However, such a stratification causes no problems.

Although the last two model classes are parametric, we can get so-called non-parametric models out of these by a suitable completion. For instance, in example 3 one such completion would give the class of all continuous densities in the unit interval. In traditional statistics some such non-parametric limiting density is assumed to have generated the data, and the statistician's role is to estimate it with, say, the histograms to be fitted to the data. This scenario creates the difficulty of having to explain away the reason why not to accept the best-fitting parametric model with the maximum number of parameters, which traditional statistics has not succeeded in doing in any logically acceptable manner.

Let us now be a bit more specific about the two complexities involved, the first of the 'noise' and the second of the model. Perhaps the intuitively most appealing way to construct a probability measure for data, given a class of models, is the so-called ML model:

$$\hat{f}(x^n) = \frac{f(x^n|\hat{\theta}(x^n))}{\int_{\hat{\theta}(y^n)\in\Omega} f(y^n|\hat{\theta}(y^n))dy^n},$$ (1)

where $\hat{\theta}(y^n)$ denotes the maximum likelihood estimate, and Ω is an open subset of the parameters such that the integral is finite. Such a probability measure has been studied in the universal coding literature for Markov chains over a finite alphabet by Davisson (1973) and Shtarkov (1987).

Although this model does not satisfy the marginality conditions of a random process exactly, it is so intuitively appealing that we took it as the primary candidate for the stochastic complexity, and we evaluated the denominator (Rissanen, 1996) with the result:

$$-\ln\hat{f}(x^n) = -\ln f(x^n|\hat{\theta}(x^n)) + \frac{k}{2}\ln\frac{n}{2\pi} + \ln\int_{\Omega}\sqrt{|I(\theta)|}d\theta + R_n,$$ (2)

where $I(\theta)$ denotes the Fisher information matrix, and R_n converges to zero as n grows. The convergence for many model classes is fast, like $O(1/n)$. The exact conditions required for equation (2) to hold are listed in Rissanen (1996); in essence, they require that the estimates of the parameters satisfy the central limit theorem.

The main theorem, mentioned above, states that no matter which kind of estimate $q(x^n)$ you form for the assumed data-generating process $f(x^n|\theta) \in \mathcal{M}$, the mean ideal code length $-\ln q(x^n)$ satisfies the inequality (Rissanen, 1986),

$$E_\theta \ln\frac{f(X^n|\theta)}{q(X^n)} \geq \frac{k-\in}{2}\ln n$$ (3)

for all positive $\in$ and almost all θ. The expectation is taken with respect to the model in the numerator. This acts as a grand Cramer-Rao inequality, for it includes even the effect of the number of parameters. Moreover, it was shown in Merhav (1994) that reachability of the lower bound, which the ML-model (1) is seen to do by (2), implies a bound for the rate with which parameters can be estimated. Further, the expectation can be replaced with an almost sure quantification, which, in effect, was shown in Dawid (1991).

If we take the mean in equation (2) with respect to a model specified by a parameter θ, the mean of the first term minus the entropy can be shown to converge to $-k/2$, which, just as the remaining terms, does not depend on the parameter θ. Hence, we have the quite remarkable fact that the Kullback–Leibler distance between any model $f(x^n|\theta)$ and the ML model $\hat{f}(x^n)$ is the same for all models and given by

$$D_n = \frac{k}{2}\ln\frac{n}{2\pi e} + \ln\int_\Omega \sqrt{|I(\theta)|}d\theta + R_n. \tag{4}$$

Moreover, this distance divided by n shrinks to zero by (3) at the fastest possible rate. Accordingly, we may take it as the mean *complexity* of the optimal model, $f(z^n|\hat{\theta}(x^n))$, picked out by the maximum likelihood estimate $\hat{\theta}(x^n)$ computed from the data; i.e. the first term in equation (2).

It is of course only prudent that the model complexity is essentially proportional to the number of independent parameters. However, it is not this number alone that determines the complexity. It also depends on the amount of available data reflecting the fact that we should not distinguish between models in an uncountably infinite set as the explanation of a finite amount of data, if they give exactly the same explanation. In other words, if we cannot tell two models apart by any estimation method in light of the available data, we must consider the models as equivalent.

The so-called Jeffreys' mixture is another way to define a probability measure with essentially the same result for many model classes. It is given by

$$f_\pi(x^n) = \int_\Gamma f(x^n|\theta)d\pi(\theta), \tag{5}$$

where π is (a generalization of) Jeffreys' prior

$$\pi(\theta) = \frac{|I(\theta)|^{1/2}}{\int_{\eta\in\Gamma}|I(\eta)|^{1/2}d\eta}.$$

It is readily seen that Jeffreys' mixture defines a random process. At least for classes of independent processes that satisfy suitable smoothness conditions, the negative logarithm $-\ln f_\pi(x^n)$ agrees with equation (2).

How do we define the shortest code length if the model class does not satisfy the smoothness conditions required for the formula (2) to hold? A most important technique is to apply a predictive algorithm, which we give in a particularly efficient form developed recently. Suppose we proceed as follows: first, order the data set in any manner, unless already done, say as $x_1, x_2, \ldots, x_n$. Next, subdivide the data into segments of length $t(1), t(2) - t(1), \ldots, t(M + 1) - t(M)$, which increases at a suitable rate. Now put

$$PMDL(x^n) = -\sum_{m=0}^{M} \sum_{t=t(m)}^{t(m+1)-1} \ln P(x_{t+1}|x^t, \hat{\theta}(x^{t(m)})), \tag{6}$$

where $t(0) = 0$, and $P(x^t|\hat{\theta}(x^0))$ is any reasonable distribution added to the model class to take care of the first $t(1)$ data points. Notice that the updates of the estimates of the parameters are done only at the end of the segments, which are then held constant for the subsequent segment. Since this can also be written as

$$PMDL(x^n) = -\ln P(x^n|\hat{\theta}(x^n)) + \sum_{m=0}^{M+1} \ln \frac{P(x^{t(m)}|\hat{\theta}(x^{t(m)}))}{P(x^{t(m)}|\hat{\theta}(x^{t(m-1)}))},$$

we see that the model complexity, consisting of the sum, which is certainly non-negative, has not been avoided despite the fact that no paramters are explicitly encoded. Instead they are given by the estimation algorithm. In fact, under suitable smoothness conditions the model complexity behaves asymptotically as equation (4). Moreover, there is no loss of optimality if we put $t(i) = [e^{\sqrt{i}}\sqrt{i}]$, where $[x]$ denotes the nearest integer to x. Since this grows faster than any polynomial only a few updates are needed for any reasonable amount of data.

3 The MDL principle

The preceding ideas suggest the MDL principle for model class comparison, which is to calculate or estimate the stochastic complexity of the observed data string, relative to each pair of suggested classes of models, and to prefer the one with the smaller stochastic complexity. Because the complexity of the optimal model is an integral part of the so-obtained yardstick, any two model classes may be compared, regardless of the number of parameters in them or whether or not the models have the same structure. This, then, provides a much more widely applicable criterion than the usual ones such as Akaike's criterion AIC, or BIC, or those where arbitrary terms are added to penalize the number of parameters in the model.

For many of the usual model classes, which do satisfy the smoothness conditions required and hence for which the formula (2) holds, the MDL criterion produces results that are unsurpassed. In the analysable cases one can prove that they have all the optimality properties one can expect. Indeed, the principle amounts to a global maximum likelihood principle, and just as in the case of the ordinary 'local' maximum likelihood principle, it can be beaten only in pathological cases. Moreover, and quite importantly, the code length criterion has a meaningful *data dependent* interpretation; in fact it has three, the first as a code length, the second as the probability the model assigns to the data, and finally, often as the true prediction error with which the data are predicted. Hence, there is no need to construct an expected value-based criterion, the expectation necessarily taken with respect to an arbitrary probability measure, which then will have to be estimated. A little reflection will show that one cannot compare model classes in a meaningful way by expected value-based criteria nor even by their estimates. In fact, take the class consisting of models parameterized by ϵ, each assigning the probability $1 - \epsilon$ to the data string consisting of all 0's and dividing the probability ϵ among the remaining strings. If you use the mean square prediction error as the criterion, the predictor $x_t = 0$ gives as small a mean error as you wish by a model in the class for small enough ϵ.

The real potentiality of the MDL principle is realized in complex modelling problems, such as classification and regression trees, various image-processing applications, and the like. Clearly, then, we cannot calculate the shortest code length by any formula. Rather, a practical way to tackle such problems is to break up the complex model class into smaller ones, for each of which either the formula (2) applies or the predictive algorithm is used. In addition we must calculate the code length needed to link the subclasses together. Such an enterprise is obviously a challenge, but a consolation is that there is little competition, for problems of that magnitude are often beyond the reach of the traditional statistical techniques.

We conclude this section with a remark on universal models. When the programs in the algorithmic theory of complexity are made self-delimiting, which amounts to the requirement that no program as a binary string is a prefix of another, the Kolmogorov complexity defines a probability measure for all strings thus $P_K(x^n) \propto 2^{-K(x^n)}$. This measure has a universality property in that it mimics any computable measure. In the same spirit, the measure (1) is universal in the given model class, and it approximates any model in the class in an asymptotically optimal manner.

3.1   An application: test for homogeneity

We conclude the chapter by illustrating the application of the ideas with an example. Consider the two data sets (Qian, Gabor and Gupta, 1994):

$X =$ 7.362   8.876   5.219   10.506   12.590   9.552   10.203   11.144
       27.296   3.105   8.995   4.955   4.065   10.822   11.097
$Y =$ 6.645   6.246   7.589   4.563   11.131   4.371   6.743   16.647
       15.412   6.202   15.134   6.951

We wish to test whether these data sets are homogeneous in the sense that they were generated by the same machinery or whether each was generated by its own. To do this we use a universal density model, introduced in Rissanen, Speed and Yu (1992).

Let x^n denote the sequence of the observed data. For m equal-width bins partitioning an interval $[a, a + R]$, let $t(i|x^t, m)$ denote the number of points in the sequence x, for $t \leq n$, that fall within the ith bin. Define the conditional density function of histogram type

$$f(y|x^t, m) = \frac{m[t(y|x^t, m) + 1/2]}{R(t + m/2)}.$$ (7)

In order to get rid of the parameter m and to obtain a smoother density function we form a convex mixture

$$f_M(y|x^t) = \sum_{m=1}^{M} \frac{m[t(y|x^t, m) + 1/2]}{RM(t + m/2)}.$$ (8)

Here we used a uniform 'prior' $\mu_M(m) = 1/M$, as it were, even though we are guided by the provably good properties of mixture densities rather than by any consideration of prior knowledge. Although we have introduced a new parameter M, the density depends on it only slightly if it is taken large. We can get rid of it completely by taking it as $M = \sqrt{n}$.

We settle the question of homogeneity of the two data sets above simply by comparing the code lengths $-\ln f(X, Y)$ and $-\ln f(X) - \ln f(Y)$, determined by the density function in (8), which are excellent approximations of the stochastic complexities, relative to the class of all continuous, once-differentiable density functions on the range given. We got the values $-\ln f(X, Y) = 77.76$, $-\ln f(X) = 43.34$ and $-\ln f(Y) = 29.80$. Since the sum 73.14 of the last two is less than the code length of the pooled data, we conclude that the samples were indeed generated by two different machineries. In fact, the first sample was generated by the Gamma (4,3) density function and the second by the uniform (4,18) distribution.

The conclusion we reached agrees with the result in Qian et al. (1994), where a different MDL density function was used with a somewhat awkward precision parameter to be selected. It was also reported in this reference that neither the Student t test nor the Smirnov test would indicate the difference between the two samples.

How could one form an idea of the confidence in the correctness of the decision made? A reasonable way is to generate new samples of the same sizes as X and Y with the two density functions adapted to the originally given samples, $f(y|X)$ and $f(y|Y)$. For each new sample pair, say X' and Y', compute the difference $\ln f(X') + \ln f(Y') - \ln f(X', Y')$ and calculate the relative frequency of the difference being positive. This serves as a measure of the desired confidence.

REFERENCES

Clarke, B. S. and A. R. Barron (1994). Jeffreys' prior is asymptotically least favorable under entropy risk. *Journal of Statistical Planning and Inference* 41 (1): 37–61.

Davisson, L. D. (1973). Universal noiseless coding. *IEEE Transactions on Information Theory* IT-19 (6): 783–95.

Dawid, A. P. (1991). Prequential analysis, stochastic complexity and Bayesian inference. *Fourth Valencia International Meeting on Bayesian Statistics*, Peniscola, Spain, 15–20 April.

Qian, G., G. Gabor and R. P. Gupta (1994). Test for homogeneity of several populations by stochastic complexity, private communication.

Li, M. and P. Vitányi (1993). *An Introduction to Kolmogorov Complexity and Its Applications*. New York: Springer.

Merhav, N. (1994). Bounds on achievable convergence rates of parameter estimators via universal coding. *IEEE Transactions on Information Theory* IT-40: 1210–15.

Rissanen, J. (1983). A universal data compression system. *IEEE Transactions on Information Theory* IT-29 (5): 656–64.

(1984). Universal coding, information, prediction, and estimation. *IEEE Transactions on Information Theory* IT-30 (4): 629–36.

(1986). Stochastic complexity and modeling. *Annals of Statistics* 14: 1080–100.

(1987). Stochastic complexity. *Journal of the Royal Statistical Society*, series B, 49 (3) (with discussions): 223–65.

(1996). Fisher information and stochastic complexity. *IEEE Transactions on Information Theory* IT-42 (1): 40–7.

Rissanen, J., T. Speed and B. Yu (1992). Density estimation by stochastic complexity. *IEEE Transactions on Information Theory* IT-38 (2): 315–23.

Shtarkov, Yu. M. (1987). Universal sequential coding of single messages. Translated from *Problems of Information Transmission* 23 (3): 3–17.

10 Rissanen's theorem and econometric time series

Werner Ploberger and Peter C. B. Phillips

1 Introduction

The twin notions of 'simplicity' and 'complexity' affect modelling throughout the social and physical sciences and are recognized as being important in most modelling methodologies, even though there may be no general agreement on methodological principles themselves. We therefore applaud the courage of the organizers of the Tilburg Conference in fostering an interdisciplinary treatment of these twin themes. The interdisciplinary nature of the subject means that most readers of this volume will be specialists in fields other than our own primary interest, which is econometrics, and are therefore most likely to be interested in the main ideas of our work on this topic rather than the technical details. Consequently, this chapter passes over most technicalities and seeks to explain why econometricians are interested in a particular aspect of Rissanen's theorem. Those readers who wish to pursue the technical details can consult our companion paper, Ploberger and Phillips (1998).

In economics, and other empirical sciences, researchers collect data – say $x^n = (x_t)_{t=1}^n$ – which do not follow any pre-ordained pattern but which can often be successfully 'explained' using a certain probabilistic framework. In particular, the data can be modelled in terms of a 'data-generating process' or DGP whereby it is assumed that the observed series x^n comprises realizations of some random variables $X_1, \ldots, X_n$ that are jointly distributed according to a probability measure P. This approach to modelling naturally turns attention to the measure P.

Usually, this probability measure arises from a theoretical model of the underlying mechanism. In most applications, however, we do not have enough prior information or 'first principles' to define all possible parameters of our model. Instead of one probability measure we have to consider a parametrized set – say P_θ – of probability measures, where

This chapter is based on a lecture given by Werner Ploberger at the Tilburg Conference in January 1997.

$\theta \in \Theta$ (the parameter space) and it is often simply assumed that the 'true' DGP is among those measures. We must now use our data x^n for inference about the parameter θ. Under this framework, a large number of applications have been developed and successfully applied in practical work, including econometrics.

This parametric statistical framework is not, of course, free from conceptual and practical difficulties, one of which is alluded to above, viz. the existence of a knowable 'true' model for x^n. A major practical difficulty that arises in most empirical applications is that the above description does not include one essential part: in many cases the parameter space itself is not fixed.

Consider a popular time series example. Often a process like x_t is influenced by its past history and a common model for such data is an autoregressive process of the form

$$x_t = a_1 x_{t-1} + ..a_p x_{t-p} + u_t$$

where the u_t are i.i.d. $N(0, \sigma^2)$. In this case, our parameter space consists of all $(p+1)$-tuples $(a_1, \ldots, a_p, \sigma^2)$. Usually one has no information about p, although in economics we can usually expect $p \geq 2$ if we are seeking to model cyclical behaviour and $p \geq 4$ when we are modelling quarterly data. In choosing p, we are aware of two immediate dangers:

1. We can specify p too small. Then, we lose the opportunity to find the 'true' model within our class. We have misspecified.
2. We can specify p too large. Then, statistical procedures become less efficient, a matter that affects estimation, inference and forecasting capability.

The loss of efficiency from p being large can be dramatic, especially in multiple time series situations where a unit increase in the lag parameter p involves m^2 additional parameters for an m-variable system. It is such an object of concern for econometricians that it is treated in standard undergraduate texts like Dougherty (1992). For this reason, it can be said that econometricians are often preoccupied with the *complexity* of the model class.

In economics, as elsewhere in the statistical sciences, many people have advocated the principle of parsimony: seek out the model with the smallest number of parameters which 'fit the data'. The principle has been successful in practical applications and it obtained a precise theoretical foundation through attempts to quantify the loss of information arising from the lack of knowledge about the parameters. Several proposals, including the AIC criterion by Akaike (1969, 1977) and the BIC criterion by Schwarz (1978), have won acceptance and been widely adopted in the empirical literature. This chapter concentrates on one of the most remarkable approaches in this class, the idea of stochastic complexity, due to Rissanen. We will be particularly concerned with a theorem in Rissanen (1987) which shows that stochastic complexity attains, in a certain well-defined sense, the best achievable rate of approach to the 'true' law of a process in a given parametric class.

Since our chapter concentrates on the application of Rissanen's theorem to econometric time series, we will shortly discuss the basic ideas underlying his approach from an econometric time series perspective. We will not pursue here the information-theoretic interpretation of the theorem (q.v. Cover and Thomas, 1991). In information theory, a probability measure is very largely a means to construct a code, or as Rissanen (1986) put it, a 'language to express the regular features of the data'. In econometrics, it is often an object of central importance in itself – one goal in the construction of models being the computation of 'probabilities' of events, for which the probability measure is an essential element. Thus, for us, the result of modelling will be – for every sample size – a probability measure – say G_n – on the sample space for x^n.

This approach allows us to consider both Bayesian and classical statistical modelling. A Bayesian statistician would use the 'Bayesian mixture' $Q_n = \int P_\theta d\mu(\theta)$, where μ is the prior distribution for the parameter θ, as the data measure. If p_θ is the density of P_θ with respect to some dominating measure, then the Bayesian mixture $q_n = \int p_\theta d\mu(\theta)$ is simply the data density, or, as it is sometimes called, the marginal likelihood. Conditional data densities for $x_{n_0}^n = (x_{n_0+1}, \ldots, x_n)$ given x^{n_0} can then be constructed from the ratios $q_{n,n_0} = q_n/q_{n_0}$, with corresponding measures Q_{n,n_0}.

Now, suppose that the conditional probabilities $P_\theta(x_t|x^{t-1})$ have densities $p_\theta(x_t|x^{t-1})$ with respect to a common dominating measure ν. A classical statistician might – for every $t \leq n$ that was big enough – use x^{t-1} to estimate θ, e.g. by the use of the maximum likelihood estimator $\hat{\theta}_{t-1}$, and then use the 'plug-in' density $p_{\hat{\theta}_{t-1}}(x_t|x^{t-1})$ to 'predict' x_t. Then the model, in our sense of a useable empirical measure, is given by the density $\hat{p}_{n,n_0} = \prod_{n_0 \leq t \leq n} p_{\hat{\theta}_{t-1}}(x_t|x^{t-1})$, where n_0 is the smallest number of observations for which $\hat{\theta}_t$ is well defined. This model corresponds to Dawid's (1984) 'plug-in forecasting system' and leads to his notion of prequential probability. Phillips and Ploberger (1994, theorem 2.3) and Phillips (1996) establish the asymptotic equivalence between these prequential DGPs and the conditional Bayesian data densities q_{n,n_0}. One can also use procedures like the Kalman filter to 'predict' the next data point and this would simply correspond to the use of a different model, in our terminology.

Since the class of possible 'models' for the data is extremely large it is natural to start thinking about ways of assessing the quality of models as statistical instruments. Since models, in the sense above, are just probability measures, we can compare them – or their densities – with the true data-generating process. There are a variety of sensible distance functions for probability measures (see Strasser, 1985, and LeCam and Yang, 1990, for an overview and discussion of their properties). One of these is the so-called Kullback–Leibler (KL) information distance. This distance measure is well known not to be a metric, since it is not symmetric, but has some useful advantages and is appealing in our context where the models are measures and we want to compare the 'likelihood' of different models. The KL distance from model G_n to the 'true' DGP P_θ is defined as $-E_\theta \log \frac{dG_n}{dP_\theta}$.

Rissanen (1987, 1996) showed that if X_t is stationary, if Θ is a regular subset of the $\mathbb{R}^k$, i.e. if

$$\dim \Theta = k,$$

and if some technical conditions are fulfilled, then the Lesbesgue measure (i.e., the volume in $\mathbb{R}^k$) of the set

$$\left\{ \theta : -E_\theta \log \frac{dG_n}{dP_\theta} \leq \frac{1}{2} k \log n \right\}$$

converges to 0 for any choice of empirical model G_n. This theorem shows that whatever one's model, one can approximate (with respect to KL distance) the DGP no better, on average, than $\frac{1}{2} k \log n$ for the typical parameter. Thus, outside of a 'small' set of parameters we can get no closer to the truth than $\frac{1}{2} k \log n$ – the 'volume' of the set for which we can do better actually converges to zero!

In a way, Rissanen's theorem justifies a certain amount of scepticism about models with a large number of parameters. Note that the *minimum achievable distance* of an empirical model to the DGP increases linearly with the number of parameters. In essence, the more complex the system is, the harder it is to construct a good empirical model. Thus, the theorem makes precise the intuitive notion that complex systems can be very hard to model, that models of larger dimension place increasing demands on the available data!

2   Stylized facts about econometric data and models

Before discussing our extension of the Rissanen theorem, we discuss some typical features of economic time series that help to motivate our generalization. We particularly want to draw attention to the following:

(a) Economic time series are often non-stationary Simple inspection of time series plots for aggregate macroeconomic data are sufficiently compelling to justify this observation. Extensive analysis of economic data, following early work by Nelson and Plosser (1982), confirms that there is good reason to believe that the trending mechanism is stochastic. However, the precise form of the non-stationarity is not so much an issue. Even if one chooses models that involve time polynomials, or breaking time polynomials as in Perron (1989), the non-stationarity of the data itself is seldom at issue.

(b) Many interesting econometric models have a 'stochastic information matrix' Following the formal development of unit-root tests (both parametric approaches like those in Dickey and Fuller, 1979, 1981, and semiparametric approaches like those in Phillips, 1987), econometricians have devoted substantial effort to analysing the particular class of non-stationary models where the stochastic trend results from accumulated shocks. The log likelihood function for such models is – after proper normalization – asymptotically quadratic, but has some special features that distinguish it from the traditional stationary case. Indeed, contrary to the standard assumption that the matrix originating from the quadratic term (i.e. the properly normalized second derivatives of the likelihood function) converges to a constant, under unit root non-stationarity this matrix converges in distribution to a 'proper' limit random matrix. Secondly, when we move away from unit root non-stationarity but stay in the local vicinity, the limit matrix also changes. In this sense, the traditional Fisher information is both random and variable in the limit, divergences from traditional theory that were pointed out in Phillips (1989). These points of difference end up having a profound effect on the extension of Rissanen's theorem.

The simplest example is as follows. Consider an autoregressive process x_t defined by

$$x_t = \theta x_{t-1} + u_t \tag{1}$$

where u_t is i.i.d $N(0, 1)$, the scale parameter being set to one and assumed to be known. The log likelihood (up to additive constants) can be written as

$$-\frac{1}{2}\sum_{t=1}^{n}(x_t - \theta x_{t-1})^2$$
$$= -\frac{1}{2}\sum_{t=1}^{n}u_t^2 + \{n(\theta - 1)\}\left\{\frac{1}{n}\sum_{t=1}^{n}x_{t-1}u_t\right\} - \frac{1}{2}\{n(\theta - 1)\}^2\left\{\frac{1}{n^2}\sum_{t=1}^{n}x_{t-1}^2\right\}. \tag{2}$$

The log likelihood function here is exactly quadratic and, in the case where we centre on $\theta = 1$ (the true DGP has a unit autoregressive root), we use the normalization factor n (in contrast to the traditional $\sqrt{n}$). The quadratic factor $\frac{1}{n^2} \sum x_{t-1}^2$ converges in distribution to a nontrivial functional of a Brownian motion and the linear factor $\frac{1}{n} \sum_{t=1}^{n} x_{t-1} u_t$ to a stochastic integral of Brownian motion (see Phillips, 1987). When we centre on $\theta = 1 + \frac{c}{n}$ in the vicinity of unity, we get the same normalization factor n, but the limit functionals involve a diffusion process. In both cases, there is random Fisher information in the limit. For a detailed discussion of the behaviour of this likelihood, see Phillips (1989) and Jeganathan (1995).

The main aim of our companion paper, Ploberger and Phillips (1998), is to generalize Rissanen's theorem to an environment that includes such examples. In doing so, we did not use the KL-distance. Instead of investigating the *expectation* of the log-likelihood ratio $\log \frac{dG_n}{dP_\theta}$, we focus on deriving bounds for $\log \frac{dG_n}{dP_\theta}$ itself. Rissanen's (1987) emphasis lay in the construction of codes which encode *the data* optimally (i.e. using the smallest number of bits). Then, the measure $E_\theta \log \frac{dG_n}{dP_\theta}$ is closely related to the amount of bits necessary to encode the data (e.g. for storage or transmission). Our primary interest is in statistical inference, not just data encoding, so we focus our attention on the log-likelihood ratio $\log \frac{dG_n}{dP_\theta}$ itself rather than its average value. In consequence, we may interpret certain aspects of our theory differently from that of Rissanen.

3   The generalization of Rissanen's theorem

Defining a 'distance' to the true model automatically establishes an ordering on sets of models: 'good' models have a 'small' distance to the true DGP measure, whereas 'bad' models have a 'large' distance. Our distance measure will be the log-likelihood ratio itself, viz. the random variable

$$\log \frac{dG_n}{dP_\theta}. \tag{3}$$

From the econometric point of view, the idea of using (3) as the basis for a distance measure between the model G_n and the DGP is an attractive one, since the resulting 'ordering' reflects established practice of choosing models. Suppose one has given two models $G_{1,n}$ and $G_{2,n}$. Statisticians are accustomed to basing inference on the value of the likelihood ratio $\frac{dG_{1,n}}{dG_{2,n}}$, measured here by the Radon Nikodym derivative of the two measures. This practice applies irrespective of the particular foundations for inference. A 'classical' statistician would use this ratio as the basis for a test in the Neyman–Pearson framework, whereas a Bayesian statistician would use this ratio as a Bayes factor in the context of posterior odds testing. In either event, if $\frac{dG_{1,n}}{dG_{2,n}}$ is 'large', $G_{1,n}$ is taken to be the better model over $G_{2,n}$, and vice versa if the ratio is 'small'. Since we can write

$$\log \frac{dG_{1,n}}{dG_{2,n}} = \log \frac{dG_{1,n}}{dP_\theta} - \log \frac{dG_{1,n}}{dP_\theta}$$

the logarithm (which is a monotone transformation) of this ratio is just the difference of our distance measure (3) for the two models.

From our point of view, it is not so important to look at the expectation $E(\log \frac{dG_n}{dP_\theta})$. Since $\lim_{x \to 0} \log x = -\infty$, the expectation can be over-influenced by small values of $\frac{dG_n}{dP_\theta}$. To illustrate, consider a series of events A_n in part of the sample space of x^n and models $G_{1,n}$ defined on the same sample space. Suppose $G_{1,n}(A_n) \to 0$ and $P_\theta(A_n) \to 0$ for all θ, but

$$P_\theta(A_n) > 0. \tag{4}$$

Then define alternate models $G_{2,n}$ by

$$\frac{dG_{2,n}}{dG_{1,n}} = \left\{ \begin{array}{l} 0 \text{ on } A_n \\ \frac{1}{1-G(A_{1,n})} \text{ on the complement of } A_n \end{array} \right\}$$

Most statisticians would consider $G_{1,n}$ and $G_{2,n}$ to be asymptotically equivalent: since their likelihood ratio converges to one – and even the variational distance between these two measures converges to zero – there is no way to distinguish them asymptotically. On the other hand, (4) demonstrates that

$$E_\theta \left(\log \frac{dG_{2,n}}{dP_\theta} \right) = -\infty,$$

so that, upon averaging, $G_{2,n}$ is taken to be one of the worst possible models!

The precise formulation and requisites for our extension of the Rissanen theorem are technical and we refer readers to our original paper, Ploberger and Phillips (1998), for details. The exposition here is intended to outline the essential features and to discuss its implications. In this regard, it is helpful to clarify the model classes under investigation.

As mentioned above, we want the likelihood function to be asymptotically sufficiently 'smooth', i.e. locally quadratic, and we start by making this statement more precise. The key conditions can be laid out as follows.

1. The parameter space Θ is an *open* and *bounded* subset of $\mathbb{R}^k$.

2. The measures P_θ on the sample space of x^n are, for all $n \in \mathbb{N}$, generated by densities $p_\theta = p_\theta(x^n)$. For $\theta \in \Theta$, the log-likelihood is defined as $\ell_n(\theta) = \log p_\theta(x^n)$.
3. There exist deterministic norming matrices D_n such that for $h \in \mathbb{R}^k$ we have the expansion

$$\ell_n(\theta + D_n^{-1}h) = \ell_n(\theta) + W_n'h - \frac{1}{2}h'M_nh + o(h'h), \tag{5}$$

uniformly for all bounded h, where

$$W_n = D_n^{-1\prime}\frac{\partial \ell_n}{\partial \theta},$$

and

$$M_n = D_n^{-1\prime}B_nD_n^{-1}, \quad B_n = -\frac{\partial^2 \ell_n}{\partial\theta\partial\theta'} \tag{6}$$

are the properly normalized first two coefficients in the Taylor-series expansion of the likelihood. (This model class is discussed extensively in e.g. LeCam and Yang (1990) and Jeganathan (1995).) An expansion that is equivalent to (5) is obtained when the second derivative matrix in (6) is replaced by the conditional quadratic variation of the score process $\partial \ell_n/\partial \theta$.
4. The components W_n, M_n defined above converge jointly in distribution to random elements (a matrix in the case of M_n) which we denote by W and M. We furthermore assume that

$$M > 0 \text{ with probability one}$$

in the matrix (positive definite) sense.
5. There exists an estimator $\hat{\theta}_n$ for which the normalized quantity $D_n(\hat{\theta}_n - \theta)$ remains bounded stochastically.

Ploberger and Phillips (1998) discuss and use some more general conditions than these. However, concentration on problems for which the likelihood satisfies the above conditions simplifies the exposition considerably, yet still allows for some non-trivial cases as the following two examples illustrate.

Example 1 Suppose x^n is a realization of a time series for which the conditional density of x_t given x^{t-1} is $f_{t\theta}(x)$ depending on the scalar parameter θ. In this case, the log-likelihood is $\ell_n(\theta) = \sum_{t=1}^{n} \log f_{t\theta}(x_t)$ and, under familiar regularity conditions (e.g. ch. 6 of Hall and Heyde, 1980), the score process $\partial \ell_n/\partial \theta = \sum_{t=1}^{n} \partial \log f_{t\theta}(x_t)/\partial \theta = \sum_{t=1}^{n} e_{t\theta}$ is a martingale. The quantity

$I_{n\theta} = \sum_{t=1}^{n} E_{t-1}(e_{t\theta}^2)$ is the conditional variance of the martingale and measures conditional information (it reduces to the standard Fisher information when the x_t are independent). Under quite general conditions, it is known (Hall and Heyde, 1980, proposition 6.1) that the normed quantity $\xi_n = I_{n\theta}^{-\frac{1}{2}} \partial \ell_n / \partial \theta$ satisfies a martingale central limit theorem and converges to the mixed Gaussian law $\eta_\theta N(0, 1)$, where η_θ is the limit in probability of $E(I_{n\theta})^{-1} I_{n\theta}$ and is generally random. This time series set-up fits our general framework when we can choose a scalar sequence D_n for which $D_n^{-2} E(I_{n\theta})$ converges to a constant, which will be the case when the $e_{t\theta}$ are stationary and ergodic martingale differences and then $D_n = \sqrt{n}$.

Example 2 The Gaussian non-stationary autoregression (1) has log-likelihood (2) and we can choose $D_n = n$. Then, it is well known from unit-root asymptotic theory (see Phillips and Xiao, 1998, for a recent review) that the normed quantities $n^{-1} \partial \ell_n / \partial \theta = \frac{1}{n} \sum x_{t-1} u_t$, and $-n^{-1} \partial^2 \ell_n / \partial \theta^2 = \frac{1}{n^2} \sum x_{t-1}^2$ converge in distribution to certain functionals of Brownian motion. Again this example satisfies all the above requirements.

We are now in a position to state the main result of Ploberger and Phillips (1998). We presume that for each $n \in \mathbb{N}$ we have a given empirical model represented by the proper probability measure G_n and that the assumptions given above apply. (Some additional technical conditions are used in Ploberger and Phillips and these too are assumed to be fulfilled.)

Proposition 1 *For all $\alpha, \varepsilon > 0$ the Lebesgue measure of the set*

$$\left\{ \theta : P_\theta \left[-\log \frac{dG_n}{dP_\theta} \leq \frac{1-\varepsilon}{2} \log \det B_n \right] \geq \alpha \right\}$$

converges to zero.

This result may be interpreted as follows. Up to a 'small' exceptional set, the empirical model G_n cannot come nearer to the true DGP than $\frac{1}{2} \log \det B_n$. Since G_n is arbitrary, the result tells us that there is a bound on how close any empirical model can come to the truth and that this bound depends on the data through B_n.

Phillips (1996) and Phillips and Ploberger (1996) show how to construct empirical models for which

$$-(\log \frac{dG_n}{dP_\theta}) / (\log \det B_n) \to \frac{1}{2}. \tag{7}$$

These models can be formed by taking G_n to be the Bayesian data measure Q_n for proper Bayesian priors. Or, in the case of improper priors, the models G_n may be obtained by taking the conditional Bayes measures Q_{n,n_0}, which will be proper for all $n_0 \geq k$, and these can be assessed against the corresponding true conditional DGP of $x_{n_0}^n$ given x_{n_0}. In the latter case, we may also take G_n to be the classical (or prequential) measure, $\hat{P}_{n,n_0}$, which is asymptotically equivalent to the conditional Bayes measure Q_{n,n_0}.

Given the feasibility of (7), it seems sensible to define 'essentially better' models as models G_n for which

$$-\left(\log \frac{dG_n}{dP_\theta}\right)/(\log \det B_n) \leq \frac{1-\varepsilon}{2}, \tag{8}$$

for some $\varepsilon > 0$. The above inequality needs to be made more precise because both $\log dG_n/dP_\theta$ and $\log \det B_n$ are random variables, and so the event $A_n = \left[-\left(\log \frac{dG_n}{dP_\theta}\right)/(\log \det B_n) \leq \frac{1-\varepsilon}{2}\right]$ may be nontrivial. However, if the probability of the event A_n converges to zero, one cannot reasonably define G_n to be essentially better because the sample space over which the inequality (8) holds has negligible probability. Therefore, for a model to be essentially better, we must postulate the existence of an $\alpha > 0$ for which $P_\theta(A_n) \geq \alpha$, and then the probability of events such as A_n is non-negligible. What the proposition tells us is that the set of such essentially better models has Lebesgue measure zero in the parameter space in $\mathbb{R}^k$ as $n \to \infty$. In this well defined sense, we can generally expect to be able to do no better in modelling the DGP than to use the models Q_n, Q_{n,n_0} or $\hat{P}_{n,n_0}$.

4   Consequences

The upshot of proposition 1 is that for time series where there is apparent non-stationarity, the smallest possible 'distance' of the empirical model from the truth is given not by the quantity $\frac{k}{2}\log n$, but by $\frac{1}{2}\log \det B_n$. When the data are stationary, these two benchmarks are asymptotically equivalent. More specifically, in the stationary and ergodic case, it is apparent that $B_n \sim nI$, where $I = -E(\partial^2 \log f_{t\theta}(x_t)/\partial\theta\partial\theta')$ is the Fisher information matrix. Then, we have $\det B_n \sim n^k \det I$ and it follows that $\log \det B_n/(k \log n) \to_p 1$.

In the non-stationary case, the two bounds are different. The distance $\frac{1}{2}\log \det B_n$ in the general case is determined by the logarithm of the determinant of the conditional variation matrix of the score process, a form of Fisher information. Moreover, (6) and the weak convergence of M_n to some non-singular matrix implies that

$$\frac{\log \det B_n}{2 \log \det D_n} \to_p 1, \tag{9}$$

so that, under our assumptions here, the asymptotic behaviour of the deterministic sequence

$$2 \log \det D_n$$

essentially determines how 'near' we can get to the true DGP.

In the stationary case, it is relatively easy to compare the 'loss' from parameter estimation in different parameter spaces. Rissanen's theorem states that the loss due to parameter estimation is essentially determined by the dimension of the parameter space.[1] In the presence of non-stationarities, however, the situation changes. It is not the dimension of the parameter space (which we can think of as the simplest quantity associated with the complexity of the model class) that determines the distance of the model to the true DGP, but the order of magnitude of the first and the second derivatives of the log-likelihood, which in our case here is essentially represented by the matrix D_n. In some commonly arising cases, the matrices D_n are diagonal and the diagonal elements are given by simple powers of the sample size, n^{α_i}, and then we have

$$\log \det D_n \sim \left(\sum_{i=1}^{k} \alpha_i \right) \log n \tag{10}$$

In the example below, we analyse the special case of a linear regression model. We show that in cases of primary interest to econometricians $\alpha_i \geqq \frac{1}{2}$, with inequality occurring for at least one diagonal element i. In such cases, the distance of the model to the DGP increases *faster* than in the traditional case. Thus, when non-stationary regressors are present, it appears to be even more important to keep the model as simple as possible. An additional non-stationary component in a linear regression model turns out to be more expensive than a stationary regressor in terms of the marginal increase in the nearest possible distance to the DGP. In effect, non-stationary regressors have a powerful signal and generally have estimated coefficients that display faster rates of convergence than those of stationary regressors. But they can also be powerfully wrong in prediction when inappropriate and so the loss from including

---

[1] Rissanen (1996) investigates the role of the information matrix for stationary processes. The dominant term, however, in that context is simply the dimension of the parameter space.

non-stationary regressors is correspondingly higher. In a very real sense, therefore, the true DGP turns out to be more elusive when there is non-stationarity in the data!

The above remarks apply regardless of the modelling methodology that is involved. Neither Bayesian nor classical techniques can overcome this bound. As the statement of the proposition itself makes clear, the bound can be improved only in 'special' situations, like those where we have extra information about the true DGP and do not have to estimate all the parameters (e.g. we may 'know' that there is a unit root in the model, or by divine inspiration hit upon the right value of a parameter). On the other hand, Phillips (1996) and Phillips and Ploberger (1996) show under conditions similar to the ones considered here (or those in Ploberger and Phillips, 1998), that the bound is attainable and can be achieved by both Bayesian models and plug-in prequential models.

Example 3 Consider the linear model

$$y_t = x_t'\theta + u_t,$$ (11)

where y_t is scalar, x_t is a k-vector and the u_t are i.i.d. Gaussian with known variance, which we set to one. We assume the x_t to be (weakly) exogenous in the sense of Engle, Hendry and Richard (1983). This condition allows us to substitute for the full joint likelihood the concentrated log-likelihood

$$\ell_n(\theta) = -\frac{1}{2}\sum(y_t - x_t'\theta)^2.$$ (12)

The function is quadratic and the conditional variance matrix of the score is

$$B_n = \sum_{t \leq n} x_t x_t'.$$

To illustrate the points made above about the growth (cf. (10)) of our bound, we start by taking the special case where x_t has the following form

$$x_t' = \left(1, t, W_1, \ldots, W_m, Z_1, \ldots, Z_p\right),$$ (13)

where $W_1, \ldots, W_m$ are (full-rank) integrated (i.e. unit-root) processes and $Z_1, \ldots, Z_p$ are stationary processes with non-singular variance matrices. It is easily seen that $D_n = diag(\sqrt{n}, \sqrt{n^3}, n, ..n, \sqrt{n}, ..\sqrt{n})$. Hence, applying formula (9), we have

$$\frac{\log \det B_n}{2(\frac{1}{2} + \frac{3}{2} + m + \frac{p}{2}) \log n} \to 1. \tag{14}$$

It follows from this formula that the inclusion of a deterministic trend 'costs' (in terms of the distance between the empirical model and the DGP) three times as much as the lack of knowledge about the constant or the coefficient of a stationary variable, whereas the inclusion of an independent stochastic trend costs twice as much. Similarly, a polynomial time trend of degree q would cost $2q + 1$ times as much as a stationary regressor.

In the general case where the regressors x_t are stationary in some directions, integrated in others and have some deterministic trend components, it is possible to transform the system into one with regressors of the form (13). Indeed, by rotating coordinates in the regressor space (cf. Phillips, 1989, and Ploberger and Phillips, 1998), we can find a non-singular matrix C for which Cx_t has the form (13). In transformed coordinates, we have the equivalent linear model $y_t = x_t^{*\prime}\theta^* + u_t$, where $x_t^* = Cx_t$ and $\theta^* = C'^{-1}\theta$. Then, formula (14) above continues to apply with p equalling the total number of stationary components (which includes the number of cointegrating vectors) and m being the number of primitive (i.e. not cointegrated) stochastic trends.

Some implications for prediction

A direct analysis of the likelihood (12) helps to establish some results about the best prediction in a linear model when the parameters are unknown. Take the classical linear regression model (11) with u_t i.i.d. $N(0, \sigma^2)$ and σ^2 known. If we knew the true parameter θ_0, the best predictor for y_t given x_t would equal $x_t'\theta_0$. In practical empirical problems, of course, the true parameter is unknown and has to be estimated. In place of the optimal predictor $x_t'\theta_0$, therefore, we have to use another predictor such as $x_t'\hat{\theta}_{t-1}$, where $\hat{\theta}_{t-1}$ is the OLS-estimator for θ based on $z^{t-1} = (y, x)^{t-1}$. Of course, we may also use more sophisticated methods relying on the past history z^{t-1}. So let us assume that we have given some predictors $\bar{y}_t = \bar{y}_t(x_t, z^{t-1})$ for y_t. Then, for fixed (t, x_t, z^{t-1}) we can consider the function

$$q_t(y_t | x_t, z^{t-1}) = \frac{1}{\sqrt{2\pi\sigma^2}} \exp\left(-\frac{(y_t - \bar{y}_t)^2}{2\sigma^2}\right),$$

which is evidently a proper density function, integrating to unity. Therefore, the probability measure G on the sample space defined by

the density $\prod_{t\leq n} q(y_t|x_t, z^{t-1})$ is a model (in our sense) for the data.[2]
Then, it is easily seen that

$$-\log\frac{dG}{dP_\theta} = \frac{1}{2\sigma^2} \sum \{(y_t - \bar{y}_t)^2 - (y_t - x_t'\theta_0)^2\},$$

namely the difference between the sums of squared prediction errors for the given predictor and the best possible predictor. Now we can apply our proposition 1 and conclude that this difference must be (for Lebesgue-almost all θ, of course) greater than our bound (14). This shows that there is a natural bound on how close we can come to the optimal predictor, in terms of mean-squared prediction error, and that this bound depends not only on the parameter count but on the trend properties of the regressors.

5   Conclusion

In a certain way, our proposition helps to quantify the well-known opinion of one of the editors of this volume that models with high-dimensional parameter spaces are to be avoided. Increasing the dimension of the parameter space carries a price in terms of the quantitative bound of how close we can come to the 'true' DGP and, in consequence, how closely we can reproduce the properties of the optimal predictor. Our proposition shows, further, that this price goes up when we have trending data and when we use trending regressors. The price no longer follows the (parameter count)*(logarithm of sample size) law, and it becomes necessary to multiply the parameter count by an additional factor that depends on the number and the type of trends in the regressors.

No methodology can break this curse of dimensionality, at least for almost all of the elements of the parameter space. The new element that emerges from the present theory is that the curse is exacerbated when non-stationary regressors and trending data are involved. Both in modelling and in prediction, our results indicate that there are additional gains to be had from parsimony in the formulation of models for trending time series.

---

[2] Strictly speaking, we should define a measure on the space of all y_t, x_t. But, we can use the concept of *exogeneity* mentioned earlier to restrict attention to conditional measures.

REFERENCES

Akaike H. (1969). Fitting autoregressive models for prediction. *Annals of the Institute of Statistical Mathematics* 21: 243–7.

(1974). Stochastic theory of minimal realization. *IEEE Transactions on Automatic Control* AC-19: 667–74.

Cover, T. M. and J. Thomas (1991). *Elements of Information Theory*. New York: Wiley.

Dawid, A. P. (1984). Present position and potential developments: some personal views, statistical theory, the prequential approach. *Journal of the Royal Statistical Society* A-147: 278–92.

Dickey, D. and W. Fuller (1979). Distribution of the estimators for autoregressive time series with a unit root. *Journal of the American Statistical Association* 74: 427–31.

(1981). Likelihood ratio tests for autoregressive time series with an unit root. *Econometrica* 49: 1057–72.

Dougherty, C. (1992). *Introduction to Econometrics*. New York: Oxford University Press.

Engle, R. F., D. F. Hendry and J. F. Richard (1983). Exogenity. *Econometrica* 51: 277–304.

Hall, P. and C. C. Heyde (1980). *Martingale Limit Theory*. San Diego: Academic Press.

Jeganathan, P. (1995). Some aspects of asymptotic theory with applications to time series modeling. *Econometric Theory* 11: 818–87.

LeCam, L. and G. Yang (1990). *Asymptotics in Statistics: Some Basic Concepts*. New York: Springer.

Nelson, C. and C. Plosser (1982). Trends and random walks in macroeconomic time series. *Journal of Monetary Economics* 10: 139–62.

Park, J. Y. and P. C. B. Phillips (1988): Statistical inference in regressions with integrated processes: Part 1. *Econometric Theory* 4: 468.

Perron, P. (1989). The great crash, the oil price shock and the unit root hypothesis. *Econometrica* 58: 1361–401.

Phillips, P. C. B. (1987). Time series regression with a unit root. *Econometrica* 55: 277–301.

(1989). Partially identified econometric models. *Econometric Theory* 5: 181–240.

(1996). Econometric model determination. *Econometrica* 64: 763–812.

Phillips, P. C. B. and W. Ploberger (1994). Posterior odds testing for a unit root with data-based model selection. *Econometric Theory* 10: 774–808.

(1996). An asymptotic theory of Bayesian inference for time series. *Econometrica* 64(2): 381–412.

Phillips, P. C. B. and Z. Xiao (1998). A primer in unit root testing. *Journal of Economic Surveys* (forthcoming).

Ploberger, W. and P. C. B. Phillips (1998). An extension of Rissanen's bound on the best empirical DGP. Mimeographed paper, Yale University.

Rissanen, J. (1986). Stochastic complexity and modelling. *Annals of Statistics* 14: 1080–100.

(1987). Stochastic complexity (with discussion). *Journal of the Royal Statistical Society* 49: 223–39, 252–65.

(1996). Fisher information and stochastic complexity. *IEEE Transactions on Information Theory* 42(1).

Schwarz, G. (1978). Estimating the dimension of a model. *Annals of Statistics* 6: 461–4.

Strasser, H. (1985). *Mathematical Theory of Statistics*. New York: Walter de Gruyter.

11 Parametric versus non-parametric inference: statistical models and simplicity

Aris Spanos

1 Introduction

The main objective of this chapter is to compare and contrast the two main approaches to modern (frequentist) statistical inference, known as *parametric* and *non-parametric*. The comparison focuses on their *effectiveness* in empirical modelling, i.e. how effective these two approaches are in enabling the modeller to learn about observable stochastic phenomena of interest. By interpreting *simplicity* of a statistical model in terms of *parsimony* and *informational content*, as they relate to the statistical information contained in the observed data, we proceed to compare parametric and non-parametric models. The main conclusion is that parametric models not only have a clear advantage over non-parametric models on simplicity grounds, they are also better suited for giving rise to *reliable* and *precise* empirical evidence.

In section 2 we explain the main difference between *parametric* and *non-parametric* models as they pertain to statistical inference. In section 3 we discuss the notion of simplicity as it relates to statistical modelling. In section 4 we compare parametric and non-parametric modelling in relation to statistical adequacy (the assumptions defining the models are not rejected by the observed data) and robustness. In section 5 we discuss the precision of inference as it relates to parametric and non-parametric modelling. In section 6 we consider an empirical example of descriptive correlation analysis in order to illustrate some of the issues raised in the previous sections. Section 7 discusses briefly the *probabilistic reduction approach* (see Spanos, 1989) to empirical modelling, which is designed to take full advantage of the strengths of the parametric approach in order to enhance the *reliability* and *precision* of empirical evidence.

2 Statistical models

Modern statistical inference, as formalized by Fisher (1922, 1925), commences with the modeller putting forward a **statistical model** aspiring to

181

Table 11.1. *A generic parametric statistical model*

[i]	Probability model:	$\Phi_\theta = \{f(x; \theta), \theta \in \Theta, x \in \mathbb{R}_x\}$,
[ii]	Sampling model:	$(X_1, X_2, \ldots, X_n)$ is a Random Sample.

describe an 'idealized' stochastic mechanism that gave rise to the observed data. Putting forward a statistical model and interpreting the observed data as a *realization* of the 'idealized' stochastic mechanism constitutes the cornerstone of modern statistical inference. It is important to emphasize at the outset that *non-parametric* models are proper statistical models in the context of modern statistical inference. They differ from *parametric* models in so far as they make less specific probabilistic assumptions.

For the purposes of the discussion that follows, it suffices to concentrate on the simplest form of a statistical model in order to focus on the methodological issues without the technical difficulties. Following Spanos (1986), statistical models in this chapter are specified exclusively in terms of the observable random variables involved. The simplest form of a parametric statistical model is given in table 11.1.

The probability model represents a family of density functions (or cumulative distribution functions (cdf) $F(x; \theta)$ for added generality) indexed by a set of unknown parameters θ (hence the term *parametric model*). The sampling model, in this particular example, is assumed to be a set of Independent and Identically Distributed (IID) random variables. Postulating such a statistical model can be seen as *narrowing down* the set of all possible models $\mathcal{P}$ (an infinite dimensional space) to a proper subset $\mathcal{P}_\theta := \Phi_\theta$.

Parametric inference refers to modern statistical inference based on postulating a parametric statistical model, such as the one in table 11.1. Modern parametric statistical inference is dominated by the concept of a likelihood function because the statistical model is prespecified in a form which enables the modeller to determine the likelihood function completely. Indeed, the machinery built for assessing optimality for estimators, tests and predictors is inextricably bound up directly or indirectly with the notion of the likelihood function; see Gourieroux and Monfort (1995).

In this chapter the term **non-parametric** (or distribution free) is used to denote a statistical model whose simplest generic form is given in table 11.2, where $\mathcal{P}_F$ denotes a proper subset of the set of all possible distributions $\mathcal{P}$. In non-parametric models $\mathcal{P}_F$ is not defined directly in terms of a

Table 11.2. *A generic non-parametric statistical model*

[i]	Probability model:	$f(x) \in \mathcal{P}_F \subset \mathcal{P}$,
[ii]	Sampling model:	$(X_1, X_2, \ldots, X_n)$ is a Random Sample.

specific parametric family of distributions (Normal, Gamma, etc.) but indirectly using assumptions relating to features of the distribution such as:

(a) whether the random variable(s) is discrete or continuous,
(b) the nature of the support set of the distribution: $\mathbb{R}_X^* = \{x : f(x) > 0, x \in \mathbb{R}_X\}$,
(c) the existence of certain moments, and
(d) the smoothness of the distribution (continuity, differentiability).

These indirect distribution assumptions aim at narrowing down the set of all possible distributions $\mathcal{P}$ to a feasible subset.

Non-parametric inference belongs to statistical inference proper (within the Fisher paradigm), based on statistical models whose only difference from parametric inference is the use of implicit (instead of explicit) distribution assumptions. By its very nature, non-parametric statistical inference cannot utilize the concept of the likelihood function because the latter requires an explicit parametric form for the distribution underlying the statistical model in question. In view of the fact that modern statistical inference relies on sampling distributions of statistics (estimators, tests and predictors), the question that naturally arises is how are these sampling distributions determined in the absence of a prespecified probability distribution? The short answer is that it relies mostly on inequalities and asymptotic results. As argued below, the reliance of non-parametric methods on probabilistic inequalities and asymptotic results has a detrimental effect on the precision of the resulting inference.

Non-parametric inference based on ranks. The early literature on non-parametric inference was launched by the classic paper by Wilcoxon (1945) and concentrated mostly on finding alternatives to the classic t-test without the reliance on the Normality assumption. This literature made extensive use of the so-called *rank-order statistics* in the case of a simple non-parametric model as given in table 11.2, where the probability model often takes the form:

$$\mathcal{P}_F = \{F(x) : F(x) \text{ is continuous and symmetric around the median}\};$$

(see Lehmann, 1975). This indirect distribution assumption narrows down the set of all possible distributions by excluding any non-continuous and non-symmetric distributions. Given a *random* sample $(X_1, X_2, \ldots, X_n)$, the ordered sample is defined by $(X_{[1]}, X_{[2]}, \ldots, X_{[n]})$ where $X_{[1]} \leq X_{[2]} \leq, \ldots, \leq X_{[n]}$. The rank R_k of an observation x_k is defined as the number of values $(x_1, x_2, \ldots, x_n)$ less than or equal to x_k. The popularity of the non-parametric tests based on ranks began with the paper by Hodges and Lehmann (1956) who demonstrated that these tests are more *robust* than the classic t-test, because they require weaker assumptions for their validity, without having to pay a big price in terms of efficiency. This literature has been extended to include linear models, taking the form of *robust estimation* based on weighted L_1 norms (see Tukey, 1960; Huber, 1981; Hettmansperger and McKean, 1998).

Non-parametric inference based on smoothing techniques. More recently, the literature on non-parametric inference has concentrated more on estimating the unspecified distribution and density functions, as well as functions thereof, such as the regression and quantile functions. The initial emphasis was mostly on *series estimators* (see Gallant, 1987; Thompson and Tapia, 1991) but more recently the emphasis has been placed on *smoothing* techniques and in particular *kernel smoothing* (see Silverman, 1986; Härdle, 1990).

3   Simplicity in statistical modelling

In this chapter we sidestep the issue of providing a precise definition or quantification of simplicity; see Keuzenkamp and McAleer (1995). Instead, we focus our attention on simplicity as it pertains to statistical modelling. As various as are the conceptions of simplicity in the literature, the idea that seems most relevant to the methodological issue here has to do with a model's informativeness and its value for testing hypotheses and learning about the phenomena of interest. This idea can be traced back to the father of modern statistics, R. A. Fisher, in his classic (1922) paper:

> the object of statistical methods is the reduction of data. A quantity of data, which usually by its mere bulk is incapable of entering the mind, is to be replaced by relatively few quantities which shall adequately represent the whole, or which, in other words, shall contain as much as possible, ideally the whole, of the relevant information contained in the original data. (Ibid., p. 311)

In Fisher's view, the primary objective of statistical modelling is the *reduction* of a large quantity of data to a few numerical values, in the form of parametric models. As Fisher emphasizes, however, this reduction should adequately summarize all the *relevant information* in the observed data. Intuitively, the simplest model in the context of statistical modelling is the one that (somehow) *compresses the systematic information in the data the most*, describing compactly as well as *reliably* the systematic statistical information exhibited by the stochastic phenomenon of interest. The principle of simplicity in this context pronounces a statistical model **simplest** if it narrows down the set of all possible models $\mathcal{P}$ to its smallest subset, say $\mathcal{P}_0 \subset \mathcal{P}$, in such a way as to ensure that all the systematic information in the data has been retained.

Simplicity in the context of a statistical model is defined in terms of two interrelated dimensions. The *first* dimension refers to the attribute known as *parsimony*: number of entities (parameters) used to specify a statistical model. The *second* dimension of simplicity concerns the informational content of a statistical model. Defining information as the *reduction in possible events*, we say that the model $\mathcal{P}_0$ is more informative than the model $\mathcal{P}_F$ if: $\mathcal{P}_0 \subset \mathcal{P}_F \subset \mathcal{P}$.

This agrees with Popper's definition of simplicity when he claims that the simpler the hypothesis the more falsifiable it is:

Simple statements, if knowledge is our object, are to be prized more highly than less simple ones because they tell us more; because their empirical content is greater; and because they are better testable. (See Popper, 1959, p. 142)

Every good scientific theory is a prohibition: it forbids certain things to happen. The more a theory forbids, the better it is. (See Popper, 1963, p. 36)

This is because the smaller the subset $\mathcal{P}_0$ the more testable and informative is the corresponding statistical model. However, as the above quotation from Fisher suggests, this 'compression of information' cannot be done in the abstract, but in conjunction with the *relevant information* in the observed data. The value of a model in learning about the phenomena of interest must be assessed on the basis of how adequately it summarizes this *relevant information*. That is, a simple model has high informational content when it provides an adequate summary of this information. A statistical model is said to be *adequate* if:

the probabilistic assumptions comprising the model are thoroughly tested and no departures are detected

The central thesis of this chapter is that the essence of the principle of simplicity (viewed in terms of parsimony/high informational content) is inextricably bound up with statistical adequacy, because if the 'compression' is achieved at the cost of ignoring systematic information in the data, it is no longer informative vis-à-vis the observable phenomenon of interest. This leads us to regard simplicity as best encapsulated by

Fisher's concept of a parametric statistical model. It is the combination of parsimony/informativeness in conjunction with statistical adequacy that gives rise to reliable and precise inferences. To be more specific, parametric models enjoy parsimony/high informational content, and at the same time they are amenable to assessing their statistical adequacy. Hence, we view parametric statistical modelling as the quintessential application of the principle of simplicity in scientific inference.

The notion of simplicity, as defined above, should not be confused with the notion of mathematical simplicity. Mathematical simplicity or elegance has nothing to do with the simplicity of a statistical model. Discussions in the literature about preferring a straight line to a curve in fitting polynomials to scatter plots constitute misleading oversimplifications of statistical modelling. Indeed, mathematical simplicity will confuse matters in the present context because it cannot be used to discriminate between the following simple parametric statistical model of the type in table 11.1:

$$X_t \sim N(\mu, \sigma^2), \quad t \in \mathbb{T}, \text{ and } (X_1, X_2, \ldots, X_n) \text{ is an IID sample} \quad (1)$$

where IID stands for 'Independent and Identically Distributed', and the non-parametric probability model of the type in table 11.2:

$$X_t \sim D(\mu, \sigma^2), \quad t \in \mathbb{T}, \text{ and } (X_1, X_2, \ldots, X_n) \text{ is an IID sample} \quad (2)$$

where $D(\mu, \sigma^2)$ is some unknown distribution with mean μ and variance σ^2. The two models are equivalent on parsimony grounds because they have the same number of unknown parameters. The only attribute that can help choose between these two models is informational content. On this basis (1) constitutes a proper subset of (2), and thus the former has higher informational content.

In summary, we argue that parametric models are simpler than non-parametric models because they are: (a) more informative, in the sense that $\mathcal{P}_\theta \subset \mathcal{P}_F$, and (b) more amenable to statistical adequacy assessment. In addition, parametric models are often more parsimonious than the corresponding non-parametric models.

4   Statistical adequacy versus robustness

4.1   *Statistical model specification*

The problem of statistical model specification can be crudely described as the choice of a subset $\mathcal{P}_*$ of the set of all possible distributions $\mathcal{P}$, underlying the observed data. In the case of parametric models, the choice $\mathcal{P}_\theta$ is made in terms of a family of distributions $f(\mathbf{x}; \theta)$, indexed by a vector of parameters $\theta \in \Theta$. On the other hand, in the case of non-parametric models, the choice of $\mathcal{P}_F$ is made indirectly via a number of features of a distribution such as the support set, the smoothness of the cdf or density functions and the existence of moments up to a certain order.

Assuming that the 'true' distribution is $F_0(x)$, statistical adequacy with respect to the distribution assumption amounts to ensuring that: $F_0(x) \in \mathcal{P}_*$, where $\mathcal{P}_*$ denotes the set of the prespecified distributions. At first sight it seems as though the non-parametric approach has a certain distinct advantage over the parametric in so far as the subset $\mathcal{P}_F$ postulated by non-parametric models is usually bigger than the one for parametric models $\mathcal{P}_\theta$: $\mathcal{P}_\theta \subset \mathcal{P}_F$, where $\mathcal{P}_F \subset \mathcal{P}$. Indeed, the great advantage often advanced in favour of nonparametric models is that the modeller does not commit herself to as many probabilistic assumptions and thus such models are less susceptible to the problem of statistical inadequacy. As argued by Scott (1992), the main objective of non-parametric inference is to:

sacrifice a small percentage of parametric optimality in order to achieve greater insensitivity to misspecification. (Ibid., p. 33)

A case can be made that this argument is not very convincing. The question of ensuring that the 'true' distribution $F_0(x)$ belongs to the postulated subset $\mathcal{P}_* \subset \mathcal{P}$ boils down to knowing how effective the narrowing down can be in the context of the two approaches. The use of an indirectly defined broad subset $\mathcal{P}_F$ is often viewed as an important safeguard against statistical inadequacy. Common sense suggests that the broader the subset the higher the likelihood of containing the 'appropriate' distribution. By the same token, the parametric approach is more susceptible to statistical inadequacy. The problem, however, is that this common-sense reasoning is flawed.

To begin with, the problem of statistical inadequacy has many dimensions, other than the distribution, such as assumptions concerning dependence and heterogeneity. For simple statistical models, departures from the *independence* and *identically distributed* assumptions are usually much more serious in their consequences for the reliability of inference than the distribution assumption. Hence, guarding against misspecification with regard to the distribution assumption, regardless of the other possible misspecifications, is not advisable (see Spanos, 1999, ch. 5). In addition, there is no reason to believe that a broader subset chosen on the basis of indirect distribution assumptions, such as the existence of moments, is more reliable than a narrower subset chosen felicitously. It all depends on the nature of the appropriate distribution and on how judicious the choice was. There are much more reliable ways to guard against misspecification than choosing a broad subset of $\mathcal{P}$.

Leaving the question of statistical adequacy aside by assuming that $F_0(x) \in \mathcal{P}_F$, there is the separate issue of the precision of inference based on $\mathcal{P}_F$. This is because the broader $\mathcal{P}_F$ is, the lower its informational content, and thus the less precise the inference based on it; the precision of inference is directly related to the informational content and inversely related to the broadness of the specified statistical model. The question which arises is whether there is an insurmountable trade-off between informational content and statistical adequacy. The answer given in this chapter is that there is no such dilemma in the context of parametric modelling. One should choose $\mathcal{P}_\theta$ to be as small as possible, but guard against misspecification by testing the assumptions of the model and establishing statistical adequacy before any inference is drawn. More specifically, guarding against misspecification is accomplished in three interrelated stages: (i) making judicious choices at the specification stage, (ii) testing the assumptions of the assumed model and (iii) respecifying (choose an alternative) when the model is rejected (see section 7).

4.2   Revisiting the non-parametric robustness argument

Let us consider the basic argument concerning *robustness* underlying non-parametric testing based on ranks:

The benefits include significant gains in power and efficiency when the error distribution has tails heavier than those of a normal distribution and superior robustness properties in general. (Hettmansperger and McKean, 1998, p. xiii)

That is, rank-based tests are more robust than the classic t-test because they require weaker assumptions for their validity, without having to pay a big price in terms of efficiency. For instance, it has been proved in this literature that the asymptotic efficiency of the Wilcoxon–Mann–Witney test relative to the t-test is (i) .864 for any continuous distribution which is symmetric around the median, (ii) .955 when the underlying distribution is Normal, (iii) 1.0 when the distribution is Uniform, and (iv) ∞ when the underlying distribution is Cauchy; see Hettmansperger (1984). The message from this literature is that the price one pays for not assuming Normality is very small when this assumption is true, but the benefits are potentially substantial when Normality is false.

Let us have a closer look at this argument. Admittedly, this is a powerful argument against the statistical modelling practice of assuming that the Normal distribution provides a universal density, whatever the structure of the observed data (see Thompson and Tapia, 1991, p. 24), but it's a very weak argument against thoughtful parametric modelling where the Normal is one of many available distributions one can choose from. To begin with, the above efficiency comparisons are asymptotic and can be misleading for small sample sizes. More importantly, the comparison between the Normal, the Uniform and the Cauchy distributions is misleading because the t-test was never meant to be applied to the latter cases. In the case of the Uniform distribution there is an analogous test concerning a shift of its mean, which, of course, does not coincide with the t-test. In the case of the Cauchy distribution the t-test is utterly inappropriate because the latter is defined in terms of the first two moments, but it's well known that the Cauchy distribution has no moments! Moreover, it's not at all obvious why one would choose to be agnostic about the underlying distribution in an attempt to reap the potential 'benefits' of the above robustness. As shown in Spanos (1999, ch. 5), distinguishing between a random sample from a Normal, a Uniform and a Cauchy distribution can be effectively done using a simple t-plot. What is more, it is well known that the t-test is indeed robust to certain departures from Normality; see Lehmann (1959). A more valuable robustness would have been with respect to the other two assumptions underlying both the t-test and the non-parametric tests based on ranks: independent and identically distributed (IID) rv's. The implications of non-Normality for the reliability of inference based on any of these tests pale in comparison to the implications of departures from the IID assumptions. Moreover, one can make a case that the t-test is more robust to certain departures from IID than the non-parametric tests.

In view of these comments, the robustness argument seems to be more relevant as a warning to a modeller who naively assumes that all data are Normally distributed, rather than as relevant advice to a thoughtful modeller prepared to entertain several (known) distributions, and test their appropriateness before any inference is drawn. It seems so much easier and more practical to test the Normality assumption using the observed data, and proceed according to whether the assumption is accepted or rejected, rather than speculate on possible departures from non-Normality without looking at the observed data, and then take decisions on the basis of one's speculation.

In conclusion, the early literature on robustness was motivated by the undue reliance of the statistical inference literature on the assumption of Normality. A prime example of this attitude is the case of the robustness of estimators and test statistics to 'outliers'. Ignoring the case where a data point has been typed incorrectly, an outlier is an unusual observation considered to be unlikely in view of a certain distribution. This, however, begs the question of what constitutes systematic information? A certain observation might be viewed as an outlier when the assumed distribution is Normal but perfectly acceptable if the assumed distribution is Student's t or Cauchy! If, indeed, the appropriate distribution is the Student's, and the modeller chooses an estimator which is robust to observations in the extreme tails, the modeller ignores the most crucial information in the sample realization; the chosen estimator is insensitive to relevant systematic information, not to potential misspecification. The same argument applies to estimators which are considered as superior because they are robust to certain forms of asymmetry of the underlying distribution. If the true distribution is non-Normal, say Beta, this constitutes important relevant information and the modeller should take it into consideration rather than devise estimators which ignore it. Pushing the notion of robustness to its extremes, the 'best' robust estimator will be the one which is completely oblivious to all systematic information in the data!

4.2.1 Is there any comfort in lack of specific knowledge? The above discussion can be extended to consider an argument similar in spirit to the one put forward by the non-parametric literature based on ranks. In an attempt to render the inference robust to certain departures, a modeller might leave the distribution assumption unspecified. For instance, instead of $X_t \sim N(\mu, \sigma^2)$, $t \in \mathbb{T}$, one assumes that $X_t \sim D(\mu, \sigma^2)$, $t \in \mathbb{T}$, where the distribution $D(.)$ is left unspecified. What possible advantages might the latter specification have over the former?

The conventional wisdom would have us believe that the latter is preferable because it's less susceptible to *statistical inadequacy* and the inference is more general; inference is derived without assuming Normality. A closer look, however, reveals that both claims of generality and robustness are questionable. The reason is that the well-known statistical inference results relating to optimality properties of moment estimators, t-tests, F-tests and associated confidence intervals, will be forgone. Instead, the modeller has to resort to asymptotic results which by definition will be approximations to the finite sample results; using the Normal instead of the Student's t for testing hypotheses about μ and the chi-square (χ^2) instead of the F distribution for hypotheses about σ^2. Not surprisingly, how good the approximations are will depend crucially on how close to Normality the 'true' distribution $D(\mu, \sigma^2)$ happened to be. For instance, if the 'true' distribution is a highly skewed Beta, the asymptotic results are likely to be much less reliable than in the case where the distribution is a symmetric Beta. Moreover, any testing concerning σ^2 will involve the estimation of the fourth central moment (μ_4) of the unknown distribution because:

$$\sqrt{n}(\hat{\sigma}^2 - \sigma^2) \underset{\alpha}{\sim} N(0, \mu_4 - \sigma^4) \text{ instead of } \sqrt{n}(\hat{\sigma}^2 - \sigma^2) \underset{\alpha}{\sim} N(0, 3\sigma^4);$$

the latter holds under Normality. This in turn will induce further noise into the approximate results via the estimated fourth moment, rendering the inference even less precise.

In addition to these problems, the question that naturally arises is why focus on the first two moments of an unknown distribution? We consider the *existence* (or otherwise) of any **moments** as an indirect *distribution assumption* in the sense that the existence of the moments depends exclusively on the 'thickness' of the tails of the density function and its *support*. In relation to any bounded *support set* $\mathbb{R}_X = [a, b]$, $a < b < \infty$, a and b being real numbers, all moments exist irrespective of the nature of $F(x)$; see Shiryayev (1984). The question is under what circumstances do the moments determine the distribution uniquely? The crude answer is that, in general, no distribution is determined by a finite number of moments, and unless we concentrate on distributions with bounded support, moments do not determine distributions uniquely even if we (somehow) use an *infinite* number of them (see Spanos, 1999, ch. 3). The usefulness of parametric models becomes apparent when one realizes that in cases where the modeller is prepared to limit himself to a specific class of parametric distributions, the problem of moments becomes trivial. For example, in the case of the Pearson family we require at most four moments to determine the particular distribution. If the modeller restricts this family further and is prepared to assume Normality, then the first two moments will suffice. Hence, assuming $X_t \sim D(\mu, \sigma^2)$, potentially systematic information is likely to be ignored unless the true distribution is characterized by its first two moments.

This discussion brings us full circle. In an attempt to ensure less susceptibility to statistical inadequacy with respect to the distribution assumption, the modeller is likely to end up with a less precise (and less incisive) inference, with the inaccuracy being a function of the departure of the 'true' distribution from the Normal. How does one evaluate this inaccuracy? The parametric modelling approach suggests testing the Normality assumption using the observed data! That is, by testing Normality the modeller, at the very least, will learn something about the phenomenon of interest; this is in the spirit of 'learning from error' (see Mayo, 1996). If Normality is not rejected, the modeller can proceed to use precise and incisive inference. If Normality is rejected, the modeller can get an idea about the precision of the asymptotic results by investigating the rejection of Normality further. For instance, if the rejection of Normality is due to skewness the asymptotic results are likely to be inaccurate for moderate sample sizes. In the case where the modeller rejects the Normality assumption, the parametric way to proceed is to postulate another, hopefully more appropriate distribution.

In conclusion, in the context of statistical modelling, vague assumptions give rise to vague inferences, and there is no comfort in ignorance.

4.2.2 Parametric robustness? It is very important to note that the more recent literature on robust statistics based on *influence functions* is at great pains to distance itself from non-parametric modelling. Hampel et al. (1986) argued:

> Robust statistics is often confused with, or at least located close to nonparametric statistics, although it has nothing to do with it directly. The theories of robustness consider neighborhoods of parametric models and thus clearly belong to parametric statistics. Even if the term is used in a very vague sense, robust statistics considers the effects of only approximate fulfillment of assumptions, while nonparametric statistics makes rather weak but nevertheless strict assumptions (such as continuity of distribution or independence). (Ibid., p. 9)

This notion of parametric robustness is of great value in assessing the sensitivity of inference to certain forms of departures from the underlying assumptions in the context of parametric modelling.

4.3   Parametric models and misspecification testing

In parametric statistical modelling one of the objectives is to be very specific about the probabilistic assumptions comprising the statistical model. For example, in the case of the simple Normal model the assumptions underlying the process $\{X_t\}_{t\in\mathbb{T}}$ are:

[1] $X_t \sim N(\mu, \sigma^2)$, $t \in \mathbb{T}$,
[2] $\{X_t\}_{t\in\mathbb{T}}$ is 't-independent',   (3)
[3] $\{X_t\}_{t\in\mathbb{T}}$ is 't-homogeneous'.

Having specified the underlying assumptions explicitly, the modeller should proceed to assess their validity before the model is used to draw any inferences. As argued in section 5, in the context of parametric statistical modelling one can assess the adequacy of the statistical model at two different stages. At the *specification stage*, the relevant probabilistic assumptions can be assessed using a variety of graphical techniques and other forms of preliminary data analysis. At the *misspecification testing* stage, after the model has been estimated, the model assumptions can be assessed using formal tests (see Spanos, 1999).

As argued in Spanos (1998, 1999) misspecification testing is very different in nature from the traditional Neyman–Pearson testing. The difference arises primarily from the fact that the latter constitutes 'testing within', and the former 'testing outside', the boundaries of the postulated statistical model. As a result the Neyman–Pearson testing assumes the postulated model $(\mathcal{P}_\theta)$ is statistically adequate and the decision boils down to choosing one of the two subsets:

$$H_0 : \mathcal{P}_\theta(\theta_0) \text{ and } H_1 : \mathcal{P}_\theta(\theta_1),$$

where the two hypotheses constitute a partition of $\mathcal{P}_\theta$, i.e.

$$\mathcal{P}_\theta(\theta_0) \cap \mathcal{P}_\theta(\theta_1) = \emptyset, \mathcal{P}_\theta(\theta_0) \cup \mathcal{P}_\theta(\theta_1) = \mathcal{P}_\theta.$$

In contrast, in misspecification testing the two hypotheses take the form:

$$H_0 : \mathcal{P}_\theta \text{ and } H_1 : \mathcal{P} - \mathcal{P}_\theta,$$

constituting a partition of $\mathcal{P}$. As a consequence, rejecting $\mathcal{P}_\theta$ does not entitle the modeller to adopt any particular alternative $\mathcal{P}_1 \in (\mathcal{P} - \mathcal{P}_\theta)$ without further investigation. Despite the fact that particular misspecification tests will have maximum power against a certain specific alternative, say $\mathcal{P}_1$, the maintained alternative set $(\mathcal{P} - \mathcal{P}_\theta)$ is usually much broader.

Because of the importance of misspecification testing in parametric inference, it is imperative to address the allegation that the modeller should be economical with the number of misspecification tests because otherwise (a) the modeller abuses the data (somehow) and (b) the modeller cannot keep track of the overall significance level. The first charge is often based on assuming that the modeller loses certain degrees of freedom every time a misspecification test is applied, although critics fail to indicate just why this is being alleged. The fact of the matter is that the probabilistic structure of the data, the assessment of which constitutes the primary objective, remains unchanged however many misspecification tests are applied. The goal is to thoroughly probe in directions of potential misspecification using tests which are effective in detecting such departures. The second charge relating to the overall significance level is misplaced because the type I and type II errors should be handled differently in the context of misspecification testing; see Spanos (1999, 2000) for further discussion.

It follows from the above discussion that one cannot even begin to consider statistical adequacy unless (i) the assumptions of the model are explicitly stated and (ii) their validity ascertained. As will be argued in the next subsection, non-parametric models fail to meet either of these conditions.

4.4   *Non-parametric models and their assumptions*

Let us consider the nature of the assumptions underlying the non-parametric models as they relate to assessing statistical adequacy. In the case of non-parametric inference based on ranks we argued above that the emphasis is not on statistical adequacy but on robustness with respect to certain departures from the Normality assumption. Indeed, the idea of testing the Normality or the IID assumptions directly runs contrary to the spirit of this approach. We know, however, that if the IID assumptions are invalid the whole approach will give rise to very misleading results because it utilizes these assumptions extensively in the derivation of the sampling distributions of the various rank statistics.

In view of the current popularity of kernel-smoothing techniques it is interesting to consider the assumptions underlying their statistical models. As in the case of the approach based on ranks, the statistical models underlying the kernel-smoothing approach retain the Random Sample assumption as shown in table 11.3 (see Thompson and Tapia, 1991, p. 46). However, the probability model assumption (a) is often unrealistic (it does not hold for the Normal, Student's t and other distributions) and assumptions (b) and (c) are unverifiable. Moreover, there is no way to assess the adequacy of the above model using the observed data. Nevertheless, this constitutes a typical example of non-parametric statistical models.

Rather than achieving the desired 'insensitivity to misspecification', it is apparent from the above discussion that the inference based on non-parametric models is often insensitive to *statistical information* and not just to misspecification. When the modeller assumes Normality but the data in question reject it as inappropriate, the modeller has *learned something* which can be exploited in respecifying the statistical model (see section 7). Being oblivious to the presence of non-Normality amounts to ignoring systematic information.

5   Precision of inference

The truism 'vague assumptions lead to vague conclusions', although crude, is particularly apt in the case of statistical modelling. Non-parametric models tend to be less specific than parametric models and as a result non-parametric inference tends to be less precise. This is because the other side of simplicity, defined in terms of parsimony/informational

Table 11.3. *A non-parametric statistical model for smoothing*

[i]	Probability model:	$F(x) \in \mathcal{P}_F \subset \mathcal{P}$,
	where $\mathcal{P}_F =$	$\{f(x) : f(x) \in \mathcal{P}\}$, and $f(x)$ has the properties:
		(a) $f(x)$ has support $[a, b]$, $a < b < \infty$,
		(b) $f(x)$ is bounded on $[a, b]$, $a \in \mathbb{R}$, $b \in \mathbb{R}$,
		(c) $f(x)$ has continuous derivatives of up to order 3, excluding the endpoints,
[ii]	Sampling model:	$\mathbf{X} := (X_1, X_2, \ldots, X_n)$ is a Random Sample.

content, is *the precision of statistical inference*. In general, given statistical adequacy, the smaller the subset $\mathcal{P}_0$ the more precise the statistical inference results. Hence, parametric models give rise to more precise and incisive statistical inference. Indirect distribution assumptions in terms of the existence of moments restrictions compel the modeller to use **inequalities**, which are often *very* crude compared with what one can get when postulating a particular distribution. The following example gives some idea of the crudeness of such inequalities when compared with specific distribution assumptions.

Example 1 Consider the case where $X \sim N(0, 1)$. The actual probability for the event: $|X| \geq c > 0$ is:

$$\mathbb{P}(\mid X \mid \geq c) \leq \frac{\left(\sqrt{\frac{2}{\pi}}\right) \exp\left(-\frac{c^2}{2}\right)}{c}.$$

For a value, say $c = 2$, $\mathbb{P}(\mid X \mid \geq c) = .054$. On the other hand, the upper bound given by the Chebyshev inequality is: $\mathbb{P}(\mid X \mid \geq 2) \leq .25$, which amounts to almost a fivefold worsening. Things are even worse in the case of non-symmetric distributions (see Spanos, 1999).

What is very important for our purposes is that as the distribution assumption becomes more specific by excluding more events, the inference gets more precise. Consider the example where we are prepared to postulate the existence of *additional higher moments*.

Example 2 Let $\{X_n\}_{n=1}^{\infty} := \{X_1, X_2, \ldots, X_n \ldots\}$ be a sequence of Independent and Identically Bernoulli distributed (IID) r.v.'s. It can be shown that: $S_n := \sum_{k=1}^{n} X_k \sim \text{Bi}(n\theta, n\theta(1 - \theta))$. Using Chebyshev's inequality (which assumes the existence of the moments up to the 2nd order) yields:

$$\mathbb{P}\left(\mid n^{-1}S_n - \theta \mid > \varepsilon\right) \le \frac{\theta(1-\theta)}{n\varepsilon^2}.$$

On the other hand, if we assume the existence of the moments up to order 4, we can use Markov's inequality which yields: $\mathbb{P}\left(\mid Y - E(Y) \mid^4 > \varepsilon\right) \le \frac{E\left(\mid Y - E(Y) \mid^4\right)}{\varepsilon^4}$. Noting that $E\left(\mid n^{-1}S_n - \theta \mid^4\right)$ $= n\theta[1 + 3\theta(1-\theta)(n-2)]$ this yields:

$$\mathbb{P}\left(\mid n^{-1}S_n - \theta \mid > \varepsilon\right) \le \frac{3}{(16)n^2\varepsilon^4}.$$

As can be seen, the estimate of the upper bound given by Markov's inequality converges much faster because it utilizes more information in relation to the existence of moments.

These bounds can be improved even further if the modeller is prepared to make additional *smoothness* assumptions such as unimodality (see Spanos, 1999).

5.1   *Goodness of fit versus statistical adequacy*

In the context of parametric inference the emphasis is on making the statistical model as parsimonious as possible and at the same time increasing its informational content as much as possible by making the subset $\mathcal{P}_\theta$ as small as possible using as many specific probabilistic assumptions as necessary. Statistical adequacy plays a very important role in this context because the informational content is assessed relative to the information contained in the observed data. The idea is that a statistically adequate and parsimonious estimated model will give rise to reliable and precise inferences.

In contrast, the emphasis in non-parametric modelling is to make as few assumptions as possible in order to increase the potential robustness of the inference to possible misspecifications. This difference in emphasis has a number of consequences which are relevant for our purposes. First, a non-parametric model $(\mathcal{P}_F)$ is usually broader than a parametric model $(\mathcal{P}_\theta)$ and thus less informative. Second, misspecification testing and statistical adequacy have no role to play in the context of non-parametric modelling. Hence, despite forsaking precision in an attempt to increase potential robustness, there is no guarantee that the inference based on such broader models is reliable. How does a non-parametric modeller justify the approach? The short answer is that non-parametric modelling tends to emphasize 'goodness of fit' instead of statistical adequacy:

Upon satisfaction with the fit, rank-based inferential procedures can be used to conduct the statistical analysis. (Hettmansperger and McKean, 1998, p. xiii)

It is well known, however, that goodness of fit does not attest to the reliability or the precision of inference. Indeed, achieving an excellent fit is very easy if one is willing to forsake the informational content of the model. In *semi-non-parametric* modelling (see Gallant, 1987) one can easily increase the goodness of fit by increasing the number of parameters of the postulated model in order to make it more inclusive. For example, a number of modelling strategies based on curve fitting, such as neural networks, Bernstein and Chebyshev polynomials and spline polynomials (see Wahba, 1990), can achieve very impressive 'goodness of fit', but often have very limited informational content; this is primarily the reason why such models do so poorly in terms of their post-sample predictive ability. A trivial example of this is when a sample realization of n observations $(x_1, x_2, \ldots, x_n)$ is modelled by a polynomial of degree $(n - 1)$ in the index variable:

$$x_t = \alpha_0 + \sum_{k=1}^{n-1} \alpha_k t^k, \, t = 1, 2, \ldots, n,$$

giving rise to a 'perfect fit' but the model has no informational content!

The conclusion is that if the aim of statistical modelling is to reach reliable and precise inferences, 'goodness of fit' is no substitute for statistical adequacy. The latter can only be established by thorough probing in directions with respect to which the postulated model might be in error; this is in the spirit of the *notion of severity* proposed by Mayo (1996). Misspecification testing enables us to detect such errors (or departures) and thus learn something about the underlying phenomenon of interest.

5.2 Whither non-parametric models?

The question that naturally arises at this stage is whether there is a role for non-parametric inference in statistical modelling. The argument in this chapter is that non-parametric models are not as appropriate for empirical modelling purposes as parametric models. Does this mean that non-parametric models have no role to play in statistical modelling? The answer is certainly not! Non-parametric inference procedures have an important role to play in empirical modelling at the *preliminary data analysis* as well as at the *misspecification testing* stages of parametric modelling.

The recently proposed smoothing techniques, especially kernel smoothing (see Silverman, 1986; Härdle, 1990; Scott, 1992), provide very powerful tools for preliminary data analysis. These techniques can be utilized to enable the modeller to make informed decisions in choosing parametric statistical models. For example, kernel smoothing in estimating density functions can be effectively used to guide the decision of a modeller on whether a certain distribution assumption is appropriate or not; see Spanos (1999, ch. 6), for an extensive discussion and several examples.

In the context of misspecification testing the modeller is faced with hypotheses of the form:

$$H_0 : \mathcal{P}_\theta \text{ and } H_1 : \mathcal{P} - \mathcal{P}_\theta,$$

where $(\mathcal{P} - \mathcal{P}_\theta)$ comprises a very large number of possible alternative models, and often a non-parametric form of $(\mathcal{P} - \mathcal{P}_\theta)$ can be more inclusive, giving rise to misspecification tests with broader probativeness. Moreover, there are very good statistical reasons to combine parametric and non-parametric misspecification tests because (a) their validity depends on different probabilistic assumptions and (b) their probing ability is often with respect to different directions of departure (often being complimentary). As a result of (a)-(b), one can argue that (c) the modeller is able to guard against circularity in misspecification testing; see Spanos (2000).

6   Non-parametric correlation analysis

It is often argued that instead of using parametric models which are liable to statistical inadequacy, we should conduct the empirical analysis using *descriptive statistics*, such as the sample *correlations* among the variables of interest. The implicit presupposition is that a descriptive correlation analysis is less susceptible to potential misspecifications (see *inter alia* Friedman and Schwartz, 1963). However, if the modeller using correlation analysis wants to derive any conclusions concerning the economy, this has to be viewed in the context of non-parametric inference. As such, correlation analysis involves a number of (implicit) probabilistic assumptions which renders it as liable to statistical inadequacy as any other form of statistical inference.

Commencing with a vector stochastic process $\{\mathbf{Z}_t, \ t \in \mathbb{T}\}$, $\mathbf{Z}_t : m \times 1$, (contemporaneous) correlation analysis involves three implicit probabilistic assumptions:

(i) the process $\{\mathbf{Z}_t, \ t \in \mathbb{T}\}$, has moments up to order 4, i.e.

$$E(|Z_{it}|^4) < \infty, \ E(|Z_{it}Z_{jt}|) < \infty, \ E(|Z_{it}Z_{jt}Z_{kt}|) < \infty, \tag{4}$$
$$E(|Z_{it}Z_{jt}Z_{kt}Z_{\ell t}|) < \infty \text{ for all } i, j, k, \ell = 1, 2, \ldots, m,$$

(ii) the process $\{\mathbf{Z}_t, \ t \in \mathbb{T}\}$, is t-uncorrelated, and
(iii) the process $\{\mathbf{Z}_t, \ t \in \mathbb{T}\}$, is t-homogeneous of order 2.

Unless these assumptions are valid, the estimated correlations:

$$\hat{\rho}_{ij} = \frac{\sum_{t=1}^{T}(z_{it} - \bar{z}_i)(z_{jt} - \bar{z}_j)}{\sqrt{\left(\sum_{t=1}^{T}(z_{it} - \bar{z}_i)^2\right)\left(\sum_{t=1}^{T}(z_{jt} - \bar{z}_j)^2\right)}},$$

$$z_i = \frac{1}{T}\sum_{t=1}^{T} z_{it}, \quad i,j = 1,\ldots,m,$$

(5)

will not be good estimators of $\rho_{ij} := Corr(Z_{it}, Z_{jt})$, $i,j = 1,\ldots,m$. This is particularly relevant in the case of time-series data which usually exhibit trending means $(E(Z_{it}) = \mu_i(t))$ as well as temporal dependence. Moreover, several speculative price time-series data exhibit enough leptokurtosis to render assumption (i) suspect. This implies that $\hat{\rho}_{ij}$ will be a very bad estimator of ρ_{ij}.

It is true that when one estimates the correlation matrix of the vector time series $\{\mathbf{Z}_t, \ t \in \mathbb{T}\}$, using (5), it is quite likely that the estimates will be close to one. The problem, however, is that the above estimator $\hat{\rho}_{ij}$ is not a good estimator of $\rho_{ij} := Corr(Z_{it}, Z_{jt})$ in most cases in practice because the (implicit) assumptions – that the data can be thought of as realizations of (temporally) Independent and Identically Distributed (IID) random variables – are usually invalid. Usually, time-series data exhibit trending means $(E(Z_{it}) = \mu_i(t))$ as well as temporal dependence. This implies that, in general, $\hat{\rho}_{ij}$ will be a bad estimator of ρ_{ij}.

Example Consider the annual USA series for the period 1947–1992 on y_t : real consumers expenditure, x_{1t} : real personal disposable income, x_{2t} : price level. In table 11.4, we present the sample correlations under three different scenarios; scenario 1 assumes IID, scenario 2 assumes Independence but allows for polynomial trends (third degree) in the mean and scenario 3 allows for both polynomial trends and Markov (two lags) dependence. As we can see, the sample correlations change dramatically from the first to the second scenario, with $\widehat{Corr}(y_t, x_{2t})$ and $\widehat{Corr}(x_{1t}, x_{2t})$ changing signs! These changes in sign and magnitude are typical of most naive correlations among time series data, and they are symptomatic of the 'non-sense correlations' problem first raised by Yule (1926).

The above empirical exercise can be profitably embedded into a parametric model, the linear regression model of the form:

$$y_t = \beta_0 + \beta_1 x_{1t} + \beta_2 x_{2t} + u_t, \ t \in \mathbb{T},$$

Table 11.4. *Sample correlation coefficients*

IID	Independence but non-ID	Markov and non-ID
$\widehat{Corr}\,(y_t, x_{1t}) = .999$	$\widehat{Corr}\,(y_t, x_{1t}) = .877$	$\widehat{Corr}\,(y_t, x_{1t}) = .654$
$\widehat{Corr}\,(y_t, x_{2t}) = .960$	$\widehat{Corr}\,(y_t, x_{2t}) = -.594$	$\widehat{Corr}\,(yt, x_{2t}) = -.307$
$\widehat{Corr}\,(x_{1t}, x_{2t}) = .953$	$\widehat{Corr}(x_{1t}, x_{2t}) = -.393$	$\widehat{Corr}(x_{1t}, x_{2t}) = -.124$

where the coefficients (β_1, β_2) denote the partial correlations, which can easily be transformed into simple correlations. Estimating this model using the above data yielded:

$$y_t = 46.015 + 0.835x_{1t} + 2.126x_{2t} + \hat{u}_t \ , R^2 = .999, T = 45.$$
$$\quad\;\;(13.993)\quad\;(.016)\quad\quad(.437)\quad\;\;(26.959)$$

As shown in table 11.5 below, the linear regression model is defined in terms of the probabilistic assumptions: [1] Normality, [2] Linearity, [3] Homoskedasticity, [4] t-homogeneity of the parameters and [5] t-independence. One can show that the above estimated model is misspecified because assumptions [2]–[5] are rejected by the data; see Spanos (1989). This renders any inference using the usual t-test of significance or/and the R^2 unreliable. Note that in terms of the R^2, the goodness of fit of the above estimated model is clearly impressive but its reliability is close to zero! Indeed, one can explain the apparent 'fit' in terms of erroneously 'inflated' second moments due to serious misspecifications due to heterogeneity and dependence as demonstrated above. The t-ratios and R^2 involve the quantities: $\sum_{t=1}^{T}(x_{1t} - \bar{x}_1)^2$, $\sum_{t=1}^{T}(x_{2t} - \bar{x}_2)^2$, $\sum_{t=1}^{T}(y_t - \bar{y})^2$, respectively. In cases where the time series $\{(y_t, x_{1t}, x_{2t}), t = 1, 2, \ldots, T\}$ exhibit trending means, these quantities will be artificially inflated, giving rise to misleading conclusions. In this case the presence of trending means will have a predictable effect on $\hat{\rho}_{ij}$: it will *overestimate* the true correlation substantially, because the estimator takes deviations from a constant mean $(\sum_{t=1}^{T}(z_{it} - \bar{z}_i)^2$ and not $\sum_{t=1}^{T}(z_{it} - \hat{\mu}_i(t))^2)$, and thus artificially inflates the variation. In the case of the above annual USA series:

$$\sum_{t=1}^{T}(y_t - \bar{y})^2 = 26334000, \qquad \sum_{t=1}^{T}(y_t - \hat{\mu}_1^3(t))^2 = 1093100,$$

$$\sum_{t=1}^{T}(x_{1t} - \bar{x}_1)^2 = 31762000, \qquad \sum_{t=1}^{T}(x_{1t} - \hat{\mu}_2^3(t))^2 = 1561200,$$

$$\sum_{t=1}^{T}(x_{2t} - \bar{x}_2)^2 = 41694, \qquad \sum_{t=1}^{T}(x_{2t} - \hat{\mu}_3^3(t))^2 = 328.88,$$

where $\hat{\mu}_i^3(t)$, $i = 1, 2, 3$ denote third-degree polynomials in t. As we can see, the artificial inflating factor in the variation of the series (y_t, x_{1t}) is over 20 and that of x_{2t} is over 126!

7   The Probabilistic Reduction approach

7.1   The Probabilistic Reduction

The various stages of the Probabilistic Reduction (PR) approach from putting forward a statistical model to drawing inferences are summarized below. The proposed sequence of modelling stages provides an overarching framework designed to enhance the reliability and precision of parametric statistical inference (see Spanos, 1986, 1989, 1995 for an extensive discussion).

(1) Specification   ⎫
(2) Estimation   ⎪
(3) Misspecification ⎬ Statistically adequate model
(4) Respecification   ⎭
(5) Testing, confidence regions
(6) Policy, Prediction

To begin with, the PR approach unifies a number of seemingly disparate procedures (specification, misspecification, respecification, identification) in a consistent and coherent way. Moreover, it provides economy of thought in the modelling process by proposing the basic taxonomy of probabilistic assumptions; all statistical models can be viewed as constructions based on three basic types of assumptions.

The PR can, in one sense, be seen as an operationalization of Fisher's view of statistics as the *reduction* of a large quantity of data to a few numerical values (parameters); 'a reduction which adequately summarizes all the *relevant information* in the original data' (Fisher, 1925, pp. 5–6); see Spanos (1989). Interestingly, the Probabilistic Reduction can also be seen as a recasting of the de Finetti-type representation theorems in the context of the frequentist (non-Bayesian) approach to statistical modelling. In the de Finetti-type representation theorems (see de Finetti, 1937), the modeller is asked to formulate degrees of belief with respect to the appropriate distribution assumption based on 'what he believes the empirical distribution function would look like for a large sample' (Bernardo and Smith, 1994, p. 179). It is argued below that this can be given an operational meaning using graphical techniques and preliminary data analysis in the context of the frequentist approach.

The de Finetti representation theorem in the case of a set of observable vectors $(\mathbf{Z}_1, \mathbf{Z}_2, \ldots, \mathbf{Z}_T)$ takes the form (see Bernardo and Smith, 1994):

$$D(\mathbf{Z}_1, \mathbf{Z}_2, \ldots, \mathbf{Z}_T) = \int_{\theta \in \Theta} \prod_{k=1}^{n} \mathbf{F}(x_k; \theta) d\mathbb{Q}(\theta). \tag{7}$$

De Finetti interpreted this representation as a way to *reduce* the objective probability and the concept of IID to that of the subjective probability and the concept of exchangeability. In this chapter we prefer to turn the argument on its head and view the representation as a way to operationalize the notion of exchangeability by relating it to that of an IID sample. This is because subjective exchangeability is not a testable assumption but IID is. Continuing this line of reasoning, we proceed to recast this representation theorem in the context of the classical approach by viewing it as a *reduction of the joint distribution of the observables* based on probabilistic assumptions. The IID assumptions constitute only a very restricted case of a more general reduction approach.

Let all the observable r.v's involved in a statistical model be denoted by $\mathbf{Z}_t$ (an $m \times 1$ vector). The joint distribution of $\mathbf{Z}_t$ for the whole of the sample period, i.e.

$$D(\mathbf{Z}_1, \mathbf{Z}_2, \ldots, \mathbf{Z}_T; \phi),$$

is called the *Haavelmo distribution*. This distribution demarcates the relevant information because it provides the most general 'description' of the data information. It has theoretical value only as a reference point for all three facets of modelling.

The reduction from the Haavelmo distribution to the statistical model takes the form of imposing several reduction assumptions on the stochastic process $\{\mathbf{Z}_t, \ t \in \mathbb{T}\}$. The reduction (probabilistic) assumptions are classified into the three broad categories (see Spanos, 1999):

(D) **Distribution**,   (M) **Dependence**,   (H) **Heterogeneity**.

To make the discussion more specific, let us consider the Probabilistic Reduction in the case of the Normal/Linear Regression model as specified in table 11.5. The vector of observables in this case is: $\mathbf{Z}_t := (y_t X_t)^\top$, and the reduction assumptions about $\{\mathbf{Z}_t, \ t \in \mathbb{T}\}$ are:

(D) **Normal**,   (M) **Independence**,   (H) **Identically Distributed**.

In order to have a clear view of the target at the outset we note that the reduction will take the form of:

$$D(\mathbf{Z}_1, \mathbf{Z}_2, \ldots, \mathbf{Z}_T; \phi) \overset{\text{NIID}}{\rightsquigarrow} \prod_{t=1}^{T} D(y_t \mid x_t; \theta), \ (x_t, y_t) \in \mathbb{R}_X \times \mathbb{R}_Y. \tag{8}$$

The details of this reduction are of interest because they bring out the role of each of the reduction assumptions and the interrelationship among the model assumptions. Let us consider the reduction by imposing these assumptions sequentially for all $(x_t, y_t) \in \mathbb{R}_X \times \mathbb{R}_Y$:

$$D(\mathbf{Z}_1, \mathbf{Z}_2, \ldots, \mathbf{Z}_T; \phi) \overset{1}{=} \prod_{t=1}^{T} D_t(\mathbf{Z}_t; \varphi_t) \overset{\text{IID}}{=} \prod_{t=1}^{T} D(\mathbf{Z}_t; \varphi) \overset{\text{IID}}{=} \prod_{t=1}^{T}$$

$$D(y_t \mid X_t; \varphi_1) \cdot D(X_t; \varphi_2). \tag{9}$$

The first equality follows after imposing the assumption of temporal independence and the second by imposing, in addition, the identically distributed assumption. The last equality involves no assumptions, just a decomposition of a joint into a marginal and a set of conditional density functions. In order to be able to disregard the marginal distribution $D(X_t; \varphi_2)$ and concentrate exclusively on $\prod_{t=1}^{T} D(y_t \mid x_t; \theta)$, we need the reduction assumption of Normality for $\{\mathbf{Z}_t, \ t \in \mathbb{T}\}$. The above reduction enables the modeller to view the Normal/Linear Regression model as specified by assumptions [1]–[5] (see table 11.5) in a broader framework which will be of considerable value in all three facets of modelling: specification, misspecification and respecification.

7.2   Reduction versus model assumptions

Having specified the Normal/Linear Regression model in terms of assumptions [1]–[5], it is imperative to draw a clear distinction between these *model assumptions* and the *reduction assumptions*. As far as the specification, the statistical adequacy and statistical inference are concerned the only relevant assumptions are the model assumptions. For purposes of misspecification analysis and respecification, however, it is of paramount importance to know the relationship between the model assumptions and the reduction assumptions.

In the case of the Normal/Linear Regression model, the two sets of assumptions are related as shown in table 11.6. This relationship suggests that the Normality of the process $\{\mathbf{Z}_t, \ t \in \mathbb{T}\}$ yields the parameterization of interest $\theta := (\beta_0, \beta_1, \sigma^2)$, ensures the weak exogeneity of X_t with respect to θ, yields the Normality of $D(y_t \mid X_t; \theta)$, the linearity of $E(y_t \mid X_t = x_t)$ and the homoskedasticity of $Var(y_t \mid X_t = x_t)$. Similarly, the t-independence of the process $\{\mathbf{Z}_t, \ t \in \mathbb{T}\}$ ensures that the sample $(y_1, y_2, \ldots, y_T)$ is t-independent. Lastly, the homogeneity of the process $\{\mathbf{Z}_t, \ t \in \mathbb{T}\}$ ensures that the parameters $\theta := (\beta_0, \beta_1, \sigma^2)$ are not changing with t.

Table 11.5. *The Probabilistic Reduction approach specification: the Normal/Linear Regression model*

$$y_t = \beta_0 + \beta_1 x_t + u_t, \, t \in \mathbb{T}.$$

[1] $D(y_t|x_t; \theta)$ is Normal,
[2] $E(y_t|X_t = x_t) = \beta_0 + \beta_1 x_t$ is linear in x_t,
[3] $Var(y_t|X_t = x_t) = \sigma^2$ is homoskedastic (free of x_t),
[4] The parameters $\theta := (\beta_0, \beta_1, \sigma^2)$ are t-invariant,
[5] $(y_1, y_2, \ldots, y_T)$ is a t-independent sample sequentially drawn from $D(y_t|x_t; \theta), \, t = 1, \ldots, T.$

Table 11.6. *Reduction versus model assumptions*

Reduction		Statistical model
$\{\mathbf{Z}_t, t \in \mathbb{T}\}$		$\{(y_t|X_t = x_t), t \in \mathbb{T}\}$
N	$\Rightarrow$	[1],[2],[3]
I	$\Rightarrow$	[5]
ID	$\Rightarrow$	[4]

The relationship between reduction and model assumptions is of foremost importance for several reasons. At the specification stage we can use the relationship between the reduction and model assumptions to assess the validity of the latter indirectly. The model assumptions are more difficult to assess directly using graphical techniques because they relate to conditional distributions, but the reduction assumptions are very easy to assess because they relate to marginal and joint distributions; see Spanos (1999, ch. 5). In addition, this relationship can be used to derive not only misspecification tests for individual model assumptions but also joint tests; see Spanos (1999, ch. 15). In the context of misspecification testing, tracing the effects of any departures from the reduction assumptions to the model assumptions will be valuable in choosing the type of misspecification tests to be applied. Respecification amounts to tracing the detected departures from the model assumptions to the reduction assumptions and changing the latter in view of the new circumstances (see Spanos, 1986, 1999).

8   Conclusion

In the context of statistical modelling, simplicity is viewed as a coin with two sides, parsimony and informational content on one side and reliability and precision of inference on the other. On simplicity grounds parametric models are clearly preferable to non-parametric models. Parametric models, as envisaged by Fisher, enjoy both parsimony and high informational content vis-à-vis the systematic information contained in the data. Moreover, they lend themselves to misspecification testing in order for the modeller to assess their statistical adequacy. In contrast, non-parametric models aim at robustness to potential departures from certain distribution assumptions. The primary goal of non-parametric models, in the form of robustness to non-Normality, is called into question and contrasted to a different kind of robustness associated with neighbourhoods of parametric models. It was argued that robustness to non-Normality is of very limited value and it diverts attention away from a potentially more serious problem, that of statistical inadequacy. The main conclusion of the above discussion is that if the modeller is aiming at reliable and precise inferences, the combination of parametric statistical models and thorough misspecification testing is the procedure of choice. Non-parametric models and techniques are better suited for preliminary data analysis and misspecification testing within the context of parametric modelling.

REFERENCES

Bernardo, J. M. and A. F. M. Smith (1994). *Bayesian Theory*. New York: Wiley.
De Finetti, B. (1937). Foresight: its logical laws, its subjective sources. Reprinted in H. E. Kyburg and H. E. Smokler (eds.), *Studies in Subjective Probability*. New York: Wiley.
Fisher, R. A. (1922). On the mathematical foundations of theoretical statistics. *Philosophical Transactions of the Royal Society A* 222: 309–68.
  (1925). *Statistical Methods for Research Workers*. Edinburgh: Oliver and Boyd.
Gallant, A. R. (1987). Identification and consistency in seminonparametric regression. In T. F. Bewley (ed.), *Advances in Econometrics: Fifth World Congress*, vol. 1. Cambridge: Cambridge University Press.
Gourieroux, C. and A. Monfort (1995). *Statistical Analysis and Econometric Models*, 2 volumes. Cambridge: Cambridge University Press.
Hampel, F. R., E. M. Ronchetti, P. J. Rousseeuw and W. A. Stahel (1986). *Robust Statistics*. New York: Wiley.
Härdle, W. (1990). *Applied Nonparametric Regression*. Cambridge: Cambridge University Press.
Hettmansperger, T. P. and J. W. McKean (1998). *Robust Nonparametric Statistical Methods*. London: Arnold.
Hodges, J. L. and E. L. Lehmann (1956). The efficiency of some nonparametric competitors of the t-test. *Annals of Mathematical Statistics* 27: 324–35.
Huber, P. J. (1981). *Robust Statistics*. New York: Wiley.
Keuzenkamp, H. A. and M. McAleer (1995). Simplicity, scientific inference and econometric modelling. *The Economic Journal* 105: 1–21.

Lehmann, E. L. (1975). *Nonparametrics: Statistical Methods Based on Ranks.* San Francisco: Holden-Day.

Mayo, D. G. (1996). *Error and the Growth of Experimental Knowledge.* Chicago: University of Chicago Press.

Popper, K. (1959). *The Logic of Scientific Discovery.* London: Hutchinson.

(1963). *Conjectures and Refutations.* London: Routledge & Kegan Paul.

Scott, D. W. (1992). *Multivariate Density Estimation.* New York: Wiley.

Shiryayev, A. N. (1984). *Probability.* New York: Springer-Verlag.

Silverman, B. W. (1986). *Density Estimation.* London: Chapman & Hall.

Spanos, A. (1986). *Statistical Foundations of Econometric Modelling.* Cambridge: Cambridge University Press.

(1989). On re-reading Haavelmo: a retrospective view of econometric modelling. *Econometric Theory* 5: 405–29.

(1995). On theory testing in econometrics: modeling with nonexperimental data. *Journal of Econometrics* 67: 189–226.

(1998). Econometric testing. In J. B. Davis, D. W. Hands and U. Maki (eds.), *The Handbook of Economic Methodology*, pp. 116–30. Cheltenham: Edward Elgar.

(1999). *Probability Theory and Statistical Inference: Econometric Modeling with Observational Data.* Cambridge: Cambridge University Press.

(2000). Revisiting data mining: 'hunting' with or without a license. *Journal of Economic Methodology* 7: 231–64.

Thompson, J. R. and R. A. Tapia (1991). *Nonparametric function estimation, modeling, and simulation.* Philadelphia: Society of Industrial and Applied Mathematics.

Tukey, J. W. (1960). A survey of sampling from contaminated distributions. In I. Olkin et al. (eds), *Contributions to Probability and Statistics I.*

Wahba, G. (1990). *Spline Functions for Observational Data.* Philadelphia: SIAM.

Wilcoxon, F. (1945). Individual comparisons by ranking methods. *Biometrics* 1: 80–3.

Yule, G. U. (1926). Why do we sometimes get nonsense correlations between time series – a study in sampling and the nature of time series. *Journal of the Royal Statistical Society* 89: 1–64.

12 The role of simplicity in an econometric model selection process

Antonio Aznar, M. Isabel Ayuda and Carmen García-Olaverri

1 Introduction

Most of the model selection strategies found in the econometric literature are based on the use of statistics defined in terms of a mix of fit and parsimony. The aim of this chapter is to analyse the form in which the different model selection criteria combine these two elements and to demonstrate the need to define a trade-off between one of them in function of the other, given that they move in opposite directions.

We will first comment on a line developed within the philosophy of science which justifies the use of the evaluation of alternative theories following a bi-polar procedure. Reference will also be made to a number of relevant contributions formulated in the same direction within economics.

We will then propose a general expression, of which the majority of the model selection criteria developed in econometrics are particular cases. This general expression explicitly combines the fit and parsimony indicators. We will also study the form adopted by the parsimony factor that corresponds to each one of the criteria.

Finally, we will propose a framework based on the use of the mean square error of prediction (MSEP) and study the conditions that the parsimony factor must comply with.

The chapter is organized as follows. In section 2 we review the developments within the philosophy of science. The general formula and the particularization of each one of the criteria is presented in section 3. Section 4 is devoted to a detailed study of the parsimony factor. In

We would like to acknowledge the comments of the participants at the 1997 Tilburg Conference on Simplicity. Our warmest thanks also go to María-Teresa Aparicio and the two anonymous referees for their helpful observations on a first version of the paper. The authors alone are responsible for any errors. We have enjoyed financial support from the Spanish Ministry of Education, DGICYT Project PB 94-0602, for which we are grateful.

section 5 we present a new approach based on the use of the MSEP. Section 6 closes the paper with the main conclusions.

2   The Bacon–Descartes Ideal[1]

In this section we will discuss some methodological developments that reinforce the arguments in favour of what we call a bi-polar approach. We are going to analyse these developments by reference to what is called the Bacon–Descartes Ideal.

What we mean by the Bacon–Descartes Ideal can best be stated as follows: 'This Ideal is bi-polar: it has the aim of deep (or ultimate) explanation at one pole, that of certainty at the other' (Watkins, 1978, p. 25).

One of the principles that underlies all activity related with an empirical science is that the conceptual schemes proposed have to be in agreement with the facts, and it is on this point that the members of the Vienna Circle placed their greatest emphasis. However, it soon became clear that agreement with the facts is a necessary, but not sufficient, condition. Agreement with the facts can take many forms, but not all of these are acceptable from the scientific point of view.

The confluence of the Induction and Duhem problems leads to the conclusion that achieving the truth via the agreement of the theories with reality is impossible. On this basis, the issue in methodology is no longer one of justification, but rather of preference. But preference in terms of what?

If agreement with the facts is not sufficient, we must think in terms of a second requirement that must be demanded of a theory. Thus, we speak of a theory having to avoid *ad hoc* hypotheses or, equivalently, that it must be informative, deep or simple. Some authors argue in these terms, saying that an ideal theory must say a lot, both in the sense of being precise, and in the sense of providing a deep knowledge of the facts (Radnitzky and Anderson, 1978, p. 3). Others say that scientists search for theoretical systems that are deep or explanatory and, at the same time, true, and on many occasions these scientists are forced to make a trade-off between both characteristics (Koertge, 1978, p. 267).

From this it seems clear that what scientists prefer is to choose those theories with a greater informative content that is well corroborated,

---

[1] The title of this section is taken from Watkins (1978). Alternatively, it might have been 'Corroboration-Verisimilitude', a term used by Popper (1959, 1980), or 'Corroborated Excess Empirical Content', as proposed by Lakatos (1978), or 'Achievement/Strength as a Representation', used by Radnitzky (1979), or 'the Certainty-Informative Approach', given in Aznar (1989).

rejecting the tendency to evade falsification of their theories by the introduction of suitable *ad hoc* auxiliary hypotheses. It is also clear that
demands for certainty and deep explanation pull in opposite directions,
so that an equilibrium is required.[2]

Since, in this chapter, we pay special attention to the concept of simplicity, it is interesting to note the different terms used interchangeably by
the authors when they speak of this concept. The following is merely a
reduced list taken from the writings of some of these authors:

- Deep knowledge (Radnitzky and Andersson, 1978)
- High degree of falsifiability (Radnitzky and Andersson, 1978)
- Deep explanation (Watkins, 1978)
- Scientific depth (Watkins, 1978)
- Explanatory power (Watkins, 1978)
- Severe testability (Worrall, 1978)
- Interesting highly informative theories (Koertge, 1978)
- Interesting (i.e. deep, explanatory, informative, simple)
  (Koertge, 1978)
- Excess empirical content (Lakatos, 1978).

The conclusion that can be drawn from this brief summary is that what
scientists pursue is the development of theoretical schemes that are simple
and, at the same time, achieve a good fit with the available evidence.

Following this line, it is of interest to consider some of the methodological contributions made within economics.

For Friedman, theories do not purport to be photographs of reality;
rather they are schemes which capture the essential features of that reality. For him, an abstract model is simpler than the real world and contains only those forces that the hypothesis asserts to be important. He
then goes on to develop the concept of simplicity associated with the
specification of a model at various points throughout his work
(Friedman, 1953).

Commenting on Marshall, Friedman writes:

Marshall took the world as it is; he sought to construct an 'engine' to analyse it,
not a photographic reproduction of it. (Friedman, 1953, p. 35)

Subsequently, when analysing the so-called 'ideal types', he states:

The ideal types are not intended to be descriptive, they are designed to isolate the
features that are crucial for a particular problem. (Ibid., p. 36)

Therefore, all scientific models imply a distancing from reality, one that
tends towards the obtaining of simple models. However, this distancing

[2] Other proposals on how to achieve an equilibrium of this type can be seen in Worrall
(1978), Radnitzky (1979) and Such (1982).

cannot be arbitrary. We must think in terms of a rule that defines an acceptable equilibrium between the degree of realism and the level of simplicity of each model.

When considering the problem of defining this equilibrium between the two indicators – realism and simplicity – Friedman provides the following answer:

Complete 'realism' is clearly unobtainable, and the question whether a theory is 'realistic' enough can be settled only by seeing whether it yields predictions that are good enough for the purpose in hand or that are better than predictions from alternative theories. (Ibid., p. 41)

All this clearly shows that Friedman, when evaluating alternative theories, is thinking in terms of a bi-polar approach that weights two forces moving in an antagonistic manner: on the one hand, the degree of realism and, on the other, the level of simplicity of each model. According to Friedman, the optimum equilibrium between these two forces has to be achieved through evaluating the predictive capacity of the models being compared.

Following this first contribution from Friedman, other economists have argued in favour of a bi-polar approach when evaluating alternative theories. For the sake of brevity, in this chapter we will limit ourselves to a short reference to the work of Keuzenkamp and McAleer (1995). These authors refer continuously to a bi-polar approach, in the sense that it is necessary to face the trade-off between simplicity and descriptive accuracy. The systems must not contradict any known facts and, at the same time, we must choose the simplest system when searching for a compromise between both principles.

The arguments presented throughout this section clearly show that, from an epistemological point of view, there are many reasons that justify a bi-polar approach.

In the following section we will analyse how econometrics has assimilated this bi-polar approach when establishing the form adopted by the proposed criteria when choosing between econometric models.

3   The tradition in econometrics

During the last twenty years or so, there have been a very large number of proposals for criteria to evaluate and compare econometric models.[3]

---

[3] The definition and characteristics of most of these criteria can be found in Leamer (1978), Geweke and Meese (1981), Engle and Brown (1985), Gourieroux and Monfort (1989), Mills and Prasad (1992), Phillips and Ploberger (1994, 1996) and Phillips (1996).

This section is dedicated to analysing some of these, paying particular attention to how they fit with the idea of the bi-polar approach mentioned in the previous section. We show that most of these criteria are particular forms of achieving the equilibrium between the two poles of fit and parsimony.

From a hedonistic point of view, the criteria differ. Some of them have been derived by assuming the Neyman–Pearson framework. The critical region is determined by specifying the size of the type 1 error. Another group has been obtained by assuming a specific statistical decision framework with a particular loss function, a decision set and a given set of states of nature.

In order to present the criteria being studied in this section, let us consider the following two nested linear models:

$$M_1 : \ y = X_1\beta_1 + u_1 \tag{1}$$

$$M_2 : \ y = X_2\beta_2 + u_2 = X_1\beta_1 + X^*\beta^* + u_2 \tag{2}$$

where y is a Tx1 vector of observations of the dependent variable; X_2 is a Txk$_2$ matrix of the observations of the k$_2$ regressors; β_1, β_2 and β^* are vectors of parameters with k$_1$, k$_2$ and k$_2$–k$_1$ elements, respectively; and u_1 and u_2 are vectors of T random disturbances. When M$_1$ is the true DGP, then u_1 is iid N(0, $\sigma_1^2 I_T$) and when M$_2$ is the true DGP, then u_2 is iid N(0, $\sigma_2^2 I_T$). It is clear that $X_2 = (X_1, X^*)$, with X_1 being a Txk$_1$ matrix of observations of the k$_1$ regressors.

Let x'_{p1} be the vector of observations of the k$_1$ regressors included in M$_1$, corresponding to an out-sample period that we denote by p, and let x'_{p2} be the corresponding vector of the k$_2$ regressors included in M$_2$.

The OLS predictor and prediction error for M$_1$ are given by:

$$\hat{y}_{p1} = x'_{p1}\hat{\beta}_1 \text{ and } e_{p1} = y_p - \hat{y}_{p1} \tag{3}$$

where: $\hat{\beta}_1 = (X'_1 X_1)^{-1} X'_1 y$

For M$_2$ we have:

$$\hat{y}_{p2} = x'_{p2}\hat{\beta}_2 \text{ and } e_{p2} = y_p - \hat{y}_{p2} \tag{4}$$

where: $\hat{\beta}_2 = (X'_2 X_2)^{-1} X'_2 y$

The OLS estimators of the disturbance variance are given by:

$$\hat{\sigma}_i^2 = \frac{\hat{u}'_i \hat{u}_i}{T - k_i} \quad i = 1, 2 \tag{5}$$

and the corresponding Maximum-Likelihood estimators can be written as:

Table 12.1. *Criteria*

Criterion	Statistic	Decision rule	Parsimony factor $h(.)$
R^2 adjusted	$\bar{R}_i^2 = 1 - \dfrac{T-1}{T-k}\left(\dfrac{\hat{u}_i'\hat{u}_i}{\sum (y_t - \bar{y})^2}\right)$	$\bar{R}_1^2 > \bar{R}_2^2$	$(T-k_1)/(T-k_2)$
F-test	$F = \dfrac{(\hat{u}_1'\hat{u}_1 - \hat{u}_2'\hat{u}_2)/(k_2 - k_1)}{\hat{u}_2'\hat{u}_2/(T-k_2)}$	$F < F_\varepsilon[(k_2 - k_1), T - k_2]$	$1 + \dfrac{(k_2 - k_1)}{T - k_2}F_\varepsilon$
Wald	$W = T\dfrac{\tilde{\sigma}_1^2 - \tilde{\sigma}_2^2}{\tilde{\sigma}_2^2}$	$W < \chi_\varepsilon^2(k_2 - k_1)$	$1 + \dfrac{\chi_\varepsilon^2}{T}$
Lagrange	$LM = T\dfrac{\tilde{\sigma}_1^2 - \tilde{\sigma}_2^2}{\tilde{\sigma}_1^2}$	$LM < \chi_\varepsilon^2(k_2 - k_1)$	$\dfrac{T}{T - \chi_\varepsilon^2}$
Likelihood-ratio	$LR = T\ln\left(\dfrac{\tilde{\sigma}_1^2}{\tilde{\sigma}_2^2}\right)$	$LR < \chi_\varepsilon^2(k_2 - k_1)$	$\exp\left(\dfrac{\chi_\varepsilon^2}{T}\right)$
Mallows	$Cp_i = \dfrac{\tilde{\sigma}_i^2}{\tilde{\sigma}_2^2} + \dfrac{2k_i}{T - k_2}$	$Cp_1 < Cp_2$	$1 + \dfrac{2(k_2 - k_1)}{T - k_2}$
Akaike	$AIC_i = \ln\tilde{\sigma}_i^2 + \dfrac{2k_i}{T}$	$AIC_1 < AIC_2$	$\exp\left(\dfrac{2(k_2 - k_1)}{T}\right)$
Phillips–Ploberger	$PIC_i = \hat{u}_i'\hat{u}_i + \dfrac{\hat{u}_2'\hat{u}_2}{T - k_2}$ $[(k_2 - k_i)\ln\tilde{\sigma}_2^2 + \ln|X_i'X_i|]$	$PIC_1 < PIC_2$	$1 + \dfrac{k_2 - k_1}{T - k_2}\ln\tilde{\sigma}_2^2 +$ $+ \dfrac{1}{T - k_2}\ln\dfrac{|X_2'X_2|}{|X_1'X_1|}$
Geweke–Meese	$BEC_i = \tilde{\sigma}_i^2 + \dfrac{k_i\ln T}{T - k_2}\tilde{\sigma}_2^2$	$BEC_1 < BEC_2$	$1 + \dfrac{\ln T(k_2 - k_1)}{T - k_2}$
Schwarz	$SBIC_i = \ln\tilde{\sigma}_i^2 + \dfrac{k_i\ln T}{T}$	$SBIC_1 < SBIC_2$	$\exp\left((k_2 - k_1)\dfrac{\ln T}{T}\right)$
MSEP	$MSEP_i = \dfrac{1}{T_1}\sum_{p=1}^{T} e_{pi}^2$	$MSEP_1 < MSEP_2$	

$$\tilde{\sigma}_i^2 = \frac{\hat{u}_i'\hat{u}_i}{T} \qquad i = 1, 2 \tag{6}$$

where $\hat{u}_i = y - X_i\hat{\beta}_i$ $i = 1, 2$.

The criteria we analyse in this chapter are contained in table 12.1. $F_\varepsilon[(k_2 - k_1), T - k_2]$ and $\chi_\varepsilon^2(k_2 - k_1)$ are the critical points corresponding to the significance level and degrees of freedom indicated.

The structure of table 12.1 is as follows: the first column contains the name of the criterion; the corresponding statistic appears in the second column, and the decision rule is contained in the third. The last column contains an alternative form of writing the decision rule corresponding to each criterion. The general form, of which all the criteria are particular cases, can be written as:

$$\hat{u}_1'\hat{u}_1 < \hat{u}_2'\hat{u}_2 \cdot h(.) \tag{7}$$

where $\hat{u}_i'\hat{u}_i$, $i = 1, 2$ are the measures of fit and $h(.)$ is a function of the size of the model and of the sample size indicating the weight assigned to parsimony in the model selection process.

Writing the decision rule in this way, the only question that remains is to compare the properties of each $h(.)$ and to extract the characteristics of the corresponding criterion. This is carried out in the following section.

4   The parsimony factor

In this section we compare the properties of $h(.)$, first for any sample size and then asymptotically.

The weight assigned to the parsimony factor in the different selection criteria is determined by the behaviour of the function $h(.)$. Let $h_{C_i}(t)$ be the parsimony factor associated with the criterion C_i; then we can say that criterion C_i is more parsimonious than criteria C_j in the interval (t_1, t_2), if:

$$\forall t \in (t_1, t_2) \quad h_{C_i}(t) \geq h_{C_j}(t)$$

Some comparisons of functions $h(t)$ are immediate. For example, the BEC (Geweke and Meese, 1981) criterion is more parsimonious than the Cp criterion (Mallows, 1973) for sample sizes larger than 8, given that $h_{BEC}(t) \geq h_{Cp}(t)$ $\forall t \geq 8$. By analogy, it can immediately be proved that:

$$h_{Cp}(t) \geq h_{\bar{R}^2}(t) \quad \forall t,$$
$$h_{SBIC}(t) \geq h_{AIC}(t) \quad \forall t \geq 8$$
$$h_{AIC}(t) \geq h_{\bar{R}^2}(t) \quad \forall t$$

Other inequalities between parsimony factors are not so immediate, although some of them can be proved graphically. For example, in figure 12.1 we have represented the surface $h_{Cp}(t) - h_{AIC}(t)$, $t \in (20, 100)$, $k_2 \in (2, 10)$, fixing $k_1 = 1$. As can be observed, the difference $h_{Cp}(t) - h_{AIC}(t)$ is always positive and increases for small sample sizes and values of k_2 further away from k_1. *Asymptotically, the difference disappears, that is to say, the two criteria are equally parsimonious.*

The representation of the parsimony factor $h(t)$ for the LM, LR and W criteria are shown in figures 12.2a–d, respectively.

Figures 12.2a and 12.2b compare the parsimony factors of the LM, LR and W criteria for $k_1 = 1$, $k_2 = 2$, with $\varepsilon = 5\%$ and $\varepsilon = 1\%$, respectively. In both cases, $h_{LM}(t) > h_{LR}(t) > h_W(t) \; \forall t$, that is to say, the LM criterion is always more parsimonious. The difference is greater for $\varepsilon = 1\%$. When the models being compared are very different, $k_1 = 1$, $k_2 = 4$, the ordering according to the parsimony factor is the same, but the differences are greater. See figure 12.2c and 12.2d for levels of significance $\varepsilon = 5\%$ and $\varepsilon = 1\%$, respectively.

For the SBIC (Schwarz, 1978) and BEC criteria, we cannot establish an ordering. For example, figure 12.3a shows the surface $h_{BEC}(t) - h_{SBIC}(t)$, $k2 \in (2, 4)$, $\in (20, 40)$, having fixed $k_1 = 1$. As can be seen, the surface can take positive or negative values. The parsimony factor of both criteria tends to take the same values as the sample size increases, as can be seen in figure 12.3b, where the representation of the surface $h_{BEC}(t) - h_{SBIC}(t)$ has been extended to the region $k_2 \in (5, 10)$, $t \in (20,100)$.

Finally, in figures 12.4a–c we analyse the parsimony factors corresponding to three criteria, the LR, the AIC (Akaike, 1973, 1974) and the BEC criteria.

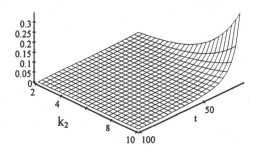

$$h_{Cp}(t) - h_{AIC}(t) = 1 + \frac{2(k_2 - 1)}{t - k_2} - \exp\left(\frac{2(k_2 - 1)}{t}\right)$$

Figure 12.1 Difference of parsimony factors of Cp and AIC

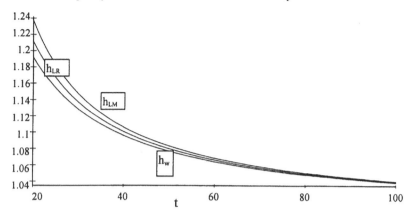

$$h_W(t) = 1 + \frac{3.84}{t} \; , \quad h_{LM}(t) = \frac{t}{t - 3.84}, \quad h_{LR}(t) = \exp\!\left(\frac{3.84}{t}\right)$$

Figure 12.2a Parsimony factors of LM, LR and W
($k_1 = 1$, $k_2 = 2$, $\varepsilon = 5\%$)

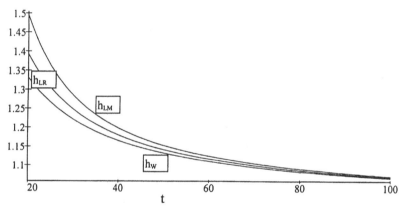

$$h_W(t) = 1 + \frac{6.63}{t} \; , \quad h_{LM}(t) = \frac{t}{t - 6.63}, \quad h_{LR}(t) = \exp\!\left(\frac{6.63}{t}\right)$$

Figure 12.2b Parsimony factors of LM, LR and W
($k_1 = 1$, $k_2 = 2, \varepsilon = 1\%$)

In figure 12.4a:

$$k_1 = 1, \; k_2 = 2, \quad \varepsilon = 5\%,$$
$$\forall t \le 46, \quad h_{AIC}(t) < h_{BEC}(t) < h_{LR}(t)$$
$$\forall t > 47, \quad h_{AIC}(t) < h_{LR}(t) < h_{BEC}(t)$$

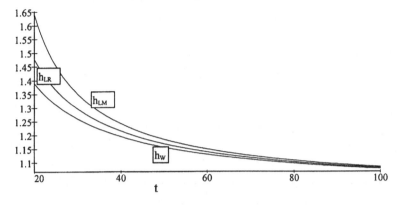

$$h_W(t) = 1 + \frac{7.81}{t}, \quad h_{LM}(t) = \frac{t}{t - 7.81}, \quad h_{LR}(t) = \exp\left(\frac{7.81}{t}\right)$$

Figure 12.2c Parsimony factors of LM, LR and W
($k_1 = 1, k_2 = 4, \varepsilon = 5\%$)

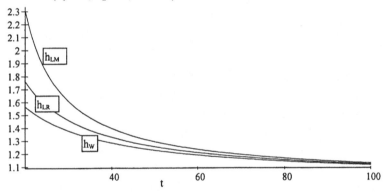

$$h_W(t) = 1 + \frac{11.34}{t}, \quad h_{LM}(t) = \frac{t}{t - 11.34}, \quad h_{LR}(t) = \exp\left(\frac{11.34}{t}\right)$$

Figure 12.2d Parsimony factors of LM, LR and W
($k_1 = 1, k_2 = 4, \varepsilon = 1\%$)

By analogy, in figure 12.4b we can observe:

$$k_1 = 1, \ k_2 = 2, \quad \varepsilon = 1\%,$$
$$\forall t \leq 766, \quad h_{AIC}(t) < h_{BEC}(t) < h_{LR}(t)$$
$$\forall t > 767, \quad h_{AIC}(t) < h_{LR}(t) < h_{BEC}(t)$$

Finally, figure 12.4c shows the differences in the parsimony for the three criteria, where:

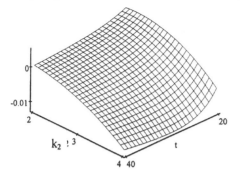

$$h_{BEC}(t) - h_{SBIC}(t) = 1 + Ln(t)\frac{(k_2 - 1)}{(t - k_2)} - \exp\left(Ln(t)\frac{(k_2 - 1)}{t}\right)$$

Figure 12.3a Difference of parsimony factors of BEC and SBIC ($k_2 \varepsilon(2,u)$, $t\varepsilon(20, 40)$)

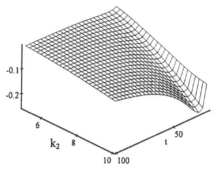

$$h_{BEC}(t) - h_{SBIC}(t) = 1 + Ln(t)\frac{(k_2 - 1)}{(t - k_2)} - \exp\left(Ln(t)\frac{(k_2 - 1)}{t}\right)$$

Figure 12.3b Difference of parsimony factors of BEC and SBIC ($k_2\varepsilon (5, 10)$, $t\varepsilon(20,100)$)

$$k_1 = 1, \quad k_2 = 4, \quad \varepsilon = 1\%,$$
$$\forall t \leq 49, \quad h_{AIC}(t) < h_{BEC}(t) < h_{LR}(t)$$
$$\forall t > 50, \quad h_{AIC}(t) < h_{LR}(t) < h_{BEC}(t)$$

Another interesting point with respect to the properties of h(.) is to determine the conditions under which a particular criterion guarantees asymptotically the selection of the DGP. These conditions are stated in the following theorem.

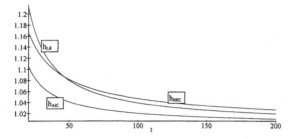

$$h_{LR}(t) = \exp\left(\frac{3.84}{t}\right), \ h_{BEC}(t) = 1 + \frac{Ln(t)}{t-2}, h_{AIC}(t) = \exp\left(\frac{2}{t}\right)$$

Figure 12.4a Parsimony factors of ATC, BEC and LR
($k_1 = 1$, $k_2 = 2$, $\varepsilon = 5\%$)

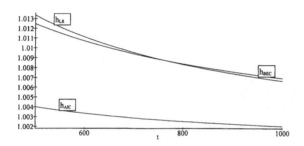

$$h_{LR}(t) = \exp\left(\frac{6.63}{t}\right), \ h_{BEC}(t) = 1 + \frac{Ln(t)}{t-2}, h_{AIC}(t) = \exp\left(\frac{2}{t}\right)$$

Figure 12.4b Parsimony factors of AIC, BEC and LR
($k_1 = 1$, $k_2 = 2$, $\varepsilon = 1\%$)

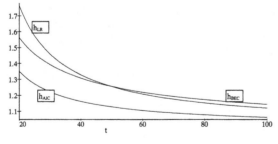

$$h_{LR}(t) = \exp\left(\frac{11.34}{t}\right), \ h_{BEC}(t) = 1 + \frac{3Ln(t)}{t-4}, h_{AIC}(t) = \exp\left(\frac{6}{t}\right)$$

Figure 12.4c Parsimony factors of AIC, BEC and LR
($k_1 = 1$, $k_2 = 4$, $\varepsilon = 1\%$)

Theorem 1 Suppose we are comparing the models written in (1) and (2) and assuming the same hypotheses on the stochastic properties of these models as stated in section 3. For a given criterion, the conditions:

$$T(h(T) - 1) \to \infty \tag{8}$$

$$h(T) - 1 \to 0 \tag{9}$$

are sufficient to guarantee the selection of the DGP.

Proof Assume first that the DGP is M_1. Conditional on this model, the probability of selecting M_1 as against M_2 is given by:

$$\text{Prob} \{\hat{u}_1'\hat{u}_1 < \hat{u}_2'\hat{u}_2 \, . \, h(.)/M_1\} \tag{10}$$

or equivalently by:

$$\text{Prob}\left\{ \frac{\hat{u}_1'\hat{u}_1 - \hat{u}_2'\hat{u}_2}{\dfrac{\hat{u}_2'\hat{u}_2}{T}} \le T(h(T) - 1)/M_1 \right\} \tag{11}$$

since, in this case, we have that:

$$\frac{\hat{u}_2'\hat{u}_2}{T} \xrightarrow{p} \sigma_1^2 \tag{12}$$

and :

$$\frac{\hat{u}_1'\hat{u}_1 - \hat{u}_2'\hat{u}_2}{\sigma_1^2} \xrightarrow{d} \chi^2(k_2 - k_1) \tag{13}$$

Introducing (12) and (13) in (11), it is clear that (8) guarantees the following:

$$\text{Prob}\{\text{selecting } M_1/M_1\} \xrightarrow{p} 1$$

where $\xrightarrow{p}$, $\xrightarrow{d}$, denote convergence in probability and convergence in distribution, respectively.

Suppose now that the DGP is M_2. Conditional on M_2, the probability of selecting M_1 as against M_2 is given by:

$$\text{Prob}\{\hat{u}_1'\hat{u}_1 < \hat{u}_2'\hat{u}_2 \cdot h(T)/M_2\} \tag{14}$$

or equivalently by:

$$\text{Prob}\left\{ \frac{(\hat{u}_1'\hat{u}_1 - \hat{u}_2'\hat{u}_2)/T}{\hat{u}_2'\hat{u}_2/T} < (h(T) - 1)/M_2 \right\} \tag{15}$$

Using standard results, we have that $\frac{\hat{u}_1'\hat{u}_1}{T} \xrightarrow{p} \sigma_2^2$ and that $\frac{\hat{u}_1'\hat{u}_1}{T\sigma_2^2}$ asymptotically follows a non-central χ^2 distribution with a non-centrality parameter given by:

$$p\lim \frac{\beta_2' X_2' M_1 X_2 \beta_2}{T} \tag{16}$$

and a variance that converges to zero. Let Z be defined as: $Z = \frac{\hat{u}_2'\hat{u}_2}{\sigma_2^2}$; this variable follows a central χ^2 distribution, so that Z/T converges to zero. Using these results, if $h(T) - 1 \to 0$, the second part of the theorem follows, since (16) is positive.

In the light of these results, we can distinguish three groups of criteria, each of them associated with a different objective. These three groups are:

Group 1 This is made up of the F, W, LM and LR criteria. The fit–parsimony combination that they implicitly incorporate seeks to guarantee that, at least asymptotically, the size of the type I error is a small value, let us say 1% or 5%, and that the power is 1.

Group 2 This is made up of the Cp and AIC criteria. In this case, the combination of fit and parsimony seeks to guarantee a consistent estimation of the risk function corresponding to a loss function. In the case of the Cp criterion, the loss function adopted is the MSEP, whilst the AIC criterion assumes the Kullback–Leibler distance.

Group 3 This is made up of the PIC (Phillips and Ploberger, 1994, 1996), BEC and SBIC criteria. Here, the fit–parsimony combination that it incorporates seeks to guarantee that asymptotically the DGP is always chosen.

On the basis of the results presented in this section, we can pose the following question: what type of recommendations can be made concerning which of the parsimony factors must be used? The reply is a straightforward one: the parsimony factor h(.) that is chosen must depend on the objective that is sought in the selection of the model.

If what is sought is to guarantee asymptotically that the size of the type I error does not exceed an amount specified *a priori*, then we must think in terms of a criterion from Group 1. If what is sought is to minimize the risk of a loss function adopted *a priori*, then use must be made of a criterion from the second group. Finally, if what is sought is to guarantee asymptotically the selection of the DGP, then we must turn to a criterion from the third group.

In this sense, the comments made in the work of Forster (1997) relative to the properties of the AIC criterion assume some relevance. Why require that the criterion always chooses the DGP if the objective for which it has been proposed is the achievement of a consistent estimation of the risk function that corresponds to the Kullback–Leibler distance?

A restriction to be imposed on h(.) is that it should be invariant to scale transformations of the explanatory variables. Otherwise, as Leamer (1978) writes: 'by a suitable change of measurement, h(.) can be made to favour any hypothesis (if each model has at least one explanatory variable not found in any of the others)'.

It can be shown that all the criteria included in table 12.1 satisfy this restriction, save for the PIC criterion. Phillips and Ploberger (1996) develop a new test procedure, the PICF criterion, that is free of this scale problem.

The criteria of the first group have been the most extensively used in applied work, but this practice has not been free of criticism, especially with respect to the choice of the level of significance. This choice has always been the subject of suspicion within the Bayesian approach, as can be seen, for example, in Leamer (1978).[4]

5   A decision framework to derive the properties of h(.)

In section 2 we proposed that, when considering how to establish the equilibrium between the fit and parsimony factors, the predictive capacity of the models being compared should be evaluated.[5] In order to illustrate this idea, we adopt a statistical decision framework with two nested linear models representing both the elements of the set of states of nature, as well as the elements of the set of decisions. The risk function is the theoretical mean square error of prediction, and we assume uncertainty with respect to which of the two models is the true DGP. The number of out-sample periods is T_1. Let

$$h_{11}^2 = \frac{1}{T_1} \sum_{p=1}^{T_1} h_{11p}^2$$

with

$$h_{11p} = x_{p2}'\beta_2 - x_{p1}'B_{12}\beta_2 \text{ and } B_{12} = (X_1'X_1)^{-1}X_1'X_2$$

Our starting point is the double-entry table 12.2. On the left-hand side we have the two decisions, and on the top the two states of nature. The cells contain the theoretical mean square error of prediction for T_1 out-sample periods. The results of the comparison for each DGP can be seen in table 12.3.

---

[4] For other criticisms of this point, see also Granger et al. (1995).
[5] In this sense, the contributions of Lakatos (1978) and Friedman (1953) were particularly significant.

Table 12.2. *Mean square error of prediction*

	DGP	
	M_1	M_2
M_1	$\dfrac{1}{T_1}\sum E_1 e_{p1}^2 =$	$\dfrac{1}{T_1}\sum E_2 e_{p1}^2 = h_{11}^2 +$
	$= \dfrac{1}{T_1}\sigma_1^2 \sum (1 + x'_{p1}(X'_1 X_1)^{-1} x_{p1})$	$+ \dfrac{1}{T_1}\sigma_2^2 \sum (1 + x'_{p1}(X'_1 X_1)^{-1} x_{p1})$
M_2	$\dfrac{1}{T_1}\sum E_1 e_{p2}^2 =$	$\dfrac{1}{T_1}\sum E_2 e_{p2}^2 =$
	$= \dfrac{1}{T_1}\sigma_1^2 \sum (1 + x'_{p2}(X'_2 X_2)^{-1} x_{p2})$	$= \dfrac{1}{T_1}\sigma_2^2 \sum (1 + x'_{p2}(X'_2 X_2)^{-1} x_{p2})$

Before we derive the conditions that h(.) should satisfy, we need a rule that allows us to judge the goodness of any model selection process. The rule we adopt says that a model selection criterion is good when it chooses the model that minimizes the risk function, no matter which model is the true state of nature, i.e. the model that is the DGP.

Taking this rule as given, and using the results contained in table 12.3, the conditions that h(.) should satisfy are the following:

- Asymptotically: h(.) should be such that, independent of whatever model is the DGP, the corresponding criterion always selects the DGP.
- Finite samples: the conditions that h(.) should satisfy depend on whether the DGP is either M_1 or M_2.

If the true DGP is the restricted model, M_1, then the model selection criterion should always tend to choose the restricted model.

If we denote the model selection criterion based on the minimization of $C(M_j)$ by $C(.)$, then this first requirement can be formulated as follows:

$$\text{Prob}\{C(M_1) < C(M_2)/M_1 \, true\} = 1 - \varepsilon$$

with ε being very small.

Let $C(.)$ and $C^*(.)$ be two different model selection criteria and let μ_c, μ_{c^*}, S_c, S_{c^*} be defined as:

Table 12.3. *Results of the comparison for each DGP*

DGP	Finite samples	Asymptotic
M_1	$MSEP(M_1) < MSEP(M_2)$	$MSEP(M_1) \cong MSEP(M_2)$
M_2	$MSEP(M_1) \gtrless MSEP(M_2)$	$MSEP(M_1) > MSEP(M_2)$

$$\mu_c = E[C(M_1) - C(M_2)]$$
$$\mu_{c*} = E[C^*(M_1) - C^*(M_2)]$$
$$S_c = [Var[C(M_1) - C(M_2)]]^{\frac{1}{2}}$$
$$S_{c*} = [Var[C^*(M_1) - C^*(M_2)]]^{\frac{1}{2}}$$

We can then say that the C criterion tends to choose the restricted model with a higher probability than the C* criterion when the following inequality holds:

$$\frac{-\mu_c}{S_c} > \frac{-\mu_{c*}}{S_{c*}}$$

When M_2 is the true DGP, then the predictor obtained from M_1 is biased, but has a smaller variance than the predictor defined from M_2, which is unbiased. Thus, either M_1 or M_2 may be chosen, but not in an arbitrary manner. When determining how to select one model or the other, note that:

$$\text{Prob}[C(M_1) < C(M_2)/M_2 \ true] = f(\sigma_2^2, \ bias^2(M_1))$$

where bias (M_1) denotes the bias of M_1 and is a function of the parameters of M_2.

Considering the form that the MSEP adopts, as can be seen in table 12.2, we can say that h(.) should be such that the following two inequalities hold:

$$\frac{\partial f}{\partial \sigma_2^2} > 0$$

and $\quad \dfrac{\partial f}{\partial \ bias^2(M_1)} < 0$

What can we say about the degree of accomplishment of these conditions by each h(.) contained in table 12.1?

From the asymptotic point of view, only the criteria of the second group fail to meet the stated requirements.

For finite samples, the criteria of the second group also fail to meet the requirements when M_1 is the DGP. Both the AIC and the Cp criteria tend towards the model M_2 on around 30% of occasions. The criteria corresponding to the other two groups appear to meet these requirements, more so with those of the third group than with those of the first.

An important result to be taken into account is that the final criterion that appears in table 12.1, that is to say MSEP, satisfies all these conditions provided that the number of out-sample observations is large.[6]

6   Conclusions

In this chapter, we have studied various aspects related to a bi-polar approach to the selection of econometric models. This approach is based on the definition of an equilibrium between two indicators – fit and parsimony – that move in opposite directions.

In section 2, we considered a number of developments within the philosophy of science that propose a bi-polar approach in order to evaluate alternative theoretical schemes. Following Watkins, we have called this the Bacon–Descartes approach. In this section, we have also drawn attention to the contributions made within economics in this same line.

In section 3, and using a framework with two linear nested models, we demonstrated that the selection criteria developed in econometrics are all particular cases of one general form, where the fit and parsimony indicators are explicitly taken into account. We also showed that the distinction between these different criteria lies in the form in which they define the parsimony factor.

In section 4, we compared the parsimony factors of the different criteria. The most important conclusion is that, as a generality, a specific fit–parsimony combination cannot be recommended; rather, the recommendation will depend on the objective that the researcher has in mind when discriminating between models.

Finally, in section 5 we developed a decision framework adopting the MSEP as the loss function, and we have further derived the requirements that the parsimony factor of any criterion must meet. The section closes with the suggestion that the MSEP could be the criterion to be taken into account within a framework such as that adopted here.

---

[6] For a detailed study of the properties of this criterion under different assumptions, see Wei (1992).

REFERENCES

Akaike, M. (1973). Information theory and an extension of the Maximun Likelihood Principle. In B. N. Petrov and F. Csaki (eds.), *2nd International Symposium on Information Theory*, pp. 267–81. Budapest: Akademiai Kiado.

—— (1974). A new look at the statistical model identification. *IEEE Transactions on Automatic Control* AC-19: 716–23.

Aznar, A. (1989). *Econometric Model Selection: a New Approach*. Dordrecht: Kluwer.

Engle, R. F. and Brown, S. J. (1985). Model selection procedures for forecasting. Mimeo.

Forster, M. R. (1997). The new science of simplicity. Mimeo.

Friedman, M. (1953). *Essays in Positive Economics*. Chicago: University of Chicago Press, pp. 3–46.

Geweke, J. and R. Meese (1981). Estimating regression models of finite but unknown order. *International Economic Review* 22: 55–70.

Gourieroux, Ch. and A. Monfort (1989). *Statistique et modeles econometriques*, 2 vols. Paris: Economica, vol. 1.

Granger, C. W. J., M. L. King and H. White (1995). Comments on testing economic theories and the use of model selection criteria. *Journal of Econometrics* 67: 173–87.

Keuzenkamp, H. A. and M. McAleer (1995). Simplicity, scientific inference and econometric modelling. *The Economic Journal* 105: 1–21.

Koertge, N. (1978). Towards a new theory of scientific inquiry. In G. Radnitzky and G. Andersson (eds.), *Progress and Rationality in Science*, pp. 253–78. Dordrecht: Reidel.

Lakatos, I. (1978). *Philosophical Papers*, vol. 1: *The Methodology of Scientific Research Programmes*, eds. J. Worral and G. Currie, Cambridge University Press.

Leamer, E. E. (1978). *Specification Searches: Ad-hoc Inference with Experimental Data*. New York: Wiley.

Mallows, C. L. (1973). Some comments on Cp. *Technometrics* 15: 661–75.

Mills, J. A. and K. Prasad (1992). A comparison of model selection criteria. *Econometric Reviews* 11: 201–33.

Phillips, P. C. B. (1996). Econometric model determination. *Econometrica* 64: 763–812.

Phillips, P. C. B. and W. Ploberger (1994). Posterior odds testing for a unit with data-based model selection. *Econometric Theory* 10: 774–808.

—— (1996). An asymptotic theory of Bayesian inference for time series. *Econometrica* 64: 381–412.

Popper, K. R. (1959, 1980). *The Logic of Scientific Discovery*. London: Hutchinson.

—— (1973, 1979). *Objective Knowledge: an Evolutionary Approach*. Oxford: Oxford University Press.

Radnitzky, G. (1979). Justifying a theory versus giving good reasons for preferring a theory on the big divide in the philosophy of science. In G. Radnitzky and G. Andersson (eds.), *The Structure and Development of Science*, pp. 213–56. Dordrecht: Reidel.

Radnitzky, G. and G. Andersson (1978). Objective criteria of scientific progress? Inductivism, falsificationism and relativism. In G. Radnitzky and G. Andersson (eds.), *Progress and Rationality in Science*, pp. 3–19. Dordrecht: Reidel.

Schwarz, G. (1978). Estimating the dimension of a model. *Annals of Statistics* 6: 461–4.

Such, J. (1982). Are there definitively falsifying procedures in science? In W. Krajewsky (ed.), *Polish Essays in the Philosophy of the Natural Sciences*, pp. 113–26. Dordrecht: Reidel.

Watkins, J. (1978). The Popperian approach to scientific knowledge. In G. Radnitzky and G. Andersson (eds.), *Progress and Rationality in Science*, pp. 23–44. Dordrecht: Reidel.

Wei, C. Z. (1992). On predictive least squares principles. *The Annals of Statistics* 20: 1–42.

Worrall, J. (1978). The ways in which the methodology of scientific research programmes improves on Popper's methodology. In G. Radnitzky and G. Andersson (eds.), *Progress and Rationality in Science*, pp. 45–70. Dordrecht: Reidel.

13 Simplicity in a behavioural, non-parametric context

Dirk Tempelaar

Motivation

The concept of simplicity is inextricably related to models and the process of modelling (dynamic) phenomena. For that reason, the definition of simplicity critically depends upon the modelling paradigm chosen. In this contribution, we will describe a non-parametric approach to modelling dynamic phenomena, and the role the concept of simplicity plays within that approach. But before turning to the descriptive part, we will first mention the most important sources of inspiration which led us to choose this specific modelling paradigm and the behavioural definition of simplicity that is congruent to it.

The first source of inspiration is to be found in the apparent paradox built into parametric versions of the concept of simplicity, like Schwartz's information criterion, SIC, Akaike's information criterion, AIC, or the minimal description length, MDL (see Keuzenkamp and McAleer, 1995). Concepts such as simplicity, or complexity as its mirror image, are particularly useful in modelling exercises in which economic theory only plays a rather modest role. This type of modelling application is characterized by a lack of economic theory or, just the opposite, by a rich affluence of contradicting economic hypotheses, and puts the data in the forefront when deciding upon the model structure. In so doing it creates a need for principles like Occam's razor. But at the same time, in this type of application with weak theory and strong data, deep structural parameters are scarce, or even absent. And when model parameters don't have a clear physical (economic) interpretation, one can wonder if parametric implementations of Occam's razor aren't a contradiction in themselves.

The lack of interpretability of parameter values in economic models is just one of the aspects of Kalman's critique of econometrics. In his theory of modelling, Kalman (1980, 1982a, 1983) makes a distinction between natural sciences, in which laws of nature live, and system-determined sciences, such as economics, computer science or engineering, in which system-independent laws do not exist. In the absence of laws and absolutely definable parameters, the system-theoretic paradigm of modelling becomes useful. According to this paradigm, modelling is a data-driven procedure, so as to prevent the use of any form of 'prejudice': assumptions unrelated to the data but that are imposed on the data without any check against the data (Kalman, 1982b). Prejudice can manifest itself in different ways, such as not treating all variables symmetrically, but instead assuming *a priori* classification into noiseless variables (the exogenous ones) and noisy variables (the endogenous ones); economic restrictions on parameter values to achieve over-identification and probabilistic assumptions. It is our ambition to opt for a modelling framework and an interpretation of the concept of simplicity that meets Kalman's critique and avoids untestable assumptions as much as possible.

Together with the issue of internal consistency, we should consider the external consistency of informational criteria for simplicity. In defining a concept that has so many connotations in daily life, and is used in so many different domains, one at least hopes to be able to find a definition that is congruent to its meaning in everyday language and can be transferred from one domain to another. The first problem with defining simplicity in terms of the number of adjustable parameters of the equations describing the object or concept under consideration is that this definition severely restricts its range of applicability. We more often than not use the concept in situations in which parameters and equations are alien. Moreover, information-criterion-based definitions of simplicity possess in some cases rather counter-intuitive properties. To clarify, just compare two different pieces of canvas, the first being tightly stretched within a picture frame, the second not being tightened at all and, for that reason, folded and crumpled. By all possible standards, the second canvas is more complex and less simple than the first one, being more curved, less aesthetic, and necessitating a higher dimensional space to describe it (see next section for an elaboration on these issues). However, when counting parameters, we quite surprisingly arrive at the opposite conclusion: the first canvas, being constrained in its manifestation (and realizing we need parameters to define such a constraint) is more complex than the second, being not constrained at all! The fact that simplicity is not so much defined in terms of the manifestation itself, but rather in terms of the mechanisms that constrain that manifestation, is the cause of this counter-intuitive outcome. The more constrained the manifestation, the more complex the mechanism of constraining but, at least at an intuitive level, the simpler the (class of) shapes that are left over after constraining. This property of counter-intuitive outcomes is not specific to information-criterion-based implementations of simplicity only, but can be generalized to other syntactic implementations of the concept of simplicity (as opposed to semantic construals of simplicity, for which we will opt in this contribution: see Sober, 2001).

In the modelling of dynamic phenomena from observed data, the generic case is that no (non-trivial) models exist that are able to explain the data exactly. The standard way out of the problem that all models, from a Popperian point of view, are falsified by the data is to adopt a probabilistic modelling approach. This comes down to postulating a model as a set of equations containing as yet unspecified parameters, and postulating random elements, for example by assuming that the observed variables, or observed time series, are a realization of a stochastic process. Such assumptions guarantee that every finite observed time series can occur with positive probability density and in this sense the data will no longer falsify the model. In specific applications, and thus as a general philosophy, this approach has drawbacks. For example, in many applications the lack of fit between data and any model is not in the first place due to randomness or measurement noise, but due to the fact that one consciously uses a model that is too simple: that cannot capture the complexity of the phenomenon one has observed. In such a case, it is appealing to formulate the modelling problem as a deterministic approximation problem instead (Willems, 1986b, p. 675). This raises the question of what is meant by an approximate model and how one should judge such a model against data that, in a strict sense, falsify the model. The paradigm on which approximate deterministic modelling is based are the objectives of low complexity, or high simplicity, and high accuracy, and not unbiasedness, consistency and efficiency as would be the case in the probabilistic framework.

A further source of inspiration is drawn from the apparent contradiction in the views of Popper and Jeffreys on simplicity, as chronicled by Keuzenkamp and McAleer (1995, pp. 10, 12). Keuzenkamp and McAleer demonstrate that Popper's view, implying that 'theories that are simple and easy to falsify, i.e. theories with high empirical content' are linked with improbability, is flawed, judged on its Bayesian, probabilistic consistency. As an alternative, Keuzenkamp and McAleer opt for Jeffreys' view on simplicity: 'variation is random until the contrary is shown', implying that probability is increasing with simplicity. The judgment on these two views seems to go hand in hand with the methodological framework used to assess both views. In this contribution, we will break a lance for Popper's view, this time reasoning within a behavioural framework of modelling.

Behavioural approach

In our common parlance, simplicity is related to manifestation: 'For both objects and concepts the most obvious meanings of "simple" relate to homogeneity in structure and the absence, or at least small number, of discernible parts or partitions ... A simple dress, painting, symphony, theory, or society has fewer lines, curves, colors, classes, or other internal differentiations than a more complicated one' (Slobodkin, 1992, p. 2). This description is the very first attempt by Slobodkin to capture the idea of simplicity and the starting point of what can be viewed as a kind of Bildungsroman of the concept simplicity within the domains of art, religion and science. The pinnacle of this development is to be found in the last chapter, 'Masters of Reality', where simplicity is defined as dimensionality. Plato's myth of the cave, populated by prisoners who observe only the two-dimensional shadows of the three-dimensional objects outside their cave, serves as a illuminating example (Slobodkin, 1992, p. 206). In principle, by noting the changes in shapes of these shadows, the prisoners might eventually have developed a three-dimensional theory of objects; but they lacked the ability to do that. However, Slobodkin continues:

We have now the general techniques for considering how many dimensions are relevant to analyse some sets of data. In a general sense, more complex things require more terms in their description than more simple things. The number of dimensions required to specify a situation depends on how much complexity we are willing to consider, and this may depend on what we want to do or say... It is ... often useful to ... consider how many dimensions might be relevant and how they should be arranged in 'space' in order to suggest ways of thinking about data. There is no necessary numerical limit to the number of dimensions involved. The more kinds of things we know about anything, the more likely we are able to deal with it in a realistic way. (Slobodkin, 1992, pp. 206, 207)

Opting for a semantic construal of simplicity, and also defining the complexity of a system – being the opposite of simplicity – as the dimension of the system, characterizes the modelling approach called 'behavioural modelling'. Without giving a full exposition on this approach – for that purpose we refer to the numerous publications of Willems and Heij, on which this contribution is largely based – it is our intention to provide the reader with a sufficient notion of behavioural modelling as to sense the perspective of an alternative definition of simplicity and its role in modelling. In this behavioural approach, all concepts are semantic by nature: simplicity, complexity, but also accuracy and the concept model itself. This semantic nature implies a non-parametric approach: a model is not the same thing as a structural model, consisting of mathematical equations with unknown para-meters; a model is defined in terms of its behaviour, that is, the set of all outcomes that are allowed by the system. In the dynamic case, and we will concentrate on that, these are trajectories in time. Behavioural model selection, like traditional estimation, involves a trade-off between the complexity and the accuracy of the model. Accuracy is measured as the error or misfit of the system with respect to the observed behaviour (time series). Contrary to other modelling approaches, fit isn't measured in terms of local restrictions, as in equation error methods, but in terms of the global distance from the observed time series to the nearest time series within the model. This implies a non-parametric implementation of fit: it is defined purely in terms of external behaviour and involves no parameters. As we have indicated before, complexity, the second criterion, is also defined in a non-parametric way. In the static case, the complexity is the dimension of the system, which equals the number of driving forces (inputs or exogenous variables). In the dynamic case, depending upon the repre-sentation chosen, complexity is determined by the number of states and the number of driving forces (in a state space representation), or by the number of equations and the number of lags (in a poly-nomial representation).

Before we elaborate further on the behavioural approach, we will descend one last time into Plato's cave, to discover if and to what degree the above definition of complexity, or simplicity, does indeed correspond to its usual meaning. The prisoners in the cave couldn't observe the three-dimensional world outside, but only a two-dimen-sional reduction of it, in the form of shades projected on the wall. Both in Slobodkin's language and in behavioural modelling, this reduc-tion is a simplification: the shades have a simpler form than their three-dimensional originals. One can pursue this example even one step further by assuming that Plato's cave resembles a cavern with an extre-mely narrow entrance. In that case, all shadows are one-dimensional, implying a further reduction of the behaviour compatible with the pro-jection operation. However, if we describe the behaviour by means of a parametric model, each reduction step implies the introduction of another equation containing several parameters, thus decreasing para-metric simplicity instead of increasing it.

Behavioural models and equations

Assume we have a *phenomenon* we want to model. In defining a proper language, we assume that the phenomenon produces elements in a set U

that we call the *universe*. Elements of U will be called the *outcomes* of the phenomenon. Now, a mathematical model for the phenomenon claims that certain outcomes are possible, whilst others are not. Hence a model recognizes a certain subset B of U. This subset will be called the *behaviour* (of the model). Formally: a *behavioural model* is a pair (U, B) with U the *universe* – its elements are called *outcomes* – and B the *behaviour*.

> **Example**: the price of a good being non-negative may be viewed as modelling the phenomenon price. Thus $U = \mathbb{R}$ and $B = [0, \infty)$. And a second example: the production possibilities of an economy, facing a Cobb–Douglas production function, is described by the model: $U = \mathbb{R}_+^3$ and $B = \{(Y, K, L) \in \mathbb{R}_+^3 | Y = \alpha K^\beta L^{1-\beta}; \alpha, \beta \in \mathbb{R}_+; 0 \leq \alpha; 0 \leq \beta \leq 1\}$.

In applications, models are more often than not described by equations. We will make use of them in the behavioural approach as follows: let U be a universe, E an abstract set, called the equating space, and $f: U \to E$. The behavioural model (U, B) with $B = \{u \in U | f(u) = 0\}$ is said to be described by *behavioural equation(s)*.

Whereas equations uniquely specify the behaviour, the converse is obviously not true. Since we have a tendency to think of mathematical models in terms of equations, most models being presented in that form, it is important to emphasize their ancillary role: it is the behaviour, the solution set of the behavioural equations, and not the behavioural equations themselves, which is the essential result of a modelling procedure. The equations are just a (non-unique) representation of that behaviour.

Dynamic systems

The next step is the application of this view of mathematical models to set up a language for dynamic systems. In many disciplines, there is a tendency to view systems as processors, producing output signals from input signals. There are without doubt applications where it is eminently clear what the inputs and the outputs are. However, there are also many applications where this input–output structure is not at all evident. So we will view a dynamic system in the logical context of static systems defined before as symmetric models, in which all variables are treated on the same footing. The only distinguishing feature is that now the phenomenon produces outcomes that are functions of time: the universe U is a function space. More formally, this can be described as follows: a *dynamic system* Σ is a triple, $\Sigma = (T, W, B)$, with $T \subset \mathbb{R}$ the time axis, W the signal space, and $B \subset W^T$ the behaviour of the system.

This description does not refer to input–output maps, relations or behavioural equations: a dynamic system is defined as a family of trajectories. In the triptych that constitutes a dynamic system, T is the time set of interest. Usually T is an (infinite) interval in $\mathbb{R}$ or Z, and in the discrete time series case $T = Z$ or $T = Z_+$. W is the space in which the time signals that the system produces take on their values, and B is a family of W-valued time trajectories. Whereas the sets T and W define the setting, B formalizes the laws that govern the system. According to the dynamic model Σ, time signals in B can in principle occur and are compatible with the laws of the system, while those outside B cannot occur and are prohibited.

Inherent to modelling is the use of a restricted model class. This restriction is prior in nature: independent of the data, we impose a certain structure on the models we are willing to accept. In the model selection phase, we subsequently infer additional structure from the data. The restrictions we introduce are the following: we focus on discrete time systems, so the time set equals the set of integers: $T = Z$. The system we study contains q variables that take on real values and evolve in discrete time: so the signal set is $\mathbb{R}^q$ for some integer $q \geq 1$. A system then is a set of q-dimensional time series: $B \subset (\mathbb{R}^q)^Z$. As model class we take the subclass of the systems in $(\mathbb{R}^q)^Z$ that are linear, time invariant and complete.

- A system $B \subset (\mathbb{R}^q)^Z$ is called *linear* if it is a linear subspace of $(\mathbb{R}^q)^Z$.
- A system B is called *time invariant* if its time lag LB also satisfies the laws of the system: $LB = B$.
- A system B is called *complete* if, in order to check whether a time series w belongs to B or not, it is sufficient to consider it does so for all finite time intervals. Completeness is only an interesting property when T is an unbounded subset of $\mathbb{R}$, for example in the discrete time series case $T = Z$ or $T = Z_+$. Then completeness simply says that the behaviour at plus or minus infinity is of no consequence for deciding whether or not w belongs to B (the behaviour is closed in the topology of pointwise convergence).

The class of linear, time-invariant and complete systems is of special interest since each member of this class corresponds to a linear, time-invariant, finite-dimensional system. And such systems can be represented with behavioural equations having alternative formats: each element of the model class B of linear, time-invariant and complete systems allows a representation according to each of the following parametrizations (see Willems, 1986a, Heij, 1989, or Heij et al., 1997):

- polynomial (autoregressive) representation: $R(L)w = 0$
- input/output representation: $P(L)y = Q(L)u$, $w = \text{col}(u,y)$
- state space representation: $L^{-1}x = Ax + Bv$, $w = Cx + Dv$
- input/state/output representation: $L^{-1}x = Ax + Bu$, $w = Cx + Du$, $w = \text{col}(u,y)$
- transfer function representation: $w = G(L)v$.

These representations exhibit different degrees of structure. For example, in the input/output representation a causality structure is shown, and external variables are subdivided into two classes: the inputs, the causes: free variables that are left unexplained; and the outputs, the effects: bound variables that are explained by the model. However, in the AR-representation such a causality structure is absent. State representations display the state as an auxiliary variable: the state is a memory function which shows what part of the past is relevant for the future behaviour. The input/state/output representations display both their causality and their memory structure.

The fact that each linear, time-invariant and complete system can be represented in each of the above formats implies for this class of systems that causality (and memory) is a matter of representation and not an *a priori* axiom which needs to be imposed. In other words, in this model class one can always obtain causality by properly interpreting the variables.

Modelling objectives

The selection of an approximate deterministic model involves three ingredients: the objectives of modelling, denoted by π, a set of conceivable data, denoted by D, and a model class, denoted by M. For model selection we need a procedure which for a given data set assigns a model in the prespecified class M. This *data modelling procedure* can be expressed as a map: $P: D \rightarrow 2^M$. The aim of any procedure is to find models that are optimal with respect to the objectives π.

In constructing models from data, two general objectives are placed in the forefront:

- we want to infer from the data as much *structure* as possible, and
- the model is an *accurate* description of the data.

Structure is generated by laws: the more laws a model claims, the more structure it implies. Each law imposes restrictions on the variables under consideration, and thus implies a reduction of the dimension of the solution space. For that reason, greater simplicity is a synonym for more structure, in the behavioural view. Also, a simpler model is more easily falsified, since it counts more restrictions each of which can be falsified separately. As a consequence, the *simplicity* principle, the *falsifiability* principle and the *striving for structure* are synonyms, once we accept the behavioural view on systems and modelling.

The second principle is the *corroboration* principle: although we want to infer as many laws from the data as possible, we want to accept laws only if there is sufficient evidence for them from the data. Such evidence for a law is measured applying a criterion of *fit* of the law with respect to the data.

As a next step, we assume that the objectives π can be specified by a complexity map $c: M \to C$ and a misfit map $\varepsilon: D \times M \to E$. Both spaces C and E are assumed to be partially ordered. It is desirable to design procedures that find models with both low complexity and small misfit: simple models that are corroborated by the data. However, in general these goals are conflicting. We therefore assume that π can be expressed as a utility function, that is a map $u: C \times E \to U$, where U is a partially ordered set. In this case, our selection procedure P_u picks that model for which the complexity and misfit are such that the corresponding utility is maximal.

In case the complexity space C and the misfit space E are both totally ordered, two specific modelling procedures can be classified:

- $P_{c/tol}$ or *modelling under a complexity constraint*: this procedure determines the most accurate model amongst those models that obey a prespecified maximal tolerated complexity level c_{tol}.
- $P_{\varepsilon/tol}$ or *modelling under a misfit constraint*: this procedure determines the most simple model amongst those models that obey a prespecified maximal tolerated misfit level ε_{tol}.

These two different modelling strategies show some similarities to the 'simple to general' approach and the 'general to specific' or reductionist approach to modelling, respectively.

> **Example** (see Heij, 1989, pp. 25, 28): the maximum likelihood estimation of a univariate time-series model. For instance, let M consist of the class of ARMA-models and D be the set of finite times series. For M $\in$ M we can define the complexity $c(M)$ as e.g. max $\{d_1, d_2\}$ with d_1 the degree of the AR-part and d_2 the degree of the MA-part. For M $\in$ M and $w \in D$ we define the misfit $\varepsilon(w, M)$ as the inverse of the likelihood of M for w. For given c_{tol}, the procedure $P_{c/tol}$ models the time series by means of an ARMA-model of maximum likelihood, under the restriction

max $\{d_1, d_2\} < c_{tol}$. For 'non-degenerate data', the optimal solution satisfies $d_1 = d_2 = c_{tol}$. For given minimal tolerated likelihood $1/\varepsilon_{tol}$, the procedure $P_{\varepsilon/tol}$ minimizes max $\{d_1, d_2\}$ under the likelihood constraint, which gives a solution of the model order selection problem.

Behavioural modelling

The restriction of the model class M to the aforementioned class of linear, time-invariant and finite-dimensional systems results in the following modelling problem: find a decomposition $w = \hat{w} + \tilde{w}$ of the observed q-dimensional time series w where the unobserved, latent trajectory $\hat{w}$ is the behaviour of a linear system. Such a behaviour is a subset $B \subset (\mathbb{R}^q)^Z$ of the set of all time series over Z. For 'non-degenerate data' only high-dimensional linear systems with long lag structures will model the observed data exactly. In that case $w = \hat{w}$. Linear models corresponding to simpler behaviours induce a non-zero approximation error $\tilde{w}$. As stated before, the modelling objective is to trade off the *accuracy* of the model, inversely related to the size of this approximation error with the simplicity of the model. We measure the *approximation error* by the squared distance between the data and the linear system, that is:

$$\|w - \hat{w}\|^2 = \sum_{t=1}^{T} \sum_{j=1}^{q} [w_j(t) - \hat{w}_j(t)]^2$$

with $T = [1..T]$ the time-interval of the observations.

The next step is to define the simplicity/complexity of the behavioural model. Since each behavioural model allows for several representations, we can interpret this definition in different ways. First of all, $\hat{w}$ can be represented as the solution set of the *polynomial* (autoregressive) equations:

$$R(L) \cdot \hat{w} = 0$$

with R a full row rank polynomial matrix in the lag operator L. We interpret this representation as an input–output system in polynomial form, where p, the rank of R, so the number of independent equations, equals the number of outputs, and $m := q{-}p$ the number of inputs. In this representation, we denote with n the sum of the degrees of the p polynomial equations. Those degrees are the longest lags contained in each equation, so n, being the sum of these separate lags, can be viewed as the 'total lag'. For that reason, a further interpretation of n is the minimal number of initial conditions required to express future outputs in terms of future inputs.

Alternatively, $\hat{w}$ can be represented in *state space* form:

$$x_{t+1} = A \cdot x_t + B \cdot v_t, \hat{w} = C \cdot x_t + D \cdot v_t$$

Here v is an m-dimensional auxiliary vector of unrestricted and unobserved driving variables (inputs), and x is an n-dimensional vector of unobserved state-variables. Both representations are highly non-unique. We reduce the non-uniqueness by focusing on *minimal* representations: representations that have fewer driving variables (m), or the same number of driving variables but fewer states (n), than any other representation.

A third representation is in terms of *transfer functions*:

$$\hat{w} = G(L)v$$

In this representation, m is the rank of the transfer function G, and n the so-called McMillan degree, the sum of the Kronecker indices of the q polynomials (see Heij et al., 1997).

The pair (m, n) of a minimal representation is used as a measure of the *complexity* of the system B. The intuition behind this choice of the two indices determining complexity will be clear from the preceding discussion. The complexity measure (m, n) is directly related to the dimension of the linear space B_T, the restriction of the behaviour B to the time interval $[1..T]$. That dimension equals $mT + n$. So the complexity is defined by the number of inputs and the number of states of the system when referring to a state space representation. Or by the number of inputs and the total lag (number of initial conditions) in case of a polynomial representation. The simpler a system, the fewer degrees of freedom it has. There are two different kinds of degrees of freedom: the initial ones, and the degrees of freedom at each time instant. The first equals the dimension of the state, the second equals the dimension of the input vector.

Deterministic modelling

In the static case, the modelling problem is to describe a finite number of points in $\mathbb{R}^q$ by means of a linear subspace. So data set D consists of the finite subsets of $\mathbb{R}^q$ and the model class M consists of the linear subspaces of $\mathbb{R}^q$. In this case, the state dimension $n = 0$ and the measure of *complexity of a model* $M \in M$ reduces to its dimension: $c^D(M) = \dim(M)$. So the simpler the model, the lower its dimension, the more it excludes, the easier it is to falsify. In this static case, our complexity definition results in a total ordering, thereby fulfilling the requirements of the two procedures of minimizing misfit under a complexity constraint $P_{c/tol}$ and minimizing complexity under a misfit constraint $P_{\varepsilon/tol}$. Those procedures are based on singular value decomposition of the empirical covariance matrix (see Willems, 1986a, or Heij, 1989). There is a close relationship between these procedures and total least squares.

In the dynamic case, the modelling problem is to describe a finite number of q-valued vectors in $(\mathbb{R}^q)^T$ by means of a linear, time-invariant and finite-dimensional system. As a measure of complexity, we take the pair (m, n). High complexity implies few and high-order laws: complex systems impose few restrictions on the behaviour, and are thus characterized by many degrees of freedom. In dynamic systems, this can be the result of a small number of laws, and laws that are 'loose' in nature, in the sense that they involve large lags and therefore only constrain the behaviour if long time series are considered. However, this definition of complexity only induces a partial ordering, not total ordering. So the procedure of minimizing misfit under a complexity constraint $P_{c/tol}$ and that minimizing complexity under a misfit constraint $P_{\varepsilon/tol}$ has to contain a grid-search step: for a range of complexities (m, n), the accuracy of the model is calculated and traded-off against the simplicity. $P_{c/tol}$ first finds the maximal number of zero-order relations under the misfit constraint (as is the static problem). Among the solutions, which are in general non-unique, those with minimal misfit are preferred. Subsequently the number of first-order relations is maximized, again under the misfit constraint. And so on. $P_{\varepsilon/tol}$ first minimizes the misfit of the zero-order laws that are compatible with the tolerated complexity, then continues with the truly first-order laws, and so on.

Dynamic factor models

A direct extension of the above modelling procedure is to consider stochastic systems. The extension is bought at some cost, e.g. in the form of making assumptions on the stochastic processes w, $\hat{w}$ and $\tilde{w}$. But the cost brings some additional returns: the model of behaviour $\hat{w}$ can be interpreted as a factor model. For an elaboration of this stochastic case, we refer to Heij et al. (1997) and Scherrer and Heij (1997).

Conclusion and comparisons

In this contribution an (informal) introduction to the behavioural systems framework and approximate modelling is given. This approach allows for a non-parametric definition of the concepts of simplicity, complexity and accuracy. Among other things, this approach seems to be a way out of the apparent paradox built in parametric applications of the concept of simplicity: they require parameters to be important aspects of the modelling process, but will only contribute to that process in cases where there are no obvious candidates for such structural parameters.

The second advantage of the behavioural approach is its capacity to reconcile Popper's view on simplicity and this framework of modelling (dynamic) phenomena, thereby rejecting Jeffreys' simplicity postulate. The hypothesis that all variation is random, in the sense of being unexplained by the model, is not the simplest hypothesis one can think of, it is just the reverse: it is the most complex hypothesis one can possibly suggest. The more structure is added, the more manifestations are excluded, the simpler the hypothesis gets, and the more easily it is falsified.

If we regard the opening paragraph of Keuzenkamp and McAleer (1997): 'it seems natural to consider a trade-off between simplicity and empirical validity. In order to determine such a trade-off, simplicity has to be defined precisely, and the same holds for empirical validity', as summarizing the major objective of any theory on simplicity, the behavioural approach performs its duty. And how does it relate to other contributions on the concept of simplicity? In the framework proposed by Sober (2001), behavioural simplicity is a semantic construal. Our definition even allows us to answer one of the (rhetorical) questions posed in Sober's contribution: the hypothesis of egoism is indeed simpler than the hypothesis of motivational pluralism, not because of the smaller number of postulated types of ultimate desire, but because it is more restrictive with regard to the behaviour that is compatible with the hypothesis: it restricts more, and thus is easier to falsify (the other examples in Sober's contribution are more difficult to integrate into our behavioural framework). Spanos (2001) offers a further binary classification of simplicity concepts (albeit with less appealing names). Behavioural simplicity falls into his first category.

Although the above quote from Keuzenkamp and McAleer isn't precise enough to rigorously deduce the following principle, it seems at least to suggest it: in trading off accuracy and simplicity, we trade off a property of the model alone (simplicity) and a property of both model and data (accuracy). There seem to be some attractive intuitive arguments for using a data-independent definition of simplicity, for example, why should it be obvious that adding one observation to the data sample still using the same model increases the complexity? The large watershed between the several contributions on simplicity is to be found in this characteristic: is simplicity a *property of the model* (so data-independent), or of the *data and the model* together (so data-dependent)? All information-theory-based definitions of simplicity fall into this second category: stochastic complexity (Rissanen, 2001), Kolmogorov complexity (Vitányi and Li, 2001) and Simon's parsimony principle (Simon, 2001). Given the strong ties of information theory and the application areas of coding, speech processing and signal recognition, this does not surprise. The main objective of modelling in these areas is to achieve efficiency gains in transferring data. But after the transfer has taken place, the original data is to be reconstructed. This gives a very special meaning to the word noise (see e.g. Rissanen, 2001): it is that part of the data for which no efficiency gains can be achieved. But in this area there isn't such a thing as an approximate model, so the code length of the noise is an integral part of Rissanen's stochastic complexity, and even has the same weight as the code length of the model. But then, there is in fact no real trade-off between accuracy and simplicity: the definition of simplicity by its very nature presumes full accuracy, and no accuracy-loss is tolerated. In contrast, data-independent definitions of simplicity seem to be more natural in application areas where noise is seen as error: inevitable but uninteresting, since it disturbs our view on the 'true underlying system'. In that case, the only objective is to eliminate this noise, and in no way to reconstruct it.

The view that simplicity is a model property, accuracy is a property of the relation between model and data, and the essence of modelling is the trade-off between those two concepts, shares the behavioural approach with interpretations of simplicity based on 'counting parameters' (see Keuzenkamp and McAleer, 1997, p. 553). But besides this common background, the two approaches choose sharply diverging routes in their definition of simplicity, as is illustrated in this chapter.

REFERENCES

Heij, C. (1989). *Deterministic Identification of Dynamical Systems*. Lecture Notes in Control and Information Sciences 127. Berlin, New York: Springer.
— (1992). Exact modelling and identifiability of linear systems. *Automatica – Journal of the IFAC* 28 (2): 325–44.
— (1993). System identifiability from finite time series. *Automatica – Journal of the IFAC* 29 (4): 1065–77.
— (1994). *Measurement from a System Theoretic Perspective*. Rotterdam: discussion paper Tinbergen Institute.
Heij, C., W. Scherrer and M. Deistler (1997). System identification by dynamic factor models. *SIAM Journal on Control and Optimization* 35 (6): 1924–51.
Kalman, R.-E. (1980). A system-theoretic critique of dynamic economic models. *International Journal of Policy Analysis and Information Systems* 4 (1): 3–22.
— (1982a). Identifiability and problems of model selection in econometrics. In Werner Hildenbrand (ed.), *Advances in Econometrics: Invited Papers for the Fourth World Congress of the Econometric Society at Aix-en-Provence, September 1980*, ch. 6, pp. 169–207. (Econometric Society Monographs in Quantitative Economics 2.) Cambridge: Cambridge University Press.

(1982b). System identification from noisy data. In *Dynamical Systems II*, pp. 135–64. New York, London: Academic Press.

(1983). Identifiability and modeling in econometrics. In *Developments in Statistics*, vol. 4, pp. 97–136. New York, London: Academic Press.

Keuzenkamp, H. A. and M. McAleer (1995). Simplicity, scientific inference and econometric modelling. *The Economic Journal* 105 (1): 1–21.

(1997). The concept of simplicity. *Mathematics and Computers in Simulation* 43: 553–61.

Rissanen, J. (2001). Simplicity and statistical inference. In this volume.

Simon, H. (2001). Science seeks parsimony, not simplicity: searching for pattern in phenomena. In this volume.

Scherrer, W. and C. Heij (1997). Identification of factor models by behavioural and subspace methods. *Systems and Control Letters* 32: 335–44.

Slobodkin, L. B. (1992). *Simplicity and Complexity in Games of the Intellect*. Cambridge, MA: Harvard University Press.

Sober, E. (2001). What is the problem of simplicity? In this volume.

Spanos, A. (2001). Parametric versus non-parametric inference. In this volume.

Vitány, P. and M. Li (2001). Simplicity, information, Kolmogorov complexity, and prediction. In this volume.

Willems, J. C. (1986a). From time series to linear system. I. Finite-dimensional linear time invariant systems. *Automatica – Journal of the IFAC* 22 (5): 561–80.

(1986b). From time series to linear system. II. Exact modelling. *Automatica – Journal of IFAC* 22 (6): 675–94.

(1987). From time series to linear system. III. Approximate modelling. *Automatica – Journal of IFAC* 23 (1): 87–115.

(1989a). Models for dynamics. *Dynamics Reported* 2: 171–269.

(1989b). *From Data to Model*. Berlin, New York: Springer.

(1991). Paradigms and puzzles in the theory of dynamical systems. *IEEE Transactions on Automatic Control* 36 (3): 259–94.

(1993). Laudatio for the Johann Bernoulli Lecture for Rudolf Kalman. *Nieuw Archief voor Wiskunde* 11 (1): 43–50.

14   Keep it sophisticatedly simple

Arnold Zellner

1   Introduction

Some years ago, I came upon the phrase used in industry, 'Keep it simple stupid', that is, KISS, and thought about it in relation to scientific model-building. Since some simple models are stupid, I decided to reinterpret KISS to mean 'Keep it sophisticatedly simple.' In any event, KISS is very popular in many scientific and non-scientific areas. For example, the slogan of the Honda Motor Company is, 'We make it simple.' The Dutch Schipol airport in its advertising claims that, 'It excels because it is simple and convenient.' And it is well known that Einstein advised in connection with theorizing in the natural sciences, 'Make it as simple as possible but no simpler.' Also, the famous physicist Jaynes (1985, p. 344) wrote, 'We keep our model as simple as possible so as not to obscure the point to be made and also to heed Arnold Zellner's wise advice about "sophisticatedly simple" models.'

Many, including myself, have for long advocated that workers in econometrics and statistics follow the advice of natural scientists and others to keep analyses and models sophisticatedly simple. In addition, I have pointed out that there are many important, sophisticatedly simple models and methods that work well in practice, that is in explanation and prediction, namely $s = \frac{1}{2} gt^2$, $E = mc^2$, $PV = RT$, maxent, etc. in the physical sciences and the laws of demand and supply, the Fisher equation, no arbitrage conditions, Marshall's competitive industry model, Friedman's and Becker's consumer models, the method of least squares, maximum likelihood techniques, Bayesian analysis, etc. in economics, econometrics and statistics. See Zellner (1997) for further discussion of these topics. Further, for many years, I have challenged many audiences to give me an example of a large, complicated model in any field that works well in explaining

Research financed in part by the US National Science Foundation and by income from the H.G.B. Alexander Endowment Fund, Graduate School of Business, University of Chicago.

past data and experience and in predicting new data. As yet, I have not heard of a single one.

Certainly, the many large-scale, complicated macroeconometric models of national economies, involving hundreds of non-linear stochastic difference equations have not been very successful in explanation and prediction. See, for example, Christ (1951), Friedman (1951), Cooper (1972), Nelson (1972), Nelson and Plosser (1982), Meese and Rogoff (1983), McNees (1986), Garcia-Ferrer et al. (1987) and Smyth (1983) for evidence on the forecasting performance of a sample of complicated macroeconometric models. In general, these studies found their forecasting performance to be unsatisfactory and in a number of instances no better or worse than that of random walk models and other simple, univariate time series models. As many have noted, if a large-scale model using many variables and data on them, along with much background subject-matter information and theory, cannot perform better in prediction than a simple random walk model, the large, complicated model is probably defective. Rather than complicated, large Stanley steamers that often break down and sometimes explode, we need dependable Model T or A Fords which can be improved with additional work.

Further, Adelman and Adelman (1959), Hickman (1972), Zellner and Peck (1973) and others have reported the results of simulation experiments with several, leading complicated macroeconometric models that cast doubt on their value. Indeed, with some models that have hundreds of non-linear stochastic difference equations, it is very difficult to show that they have a unique solution and their dynamic properties are hard to establish. If questions about these basic issues cannot be answered, then, in my opinion, these models should be labelled 'UNSAFE FOR USE'. Recently, after much unsatisfactory performance, US Federal Reserve officials decided to scrap the large-scale, complicated Federal Reserve-MIT–PENN model and commence construction of a new model. Similarly, the Federal Reserve Bank of Minneapolis is revising its complicated vector autoregressive (VAR, i.e., Very Awful Regression) models after their poor performance in forecasting turning points, etc. Also, on a visit to the Federal Reserve Bank of New Zealand a few years ago, I was told by researchers there that they have stopped using big, complicated models and are developing simple aggregate demand-and-supply models in attempts to understand their economy and to make good forecasts.

When James Tobin, a Nobel Prize winner in economics, was on the US Council of Economic Advisors some years ago, I asked him if he used complicated macroeconometric models in his work for the Council. He responded that he didn't because he and others could not understand the workings and output of such models and thus did not have much confidence in them. When I asked what he actually did use to analyse problems, he remarked that he used a simple multiplier–accelerator model on the back of an envelope and even though he didn't have too much confidence in it, he said at least he understood what he was doing. In addition, in personal correspondence with Jan Tinbergen I learned that he too favoured starting analyses with sophisticatedly simple models. The same can be said for other Nobel Prize winners, Gary Becker, Milton Friedman, Robert Lucas, Merton Miller, Robert Solow, George Stigler, James Tobin and many others. That this is the case with respect to these leading researchers and many others contrasts markedly with the statement in Keuzenkamp and McAleer (1995, p. 17), 'In econometrics, Zellner is a rare exception in support of the simplicity postulate; Zellner ... opposes a "top–down" (general to specific) approach.' On the contrary, there are many in econometrics and economics who oppose a 'top–down' approach and like to KISS.

In addition to many other scientists, Sir Harold Jeffreys advocated the use of simple models in his books, *Theory of Probability* (1939, 1948, 1961, 1967, 1988) and *Scientific Inference* (1931, 1957). With respect to the former book, the eminent statistician I. J. Good (1980, p. 32) has written, 'In summary, Jeffreys' pioneering work ... has had a large permanent influence on statistical logic and techniques. In my review (Good, 1962b), I said that Jeffreys' book on probability "is of greater importance for the philosophy of science and obviously of greater practical importance, than nearly all the books on probability written by professional philosophers lumped together".'

With this in the way of an introduction, I shall now provide an overview of the remaining sections of this chapter. In section 2, a brief review of the thoughts of Sir Harold Jeffreys, formerly of Cambridge University, on simplicity and its role in science will be provided.[1] Then his numerical measure of the complexity of differential equation systems will be reviewed and discussed. In section 3, Jeffreys' measure will be applied to several central time series and other models that are often used in econometrics and statistics. Some specific procedures for extending Jeffreys' measure of complexity to apply to difference equation systems, distributions of random structural and measurement errors will be provided employing engineers' state space modelling concepts. The discussion and methods of sections 2 and 3 are considered in relation to some

---

[1] In Zellner (1980), a volume dedicated to Jeffreys, leading statisticians and econometricians summarize his contributions to the philosophy of science, statistical science and Bayesian analysis.

structural econometric and time series modelling procedures that have been employed in practice in section 4. Examples will be provided to illustrate general points. Last, in section 5 some conclusions and topics that deserve further work are presented.

2   Jeffreys' views on simplicity and his measure of model complexity

In section 1 a number of prominent, important simple models and methods from several sciences were mentioned. They all have the property that they are widely used in analysing many problems and yield useful results. I believe that such impressive behaviour of relatively simple models has been appreciated by many and hence the widespread belief in the efficacy of sophisticatedly simple models. On this issue, Jeffreys (1961, pp. 4–5) has written,

It is asserted, for instance, that choice of the simplest law [or model] is purely a matter of economy of description or thought, and has nothing to do with any reason for believing the law [or model] . . . I say on the contrary, the simplest law is chosen because it is the most likely to give correct predictions; that the choice is based on a reasonable degree of belief; and the fact that deductive logic provides no explanation of the choice of the simplest law [or model] is an absolute proof that deductive logic is grossly inadequate to cover scientific and practical requirements.

Further, he points out that 'the tendency to claim that scientific method can be reduced in some way to deductive logic . . . is the most fundamental fallacy of all: it can be done only by rejecting its chief feature, induction' (p. 2). Jeffreys defines induction as generalization from past data and experience to explain past experience and data and predict future experience and data. In his book, *Theory of Probability*, he develops and successfully applies a system of inductive logic that serves the needs of scientists and applied workers in all fields.

In Jeffreys' discussion of models, he explicitly points out that including too many terms in a relation can improve fit but 'the conclusion is that including too many terms will lose accuracy in prediction instead of gaining it' (1961, p. 46). He goes on to explain,

All we have to say is that the simpler laws [or models] have the greater prior probabilities. This is what Wrinch and I called the *simplicity postulate*. (p. 47)

He remarks that he requires that laws or models be put in an order of decreasing prior probability that represents a degree of confidence in a particular law or model. As he points out,

To make the order definite, however, requires a numerical rule for assessing the complexity of a law. In the case of laws expressible by differential equations this is easy. We could define the complexity of a differential equation, cleared of roots and fractions, by the sum of the order, the degree, and the absolute values of the coefficients. (1961, p. 47)

He also mentions that, 'All the laws of classical physics are in fact expressible by differential equations, and those of quantum physics are derived from them by various systematic modifications' (1961, p. 47). It is also the case that many economic and econometric models are in differential or difference equation form.

Thus in terms of explaining a particular phenomenon, there is, in Jeffreys' view, an infinity of possible models. He indicates how to produce an ordering of models with respect to degree of complexity. Then he suggests assigning probabilities to each with simpler models given higher probabilities in a convergent sequence that is assumed to sum to one. The probabilities so assigned to models can be employed to form prior odds and used to compute posterior odds in evaluating alternative models with data. As many have noted, such model evaluation procedures incorporate 'penalties for complexity', see, e.g. Zellner and Min (1997, p. 396).

With regard to other uses of Jeffreys' complexity measure, if simpler models are given higher prior probabilities of being adequate, then in the choice between a simple model, say M1, and a complicated model, say M2, there is a preference for M1, *a priori*. Also, if the construction of M1 is less costly than that of M2, the preference for M1 is probably strengthened. Further, if M1 is chosen and found to be inadequate, many believe that it is easier to determine the causes of the inadequacy and to remedy them in the case of a simple model than in the case of a complicated model. These are considerations that seem important in the choice between M1 and M2 and Jeffreys' prior probabilities associated with simple and complicated models play an important role in this and other model choice problems.

To illustrate his measure of complexity, Jeffreys (1961, pp. 48–9) considers 'laws of the following form, $y = ax^n$ where n is restricted to be a particular integer. Cleared of the parameter a this gives the differential equation $x\frac{dy}{dx} = ny$ the complexity of which is $n + 4$.' The parameter a is cleared from the equation by differentiating $\log y = \log a + n\log x$ with respect to x which yields the equation presented above, a first-order differential equation with the sum of the absolute values of its coefficients equal to $n + 1$ and its degree equal to 2 and thus of complexity $n + 4$. Note that the order of a differential equation is the order of the highest derivative appearing in it; see, e.g. Bakker (1966, p. 101) or texts on differential equations. As regards the degree of the equation, here

Jeffreys considers it to be 2, the degree of the product $x\,dy/dx$, a convention that is widely used even though the mathematical definition of the degree of a differential equation is given in Bakker (1966, p. 94) as 'The degree of the highest order derivative.' According to this definition, the above equation is of degree 1 and it would be equal to 1 for any value of q in the following differential equation, $x^q\,dy/dx = ny$ whereas Jeffreys' value of the degree of this equation is $q + 1$, a measure that reflects the added complexity vis-à-vis, e.g. a value of $q = 0$. Given these considerations, we shall employ Jeffreys' convention in appraising the degree of differential and difference equations in what follows.

Jeffreys also considers the relation $y = ax^n$ in the case in which the value of n is 'wholly arbitrary', that is not necessarily equal to an integer. From $\log y = \log a + n\log x,\ xd^2y/dx^2 = (n/x)dy/dx$ and when $n = (x/y)dy/dx$ is substituted in this last relation, we obtain Jeffreys' equation, $xyd^2y/dx^2 + ydy/dx = xdy/dx$ which is of order 2, degree 3 and has sum of the absolute values of the coefficients equal to 3 and thus its complexity measure is 8. Note that the terms $x(dy/dx)^2$ and $xy\,d^2y/dx^2$ are each of degree 3, the degree of the equation.

Jeffreys also illustrates his complexity measure as follows. For the law, $s = a$, where s is distance and a is a constant, he states that 'it would be written as $ds/dt = 0$ [with t denoting time], with complexity $1 + 1 + 1 = 3$. $s = a + ut + \frac{1}{2}gt^2$ would become $d^2s/dt^2 = 0$ with complexity $2 + 1 + 1 = 4$ and so on' (p. 47). Note that in this last case, he employs the homogeneous, second-order differential equation for s. Solution of this homogeneous equation yields the complementary function $a + u\,t$, which when added to a particular solution of the non-homogeneous equation, e.g $\frac{1}{2}gt^2$, provides a general solution. Further for the non-homogeneous equation, $d^2s/dt^2 = g$ or $d^2y/dt^2 = 1$, where $y = s/g$, the complexity is $2 + 1 + 2 = 5$, larger than for the homogeneous equation considered above. Below, Jeffreys' complexity measure will be discussed further and used in conjunction with laws or models expressed in discrete time by use of difference equations with additive stochastic errors.

It should be emphasized that Jeffreys regards his rule as a first rough approximation to measuring complexity. If we write his rule as follows:

$$C = \text{Order} + \text{Degree} + \text{Sum of absolute values of} \qquad (1)$$
$$\text{normalized coefficients}$$
$$= O + D + S$$

where 'normalized coefficients' means that 'differential equations must be cleared of factors common to all terms' (p. 48) since otherwise 'multiplying the whole differential equation by an integer would apparently increase the complexity, though the result is exactly equivalent to the original equation' (p. 48). Very importantly, Jeffreys does *not* just count the number of parameters in a model. Rather he adds the absolute values of the parameters which of course can be expressed as their number, N, times their average absolute value. Thus a parameter that has a large absolute value contributes more to Jeffreys' measure of complexity, C, than one that has a small absolute value. To repeat, just counting the number of parameters to represent complexity is not in accord with Jeffreys' approach.

As regards the common practice of 'counting parameters' to measure complexity, Keuzenkamp and McAleer (1997, p. 554) are very critical of this practice and write,

Much of the literature in the philosophy of science and in econometrics deals with a popular definition of simplicity based on counting the number of parameters (or variables) of a model ... For example, Popper ... identifies simplicity with the paucity of parameters ... In practice, Rissanen's Minimum Description Length criterion is similar to defining a measure of simplicity by counting parameters. The paucity of parameters measure of simplicity does not seem satisfactory, in general, as several simple examples will demonstrate.

We shall consider some of these simple examples below and show that Jeffreys' measure is useful in distinguishing between or among models that have the same number of parameters with respect to their relative complexity. As indicated above, just counting the parameters does not take account of their magnitudes nor of other properties of the models in which they are embedded, e.g. order and degree of differential or difference equations. However, as pointed out above, the number of parameters appearing in a model is one ingredient of Jeffreys' measure of complexity.

To illustrate Jeffreys' rule further, consider a model that is often used to represent the growth of human and other populations, the differential equation with solution the logistic growth curve, namely,

$$dN/dt = r\,N\,(1 - N/K) \tag{2a}$$

or

$$d(N/K)/dt = r\,(N/K)(1 - N/K) \tag{2b}$$

where $N = N(t)$, population at time t, and r and K are parameters, the latter the limiting, equilibrium population. (2b) is a first-order differential equation of degree 2 with the sum of the parameter's absolute values $1 + 2r$. Thus Jeffreys' complexity measure is $1 + 2 + 1 + 2r = 4 + 2r$. A discrete-time version of (2b) is

$$N(t)/K - N(t-1)/K = r[N(t-1)/K][1 - N(t-1)/K] \qquad (3)$$

which is a first-order difference equation of second degree and thus the Jeffreys' measure of complexity is 4+2r. If the discrete time model that best approximates the continuous time model in (2) were to be considered, it would be more complicated than the model given in (3). Open problems are whether the differential equation is more complicated than the difference equation in this and other cases and how to measure the complexity of a mixed difference–differential equation model, say the model in (2), with a finite gestation lag introduced that can yield a solution with damped oscillatory solutions whereas (2) does not have oscillatory solutions.

Another simple example is the Harrod–Domar growth model for total real income, Y, namely $S = sY$, the savings equation and $I = vdY/dt$, the investment equation and $I = S$, the equilibrium condition. Then we obtain $vdY/dt = sY$ or $dz/dt = 1$, with $z = (v/s)\log Y$. Thus we have the complexity $C = 1 + 1 + 2 = 4$. If the savings function is elaborated to permit the parameter s to depend on Y – see Zellner and Moulton (1985) for some empirical evidence on this point – so that $S/Y \to 0$ as $Y \to 0$, and $S/Y \to 1$ as $Y \to \infty$, let us see how this alters the complexity of this model. Let $s = Y^\lambda/(Y^\lambda + A)$ with $A, \lambda > 0$, then $v(Y^\lambda + A)dY/dt = Y^{\lambda+1}$, or $r = d \log Y/dt = Y^\lambda/v(A + Y^\lambda)$ is the equilibrium condition, a non-linear first-order differential equation that is more complicated than that above.

Of course Jeffreys' rule in (1) is in a simple linear form with all terms receiving the same weight. Many other forms of (1) can be contemplated but true to his philosophy, Jeffreys starts with the simplest form and points to the need to investigate the extent to which it performs satisfactorily and would modify it if necessary to produce improved performance in measuring complexity. For example, one could consider various monotonic functions of C, say $f(C)$ as a measure of complexity rather than C itself. Or one might contemplate that C, the measure of complexity is related to order (O), degree (D) and sum of normalized coefficients, S, by $C = h(O, D, S)$ with h being a homogenous function of a given degree or perhaps a non-homogenous function. See Zellner and Ryu (1998) for some differential equations defining production functions' forms that can be ordered with respect to complexity that may be helpful in characterizing complexity functions. As with the forms of utility functions, loss functions, production functions, etc., choice of an appropriate functional form is an important issue that is usually approached by starting with simple forms and seeing how well they work in applications and modifying them if necessary. In this connection, see Tinbergen's discussion of the forms of social welfare functions for use in policy-making, Arrow's, and Solow's work on the CES production function, Friedman's, Becker's, Tobin's and Modigliani's consumer models and Lucas's rational expectations model to appreciate how these leading researchers in economics developed sophisticatedly simple models, much in the spirit of the approach described by Jeffreys. Namely, start simply and complicate the model only if necessary. Indeed, learning how and why a simple model performs poorly is important information in attempts to improve it.

Last, as is obvious, sophisticated simplicity is a relative term. It has to be considered in connection with our current state of knowledge. A random walk model may be a sophisticatedly simple model when little knowledge is available about the subject under consideration. However, in areas in which there is much subject-matter information, a random walk model is probably a stupid model. And other simple models that are known to be at variance with our knowledge are also stupid. A sophisticatedly simple model will not be in conflict with what is known and provides more in the way of understanding than currently available models. In this connection, Jeffreys' (1967, p. 50) comments on the Schrödinger partial differential wave equation in physics are illuminating,

One reviewer of *Scientific Inference* argued that on my theory Schrödinger's equation would have so high a complexity, and therefore so low an initial probability, that it could never have acquired a high probability. This argument overlooks the greater part of the book, which shows how by consideration of different types of data in turn and corresponding modification of the laws Schrödinger's equation is actually reached. Besides those mentioned as stages in the approximation hosts of others have been excluded as having negligible posterior probabilities, and it may well be true that Schrödinger's equation is the simplest of the survivors.

With this said about Jeffreys' views and his measure of complexity, the issue of how his measure works in connection with widely used time series models in econometrics and statistics will now be considered.

3   Measures of complexity for time series models

Herein, we apply Jeffreys' measure of complexity to some time series models encountered in econometrics and statistics. Then we shall consider measures of complexity for the distributions of error terms and relate these measures to our past work on producing forecasting and structural models for eighteen countries' output growth rates; see Garcia-Ferrer et al. (1987), Zellner and Hong (1989, 1991), Hong (1989), Zellner, Hong and Gulati (1991), Zellner, Hong and Min

(1991), Min (1992) and the review paper summarizing work in these and other papers, Zellner (1994).

Consider the following deterministic autoregressive models of order 1 and 2, denoted by AR(1) and AR(2), namely, $y(t) = ay(t-1)$ and $y(t) = ay(t-1) + by(t-2)$. Jeffreys' measure of complexity for the AR(1) and AR(2) are $O = 1, D = 1$ and sum of the absolute values of the coefficients, $1 + |a|$, that is $3 + |a|$ and $4 + |a| + |b|$, respectively and thus the AR(2) is more complex than the AR(1) given that the coefficient of $y(t-1)$ is the same in the two models. If it is not, then it is possible that the AR(2) model can have a complexity measure that is smaller in value than that for the AR(1) model. An example is $y(t) = by(t-2)$ which may be less complex than the above AR(1) model given that a is much larger than b in absolute value. Further, this last AR(2) containing just one parameter b is simpler than an AR(2) model containing two parameters, a and b. Also in terms of an AR(1) model, a model with the absolute value of larger than one, namely an explosive model, is more complicated than an AR(1) model with the absolute value of a less than one, that is a non-explosive process. Similar considerations apply to AR(2) models in that explosive models will tend to be more complicated than non-explosive models. See Zellner (1996, p. 196) for a plot of regions of the parameter space associated with explosive and non-explosive oscillatory and non-oscillatory solutions of an AR(2) process. And if we consider an m'th order AR process, it will usually be more complex in terms of Jeffreys' measure than lower-order processes. In summary, it is clearly the case that Jeffreys' complexity measure can be applied to deterministic AR processes without difficulty and appears to yield sensible results.

We now add an error term to our AR process, e.g. $y(t) = ay(t-1) + u(t)$. Then to evaluate Jeffreys' complexity measure, we can consider the homogenous part of the AR process, namely $y(t) = ay(t-1)$ and proceed as in the previous paragraph to evaluate his measure of complexity. Note however that if $u(t)$ is not white noise, e.g. it might be generated by an invertible AR(1) process, $u(t) = cu(t-1) + e(t)$ or $u(t) = e(t)/[1 - cL]$, where L is the lag operator such that $Lu(t) = u(t-1)$, we have, $[1 - aL][1 - cL]y(t) = e(t)$. It is seen that the homogenous part of this last equation is a second-order AR with complexity $3 + |a + c| + |ac|$. This AR process with an AR error term has been called an ARAR model in Carter and Zellner (1996). On the other hand, the error term $u(t)$ might be generated by an invertible moving average process of order one, say $u(t) = e(t) - q\,e(t-1) = [1 - qL]\,e(t)$, where $e(t)$ is white noise and it is assumed that $1 - qL$ is invertible, that is $-1 < q < 1$. Then from $[1 - aL]y(t) = [1 - qL]e(t)$, $\{[1 - aL]/[1qL]\}y(t) = e(t)$. The lefthand side of this last equation, the homogeneous difference equation, is an *infinite-order* AR process, as is well known, and thus extremely complicated according to Jeffreys' complexity measure, much more complicated than the ARAR model considered above that has a finite second-order homogeneous difference equation even though the two equations have the same number of parameters, as pointed out by Keuzenkamp and McAleer (1997). Researchers have recognized complications of working with moving average error terms, e.g. multimodal likelihood functions, 'piling up' phenomena, etc. In Carter and Zellner (1996) many comparisons of ARAR and ARMA models are made in univariate and multivariate cases and the general result is that ARAR models are simpler to interpret and implement. Model selection techniques and data are employed to compare ARAR and ARMA models to determine which is better supported by the information in the data, see, e.g. Zellner and Geisel (1970).

Note that in the above stationary ARAR model, $(1-aL)(1-cL)y(t) = e(t)$, the sum of the absolute values of the parameters is $1+|a+c|+|ac|$, where $-1 < a, c < 1$. In an unrestricted second-order AR(2), the sum of the absolute values of the unrestricted parameters can obviously be larger than that for the above ARAR model which is then less complex and has higher prior probability than an unrestricted AR(2) process.

Jeffreys' measures of complexity can be applied to higher-order AR, ARAR and ARMA models. It was mentioned that the AR representation of invertible ARMA models is an *infinite* autoregression whereas that of the ARAR model is a *finite* autoregression. Thus Jeffreys' complexity measure has a greater value for the ARMA model than for the ARAR model since the order of the former is infinite, unless truncated in which case the order will generally be very high. For a particular transfer function, $a(L)y(t) = b(L)x(t)$, an analysis similar to that above indicates that those with MA(q) error terms are in general more complicated than those with AR(q) error terms. And both of these models will be simpler than the above transfer function with ARMA (p, q) error terms.

As regards the densities for the error terms introduced above, it is well known that many probability density functions can be produced as solutions of differential equations. For example the solution to $d\log f/dx = -1$ is the exponential density, $f(x) = \exp(-x)$, to $d\log f/dx = -x$, the normal density, $f(x) = [1/\sqrt{2\pi}]\exp\{-x^2/2\}$, to $d\log f(x)/dx = -(1 + ax + bx^2 + cx^3)$, the exponential quartic density. Further, the Pearson system of densities can be obtained as solutions to the following differential equation; see, e.g. Jeffreys (1967, p. 74),

$$d \log f/dx = -(x - a)/(b_0 + b_1 x + b_2 x^2) \tag{4}$$

Clearly, Jeffreys' measure of complexity can be evaluated for these differential equations and leads to the conclusion that for the uniform density, $d\log f/dx = 0$ is the simplest, with $C = 3$, while $C = 4$ and 5 for the exponential and normal densities. Also, it is the case that maxent densities that arise from maximizing entropy, $-\int f(x) \log f(x) dx$, here defined relative to uniform measure, with respect to choice of $f(x)$ subject to moment side conditions, $\int x^i f(x) dx = \mu_i$, $i = 0, 1, \ldots, m$, $\mu_i's$ having known values, have the form $f(x) = \exp\{-(\lambda_0 + \lambda_1 x + \lambda_2 x^2 + \ldots + \lambda_m x^m)\}$ where the $\lambda's$ are Lagrange multipliers. On logging this last expression and differentiating by x, an explicit differential equation involving $d\log f/dx$ and powers of x is obtained and its complexity can be measured using Jeffreys' complexity measure. Note that the maxent solution may be a density for the subject-matter part of a model or for the error term.

Thus adding error terms to models involves increasing their complexity. If the differential equation for the error term density has complexity C', this can be added to the complexity for the model's differential equation, C, to obtain an overall measure $C + C'$. As noted above, many other possible ways of combining C and C' can be considered.

While many model builders just add random error terms to their models, state space engineers, statisticians and econometricians add measurement equations, deterministic or stochastic, to their state equation models. The measurement equations link the variables of the model, the so-called state variables, to the measurements or measured variables. To illustrate, consider Friedman's (1957) model for the state variables, permanent consumption Cp and permanent income Yp, $Cp = kYp$, with k assumed constant. This is a state equation with no error term. One could write $Cp = kYp + u^*$, where u^* is a state equation error term. The complexity of this relation and of its error term density can be evaluated as shown above. But this model is not sophisticatedly simple since Cp and Yp are not observable. Friedman presented the following measurement equations to make his model operational, $C = Cp + u$ and $Y = Yp + v$, where C and Y are measured real consumption and real income and u and v are the measurement equation error terms that Friedman calls temporary consumption and temporary income, respectively. Additional assumptions about the properties of u and v have to be introduced to make the model operational, say u and v are independent normal variables with zero means and finite variances. These assumptions have to be adequate to identify the key parameter k and other parameters of the model. If they are not, the model is not sophisticatedly simple. Note that in this 'errors in the variables' model with no state space error term, having the intercept parameter in the state equation be equal to zero, a key economic property of the Friedman model, is adequate to identify the model's parameters; see, e.g. Zellner (1996, pp. 128ff) for discussion of this identification problem.

The assumed measurement equations of the Friedman model are relatively simple and have been made more general in applications by the introduction of proxy or instrumental variables to represent Yp, or by the introduction of adaptive or rational expectations models as well as seasonal time series models to provide time series proxies for Yp. If the measurements come from survey data, then the measurement equations may have to be elaborated to take account of systematic reporting errors, the design of the survey, and other features of the process generating the data, e.g. non-random attrition, missing observations, etc., etc. It is clear that if there are no good simple measurement models relating Cp and Yp to the measurements, the overall model would not be operational and hence would be only a theoretical model, perhaps empirically useful in the future. One strength of the Friedman model is that it is readily implementable with available data and makes predictions, many of them verified with data.

One other consideration that must be taken into account is the constancy of the parameters of models. In Friedman's model the parameter k is sometimes assumed constant, particularly in cointegration analyses. However, Friedman's theory indicates that k is a function of the interest rate, ratio of non-human wealth to total wealth, family size, tastes and preferences, etc. Perhaps the parameter k above is a time-varying parameter that should be modelled, as in state space models with time-varying parameters. If a time series model for k is added to the model, that indeed would add to the complexity of the model but in certain circumstances might improve its performance. For example, in explaining Kuznets' finding of a relatively constant savings rate for the US since the turn of the century until after World War II, Friedman did not just point to the constancy of the parameter k. He pointed out that two main offsetting influences kept S/Y relatively constant, namely, the fall in average family size and the decline in the proportion of farmers and other entrepreneurs in the labour force; see Friedman (1957). In addition, aggregation effects, Lucas effects, changes in tastes and technology and other factors can cause parameters' values to change through time.

At this point, we recognize that in modelling in the sciences, there are at least six components, (1) state equations, (2) state equations' parameters, (3) state equations' errors, (4) measurement equations, (5) measurement equations' parameters and (6) measurement equations' errors. As indicated above, Jeffreys' measure of complexity is operational in connection with (1)–(6) insofar as components are in differential or difference equation form. Adding these measures of complexity will provide a first approximation to the overall complexity. If a weighted average or some other combination of the above components of complexity can be shown superior to the simple sum, then of course it should be employed.

We now turn to review some work in modelling to show the roles played by the above concepts in actual analyses of macroeconomic data relating to eighteen industrialized countries' economies.

4   Structural and time series modelling procedures and results

In section 1, some remarks were made about certain macroeconomic modelling procedures. Some years ago, Franz Palm and I (Zellner and Palm, 1974) investigated the relation between multivariate time series (TS) models and dynamic structural econometric models (SEM) in an effort to produce improvements in modelling strategy. We began by considering Quenouille's (1957) multivariate ARMA model,

$$H(L)z(t) = F(L)e(t) \tag{5}$$

where $H(L)$ and $F(L)$ are invertible matrix polynomial lag operators, $z(t)$ is an $m \times 1$ vector of variables, e.g. output, prices, consumption, etc. in period t, and $e(t)$ is an $m \times 1$ vector of zero mean white noise errors, $Ee(t) = 0$ and $Ee(t)e(t)' = Im$ for all t. If $F(L) = Fo$, an $m \times m$ non-singular matrix, the process is a VAR. Also, Quenouille's system can incorporate cointegration relations along with other relations. Now, Palm and I asked, if we start with this complicated MVARMA or VAR process, what are its implications and are they sophisticatedly simple? One easy operation is to solve the m-equation system to determine the implied processes on individual variables. By multiplying both sides by the inverse of $H(L) = $ adjoint matrix of $H(L)/$determinant of $H(L) = H^*/Hd$, we have $z(t) = (H^*/Hd)F(L)e(t)$ or $Hd\, z(t) = H^* F(L)e(t)$. For an individual component of $z(t)$, say $z_i(t)$, the implied process is $Hd\, z_i(t) = b_i'e(t)$, where b_i is the i'th row of $H^* F(L)$. For many values of m, say $m = 5$ or $m = 10$, the determinant Hd will usually be an extremely high-degree polynomial in L giving rise to an extremely high-order AR on $z_i(t)$. Similarly, the elements of b_i' will be high-degree polynomials in L giving rise to a high-order MA process for the error term in this 'final equation'. Thus the unrestricted general linear MVARMA model or VAR model implies very, very complicated, according to Jeffreys' measure, ARMA models for individual variables. Since such highly complicated models have not generally been identified using annual data, the complicated implications of these general models do not square with the data.

To simplify somewhat the complicated MVARMA model, econometricians generally assume that some of the variables in the $m \times 1$ vector $z(t)$ are endogenous, denoted by $y(t)$ and the remainder are exogenous, denoted by $x(t)$, or $z(t)' = (y(t)', x(t)')$ and with a corresponding partitioning of $H(L)$ and $F(L)$, the system becomes:

$$H_{11}(L)y(t) + H_{12}(L)x(t) = F_{11}(L)e_1(t) \tag{6}$$

and

$$H_{22}(L)x(t) = F_{22}(L)e_2(t) \tag{7}$$

where (6) is the dynamic linear structural equation system and (7) is the MVARMA process for the exogenous variables, $x(t)$ implied by the overall ARMA process in (5). The assumption that $x(t)$ is exogenous imposes the restrictions that a submatrix of $H(L)$, $H_{21}(L)$ and two submatrices of $F(L)$, $F_{12}(L)$ and $F_{21}(L)$, are identically equal to zero, simplifying assumptions that reduce the number of unknown parameters considerably. However, without further assumptions, the parameters in the structural equation model in (6) are not identified. Also, when Palm and I solved for the marginal processes for individual variables, they were still very complicated ARMA processes. Also, (6) can be solved for the transfer equations associated with the dynamic SEM. These relate single endogenous variables to current and lagged values of the exogenous variables and have the general form, obtained by multiplying both sides of (6) by the inverse of $H_{11}(L)$ and solving for $y_i(t)$, the i'th endogenous variable,

$$|H_{11}(L)|y_i(t) = b(L)'x(t) + c(L)'e_1(t) \tag{8}$$

where $b(L)$ and $c(L)$ are vectors the elements of which are polynomials in the lag operator L. See Zellner and Palm (1975) for the transfer functions associated with several variants of Friedman's monetary macroeconomic model, Hong (1989) for those associated with several variants of a Keynesian IS-LM model and Min (1992) for those associated with several generalized real business-cycle models.

Since transfer functions represent the variation of a single variable that is related to past values of itself and just possibly current and lagged values of exogenous variables, they are somewhat simpler than reduced-form equations and also equations of VAR models. Thus it is a possible, simple starting point for model construction. That is, empirically determine the forms of (8) for each endogenous variable and then try to determine the form of the SEM system in (6) that algebraically yields the empirically determined transfer functions. See the references in the previous paragraph for some results.

One important endogenous variable is the rate of growth of an economy's total output as measured by real GDP. Since there may be biases in measuring real GDP, in our empirical work, Garcia-Ferrer et al. (1987) and Zellner (1994), we logged measured real GDP and first-differenced log GDP to get the rate of growth of GDP. The logging and differencing was thought to help remove certain types of systematic biases in measured real GDP, a simple but important reason for doing it, and also because there is great interest in the rate of growth of real GDP, denoted by y_{it} for the i'th country in the t'th year. After finding that a simple AR(3) model for this variable did not work because it missed in forecasting turning points, we added several leading indicator variables to the model, namely the lagged rates of growth of real money and real stock prices, variables that Burns and Mitchell empirically discovered tended to lead in the business cycles for France, Germany, the UK and the US using pre-World War II data. In addition, we added the lagged annual median growth rate of real stock prices for the countries in our sample to the equation, a proxy for the world rate of return. This common-effect variable took most of the contemporaneous correlation out of our country error terms which very importantly reduced the number of non-zero parameters in our 18×18 covariance matrix for the eighteen countries in our sample by making it diagonal. The autoregressive model containing lagged leading indicator variables is called an ARLI model. In forecasting experiments with the ARLI model, it was found to be superior to various random walk models, AR(3) models, the famous Nelson–Plosser ARIMA model, and to several OECD macroeconometric models for various countries. The root mean squared error of forecast for our out-of-sample forecasts were employed in these computations. Further, it was found that Stein shrinkage, that involves assumptions regarding the distribution of countries' coefficient vectors, namely that they are concentrated about some central value, to be estimated, improved forecasts considerably. Here by making the individual country parameters random and time-varying and integrating them out to express our models in terms of relatively few hyperparameters, we reduced the complexity of our models and obtained improved results. See also the paper by Putnam and Quintana (1995) who review forecasting in the financial economics area and comment favourably on some of our procedures that they have found quite useful.

Not only were the annual point-forecasting results produced by our methods and models encouraging but also their turning-point forecasts are surprisingly good, namely about 70 per cent or more of 158 turning points, 1974–86, correctly forecasted; see Zellner, Hong and Min (1991) for the new Bayesian decision-theoretic turning-point forecasting methods employed and results. In recent work, Zellner and Min (1998), the data were extended to include 211 turning points and the former favourable results were still encountered. In this work, the models' turning-point forecasts were shown to be better than those of various naive models' forecasts, e.g. a coin flipper, an eternal optimist, who always forecasts no downturn and upturn, an eternal pessimist, who always forecasts downturn and no upturn, and a deterministic four-year-cycle forecaster, who always forecasts downturn at the top and upturn at the bottom.

Thus these relatively simple variants of a basic ARLI model work reasonably well but, as with almost all models, still need improvement. Again a simple solution is being investigated, namely disaggregation by industrial sector, namely agriculture, construction, manufacturing, wholesale trade, retail trade, etc. As an engineer might put it, instead of viewing the economy as one big oscillator, we view the economy as made up of coupled sectoral oscillators. For each sector, sophisticatedly simple and useful Marshallian demand, supply and entry (DSE) models have been formulated and will be implemented to forecast sectoral outputs. Then the sectoral output forecasts will be aggregated to obtain a forecast for aggregate output that can be compared with the forecasts obtained from various models for aggregate output. Since use of the sectoral data involves increasing the sample size and introducing specific, important sectoral variables and linkages, it is expected on theoretical and intuitive grounds that improved forecasts will be obtained. See consideration of these issues in the discussion of Zellner (1994). All of this contrasts markedly with a strategy of starting with an 'encompassing' or general MVARMA model or a VAR model and testing downward. As Keuzenkamp and McAleer (1995, p. 17) rightly stated, I and many others do not favour such a strategy for the simple reason that in decades during which it has been used, it has not as yet produced macroeconometric models that perform well in explanation and prediction. In my opinion, it is much more fruitful to KISS and complicate only if necessary. Needless to say, this conclusion owes much to the wisdom and analysis of Harold Jeffreys and many other leading researchers mentioned earlier.

5   Summary and conclusions

In this chapter, I have attempted to summarize Jeffreys' views on simplicity and to review and extend his measure of complexity. On the latter topic, Jeffreys' measure of complexity has been extended to apply to difference equation models and differential equations defining probability density functions. Thus it becomes possible to measure the complexity of state equations, measurement equations and the density functions for their error terms. Bringing in the complexity of probability density functions and of measurement equations is important in terms of appraising the overall complexity of a model that purports to explain the past and predict the future.

Further, I have emphasized the virtues of sophisticatedly simple models and pointed out that simple models that contain logical errors, are at variance with known facts etc. are simply stupid. A sophisticatedly simple model takes appropriate account of the techniques and knowledge present in a field and is logically sound. It is suggested that it is more worthwhile to develop sophisticatedly simple models than to develop complex models. When a sophisticatedly simple model does not work well, some added, well-chosen complexity may improve the situation. For example, disaggregating total output by sector and modelling coupled sectors is probably a better strategy for understanding and predicting total output than by modelling total output in an aggregate model. The former strategy represents a complication of the latter that will probably be justified in terms of superior performance in explanation and prediction. In such a case, added sophisticated complexity, not too much, may be justified.

There is much more work to be done on the appropriate ways to combine the elements of Jeffreys' measure of complexity and of the broadened measures presented in this chapter. More analysis of the sequential decision problem of model choice and subsequent improvement using appropriate prior probabilities and criterion functions would be welcome. And last, not much has been said about the important issue of how new, sophisticatedly simple models are conceived and developed, the objective of reductive inference that I have briefly discussed in Zellner (1996, pp. 5ff.). How important, new sophisticatedly simple models that work well in explanation and prediction are produced is a topic that deserves much attention.

REFERENCES

Adelman, I. and F. L. Adelman (1959). The dynamic properties of the Klein–Goldberger model. *Econometrica* 27: 569–625.

Bakker, C. C. T. (1966). *Dictionary of Mathematics*. New York: Hart Publishing Co.

Carter, R. A. L. and A. Zellner (1996). The ARAR model for time series. *Proceedings of the American Statistical Association's Section on Bayesian Statistical Science*, pp. 226–31.

Christ, C. F. (1951). A test of an econometric model for the United States, 1921–1947. In *Conference on Business Cycles*, pp. 35–107. New York: National Bureau of Economic Research, Inc.

(1975). Judging the performance of econometric models of the US economy. *International Economic Review* 16: 54–74.

Cooper, R. L. (1972). The predictive performance of quarterly econometric models of the US economy. In B. G. Hickman (ed.), *Econometric Models of Cyclical Behavior*, vol. 2, pp. 813–926. New York: Columbia University Press.

Friedman, M. (1951). Comment on 'A Test of an Econometric Model for the United States, 1921–47' by Carl Christ. In *Conference on Business Cycles*, pp. 107–14. New York: National Bureau of Economic Research, Inc.

(1957). *A Theory of the Consumption Function*. Princeton: Princeton University Press.

Garcia-Ferrer, A., R. A. Highfield, F. C. Palm and A. Zellner (1987). Macroeconomic forecasting using pooled international data. *Journal of Business and Economic Statistics* 5: 53–67.

Good, I. J. (1980). The contributions of Sir Harold Jeffreys to Bayesian Inference. In A. Zellner (ed.), *Bayesian Analysis in Econometrics and Statistics: Essays in Honour of Harold Jeffreys*, pp. 21–34. Amsterdam: North-Holland.

Hickman, B. G. (ed.) (1972). *Econometric Models of Cyclical Behavior*. New York: Columbia University Press.

Hong, C. (1989). Forecasting real output growth rates and cyclical properties of models: a Bayesian approach. PhD thesis, Dept. of Economics, University of Chicago.

Jaynes, E. T. (1985). Highly informative priors. In J. M. Bernardo et al. (eds.), *Bayesian Statistics* 2, pp. 329–52. Amsterdam: North-Holland.

Jeffreys, H. (1939, 1948, 1961, 1967, 1988). *Theory of Probability*. Oxford: Oxford University Press.

(1931, 1957). *Scientific Inference*. Cambridge: Cambridge University Press.

Keuzenkamp, H. A. and M. McAleer (1995). Simplicity, scientific inference and econometric modelling. *Economic Journal* 105: 1–21.

(1997). The complexity of simplicity. *Mathematics and Computers in Simulation* 43: 553–61.

Litterman, R. B. (1986). Forecasting with Bayesian vector autoregressions: five years of experience. *Journal of Business and Economic Statistics* 4: 25–38 (with discussion).

McNees, S. K. (1986). Forecasting accuracy of alternative techniques: a comparison of US macroeconomic forecasts. *Journal of Business and Economic Statistics* 4: 5–23 (with discussion).

Meese, R. and K. Rogoff (1983). The out of sample failure of empirical exchange rate models: sampling error or misspecification? In J. A. Frenkel (ed.), *Exchange Rates and International Economics*. Chicago: University of Chicago Press.

Min, C. (1992). Economic analysis and forecasting of international growth rates using Bayesian techniques. PhD thesis, Dept. of Economics, University of Chicago.

(1993). Bayesian and non-Bayesian methods for combining models and fore-casts with applications to forecasting international growth rates. *Journal of Econometrics* 56: 89–118.

Nelson, C. R. (1972). The predictive performance of the FRB-MIT-PENN model of the US economy. *American Economic Review* 62: 902–17.

Nelson, C. R. and C. I. Plosser (1982). Trends and random walks in macroeco-nomic time series. *Journal of Monetary Economics* 10: 139–62.

Putnam, B. and J. M. Quintana (1995). The evolution of Bayesian forecasting models. In B. Putnam (ed.), *Applying Quantitative Discipline to Asset Allocation*. London: Euromoney Publications.

Quenouille, M. H. (1957). *The Analysis of Multiple Time Series*. New York: Hafner.

Smyth, D. J. (1983). Short-run macroeconomic forecasting: the OECD perfor-mance. *Journal of Forecasting* 2: 37–49.

Zellner, A. (ed.) (1980). *Bayesian Analysis in Econometrics and Statistics: Essays in Honor of Sir Harold Jeffreys*. Amsterdam: North-Holland.

(1994). Time-series analysis, forecasting and econometric modelling: the struc-tural econometric modelling, time-series analysis (SEMTSA) approach. *Journal of Forecasting* 13: 215–33.

(1996). *An Introduction to Bayesian Inference in Econometrics*. New York: Wiley. (Wiley Classics Series, reprint of 1971 edn).

(1997). *Bayesian Analysis in Econometrics and Statistics: the Zellner View and Papers*. Cheltenham, UK: Edward Elgar.

Zellner, A. and M. S. Geisel (1970). Analysis of distributed lag models with applications to consumption function estimation. *Econometrica* 38: 865–88.

Zellner, A. and C. Hong (1989). Forecasting international growth rates using Bayesian shrinkage and other procedures. *Journal of Econometrics, Annals,* P. Schmidt (ed.), *Issues in Econometric Forecasting* 40: 183–202.

(1991). Bayesian methods for forecasting turning points in economic time ser-ies: sensitivity of forecasts to asymmetry of loss structures. In K. Lahiri and G. Moore (eds.), *Leading Indicators: New Approaches and Forecasting Records*, pp. 19–40. Cambridge: Cambridge University Press.

Zellner, A., C. Hong and G. M. Gulati (1991). Turning points in economic time series, loss structures and Bayesian forecasting. In S. Geisser, J. Hodges, S. J. Press and A. Zellner (eds.), *Bayesian and Likelihood Methods in Statistics and Econometrics: Essays in Honor of George A. Barnard*, pp. 371–93. Amsterdam: North-Holland.

Zellner, A., C. Hong and C. Min (1991). Forecasting turning points in interna-tional output growth rates using Bayesian exponentially weighted autore-gression, time-varying parameter, and pooling techniques. *Journal of Econometrics* 49: 275–304.

Zellner, A. and C. Min (1997). Bayesian analysis, model selection and prediction. In Zellner, 1997, pp. 389–400.

(1999). Forecasting turning points in output growth rates: a response to Milton Friedman. *Journal of Econometrics* 88: 203–6.

Zellner, A. and B. R. Moulton (1985). Bayesian regression diagnostics with appli-cations to international consumption and income data. *Journal of Econometrics* 53: 187–211.

Zellner, A. and F. Palm (1974). Time series analysis and simultaneous equation econometric models. *Journal of Econometrics* 2: 17–54.

——— (1975). Time series analysis of structural monetary models of the US economy. *Sankhga* Series C: 12–56.

Zellner, A. and S. Peck (1973). Simulation experiments with a quarterly macroeconometric model of the US economy. In A. A. Powell and R. A. Williams (eds.), *Econometric Studies of Macro and Monetary Relations*, pp. 149–68. Amsterdam: North-Holland.

Zellner, A. and H. Ryu (1998). Alternative functional forms for production, cost and returns to scale functions. *Journal of Applied Econometrics* 13: 101–27.

15   Communication, complexity and coordination in games

Mattias Ganslandt

1   Introduction

This chapter investigates how the transmission of information determines collective behaviour in coordination games. Pre-play communication should help players to avoid coordination failures. Furthermore, transmission of information should help players to optimize their collective behaviour. Does this mean that pre-play communication guarantees successful coordination? Moreover, does pre-play communication favour Pareto-optimal Nash equilibria in the underlying game?

Most coordination games that are studied in the game-theoretic literature exhibit multiple strict Nash equilibria.[1] While intuition might suggest that players should be able to coordinate in a Pareto-optimal equilibrium, the traditional refinements in game theory fail to select an efficient outcome. Still worse, they even fail to select a unique outcome. All strict equilibria survive even the strongest refinements. This conflict between intuition and formal analysis has given birth to several efforts among game theorists.

The first approach allows agents to send costless pre-play signals before they choose actions. This costless pre-play communication is called *cheap talk*. Unfortunately, cheap talk does not help players to coordinate in the efficient outcome. There exist equilibria in which players have decisions rules that are constant and therefore unaffected by the message received from the other players (cf. Weibull, 1995, p. 61).

The author is grateful to Hans Carlsson, Håkan Holm, Roy Radner and seminar participants at the Stockholm School of Economics, University of Lund and the seventeenth Arne Ryde Symposium for valuable comments. Financial support from the Marianne and Marcus Wallenberg foundation is gratefully acknowledged.

[1] Much recent discussion in game theory has focused on simple coordination experiments. Coordination problems have been used by game theorists to test various hypotheses on learning, equilibrium selection and strategic uncertainty. For examples and references see van Huyck, Battalio and Beil (1990), (1991), (1993); van Huyck et al. (1995); van Huyck, Battalio and Rankin (1997) and van Huyck, Cook and Battalio (1997).

Hence, both problems of coordination, i.e. the problem of equilibrium selection and the problem of social inefficiency, remain unsolved.

The second approach suggests that if an equilibrium arises as the result of costless negotiations between the players, then team members should be able to coordinate in a Pareto-optimal outcome. It is argued that it must not be profitable for any player to propose that a strategy combination be abandoned for another equilibrium in which everybody is better off. Only Pareto-optimal equilibria are *renegotiation-proof* (Fudenberg and Tirole, 1991, pp. 174f). Renegotiation-proofness predicts complex behaviour in situations when complex behaviour is collectively optimal.[2]

It could be argued that players do neither as poorly as some cheap talk models suggest in terms of equilibrium selection, nor as well as renegotiation-proofness predicts in terms of efficiency. Therefore, we suggest that some underlying assumptions must be changed.

We analyse how the structure of a common language influences the equilibrium selection problem in coordination games when players are allowed to transmit messages to coordinate their behaviour in a language, i.e. a labelling procedure and a code, which is optimal for a class of coordination games. In order to simplify the analysis we assume that the coordination game involves neither conflicts of interest, such as the Battle of Sexes, nor problems of trustworthiness, as in the Stag Hunt game.[3] Instead, we focus on a variant of Binmore's (1994) Dodo game. All players have identical interests and there are no incentives to send insincere messages. The game has many strict Nash equilibria, and players have asymmetric information. The informed player knows the relative Pareto ranking of all Nash equilibria before players choose actions, while the uninformed player expects all symmetric pure strategy combinations to be strict Nash equilibria with the same payoff *ex ante*.

We model the pre-play communication in two steps. Before one player is informed about the ranking of equilibria both players communicate without cost. Once the informed player has learned the Pareto-ranking of equilibria every message is costly. In this game players can use communication both to coordinate their expectations in a specific equilibrium

---

[2] Harsanyi and Selten's (1988) 'general theory of equilibrium' selection discriminates between strict equilibria. In this theory payoff-dominance should have absolute precedence and players should have no trouble coordinating their expectations at the commonly preferred equilibrium point. Thus, Harsanyi and Selten's theory predicts the same outcome as renegotiation-proofness in games of mutual interests.

[3] In some games each player is better off if he can convince the other players to choose a high effort, regardless of his own intended play. Aumann (1990) argues that it is not clear that players should expect that their opponents believe their announcements.

and to optimize their collective behaviour. We can illustrate our basic results in a simple version of the game:

	H	L			H	L
H	2, 2	0, 0		H	1, 1	0, 0
L	0, 0	1, 1		L	0, 0	2, 2
	G_1				G_2	

In this Dual-Dodo game two players choose H or L. Player 1 selects a row and player 2 selects a column and Nature determines the state of the world (G_1 or G_2). The payoffs are given as the intersection of a row and a column, where player 1's payoff is specified first. Before either player is informed about Nature's choice they can meet and decide how to communicate after Nature has told player 1 about its choice. Assume that they decide to play (H, H) if no information is transmitted. In other words they choose the H strategy as a 'convention'. Next, they can decide that if player 1 transmits a signal to player 2 they should both change their strategies to L, i.e. (L, L).

If Nature selects G_1 they are both happy with the tacit convention and no information is transmitted, but what if the other state of the world occurs? It immediately follows that players are ready to give up one unit of utility each to transmit a message which would trigger L-play. If the cost is higher they will remain in the (H, H) equilibrium.

Thus, if the cost of communication is sufficiently high, players would choose the strategy described by the empty string. This equilibrium is the most simple in two ways. First of all, the empty string is the shortest description available in the language chosen by players. In that sense the equilibrium is the most easy to describe. Second, the equilibrium is simple because the behaviour is not conditional on the state of the world: players would choose the same action independent of Nature's choice. In the remainder of this chapter we will generalize this analysis.

The rest of the chapter is organized as follows. In section 2 we describe the main features of the general model. The labelling and coding procedures are described in section 3 and 4, respectively. Section 5 presents the results and section 6 concludes the chapter.

2   The binary choice game

Now, consider a simple coordination problem in which two players are required to choose one or the other of two actions, called a_1 and a_2. Before players choose actions Nature has decided which of the two equilibrium profiles is dominant, i.e. which strategy profile is associated with a 'superior' and 'inferior' outcome respectively. When Nature selects A_1, strategy profile (a_1, a_1) dominates (a_2, a_2) and when it chooses A_2 the dominance relation is reversed. In a superior equilibrium each player gets x and in an inferior equilibrium both get 1 each. If players fail to coordinate they both get 0. The two payoff matrices A_1 and A_2 are defined as follows:

	a_1	a_2
a_1	x, x	$0, 0$
a_2	$0, 0$	$1, 1$

A_1

	a_1	a_2
a_1	$1, 1$	$0, 0$
a_2	$0, 0$	x, x

A_2

$$(2.1)$$

where $x > 1$. In this game both symmetric strategy profiles are strict Nash equilibria.

The binary choice game is a meta-game in which the players face the coordination problem described above T times.

As in Gauthier (1975) each player will choose an option under a description. We consider the coordination problem to be defined by the agents' description of the game. It is assumed that all players make a mutual distinction between the one-period actions a_1 and a_2 before the game starts. Following Sugden (1995), we shall use the term label for the description by which players recognize pure strategies. A labelling is a function L_i which assigns a label $L_i(s_i)$ to each strategy $s_i \in S_i$ of each player i, such that for each player, each of her pure strategies has a distinct label. Now, the rules of the meta-game are defined as follows.

First, players construct a *common language*, i.e. a labelling and a code, before the number of periods in the game is determined and a specific payoff structure is chosen. We assume that player 1 can transmit a message to player 2 through a channel which admits transmissions in binary code only.[4] For this purpose fix an alphabet $\mathcal{A} = \{0, 1\}$. Let $\mathcal{A}^*(c)$ denote the set of all strings $z = z_1 z_2 z_3 ... z_c$ of length c with elements $z_k \in \mathcal{A}$. Define the union of all strings $\mathcal{A}^* = \bigcup_{c \geq 1} \mathcal{A}^*(c)$. The message which is transmitted from player 1 to player 2 is a suggestion about what players should do in the coordination game. A suggestion is a list specifying a strategy for each player. The suggestion is *consistent* if the strategy profile is a mutual best response (see Farrell, 1988). We assume that player 1 will only make consistent suggestions. As any strict equilibrium is a symmetric pure strategy profile, this assumption implies that a consistent suggestion can be reduced to a description of a single pure strategy.

---

[4] Consequently, only a few strategies can be described with short code strings, so the descriptions of equilibrium strategies vary in complexity, cf. Chaitin (1975).

Second, the number of periods in the game is drawn, i.e. $T \in \Omega$, where $\Omega = \{1, 2, ..., \widehat{T}\}$. It is assumed that there is a probability function $\pi : \Omega \to (0, 1)$, such that $\sum_{T \in \Omega} \pi(T) = 1$ and $\pi(T) > 0$ for all $T \in \Omega$. Next, Nature selects a sequence of matrices which determines payoffs in every period. Let $A^t \in \{A_1, A_2\}$ be the payoff matrix in period t and $A = (A^1, ..., A^T)$ be the sequence of matrices which defines the payoff structure. There is a probability function $p_T : \times_{t \in T} \{A_1, A_2\} \to (0, 1)$, such that $p_T(A) = 2^{-T}$ for all $A \in \times_{t \in T} \{A_1, A_2\}$. At the end of the second stage player 1 is informed about A and T without noise.

Third, the informed agent, i.e. player 1, can send a message m coded in alphabet $\mathcal{A}$ which is received by player 2. The complexity of a message m coded in $\mathcal{A}$ is defined as the length of the string. The cost of transmission is w per bit.

Fourth, players choose strategies. A strategy of player i is an ordered string of actions, written $s_i \in S_i$, where $S_i = \times_{t \in \hat{T}} \{a_1, a_2\}$. We assume that in a T period game the sequence of actions is truncated after the T'th element. Finally, the game is played T periods and players receive payoffs. The payoff is the average period revenue minus the cost of communication. There is no observation of actions or payoffs until the game ends.

3   Labels

The players will choose an appropriate language for the entire class of payoff structures. To do this the players can proceed in the following manner. They attach one label to each action in the games in one period, call them y_1 and y_2. Moreover, the players will associate the two labels with two pure strategies in every game in $\widehat{T}$ periods. Next players will choose labels for the sequences of actions in the two-period games which remain to be named, call them y_3 and y_4. These labels are also associated with two pure strategies in every game in more than two periods. Next players will choose four labels in the games in three periods, for sequences of actions which remain unnamed, call them $y_5, ..., y_8$. Continue in this way to name 2^{k-1} sequences of actions in the k-period games and let these labels be associated with strategies in every game in $\widehat{T}$ periods. Denote the set of all labels with $Y = \{y_1, y_2, ...\}$.

The procedure described above leaves many questions unresolved. The procedure only implies that when k is small a label y_k is used in a wider range of games. For instance y_1 and y_2 must be attached to the actions in the one-period game but it is arbitrary which strategies these labels are used for in games in more than one period. However, we can apply one more assumption to provide more structure to the code.

To both players a T-period game can be decomposed in $\lceil T/k \rceil$ games in k periods, where the last game is possibly truncated.[5] Consider a strategy called $\tilde{y}$ in a k-period game. This strategy is a sequence of actions. Repeat this sequence $\lceil T/k \rceil$ times. This results in a sequence of actions which is a strategy in the T-period game. The resulting sequence is labelled $\tilde{y}$ in the T-period game. We refer to this as *invariance with respect to decomposition*.

This assumption implies that our labelling procedure is highly structured. Indeed there is a unique labelling, up to symmetric transformations, which satisfies this condition. For instance, the one-period game labels y_1 and y_2 would describe uniform sequences of actions in any T-period game. Any T-period game can be decomposed in T one-period games with a uniform action labelled y_1 or y_2. Denote repetition with $*$. Labels y_1 or y_2 refer to $(a_1)*$ and $(a_2)*$. Correspondingly, labels y_3 or y_4 refer to $(a_1, a_2)*$ and $(a_2, a_1)*$. We can proceed to construct this labelling in the same manner for y_5, y_6 etc.

4   Optimal coding

Now, we can proceed to the problem of coding. A *code* is a function $\varphi : Y \to \mathcal{A}^*$ and the elements of $\varphi(Y)$ are called code-strings.

The players' goal is to find a code which maximizes the expected payoff. Now, introduce the function $bin : \mathbb{N} \to \mathcal{A}^*$, where bin is a binary expansion of $n \geq 0$, such that $(n)_2 = 1bin(n)$. By definition $bin(1) = \lambda$. To simplify notation let $\log k \equiv \lfloor \log_2(k) \rfloor$, where $\lfloor \cdot \rfloor$ denotes the 'floor' of the real (rounding downwards). Define $\log 0 \equiv 0$.

We consider two situations. In the first case the empty string can be used as a message, in the second case it cannot be used as a message. We define the following condition:

(C) λ is a code-string

where λ is defined as the empty string. Condition C is satisfied in the first case and violated in the second. For the first case we obtain the following result:

Proposition 1 *If condition C applies then* $\varphi(y_k) = bin(k)$ *for* $k = 1, 2, \ldots$ *is an optimal code.*

---

[5] $\lceil \alpha \rceil$ denotes the 'ceiling' of the real α (i.e. rounding upwards).

The probability distribution over sequences of payoff matrices is uniform. Therefore, all pure equilibrium strategies are identical with respect to expected revenue. We will make use of the following simplifying lemma.

Lemma 1 *The expected revenue in any equilibrium in pure strategies is $\frac{1}{2}(x+1)$ before Nature has selected A*

Proof The expected revenue in any equilibrium before Nature has selected A is

$$E[u] = \frac{1}{T}2^{-T}\sum_{k=0}^{T}\binom{T}{k}((T-k)\,x+k) = \frac{1}{2}(x+1)$$

which concludes the proof.

We can now provide the proof of the main result.

Proof *Step 1.* There are 2^n unique code-strings of length n in φ and in $\mathcal{A}^*\bigcup\{\lambda\}$ for all $n \geq 0$. Thus, φ uses all strings in $\mathcal{A}^*\bigcup\{\lambda\}$. *Step 2.* The length of a code-string $\varphi(y_k)$ is $|\varphi(y_k)| = |bin(k)| = \log k$, which is increasing in k. *Step 3.* Using the lemma the expected value of the sequence of equilibria generated by the labels (y_k, y_k) for $T \geq 1 + \log(k-1)$ is

$$\sum_{t=1+\log k,\dots,\hat{T}}\left[\pi(t)\frac{1}{2}(x+1) - \pi(t)\cdot w\cdot |\varphi(y_k)|\right].$$

The expected revenue (the first part in the squared brackets) is independent of the code. Therefore we can reduce the problem of finding an optimal code to a minimization problem of the expected cost. The optimal code must solve:

$$\min_{\varphi} w\sum_{k=1}^{2^{\hat{T}}}\left(\sum_{t=1+\log k}^{\hat{T}}[\pi(t)\cdot|\varphi(y_k)|]\right)$$

From *step 1* it follows that all code-strings in $\mathcal{A}^*\bigcup\{\lambda\}$ are used. Therefore, the assumption that $\pi(t) > 0$ for all t implies that short code-strings must be used for small k, i.e. $|\varphi(y_k)|$ must increase monotonically in k, which is shown in step 2.

As condition C is met, players decide to associate the empty string with a strategy in the one-period game and therefore in any game in more periods. If the players wish to play this strategy they do not need to transmit any information through the channel. It is as if they had chosen a convention in the game. Under the assumption of invariance with respect to decomposition that means that the players had decided to define a uniform sequence of actions, $(a_1)*$ or $(a_2)*$, as the convention.

For the second case when condition C is not applied we obtain a similar result:

> **Proposition 2** *If condition C does not apply then $\varphi'(yk) = bin$ $(k+1)$ for $k = 1,2,\ldots$ is an optimal code.*

> **Proof** *Step 1.* There are 2^n unique code-strings of length n in φ and in $\mathcal{A}^*$. Thus, φ uses all strings in $\mathcal{A}^*$. *Step 2.* The length of a code-string $\varphi'(y_k)$ is $|\varphi'(y_k)| = |bin(k + 1)| = \log(k + 1)$, which is increasing in k. *Step 3.* Using the lemma we can see that the expected value of the sequence of equilibria generated by (y_k, y_k) for $T \geq 1 + \log(k - 1)$ is

$$\sum_{t=1+\log k, \ldots, \hat{T}} \left[\pi(t) \frac{1}{2}(x + 1) - \pi(t) \cdot w \cdot |\varphi'(y_k)| \right]$$

> The expected revenue (the first part in the squared brackets) is independent of the code. Therefore we can reduce the problem of finding an optimal code to a minimization problem of the expected cost. The optimal code must solve:

$$\min_{\varphi} w \sum_{k=1}^{2^{\hat{T}}} \left(\sum_{t=1+\log k}^{\hat{T}} \left[\pi(t) \cdot |\varphi'(y_k)| \right] \right)$$

> From step 1 it follows that all code-strings in $\mathcal{A}^*$ are used. Therefore, the assumption that $\pi(t) > 0$ for all t implies that short code-strings must be used for small k, i.e. $|\varphi'(y_k)|$ must increase monotonically in k, which is shown in step 2.

In the second case we obtain a symmetric code. Both strategies in the one-period game are associated with one-bit code strings. This situation is reasonable if player 2 is genuinely uninformed. For instance, we can think of a situation when both players know the rules of the game but the uninformed player does not know at which point in time the game will occur. In that case the first bit of the message has a very high coordination value.

The results in propositions 1 and 2 are not surprising. Players will use all strings of length zero before they use code-strings of length one, and strings of length one before they use code-strings of length two, and all strings of length two before strings of length three etc. In other words: they will attach a label to each node in a binary tree. Thus, the problem of finding a code is reduced to the problem of associating code-strings of a given length with some particular labels. To minimize the expected average length it suffices to attach the most likely labels with the shortest strings. The two codes φ and φ' are two such examples.

5   Simplicity and efficiency

Player 1 can send a message m coded in an alphabet A to player 2. After communication, players 1 and 2 each choose a strategy s_1 and s_2, respectively. Players choose strategies simultaneously and for all periods. No observations are made until the game ends. Finally, players receive payoffs determined by A and strategies s_1 and s_2. The cost of transmission is w per bit.

If the efficiency gains are small and communication is costly it is always profitable to coordinate in a Nash equilibrium with the shortest description. Now, we can present the following result:

> **Proposition 3** *Assume condition C applies. If $x - 1 < w$ then player 1 would choose to transmit λ as a message to the uninformed player. None of the players would incur any cost of communication.*

> **Proof** (i) The minimum payoff of the least complex message is $\underline{u} = 1$. The maximum payoff transmitting further steps of a more complex message is $\bar{u} = x - w$. Now, $x - w < 1$ if $x - 1 < w$.

Second, we can proceed to the case in which the empty string cannot be used as a message. A similar result holds if condition C does not apply:

> **Proposition 4** *Assume condition C does not apply. If $x - 1 < 2w$ then player 1 would choose to transmit a 1-bit code-string to the uninformed player.*

> **Proof.** (i) The minimum payoff of the least complex message is $\underline{u} = \frac{1}{2}(x + 1) - w$. The maximum payoff transmitting further steps of a more complex message is $\bar{u} = x - 2w$. Now, $\frac{1}{2}(x + 1) - w > x - 2w$ if $x - 1 < 2w$.

It is worth noting that the value of communication is high in both cases. If players were choosing an equilibrium strategy at random the expected payoff would be $\frac{1}{4}(x + 1)$, which is clearly lower than the expected payoff in the first case and lower than the expected payoff in the second case if

$w < \frac{1}{4}(x + 1)$. Second, as we restrict our attention to a labelling that satisfies the principle of invariance with respect to decomposition, the Nash equilibrium with the shortest description is a strategy profile with a sequence of actions with the most regular pattern. In that case we can expect players to choose the same action in every period if the cost of transmitting information is high.

> **Corollary 1** *As the labelling satisfies invariance with respect to decomposition, the expected equilibrium strategy is a sequence of actions which is uniform, i.e. $(a_1)*$ or $(a_2)*$, if (i) $x - 1 < w$ and condition C applies, or, (ii) $x - 1 < 2w$ and condition C does not apply.*

The results in propositions 3 and 4 suggest that high costs of communication and small differences between the revenues in different equilibria give both players incentives to keep the transmission of information at a minimum level. Both results are rather extreme in the following sense: players would not transmit more than the minimum number of bits even if that would result in successful coordination in the equilibrium with the highest revenue. If communication costs are high they prefer to transmit the shortest string available even if they only succeed in coordinating in the least efficient equilibrium. The reason is that the efficiency gains are outweighed by the additional cost of transmitting extra bits. In the game studied in this chapter this is equivalent to choosing the most regular pattern of behaviour if the labelling is invariant with respect to decomposition.

However, short descriptions and simple strategies do not exist merely at high communication costs. At lower levels of the communication cost the problem of choosing an optimal equilibrium is a trade-off between ease of describability and efficiency. This is possible to illustrate with two simple examples.

> **Example 1** Consider a labelling which is invariant with respect to decomposition. Let y_3 denote $(a_1, a_2)*$. As condition C applies, the code-string for this label is one bit. Of course, for this strategy there exists exactly one state of the world for which the sequence of actions is optimal with respect to revenues. However, for every T there exist T sequences of payoff matrices in which $(a_1, a_2)*$ is almost optimal in terms of revenue, i.e. it is optimal in every period except one. For each of these sequences approximately half of the matrices are A_1 and A_2, respectively.[6]

---

[6] There is at least $\frac{1}{2}(T - 3)$ matrices of each kind in every sequence.

Naturally, that means a uniform sequence of actions, $(a_1)*$ or $(a_2)*$, is far from optimal with respect to revenues. If the number of periods is large, $T > 7$, then the sequences of actions with the shortest descriptions are never optimal in more than $T - 3$ periods.

Now, if the state is one of the sequences close to $(a_1, a_2)*$ the first bit transmitted from the informed to the uninformed player would increase each agent's revenue by at least two times the difference between the revenues in the inferior and superior subperiod outcome at the cost of w. The second bit transmitted would only increase the revenues by half as much, but at the same cost. More precisely, an intermediate communication cost,

$$w \in \left(\frac{1}{8}x - \frac{1}{8}, \frac{1}{4}x - \frac{1}{4} \right) \tag{5.1}$$

is a sufficient condition to ensure that it is optimal for the informed player to choose the equilibrium strategy with the 1-bit code-string, $\varphi(y_3)$, rather than try to coordinate in the equilibrium with the highest revenue or the equilibrium with shortest description (the empty string λ). Indeed, the optimal choice of both players is a trade-off between ease of describability and efficiency. Players approximate the perfect fit with some sequence of actions that is easy to describe in order to save communication costs.

Example 2 The previous example was devoted to showing how the players can approximate some specific strategy with a sequence of actions with short description. Now, this example will show how players choose messages at some given number of time periods as the cost of communication varies. We are interested in the expected average length of the message.

To this aim we define the average length of the code-string with respect to p_T to be the number:

$$L_\varphi(w) = \sum_{A \in \times \{A_1, A_2\}} \left[p_T(A) | \varphi(y(A, w)) | \right] \tag{5.2}$$

where $\varphi(y(A, w))$ is the optimal code-string in state A at cost w.

Again, consider a labelling which is invariant with respect to decomposition. Assume that condition C applies and let $T = 8$ and $x = 1.5$. We can easily solve for the two extreme cases. As the communication cost is zero, $w = 0$, the players would naturally choose to coordinate in the revenue-maximizing outcome in

Table 15.1. *Numerical simulation*

w	L_φ	$\tilde{n}$	$\tilde{n}_1$
0.00	6.012	0	0
0.01	5.902	4	4
0.02	4.484	77	16
0.03	2.492	185	31
0.04	1.629	219	60
0.05	1.105	2.35	86
0.07	0.637	247	111
0.10	0.559	250	120
0.20	0.184	252	208
0.30	0.035	254	246
0.40	0.004	254	254
0.50	0.000	255	255

any state of the world. The average length of the message transmitted would be $L_\varphi(0) \approx 6.01$. At the other extreme, when the cost of communication is high, $w > 0.5$, the informed player would choose the empty string as a message in every state of the world. In this case the average length of the message transmitted would be $L_\varphi(0.5) = 0$.

To see what the average code length would be at intermediate levels of the communication cost we have conducted some numerical simulations. Let $\tilde{n}$ denote the number of states in which players choose a different strategy than the most efficient in terms of revenues and, correspondingly, let $\tilde{n}_1$ denote the number of states in which the players choose λ rather than the most efficient strategy in the underlying game. The number of deviations from the revenue-maximizing strategy, i.e. $\tilde{n}$ and $\tilde{n}_1$, should be related to the total number of states which is 256.

The results of our simulations are reported in table 15.1. The average length of the code-string transmitted decreases monotonically as the cost of communication increases. It is worth noting that players do not alter to the shortest description at some threshold, but rather change their behaviour gradually. At relatively low levels of w, players would start to play more easily described strategies. For instance, when $w = 0.04$ the probability that players would play a more easily described strategy is 0.86. Hence, players are very likely to alter from the revenue-maximizing strategy to some more easily described sequence of actions.

However, the probability that they would play the strategy with the shortest description is only 0.23. In 159 of 256 states the informed player would transmit some, but not all, information about the payoff structure to the uninformed player.

In terms of communication, players would start from a situation with zero communication cost when the uninformed player learns the Pareto-optimal behaviour perfectly and then change gradually to a situation when the uninformed player remains without any knowledge about the state of the world at very high cost of transmission of information. In terms of communication costs, players would not incur any cost of transmission at zero and very high costs. At intermediate levels, however, they would use the channel for transmission of information and the expected cost of communication is strictly positive.

6   Conclusions

It is shown that simplicity can select among multiple strict Nash equilibria. Not surprisingly, choosing a message (and an equilibrium) is a trade-off between efficiency and ease of describability. Simple patterns of behaviour occur if talk is costly.

As communication is costly players will coordinate in a Nash equilibrium in which the sequences of actions have descriptions that occur in games in few as well as many periods. The equilibrium appears to be simple to the players since it is obtained with a description that occurs in a wide range of games, including the least complex coordination problems (with few strict Nash equilibria). In this way the observed equilibrium behaviour is: (i) easy to describe because the code-string attached to the strategy is short, and (ii) simple because it is a replication of a behaviour from a much less complex decision problem. We expect team-behaviour to be highly regular. In Herbert Simon's (1959) words, man is not only a concept-forming, but also a pattern-finding animal.

REFERENCES

Aumann, R. (1990). Communication need not lead to a Nash equilibrium. Hebrew University of Jerusalem Working Paper.
Binmore, K. (1994). *Playing Fair: Game Theory and the Social Contract.* Cambridge, MA: MIT Press.
Crawford, V. P. (1995). Adaptive dynamics in coordination games. *Econometrica* 63: 103–43.
Chaitin, G. (1975). Randomness and mathematical proof. *Scientific American* 232: 47–52.

Farrell, J. (1988). Communication, coordination and Nash equilibrium. *Economics Letters* 27: 209–14.

Fudenberg, D. and D. K. Levine (1995). Theory of learning in games. Mimeo.

Fudenberg, D. and J. Tirole (1991). *Game Theory*. Cambridge, MA: MIT Press.

Gauthier, D. (1975). Coordination. *Dialogue* 14: 195–221.

Harsanyi, J. C. and R. Selten (1988). *A General Theory of Equilibrium Selection in Games*. Cambridge, MA: MIT Press.

Kandori, M., G. Mailath and R. Rob (1993). Learning, mutation, and long-run equilibria in games. *Econometrica* 61: 29–56.

Simon, H. (1959). Theories of decision-making in economics and behavioral science. *American Economic Review* 49: 253–83.

Sugden, R. (1995). A theory of focal points. *The Economic Journal* 105: 533–50.

Van Huyck, J., R. Battalio and R. Beil (1990). Tacit coordination games, strategic uncertainty, and coordination failure. *American Economic Review* 80: 234–48.

    (1991). Strategic uncertainty, equilibrium selection, and coordination failure in average opinion games. *Quarterly Journal of Economics* 106: 885–911.

    (1993). Asset markets as an equilibrium selection mechanism: coordination failure, game form auctions, and forward induction. *Games and Economic Behavior* 5: 485–504.

Van Huyck, J., R. Battalio, S. Mathur, A. Ortmann and P. Van Huyck (1995). On the origin of convention: evidence from symmetric bargaining games. *International Journal of Game Theory* 24: 187–212.

Van Huyck, J., R. Battalio and F. Rankin (1997). On the origin of convention: evidence from coordination games. *Economic Journal* (107:576-96).

Van Huyck, J., J. Cook and R. Battalio (1997). Adaptive behavior and coordination failure. *Journal of Economic Behavior and Organization* (32:483-503).

Weibull, J. (1995). *Evolutionary Game Theory*. Cambridge, MA: MIT Press.

Young, P. (1993). Evolution of conventions. *Econometrica* 61: 57–84.

16 The simplicity of an earnings frontier

Uwe Jensen

1 Introduction

In Jensen (1996, 2000), an extended human capital model with imperfect information on the employees' side is estimated as a stochastic earnings frontier with data from the German socioeconomic panel. The costs for the information imperfection are measured by the inefficiency terms of the frontier model. This individual inefficiency in finding suitable jobs is shown to be considerable. The approach leads to a sensible interpretation of the deviations of empirical income from estimated maximum possible income. Distinguishing between 'potential human capital' and 'active human capital' accounts for the partial failure of human capital models when estimated as average functions.

Keuzenkamp and McAleer (1995, 1997) have revived the discussion about simplicity, a wide-ranging concept in contrast to the well-known but narrow criterion of parsimony. In the present chapter, this concept will be applied in analysing the question of whether the 'standard OLS approach' or the frontier approach is to be preferred. The trade-off between simplicity and descriptive accuracy will be examined. The comparison of the models will be conducted verbally because there is no computable simplicity criterion at present.

The simplicity concept helps in the comparison of the OLS and the frontier model, and the comparison of these models demonstrates the rightness of the methodological theses of Keuzenkamp and McAleer (1995, 1997), who hold that simplicity should not be identified with the narrow criterion of parsimony and that Hendry's reductionism is a very narrow methodology. The new methodological approach pushed ahead by Keuzenkamp and McAleer, emphasizing the simplicity of econometric models, is discussed shortly.

Thanks for helpful comments are due to Gerd Hansen, Stefan Mittnik, Wolfgang Wetzel and the participants at the Conference on Simplicity in Tilburg. All remaining errors are my own.

The following section summarizes the results of Jensen (1996, 2000) on the stochastic earnings frontier required for the subsequent methodological discussion. Section 3 gives some information on the simplicity concept and explains why parsimony should only be a proper subset of simplicity. A detailed discussion of the simplicity and descriptive accuracy of the frontier approach in comparison to the competing OLS approach follows in section 4. The subsequent section shows why Keuzenkamp and McAleer (1995, 1997) are right in criticizing Hendry's theory of reduction and attempts to automate science. Conclusions are drawn in the last section.

2   Stochastic earnings frontier

This section summarizes the results of Jensen (1996, 2000) on the estimation of a stochastic earnings frontier which are necessary for the following methodological discussion.

Since the pathbreaking work of Mincer (1958) and Becker (1964), human capital theory has been the most popular approach for explaining individual income. Schooling is seen as investment in human capital because it means renouncing present consumption for higher future income by increasing the individual resources. The basic model devised by Mincer is

$$LI = \beta_0 + \beta_1 S + \beta_2 E + \beta_3 E^2 + v, \quad \beta_0, \beta_1, \beta_2 > 0, \quad \beta_3 < 0 \quad (1)$$

where LI is the natural logarithm of individual wage income, S is schooling (years of education) and E is experience (age-education-6).

For all the success and broad applicability of this approach, there are some limitations to it; for example, even in extended human capital models the portion of unexplained variance remains persistently near 50% of the total variance. In Jensen (1996, 2000), the number of exogenous variables is heavily augmented, too. But, in addition, a frontier function approach is applied for explaining the deviations between estimated and empirical earnings. Following Daneshvary et al. (1992), individual wages y are assumed to depend upon personal characteristics H augmenting human capital stock, job characteristics C and information I on labour market conditions, the wage distribution and job search methods. Individuals stop their search when a wage offer exceeds the reservation wage y_r. For any set of H and C and perfect information I^*, a potential maximum attainable wage y^* exists. Then, $y = y(H, C, I)$ is estimated as stochastic earnings frontier

$$y_i = \alpha + \sum_{j=1}^{k} \beta_j x_{ij} + e_i, \quad e_i = v_i - u_i, \quad u_i \geq 0, \quad i = 1, \ldots, n \quad (2)$$

Frontier functions have originally been developed for the estimation of production functions – see Aigner et al. (1977) and Meeusen and van den Broeck (1977) for the stochastic production frontier and Greene (1993) for a survey. The econometric task is to estimate a function lying 'on top of the data cloud'.

In this application, y is empirical gross wage income in logs and $\hat{y}_i = y_i^*$ is estimated maximum possible income. x is a vector of $k = 24$ variables shown in table 16.1. The composed error term e_i consists of the symmetric part v_i representing statistical noise and the one-sided inefficiency term u_i interpreted as cost of imperfect information becoming apparent in the underemployment or overeducation of individual number i. In this way, the approach can distinguish between the underemployed 'potential human capital' produced through the education process and the 'active human capital' used as a factor of production. v_i and u_i are assumed to be independent with the distributional assumptions

$$v \sim N(0, \sigma_v^2) \quad and \quad u \sim |N(0, \sigma_u^2)| \quad (3)$$

The data set consists of $n = 1334$ individuals from the tenth wave (1992) of the German socioeconomic panel (SOEP). Estimation has been carried out by the econometric computer package LIMDEP (Greene, 1989), where the likelihood function

$$l(\alpha, \beta, \sigma, \lambda) = -n \ln(\sigma) - const + \sum_{i=1}^{n} \left[\ln \Phi \left(\frac{-e_i \lambda}{\sigma} \right) - \frac{1}{2} \left(\frac{e_i}{\sigma} \right)^2 \right]$$

$$(4)$$

$$\lambda = \frac{\sigma_u}{\sigma_v} \quad \sigma^2 = \sigma_v^2 + \sigma_u^2 \quad (5)$$

is iteratively maximized with OLS starting values.

The alternative for the frontier approach is the OLS regression

$$y_i = \beta_0 + \sum_{j=1}^{k} \beta_j x_{ij} + v_i, \quad i = 1, \ldots, n \quad (6)$$

with standard assumptions. An adjusted R^2 of 0.60 is in line with the low explanatory power of average earnings functions in the literature. Table 16.2 shows that the step from OLS to the frontier does not turn the coefficients and t-ratios upside down – they just change a bit. The yield

Table 16.1. *Exogenous variables*

Label	Explanation
QUUN	Schooling dummy: 1 for **QU**alification for **UN**iversity entrance
TRAP	Professional **TR**aining dummy: 1 for **AP**prenticeship, technical schools, etc.
TRPS	Professional **TR**aining dummy: 1 for **P**ublic **S**ervice education
STCC	**ST**udies dummy: 1 for Technical **C**ollege
STUN	**ST**udies dummy: 1 for **UN**iversity
AGE1	Experience: **AGE** in years divided by **10**
AGE2	Experience: **AGE1** squared
JTNO	On-the-Job-Training dummy: 1 for '**NO** interest'
JTNC	On-the-Job-Training dummy: 1 for **N**o interest at one's own **C**ost'
SAHL	**SA**tisfaction with one's own **H**ealth and **L**ife: 0 (no) to 20 (yes)
FATH	Gifts, predisposition: status of the job of the **FATH**er
PCHA	Probability of **CHA**nging the occupation: 1 (yes) to 4 (no)
PDET	Probability of **DET**erioration in the same firm: 1 (yes) to 4 (no)
SATW	**SAT**isfaction with **W**ork: 0 (no) to 10 (yes)
MALE	Dummy: 1 for **MALE**
MARR	Dummy: marital status: 1 for **MARR**ied
RESI	Size of the **RESI**dence: 0 (large cities) to 6 (small places)
SIZE	**SIZE** of the firm: number of employees divided by 1000
EMPL	Dummy: 1 for salaried **EMPL**oyees
SERV	Dummy: 1 for public **SERV**ants
STAT	**STAT**us of the job
HOUR	Weekly working **HOUR**s including overtime
SENI	**SENI**ority: years of affiliation to the firm
PROP	**PROP**erty: interest and dividend income

of the frontier model lies in the better interpretation of the deviations of the observations from the estimated function.

The high significance of the ratio

$$\lambda = \frac{\sigma_u}{\sigma_v} \tag{7}$$

means that the variation of the inefficiency terms u_i in relation to the variation of the noise v_i is reasonably large. $\lambda = 0$ would lead to the simple OLS model because there are no inefficient individuals in this case.

Table 16.2. *Estimation results*

Method	OLS		Frontier	
Adjusted R^2	0.6016			
Variable	Coefficient	t-ratio	Coefficient	t-ratio
Constant	8.56200	56.498	8.85160	59.988
QUUN	0.07614	2.665	0.07559	2.507
TRAP	0.05908	2.709	0.05502	2.594
TRPS	0.07315	1.876	0.08549	2.251
STTC	0.10015	2.347	0.09697	2.043
STUN	0.23441	5.978	0.24188	6.213
AGE1	0.54392	8.638	0.50281	7.941
AGE2	−0.05877	−8.061	−0.05441	−7.319
JTNO	−0.05795	−2.979	−0.04884	−2.580
JTNC	−0.06603	−4.120	−0.06969	−4.345
SAHL	−0.00221	−0.716	−0.00199	−0.614
FATH	0.01115	0.432	0.00310	0.119
PCHA	0.04106	2.792	0.03921	2.913
PDET	−0.04315	−2.938	−0.04041	−2.752
SATW	0.01688	3.337	0.01621	3.375
MALE	0.20714	10.898	0.20679	10.862
MARR	0.08087	3.433	0.07253	2.983
RESI	−0.00783	−2.058	−0.00714	−1.888
SIZE	0.00989	6.298	0.00931	5.605
EMPL	0.09566	4.533	0.09640	4.741
SERV	−0.12591	−3.557	−0.13828	−3.825
STAT	0.35893	9.904	0.35701	11.180
HOUR	0.01084	9.213	0.01212	13.381
SENI	0.00540	5.363	0.00514	5.063
PROP	0.00655	4.041	0.00699	4.138
σ_u/σ_v			1.52190	12.571
$\sqrt{\sigma_u^2 + \sigma_v^2}$			0.35832	37.601

Note that σ_u is not the standard deviation of u because of definition (3). From the estimated coefficients in the last two lines of table 16.2 we can calculate $\sigma_u = 0.2995$ and $\sigma_v = 0.1968$. This leads to the estimates for mean and standard deviation of u

$$E(u) = \sqrt{\frac{2}{\pi}}\,\sigma_u = 0.2389 \quad and \quad Std(u) = \sqrt{\frac{\pi - 2}{\pi}}\,\sigma_u = 0.1805$$

(8)

(see e.g. Aigner et al., 1977) meaning that on average the individuals receive only $exp(-0.2389) \cdot 100 = 78.75\%$ of the maximum possible income.

The frontier model includes the important but hardly measurable human capital investment 'search for information' and it explains an essential part of the deviations of empirical income from estimated income. The extended human capital model only explains potential income sufficiently but individuals do not obtain their maximum possible income because of imperfect information on labour market conditions, the wage distribution, and job search methods. The more or less under-employed 'potential human capital' produced through the education process distinguishes substantially from the 'active human capital' used as a factor of production.

So, the reason for applying the frontier approach instead of the OLS approach is very simple: the latter does not take into account the considerable amount of individual inefficiency in finding suitable jobs and therefore falsely interprets inefficiency as misspecification.

See Jensen (1996, 2000) for more details on the data, the results and a critical assessment of the underlying model common to the frontier and the average function. We will now concentrate on the methodological distinctions between the OLS and the frontier model. Which arguments could be put forward for applying the 'standard' OLS approach instead of the frontier approach? Some researchers are perhaps only interested in estimating average income, not in estimating maximum possible income: we will comment on this reservation in section 4. Others may consider the OLS model to be much simpler than the frontier model. Is this true? What is simplicity? Are there any trade-offs? We will try to give an answer to these questions in the remaining sections.

3   About simplicity

The principle of Occam's razor, 'Entia non sunt multiplicanda praeter necessitatem', is ascribed to William of Occam (1285–1347). The Law of Parsimony, 'Frustra fit per plura, quod potest fieri per pauciora', can also be found in his writings. Since that time, it has been accepted as a methodological rule in many sciences to try to develop simple models. This rule is valid in econometrics, too, where Keuzenkamp and McAleer (1995, 1997) have revived discussion about the simplicity concept.

They illustrate why simplicity should not be identified with parsimony, a very narrow criterion meaning paucity of parameters. The task in this chapter, i.e. the comparison of an OLS function and a frontier function, demonstrates for the rightness of their demand. Simply counting the parameters cannot take into account the complexity – the counterpart of simplicity – originating, for example, from the different specification of the error term in the frontier case, i.e. the complexity of a composed error including a truncated distribution. Therefore, a sound comparison of OLS and frontier has to analyse additional aspects of simplicity.

Parsimony is a proper subset of simplicity. But whereas parsimony is well-defined and easily calculated, there is no agreement among econometricians about the further ingredients of simplicity let alone about their weights in a future 'simplicity formula'. The discussion about these questions is in its infancy. Keuzenkamp and McAleer (1995) inform about the Bayesian or information-theoretical background of simplicity measures. It is important to bear in mind the trade-off between simplicity (or parsimony) and descriptive accuracy of a model. But because simplicity is hardly quantifiable in complicated problems, we cannot expect to have criteria like AIC or SC for the weighing of simplicity and descriptive accuracy in our econometrical toolkit in the near future. The 'principle of minimum description length' of Rissanen (1983), a generalization of AIC and SC, is only a first step in this direction.

Parsimony is a one-dimensional notion (and real numbers are easily ordered), whereas simplicity is a multidimensional concept. Vectors are not easily ordered but the possible components of such a simplicity vector will be explored in the next section. We should not deplore the multidimensionality of simplicity but accept this as a natural property of versatile econometric models.

Because of the difficulties with the definition and measurement of simplicity, some econometricians are quite reserved in considering the 'difference between simplicity and parsimony' when building econometric models. Keuzenkamp and McAleer (1997) illustrate why this attitude is not recommendable. Boltzmann wrote that 'a hypothesis is false if a simpler hypothesis is superior in representing the data' (Keuzenkamp and McAleer, 1997). Zellner (1982) writes: 'Economic reality, whatever this is, may seem to be complicated because it is not understood. Understanding in my view involves simplification, not complication.' And we have seen in this section that parsimony is too simple to manage the comparison of a frontier with an OLS function. Scientific progress originates from dealing with todays intractable problems. Therefore, we will try to explore the dimensions of simplicity of an earnings frontier in the next section.

4   **The simplicity of the approach**

In the absence of a tractable criterion for simplicity, we will follow the aspects listed in Keuzenkamp and McAleer (1997) and discuss them verbally. The authors also indicate some aspects which should not be included in a formal definition of simplicity. Examples are the elegance or beauty of an approach because they are highly subjective, or the ease of communication because it depends on the subjects which communicate. Little or no acquaintance with the frontier concept should be no reason for rating frontiers as too complex because this rating depends on persons and time. Simplicity ratings should not be established by opinion polls.

In the following, the notation Frontier ≻ OLS means that the frontier approach is more complex (or less simple) than OLS in the particular aspect, ~ stands for similar simplicity.

1. Number and type of parameters: Frontier ≻ OLS
   This is the parsimony criterion. Both the OLS and the frontier approach apply the same extended human capital model. One could call for more parsimonious extensions of the basic model, but this would not affect the OLS/Frontier comparison. Nevertheless, OLS is simpler than the frontier approach because of one additional variance that has to be estimated for the latter (see equation 4).
2. Specification of the error term: Frontier ≻ OLS
   Generally, it is not easy to achieve agreement about the simplicity of different specifications of the error terms or about different distributions (see Keuzenkamp and McAleer, 1997). But in this case, the normal distribution of the OLS error in equation (6) is extended to a composed error with an additional half-normal component in (2) allowing an easy and clear decision on simplicity.
3. Specification of the functional form: Frontier ~ OLS
   What is a frontier? Is it an OLS function which has been shifted upwards and rotated slightly? Should it be more (cf. Kalirajan and Obwona, 1994)? In any case, there is no higher complexity in the functional form of the present earnings frontier than in the corresponding average earnings function. And the lower acquaintance of many econometricians with the frontier concept cannot be a sensible simplicity criterion (see above).
4. Availability of diagnostic tests: Frontier ≻ OLS
   Besides the fact that the theory on frontier functions is not as developed as the theory on OLS functions which is time-dependent and

therefore meaningless for our simplicity analysis, there are some systematic difficulties for the development of theoretical results about e.g. diagnostic tests. It is well known since Schmidt (1976) that estimating frontiers often means running into problems of irregularity. A typical example is that the ratio $\lambda = \sigma_u/\sigma_v$ in equation (5) cannot be employed for the construction of a test for 'significant inefficiency' in the model 'because the polar value, $\lambda = 0$, is on the boundary of the parameter space' (Greene, 1993, p. 77). There is no problem computing LM or Wald test statistics but interpreting them.

5. Estimation and computation: Frontier $\succ$ OLS
   The iterative ML estimation procedure with OLS starting values (see section 2) certainly is more complex than estimation by OLS.

6. Data availability: Frontier $\sim$ OLS
   The data sets are identical.

7. Robustness: Frontier $\succ$ OLS
   Working with highly sensitive results certainly is not simple. It is well known from the literature on robustness that OLS estimation is not robust, but the situation for frontiers is even worse. An earnings frontier provides the maximum possible income for given human capital stock and job characteristics (see section 2). This is no 'absolute frontier' for all theoretically possible individuals, but a so-called 'best-practice frontier' for the individuals in the sample (see Førsund et al., 1980). That is why frontiers are especially sensitive to changes in the efficient part of the data set.

8. Consistency: Frontier $\succ$ OLS
   The inconsistency of estimators also reduces the simple applicability of an approach. The parameter estimators in the present comparison show the standard consistency properties of ML or OLS estimators. The frontier problem lies in the estimation of the individual inefficiencies u_i. Because only the composed error e_i – see equation (2) – and not u_i itself can be observed, the individual inefficiencies have to be estimated indirectly by the modus or expectation of the conditional distribution of u_i for given e_i following Jondrow et al. (1982). This device provides unbiased but inconsistent estimates of u_i because the variance of the estimates does not approach zero for large n.

9. Efficiency: Frontier $\sim$ OLS
   Again, working with inefficient results reduces simplicity. And Keuzenkamp and McAleer (1997) point out that 'adding possibly redundant variables to models without bothering about their redundancy generally leads to a loss of efficiency' whereas 'omitting relevant variables through excessive parsimony may yield inconsistent

estimates of the parameters of interest'. But in our OLS/frontier comparison, the set of exogenous variables is identical and a comparison of the theoretical results on the efficiency of the respective estimators seems to be hardly possible.

10. Valid inference: Frontier $\succ$ OLS

Keuzenkamp and McAleer (1997) emphasize the relation between simplicity and valid inference requiring consistent estimation of the model parameters and their variances. Incorporating e.g. heteroscedasticity into the model unfortunately enlarges its complexity. Again, frontiers are not as well behaved as average functions: Caudill and Ford (1993) note that heteroscedasticity in the frontier model leads not only to inefficient but also biased estimators.

11. Interpretability: Frontier $\prec$ OLS

Finally, we come to probably the most controversial part of the valuation. Good interpretability certainly is an important aspect of the simplicity of a model. The problem is to pass a judgment which does not depend on personal taste, time or 'scientific trends'. OLS advocates should take care not to have a low opinion of the earnings frontier because this approach is new and not well known.

The earnings frontier is rated as simpler than the average earnings function because the frontier approach does not try to explain the actual income, but admits that it is only possible to estimate the possible income for given human capital stock and job characteristics. Individuals have been seen to be inefficient in their job search. Potential human capital produced through the education process has been seen to differ substantially from active human capital used as a factor of production. Of course, some additional assumptions have to be made in the frontier model, but these assumptions are not arbitrary.

What about those researchers maintaining to be interested only in estimating average income, not in estimating maximum possible income? The OLS model claims to be able to explain average income. Deviations from the average are identified to be white noise. But this model does not care about the realization of this average income. Individuals acquire the capability of earning a certain income during the education process, but the efficiency of the job search is crucial for really attaining this possible income. The OLS model ignores this last step and therefore partly mixes up inefficiency and white noise which complicates the interpretability of its results.

In the absence of a computable simplicity criterion, we have to combine the results on the different aspects of simplicity verbally. Although we cannot be sure to have considered all relevant aspects of simplicity and although the final judgment depends on the weights given to the aspects, it could be seen that the OLS model is actually simpler than the frontier model.

'The overly simple or overly complex is boring and ugly' (Simon, 2001). For the estimation of the trade-off between simplicity and descriptive accuracy, we now have to analyse the latter. It has been shown that the frontier model – unlike the OLS model – includes the important but hardly measurable human capital investment 'search for information'. By this means, the earnings frontier explains an essential part of the deviations of empirical income from estimated income.

Unfortunately, there is no analog to the R^2 of the OLS model in the frontier approach. Therefore, there is no frontier result comparable to the 40% unexplained variance in the OLS case. However, as inefficiency turns out to be considerable, the gain in explanation power seems to be considerable, too. Our conclusion is that the descriptive accuracy of the earnings frontier is superior to that of the average function.

That is why the estimation of the trade-off between simplicity and descriptive accuracy remains an open question. Without agreement on the definition of simplicity, without a computable simplicity criterion, the contest between the two approaches cannot be settled. Such a criterion certainly will not be developed tomorrow. And if some generally applicable criterion were available, the author's experience – see Jensen (1995) – with the necessity of model regularity for obtaining sufficient results suggests that this criterion would not be applicable to the irregular frontier model.

5   Methodology

Finally, some methodological remarks will be given about the process of development of the human capital earnings frontier. In recent years, it seems that econometricians have payed more attention to econometric methodology. This is sensible because it is very important for the individual econometrician to convince colleagues or economists applying econometric methods of the feasibility of newly developed models and techniques. This conviction can be achieved by making the reason for developing econometric methods and the development itself clear.

Surveys like Pagan (1987) or Hayo (1997) mention several econometric methodological approaches: the traditional Cowles commission approach, Hendry's 'from the general to the specific', Sims' VAR and Leamer's sensitivity analysis. This set has been enlarged by a new approach pushed ahead by Keuzenkamp and McAleer (1995, 1997) emphasizing the simplicity of econom(etr)ic models.

Keuzenkamp and McAleer (1995) criticize Hendry's reductionism proceeding 'from the general to the specific' by 'testing down' following 'the three golden rules of econometrics ... test, test, test' (Hendry, 1980, p. 403). Keuzenkamp and McAleer (1995) argue: 'The idea that the only valid way of inference proceeds by testing downward, starting from maximal attainable complexity, rests on a misconception of scientific inference' (p. 17). '... the search for the "Data Generating Process" ... is in vain. Such a process does not exist' (p. 15). '... one cannot estimate the DGP, even if it were to exist' (p. 17).

The search for the final earnings frontier model in Jensen (1996, 2000) demonstrates the rightness of the methodological critique just mentioned. Following the theory of reduction, there seems to be no way to arrive at the earnings frontier model presented in this chapter. Of course, one cannot start every econometric analysis with a frontier model testing for inefficiency. And there is no general model including all variants of econometric models. If it were to exist, limited degrees of freedom would prevent its use. Therefore, one cannot arrive at the earnings frontier model 'from the top'. 'Testing downward is sensible if one favours parsimony' (Keuzenkamp and McAleer, 1995, p. 16). We have seen that the criterion of parsimony is often too narrow. Hendry's reductionism leads to restrictions to narrow model classes as well.

For the same reason, Keuzenkamp and McAleer (1995) are right in criticizing attempts to 'automate science'. Rissanen (1987, p. 96) advocates this, arguing that 'the introduction of subjective judgements in inferential problems makes the resulting inferences strictly speaking unscientific'. The answer by Keuzenkamp and McAleer (1995) is that 'such objectivity is misleading (this is particularly true for economic inference, where data information is limited and value judgements are inevitable)' (p. 18). 'The skilful (but subjective) hand of the econometrician is indispensable' (p. 17). There seems to be no automatic and generally applicable way to arrive at specifications like the present one.

Instead of reductionism and automatism, Keuzenkamp and McAleer (1995) recommend an iterative model-building process starting with relatively *simple* models and then combining extension, approximation and reduction when the models are insufficient or new data are available. This is exactly the path from the basic human capital model devised by Mincer (1958) to the final specification in Jensen (1996, 2000). Mincer approximated the data by a simple average human capital model with a solid microeconomic foundation. Over the years, this model was extended by several exogenous variables because of insufficient explanatory power.

Then, the frontier model was chosen because the extended average human capital model still seems to be insufficient as it explains the 'wrong' income.

All this requires econom(etr)ic intuition and a skilful hand. Nevertheless, it is not jugglery that is needed in this process but the ability and the intention to make the process clear to everybody. The aim is not to find a 'true DGP' or to falsify economic hypotheses but simply to help further the understanding of economic phenomena.

6   Conclusions

In this chapter, the simplicity concept discussed by Keuzenkamp and McAleer (1995, 1997) has been applied to analyse the decision in Jensen (1996, 2000) for a stochastic earnings frontier instead of the traditional average earnings function. For want of a computable simplicity criterion, the comparison of the models has been conducted verbally. It came out that the OLS model is simpler than the frontier model, whereas the latter has the higher descriptive accuracy. But since the trade-off between simplicity and descriptive accuracy cannot be quantified, a final decision as to which method should be preferred is impossible at present.

Apart from that, the comparison with a frontier model has turned out to be a good training ground for exploring the manifold aspects of multidimensional simplicity. It has been shown that simplicity should not be identified with the narrow notion of parsimony and that, for example, the larger model can be simpler in some respects (here: interpretative simplicity). Finally, the frontier model demonstrates the rightness of the methodological theses of Keuzenkamp and McAleer (1995, 1997) in criticizing Hendry's theory of reduction and attempts to automate science.

It seems that simplicity considerations are a fruitful field for econometric methodology as well as a helpful instrument for econometricians in a successful communication with fellow econometricians or economists applying econometric models.

REFERENCES

Aigner, D. J., C. A. K. Lovell and P. Schmidt (1977). Formulation and estimation of stochastic frontier production function models. *Journal of Econometrics* 6: 21–37.
Becker, G. S. (1964). *Human Capital*. New York: NBER.
Caudill, S. B. and J. M. Ford (1993). Biases in frontier estimation due to heteroscedasticity. *Economics Letters* 41: 17–20.

Daneshvary, N., H. W. Herzog, R. A. Hofler and A. M. Schlottmann (1992). Job search and immigrant assimilation: an earnings frontier approach. *Review of Economics and Statistics* 74: 482–92.

Førsund, F. R., C. A. K. Lovell and P. Schmidt (1980). A survey of frontier production functions and of their relationship to efficiency measurement. *Journal of Econometrics* 13: 5–25.

Greene, W. H. (1989). LIMDEP. New York: Econometric Software Inc.

(1993). The econometric approach to efficiency analysis. In H. O. Fried, C. A. K. Lovell and S. S. Schmidt (eds.), *The Measurement of Productive Efficiency*, pp. 68–119. New York: Oxford University Press.

Hayo, B. (1997). Alternative methodologische Ansätze in der Ökonometrie: eine Einführung. *Allgemeines Statistisches Archiv* 81: 266–89.

Hendry, D. F. (1980). Econometrics – alchemy or science? *Economica* 47: 387–406.

Jensen, U. (1995). A review of the derivation and calculation of Rao distances with an application to portfolio theory. In G. S. Maddala, P. C. B. Phillips and T. N. Srinivasan (eds.), *Advances in Econometrics and Quantitative Economics*, pp. 413–62. Oxford: Blackwell.

(1996). Estimation of an earnings frontier with data from the German socio-economic panel. Arbeiten aus dem Institut für Statistik und Ökonometrie, Nr. 92, Universität Kiel.

(2000). Measuring earnings differentials with frontier functions and Rao distances. In P. Marriott and M. Salmon, *Applications of Differential Geometry to Econometrics*, pp. 184–213. Cambridge: Cambridge University Press.

Jondrow, J., C. A. K. Lovell, I. S. Materov and P. Schmidt (1982). On the estimation of technical inefficiency in the stochastic frontier production function model. *Journal of Econometrics* 19: 233–8.

Kalirajan, K. P. and M. B. Obwona (1994). Frontier production function: the stochastic coefficients approach. *Oxford Bulletin of Economics and Statistics* 56: 87–96.

Keuzenkamp, H. A. and M. McAleer (1995). Simplicity, scientific inference and econometric modelling. *Economic Journal* 105: 1–21.

(1997). The complexity of simplicity. *Mathematics and Computers in Simulation* 43: 553–61.

Meeusen, W. and J. van den Broeck (1977). Efficiency estimation from Cobb–Douglas production functions with composed error. *International Economic Review* 18: 435–44.

Mincer, J. (1958). Investment in human capital and personal income distribution. *Journal of Political Economy* 66: 281–302.

Pagan, A. (1987). Three econometric methodologies: a critical appraisal. *Journal of Economic Surveys* 1: 3–24.

Rissanen, J. (1983). A universal prior for integers and estimation by minimum description length. *Annals of Statistics* 11: 416–31.

(1987). Stochastic complexity and the MDL principle. *Econometric Reviews* 6: 85–102.

Schmidt, P. (1976). On the statistical estimation of parametric frontier production functions. *Review of Economics and Statistics* 58: 238–9.

Simon, H. A. (2001). Science seeks parsimony, not simplicity: searching for pattern in phenomena. In this volume.

Zellner, A. (1982). Basic issues in econometrics: past and present. *The American Economist* 26: 5–10.

17 Simplicity: views of some Nobel laureates in economic science

Michael McAleer

1 Preamble

Inspired by the chaos of opinion regarding the meaning and importance of simplicity in scientific research, including economics and econometrics, the Tilburg Simplicity Conference was held in January 1997 in an attempt to shed some light on this important topic. In preparing for the conference, a survey was conducted in late 1995 among the living Nobel laureates in economic science about their views as to the meaning and importance of simplicity in their own research. Specifically, the editors of this monograph requested the views of the Nobel laureates on the following three questions:

1. What is the meaning of simplicity?
2. Has simplicity played a role in their research?
3. Is simplicity a desirable, undesirable or irrelevant feature of economic theories and models?

For the 27-year period 1969–95, there were forty Nobel laureates (eighteen were sole recipients, two awardees shared the prize on eight occasions, and three awardees shared the prize on two occasions). Of the forty awardees, twenty-five of the twenty-six still living were sent the survey request. There were nine respondents with seven detailed responses, of whom one (Herbert A. Simon) sent a paper that appears in the monograph.

It is instructive that, of the twenty-seven citations for the laureates, not one mentions 'simplicity' and only one mentions 'complexity', as follows:

Milton Friedman [awarded 1976], for his achievements in the fields of consumption analysis, monetary history and theory and for his demonstration of the complexity of stabilization policy.

(Unfortunately, Professor Friedman was unable to submit an answer to the three questions as he felt that there was insufficient time to 'give the kind of serious answers that your questions deserve'.)

The primary contributions of the Nobel laureates for the period 1969–95, as contained in their citations, embrace the development and application of dynamic models, raising the levels of analysis, focusing on empirically founded interpretations, development and application of the input–output method, demonstration of the complexity of stabilization policy, analysis of financial markets, incorporation of new analytical methods and rigorous reformulations, discovery of new theories, clarification of existing ideas, extending the domain of knowledge, and renewing research in economic history. These fundamental contributions can be summarized as follows (with frequencies given in parentheses):

> {Pioneering/pathbreaking/fundamental/penetrating}
>   {contributions/research/analysis/work} (10)
> {Development/creation} and application (4)
> Clarification and {analyses/discovery} (2)
> Contributions (2)
> Development and contribution (1)
> Development (1)
> Seminal studies (1)
> New and deepened insight (1)
> Achievements (1)
> Analysis (1)
> Rigorous formulation (1)
> Extended domain of analysis (1)
> Renewing research (1)

In the following section, insightful replies from six Nobel laureates emphasize the importance of simplicity in their research, as well as its role in testing economic theories and models.

2   Views of the laureates

The views of the six Nobel laureates are given in the chronological order in which the prizes were awarded. Kenneth J. Arrow (born 1921) and Sir R. John Hicks (1904–89) shared the 1972 prize 'for their pioneering contributions to general economic equilibrium theory and welfare theory'. According to Arrow (7 February 1996):

'Simplicity' is a very complex subject! I have not thought deeply about it, although it certainly plays a great role in my thinking and that of my colleagues. I know certainly that the term has a number of different meanings.

Wassily Leontief (born 1906) was awarded the 1973 prize 'for the development of the input–output method and for its application to important economic problems'. Leontief wrote (22 January 1996):

I sympathize with your concern for the increasing complexity of academic economics. However, an argument that appears to be difficult to follow for one reader might appear to be simple from the point of view of another. As you possibly know, I have always objected not to complexity but to irrelevance of many 'mathematical' articles published in leading economic journals.

The 1986 prize was awarded to James M. Buchanan Jr (born 1919) 'for his development of the contractual and constitutional bases for the theory of economic and political decision-making'. Buchanan responded as follows (4 January 1996):

The projected conference topic is a fascinating one. You explicitly solicited my views on specific questions. Let me preface my remarks by disclaiming any and all expertise in statistics or econometrics. I respond only as an economist, the old-fashioned variety. In my own analytical work, I have always found it helpful to get to the simple elements of the problem addressed, to get to the elementary logic if you will. Complexity for the sake of complexity or even for the formal completeness has always seemed a waste of effort.

But let me suggest an issue that I have been thinking about recently, one that does raise problems of just what simplicity means. Take the elementary problem involved in explaining why exchange takes place. There are two contrasting approaches here.

1. Assume all persons are identical in both preferences and in capacities. Then exchange emerges because there are advantages to specialization. This is the basic Adam Smith model.
2. Assume all persons are identical in preferences but that persons differ in natural capacities. Exchange emerges as persons recognize their comparative advantages. This is the Ricardian trade model.

We know, of course, that, empirically, persons differ in both preferences and in capacities (endowments). But which model meets precepts dictated by Occam? Is it 'simpler' to postulate uniformity? Or is it 'simpler' to start with empirical reality?

Robert M. Solow (born 1924) received the 1987 prize 'for his contributions to the theory of economic growth'. His detailed response (9 February 1996) is as follows:

[T]he concept of simplicity in scientific research ... is actually a question that interests me a lot.

1. One could be quite sophisticated about the meaning of 'simplicity' in this context, but I will not try. To be brief – simple? – I would come close to equating simplicity with transparency. A simple model or theory is one

whose inner workings can be seen *and interpreted* by a knowledgeable person. 'Oh yes, I see how and why that works.' Some qualification is needed because a very large cascade of simple relations eventually gets too complicated; but maybe that is included in my version, just as very many layers of glass, each transparent, become an opaque mass if stacked one on another.

2. I am addicted to simple models. In my own research I try very hard to formulate simple models, so that in the end I think I 'understand' how the final conclusions come about. I am unhappy if I have to say to myself: 'Well, I don't understand why a change in this parameter causes just that change in the behaviour of yonder variable; it just does.' Sometimes that cannot be avoided, but it gives a bad feeling.

3. Obviously, then, I think simplicity is a desirable characteristic of a model. But again a qualification is needed. I am prepared to believe that some things one might like to model are inherently complex, and will not yield to simplicity. In that case it would be just foolish to insist on simplicity. The choice is either to find another problem, or to accept a loss of transparency. (Obviously there are complex phenomena that yield to simple models. Chaotic dynamics has taught us that. I am speaking of phenomena whose underlying analysis is inherently complex, which is different.)

I hope you find these brief and casual remarks useful.

An interesting illustration of simplicity is the current debate regarding alternative models of economic growth. Robert E. Lucas Jr was awarded the 1995 prize 'for having developed and applied the hypothesis of rational expectations'. He provides evidence (*Journal of Monetary Economics* 22 (1988), 3–42) that the neoclassical growth model of Solow (*Quarterly Journal of Economics* 70 (1956), 65–94) fits US data as well as a Lucas augmentation of the Solow model, which includes a measure of human capital accumulation in the form of the general skill level of a given worker. As the Lucas augmentation has considerably greater mathematical complexity, simplicity could be used to argue in favour of the Solow model.

The Economist (30 September 1995, p. 96) provides a journalistic flavour of such an argument as follows:

Many economists argue that they can answer such questions by making their growth models more complex. Others, however, believe that simplicity is the key.

John C. Harsanyi (born 1920), John F. Nash Jr (born 1928) and Reinhard Selten (born 1930) shared the 1994 prize 'for their pioneering analysis of equilibria in the theory of non-cooperative games'. Harsanyi argued (11 January 1996) that:

In my view, one theory should be regarded as *simpler* than another if it involves a *smaller number* of independent assumptions. It seems to me that *simplicity* (and mathematical elegance) should be considered as important *heuristic criteria*.

Other things being equal, a simpler theory will be *preferable* to a less simple theory.

For in the case of *empirical theories*, whenever we add a *new* empirical assumption to a given theory we will always reduce the prior probability that *all* our assumptions will be found consistent with the actual facts ('Popper's improbability criterion for the choice of scientific hypotheses', *Philosophy* 25 (1960), 332–40). On the other hand, in the case of normative theories, whenever we add a new normative postulate to our theory we always run the risk that the latter will be really unnecessary or will actually reduce the plausibility of our theory from a normative point of view. In my own normative work in decision theory, game theory and ethics, I have taken the view that simplicity and mathematical elegance are always strong recommendations for any given solution concept. In our joint work with Reinhard Selten both of us have been using these two criteria.

Of course, we have no guarantee that all normative problems will have particularly simple and mathematically elegant solutions. Yet, even so, it seems to me that, in decision and game theory as well as in ethics, simplicity and elegance can be very helpful heuristic criteria.

Nash sent his reactions by email message (17 April 1996):

Yes, I have definitely had appreciation of principles of simplicity and this is well illustrated in economic theory, in my case … [I]t is easy enough to realize also in a field like economics that there is often the danger of 'oversimplification'. How could a simple theory that could be easily understood and used by all speculators be expected to predict the future movements of prices on a major stock exchange? Human competitiveness, with knowledge of the theory, would act against and sabotage it.

Good examples, in economic or economics-related theory, are my axioms for bargaining solutions or Shapley's axioms giving the 'Shapley value'. But to go further into this question might bring in unnecessarily the effective function of an historian of science or a psychologist of science (if there is such a discipline).

It is certainly true that simplicity has a major function but also it's difficult to think that a simple 'rule of simplicity' can be given so that, by simply using that rule, it would be easy to produce good scientific research!

Index

Ackermann function, 150–1
adaptive systems, 62
adjustable parameters, 85, 90–1, 109–11
algorithmic information content, 138
Akaike Information Criteria (AIC), 20–1,
    29, 84, 89–90, 93, 97–9, 106–17,
    129–30, 214, 220
    consistency/inconsistency of, 113–15
Always-Complex rule, 107–8
Always-Simple rule, 107–8, 110
approximation, 35, 53
AR-processes, 158, 234–5, 251–2, 255–6
Archimedes, *The Sand Reckoner*, 139
artificial economy, 80
artificial intelligence, 74, 80
axiomatic procedure, 74–5

background information, 96
BACON, 40–5
Becon–Descartes Ideal, 208
Balmer's Law, 38
Bayes' rule, 136, 142
Bayesian Information Criteria (BIC), 20–1,
    29, 90, 93, 106–17, 214, 220, 227
Bayesianism, 27–8, 88–9, 137, 145, 167
beauty, 33, 36, 284
behaviour
    choice, 55
    exceedingly complex, 63
    human, 62
    in organizations, 58
belief, 145, 202
Bernoulli
    class, 158
    distribution, 157
bi-polar approach, 208–11
bias/variance trade-off, 105–6
Binmore's Dodo game, 264–5
black boxes, 81
Black's Law, 42, 44
block triangular systems, 64–5
Bode's Law, 38

Bohr's quantum model of the hydrogen
    atom, 39
bounded rationality, 57, 59–60, 64, 67
budget, 56–7

calibrating data set, 96–7
Cauchy distribution, 189
causal belief, 15
causal chains, 125
causal ordering, 65, 76–80
cause and effect, 39, 50
central limit theorem, 106, 159
chaos, 1, 47
cheap talk, 263–4
Chebyshev inequality, 195
chromosomes, 53–4
Cobb–Douglas production function, 232
code length, 158, 162–3, 274
code-strings, 268–74
coding, 268–9
common cause, 26
complex systems, 46, 75–6, 81
    evolution of, 68–9
complexity, 3, 34
    algorithmic theory of, 156–7, 162
    computational, 47
    of an equilibrium, 9
    increase of, 122–3
    macroeconomic approach to, 73
    measurement of, 4, 34–5, 238
    monotone, 149
    in nature, 120–1
    non-parametric, 231
    in society, 121
    stochastic, 157–9, 161, 163, 239–40
compressible object, 126
compression of descriptions, 137
compression
    data, 151, 185
    maximal, 153
convenience, 9
correlation anaylsis, 198

corroboration principle, the, 235
cost of communication, 274–5
cost of transmission, 271
counter-intuitive outcomes, 228
counting, 14–15, 248, 283
Cowles approach, 73–4, 76, 287
Cramer–Rao inequality, 159
cross-validation, 96
curve-fitting, 13, 98–9, 101, 197
curves
    bumpy and smooth, 14
    cost, 60–1
    low-order polynomial, 156
    optimal, 112
    predictively accurate, 98
    specific, 27–8

data
    comparison with theory, 44
    modelling procedure, 234
    non-degenerate, 236
    observed, 236
    theory of, 35
data-generating process (DGP), 165–6,
    175–6, 219–20
decision framework, 221
decision-making, 57
decision rules, 263
decision-theoretic approach, 95–6
decomposable systems, 75
de Finetti-type representation theorems,
    201–2
degrees of freedom, 48, 237–8, 288
descriptive accuracy, 8, 283
diagonal dynamic systems, 64
difference equation, 244
differential equation, complexity of, 27,
    246
dimensionality, 178
discovery, 39–40
    data-driven, 40
    normative theories of, 40
    theory-guided, 44
distribution, 191
domain of prediction, 98–9, 116
Duhem problem, 208
dynamic systems, 232–3

earnings frontier, 277–8
econometrics, 122–3, 165, 210, 227
    complexity of, 125
    simplicity of, 277, 287
    time series, 165, 167, 199, 250
Edwards, A. W. F., *Likelihood*, 128–30
Einstein's theory of time, 46
empirical truth, 33

EPAM, 62–3
equation
    difference, 244
    differential, 27, 246
    homogeneous/non-homogeneous, 246
    measurement, 253–4
    quadratic, 36
    simultaneous, 46
    state, 253–4
equilibrium
    Nash, 263–6, 272
    optimal, 272
    Pareto-optimal, 263–4
    renegotiation-proof, 264
    selection, 264
    superior/inferior, 266
    strategies, 269
error terms, 45
estimator, biased/unbiased, 29
experiments
    exploratory, 48–9
    well-structured, 48
expertise, theory of, 63

factoring, 46
falsifiability, 43–4, 54, 185, 235
firm size, 60–1
Fisher information matrix, 174–5
Fisher's theory of reduction, 5, 184
Fisher's Principle of Maximum Likelihood,
    22, 25, 128
Fleming, Alexander, 49–50
Fourier's series, 48
Friedman, Milton, 73, 242, 292
Friedman's principle of unrealism, 52, 68,
    209–10
frontier approach, 284–7
functional form, 249

Galileo's law of uniform acceleration, 52–3
game theory, 263–75
games
    binary choice, 265–7
    coordination, 263–5
    T-period, 268
General Problem Solver (GPS), 63
germ theory of disease, 54–5, 57
Geweke-Meese BEC, 213–14
Gibrat assumption, 60–1
Goodman's riddle of induction, 3, 15
goodness-of-fit, 6, 13–14, 20, 28, 35, 42,
    196–7, 200

Haavelmo distribution, 202
Harrod–Domar growth model, 249
heuristic approach, 50, 59, 63

hierarchic systems, 8, 65–8, 74–5, 79, 80,
    103, 112–15
hierarchic decomposition, 81
homogeneity test, 163
hypothesis
    arbitrary, 99–100
    equilibrium, 209
    fixed, 100
    predictively most accurate, 101–3, 105
    space, 145
hypothesis-generation, 42–3

identification, 45
independent and indentically distributed
    (IID), 189, 199
    assumptions, 194
incompressibility, 144
indirect distribution, 184
induction, problem of, 83, 90–1, 208
inequality, 195
    backwards/forwards, 26
inference, 25, 30, 32
    inductive, 146–7
    matching, 467
    parametric/nonparametric, 181–4, 186–9,
        193–8
    precision of, 194
    statistical, 182, 195, 201
infinity, 144
information theory, 167
input–output systems, 232–6
insiders/outsiders, 125
invariance with respect to decomposition,
    268, 270, 272
isotopes, 38

Jeffrey's measure of complexity, 247–53
Jeffreys' mixture, 160
Jeffreys, Harold, 3–4, 27, 239, 246
    Scientific Inference, 128, 244, 250
    Theory of Probability, 244–5
Jeffreys–Wrinch simplicity postulate, 81,
    245

Kalman's theory of modelling, 227
Kepler's Third Law, 32, 37, 40, 42, 44
Keynes, John Maynard, 124
KISS, 242, 258 (*see also* SEMTSA)
Kolmogorov complexity, 4, 9, 135–41, 152,
    156, 162, 239
Kraft's inequality, 142–3
Kuhn's pattern of normal science, 49
Kullback–Leibler distance, 89, 148, 160,
    168, 170, 220

labels, 267–8, 273

Lagrange multipliers, 253
language, 266
large numbers, 139, 145
laws of qualitative structure, 54, 57–9, 62,
    66
Lebesgue measure, 168, 173–4
likelihood, 24–7
    average, 29
    concentrated log, 176
    function, 182–3
    joint, 176
    maximum, 91, 94, 101–2, 107–8, 115,
        211–12
    testing, 171–2
LIMDEP, 279
linear equation systems, 77
Lorenz transformations, 46

marginal liklihood, 167
marginal utilities, 56
Markov chains, 159
Markov inequality, 196
Martin-Löf, Per, 144
Maxwell's equations, 46
mean square error of prediction (MSEP),
    221–4
measurement
    of demand elasticities, 56
    of fit, 99–100
    semantic, 16–17, 229–30
    syntactic, 4, 16–17
MECHEM, 43
Mendel's probabilistic law of inheritance,
    53
method of maximum likelihood (MML),
    129
Michelson–Morley experiments, 61
minimal complete proper subsets, 76–7
minimum achievable distance, 168
minimum description length (MDL)
    criterion, 86, 90, 136–7, 152–3, 161–2,
        283
misspecification, 188
    testing, 192–3, 196–8, 203–4
model
    accuracy, 231
    bias, 105–6, 109–12, 116
    comparison, 97
    complexity, 237
    evaluation, 246
    fit, 231
    ordering, 170, 246
    representation, 237
    sampling, 182
    structure, 234–5

model selection, 26, 29, 83–7, 100–4, 111, 116, 213, 221–2, 233–4
  behavioural, 231
  complexity of, 160
  criteria for, 86, 90, 97, 99, 106, 207, 212
  explanation of, 88
  goal, 88, 97, 101
  method of, 91
  modelling of, 89
modelling, 165, 227–8, 235
  approximate, 238
  behavioural framework of, 229–32, 235–9
  components of, 254
  deterministic, 229, 234, 237
  empirical, 6
  macroeconomic, 73
  non-parametric approach to, 230–1
  probabilistic framework of, 229
  procedures of, 234–5
models
  autoregressive (AR), 252, 257–8
  behavioural, 233
  deterministic, 234
  difference equation, 244
  dynamic factor, 238
  interconnected, 86
  frontier, 282, 287–9
  human capital, 277–8, 282, 287–9
  linear regression, 200
  macroeconometric, 243
  mathematical, 232
  multiplier-accelerator, 244
  nested/non-nested, 94, 109
  normal/linear, 202–4
  ordinary least squares (OLS), 282, 287
  parametric/nonparametric, 181–4, 186–9, 192–7, 200
  probability, 182
  random walk, 250
  Ricardian trade, 294
  simultaneous equations, 76
  statistical, 181–6
  stochastic, 238
moments, 191, 195

Nash equilibria, 263–6, 271–2
nearly block diagonal matrix, 65–6
nearly completely decomposable systems, 64–8
nearly decomposable systems, 75, 78–9, 81
nested hierarchy of models, *see* hierarchic systems
Newtonian models of motion, 101
Newton's laws, 44, 46

Neyman–Pearson hypothesis testing, 91–3, 170, 193, 211
Nobel laureates, 292–6
normal science, 125
normality, 188–90
normality assumption, 87, 106, 183, 191, 194
normal condition, 102
Nowak, Leszek, 127–7

Occam's bonus, 128–31
Occam's razor, 1, 96, 136, 142, 282
Occam's Law of Parsimony, 282
Ohm's Law, 42, 44–5
optimum rule, 109–10
ordinary least squares (OLS)
  approach, 277, 284–7
  estimators, 211
outliers, 189–90
overfitting, 30, 105–6, 110–11
over-identification, 45

parameter estimation, 99, 101
parameter space, 166, 175, 178
Pareto distribution, 37, 60
parsimony, 32–7, 39, 41–8, 61–2, 69, 185–6, 283
  paucity of, 283
  principle of, 166
Pasteur, Louis, 49
pattern, 33–7, 39, 68
  approximate, 39
  exact, 39
  in data, 33, 35, 37
  in phenomena, 32–3
  of behaviour, 9
  parsimonious, 33
  perceived, 33
  rank-size, 37
  unexpected, 49–50, 52
payoff structures, 267
Peano's Axioms, 41
Pearson's chi-squared, 130
perturbation theory, 81
Plato's cave, 230–1
plausibility, 25
  of hypotheses, 18–20, 24, 26–7, 81
pluralism, 15, 239
Popper, Karl, 32, 239
posterior odds testing, 171
prediction, 8, 32, 48, 146, 178
predictive accuracy, 29, 87, 92, 94–111, 113–16
prefixes, 140–1
pre-play communication, 263–4
probabilistic reduction (PR), 201–2

probability, 22–3, 89, 98, 167
  inferred, 145
  measure, 160
  mode, complexity of, 129
  posterior, 24, 94
  prequential, 167
  prior, 24–8, 30, 88, 94, 146
  theory, 138, 142, 144
  universal, 146
progress, 123
proper/improper priors, 174
Prout's Law, 38
psychological egoism, 15

Radon Nikodym derivative, 170
random matrix, 169
random process, 160
random sample assumption, 194
randomness, 139
  individual, 140
  Martin-Löf tests for, 140, 144, 152
rank-order statistics, 183
recursive chain models, 76
reduction, 203–4, 231, 235, 288
redundancy, 36, 43
revenue-maximizing strategy, 274
Rissanen's theorem, 6, 165, 167–70, 175
robust estimation, 184
robustness, 188–90
  parametric/non-parametric, 188, 192

SBIC, *see* Bayesian Information Criteria
  (BIC)
scale transformations, 221
Schultz, Henry, 56
science
  basic/applied, 32
  as art, 33
scientific interference, 10
semimeasures, 147, 151
SEMTSA, 74, 81
sequence of actions, 273–4
severity, 197
Shannon–Fano code, 137
Shannon's information theory, 139
Shapley value, 296
SIC, *see* Bayesian Information Criteria
  (BIC)
significance structure, 126
Simon–Ando Theorem, 64, 66
Simon, Herbert, 74–7
  Causal Ordering and Identifiability, 76
  Sciences of the Artificial, 80
  The Architecture of Complexity, 75
Simon's parsimony principle, 239
simple primitive function, 42

simplicity, 1–2
  criteria for, 126
  data-independent, 239
  in theory, 121
  is falsifiability, 235
  multidimensionality of, 283
  trade-off, 14–15, 19–20, 24–5, 30, 41, 83,
    86, 91, 210, 236, 238–9, 277, 283,
    287
simulation, 47
smoothing, 184, 194, 196–7
Snell's law of refraction, 42
Solomonoff, R. J., 34, 148, 156
Solomonoff's prediction method, 137
Solomonoff's universal prior, 136, 146
specific hypothesis, 49
stationarity/non-stationarity, 169, 175–8
statistical adequacy/inadequacy, 187, 190,
    196, 198
state space, 237
stochasticity, *see* randomness
straight lines, 28
strings, 135–6
structural equation systems, 45, 56
structural relations, 51
subjective expected utility (SEU), 56, 70
  maximization hypothesis, 58–61
Submartingale Covergence Theorem, 148
supply/demand, 125, 243
systematic information, 190

Taylor expansion, 130
Taylor's series, 48
theory building, principles of, 55
theory verification/falsification, 34, 44
Thurstone Letter Series Completion task,
    51
Tinbergen, Jan, 244
Tobin, James, 243
transfer functions, 237, 256
transparency, 294
trend, 177
trending data, 178, 199, 200
Turing computable, 136
Turing machine, 141–2, 152

uniform distribution, 189
universal density, 163, 188
universal distribution, 142, 147, 152
utility function, 55–6
utility maximization, 55, 59, 64

variables, noisy/noiseless, 228
verification, 39, 44
Viner–Wang theory, 60–1

von Neumann, 'The General Theory of
   Automata', 74–5

Walrasian equilibrium, 80

Walrasian programme, 73
weighting, 29
   assigned to parsimony, 213–4
Wilcoxon–Mann–Witney test, 188